AF564685

REGIONAL DISPARITIES IN DEVELOPMENT

REGIONAL DISPARITIES IN DEVELOPMENT

Editors

RAJ KUMAR SEN

BISWAJIT CHATTERJEE

Published on behalf of the
BENGAL ECONOMIC ASSOCIATION

DEEP & DEEP PUBLICATIONS PVT. LTD.

F-159, Rajouri Garden, New Delhi - 110027

REGIONAL DISPARITIES IN DEVELOPMENT

ISBN 978-81-8450-364-7

Typeset by THE LASER PRINTERS, 8/15, 3rd Floor, Subhash Nagar, New Delhi-110027.

Printed in India at MAYUR ENTERPRISES, WZ Plot No. 3, Gujjar Market, Tihar Village, New Delhi - 110 018

Published by DEEP & DEEP PUBLICATIONS PVT. LTD.,
F-159, Rajouri Garden, New Delhi-110027. Phones: 25435369, 25440916.
E-mail: ddpbooks@yahoo.co.in • ddpubs@gmail.com
Sales Showroom: 2/13, Ansari Road, Daryaganj, New Delhi-110002
Phone/Fax: 23245122

Contents

PART II
Agriculture

PART III
Human Development

PART IV
Infrastructure, Urbanization and Small Scale Industries

List of Contributors

1. **Dr. Biswajit Guha,** Former Reader and Head, Department of Economics, Netaji Nagar Day College, Kolkata.
2. **Dr. Debendra Narayan Bhattacharyya,** Former Head, Department of Economics, Dinabandu Andrews College, Kolkata.
3. **Professor Dhires Bhattacharya,** Former Head, Economics Department, University of Calcutta, Kolkata.
4. **Dr. Puspa Tarafdar,** Former Reader in Economics, Sarojini Naidu College for Women, Kolkata.
5. **Abhijit Dutta,** Associate Professor in Economics, Chandernagar College, W. Bengal.
6. **Dr. Gunendra Prasad Pal,** Reader in Economics, Umes Chandra College, Kolkata.
7. **Pavel Chakraborty,** Research Associate, The Energy and Resource Institute, New Delhi.
8. **Debashis Chakraborty,** Assistant Professor, Indian Institute of Foreign Trade, New Delhi.
9. **Dr. Kalipada Basu,** Joraghat, Hooghly.
10. **Dr. Jayanta Sen,** Lecturer, Department of Economics, West Bengal State University, Barasat, West Bengal.
11. **Professor D.P. Pal,** Department of Economics, University of Kalyani, West Bengal.
12. **Dr. Ruma Bhattacharya,** Calcutta Girls' College, Kolkata.

13. **Professor Biswajit Chatterjee,** Department of Economics, Jadavpur University, Kolkata.
14. **Dr. Arpita Ghose (nee Dhar),** Reader, Department of Economics, Jadavpur University, Kolkata.
15. **Sri Dipyaman Pal,** Lecturer, Department of Economics, A.B.N. Seal College, Coochbihar, West Bengal.
16. **Sri Debesh Bhowmik,** Pritinagar, Nadia, West Bengal.
17. **Dr. Sushil K. Halder,** Reader, Department of Economics, Jadavpur University, Kolkata.
18. **Sm. Kajari Roy,** Research Scholar, Department of Economics, Jadavpur University, Kolkata.
19. **Dr. Prankrishna Pal,** Reader, Department of Economics, Rabindra Bharati University, Kolkata.
20. **Dr. Dhiraj Kumar Bandyopadhyay,** Research Associate in Economics, Centre for Urban Economic Studies, University of Calcutta, Kolkata.
21. **Professor Dhirendra Nath Konar,** Department of Commerce, Kalyani University, West Bengal.
22. **Sri Debasish Bera,** Research Associate, National Institute for Transport and Urban Environmental Studies (NITUES), Delhi.
23. **Dilip Halder,** Former Professor, Department of Economics, Jadavpur University, Kolkata.
24. **Mohasin Mallick,** Lecturer, Department of Commerce, P.N. Das College, West Bengal, Siliguri.
25. **Professor Kanak Bagchi,** Head, Department of Economics, University of North Bengal.
26. **Sri Satyen Sarkar,** Lecturer, A.C. College of Commerce, Jalpaiguri, West Bengal.
27. **Professor Sumit Mukherjee,** Department of Political Science, Kalyani University, West Bengal.

Regional Disparities in Development: An Introduction

Development experiences in India are diverse and there exist wide disparities across regions and states of India in terms of wide range of indicators, viz. income, growth, employment, poverty, human deprivations and living conditions, including education, health and other infrastructure. The reasons for such disparities at a time and over time have been investigated in the literature of economic development of India. But there are also wide disparities across different regions within a state in terms of selected indicators and attempts to understand the reasons for such disparities within the political boundary of a state in Indian federation are not many. The present collection which portrays wide ranging disparities within the state of West Bengal, provides one such attempt. Born out of the papers presented in the 26th Annual Conference of Bangiya Arthaniti Parishad, the present collection provides an important amalgam of issues that needs attention of economists and policy-makers.

The book is divided in five parts. Part I deals with disparity in development experiences within West Bengal. The six papers in this part deal with development issues like rural-urban disparity, disparity in human development, inter-district disparities in income level and growth, the issue of growth acceleration with instability of growth process and inequalities across production sectors across districts within West Bengal.

Part II of the book deals with diversity in agricultural sector of West Bengal and the trends in regional disparity in agricultural productivity in the districts of the state—food and non-foodgrains.

The issues of disparity in agricultural wage rates across the districts as well as the trend for their convergences are also examined in this section.

Part III of the book deals with human development and disparities associated with it. The role of infrastructure in meeting the inter-district variations in human poverty in West Bengal has carefully been examined by two authors in Chapter 10 of the book, while chapters 11 and 12 discussed the disparities in health-education measures in the districts of the state.

Part IV of the book contains four articles which discussed urbanization in the districts and the role of infrastructural development like development of road and transport system. The fourth paper by Kalipada Basu discusses the main reasons for the pathetic state of disparities in infrastructural development in the districts of the state in terms of politico-economic factors.

Part V of the book focuses on the backwardness in North Bengal districts, the reasons for wide disparities and the strategies of economic revival, and the implications of such apalling poverty on the sessionist political movements that have been encouraged in recent years.

Altogether the eighteen papers in the volume address the question of regional disparity within the progressive state of West Bengal and studies are on implications for policy intervention by the state government.

The articles included in this book are expected to provide an exhaustive analysis for regional disparity and consequences with policy prescriptions so far as state of West Bengal is concerned. Researchers, academicians, policy-makers and general readers interested in this subject will find this book quite useful and both light and fruit bearing. State specific analysis is expected to fill-up the important gaps in the economic history of different regions of India. An analysis of the West Bengal economy is further important as it is the most densely populated in India and hence produce the longest impact on the people due to intra-region disparity between the different regions of the state.

We are thankful to the authors of the selected articles who have raised papers for publication in this volume. We are also thankful to the authorities to the Bengal Economic Association to request the present editors to do this job. Special thanks are necessary to

Dr. Asim Kumar Karmakar for his valuable help in this matter. Last but not the least special thanks are due to Mr. G.S. Bhatia of Deep & Deep Publications Pvt. Ltd., New Delhi to undertake this job and complete it in meticulous manner.

THE EDITORS
Raj Kumar Sen
Biswajit Chatterjee

PART I

DISPARITY IN DEVELOPMENT

Regional Disparities

BISWAJIT GUHA

This paper aims to study the following different types of disparity in West Bengal:

(i) Environmental, (ii) Demographic, (iii) Social Sector, (iv) Standard of Living, (v) Economic on the basis of mainly secondary and official data, statistical measures like range and coefficient of variation help to show the extent of disparities among the districts of West Bengal. This paper has also attempted to examine whether there has occurred a gradual convergence and divergence of development indicators like HDI and per capita income among these districts. A standard of living index has been constructed to focus the level of development among the districts of West Bengal. However, Kolkata has been excluded from this analysis as it is the capital city of the state and there is no rural population here. On the other hand exception Kolkata, Haldia, Durgapur and Asansol any significant development of industries did not occur in other areas of the state.

I. INTRODUCTION

All historians, Indian and foreign, agree that Bengal was the wealthiest province at the time of arrival of the British in India. The British were very much attracted by the flourishing agriculture, industry and trade of Bengal. After the battle of Plassey in 1757, Clive marched triumphantly into Murshidabad, the then capital city of Bengal. He was struck by the affluence of the city and he wrote in his diary about the city: "This city is as extensive, populous and rich as the city of London with this difference that there are individuals in the first possessing greater property than in the last city" (*Roy*, 1972, p. 11). It was Clive who started the British plunder of Bengal which gradually changed its forms and continued till 1947. But it is alleged that partition of Bengal in 1947, step-motherly attitude of the central government towards West Bengal in many cases including the Freight Equalisation Policy, several failures of the Government of West Bengal etc. together caused rapid decline of the economy of the West Bengal since the attainment of independence in 1947. This process of economic deceleration has also been associated with disparity in the nature and scale of development of different regions of West Bengal. This paper has examined the present scenario of regional disparity in West Bengal.

II. OBJECTIVES AND METHODOLOGY

This paper aims to study the following different types of disparity in West Bengal:

(i) Environmental Disparities, (ii) Demographic Disparities, (iii) Social Sector Disparities, (iv) Standard of Living Disparities, and (v) Regional Economic Disparities.

The statistical data published in different reports of the Government of West Bengal and of the Government of India have been used for the purpose of this study. The range of variation of these data in each separate table clearly shows the extent of disparities among the districts of West Bengal. The coefficients of variation have been calculated with respect to a few fields and these have been accordingly considered as a measure of index of disparity.

These different tables also show the process of gradual development of all the different districts. An attempt has been made to examine whether there has occurred a gradual convergence or divergence of development indicators among these districts. Since the state of development of any district is ultimately reflected in its figures of Human Development Index and Per Capita Income, the Coefficients of Variation, as the index of disparity, have been constructed in cases of these two important indicators of development.

This study has compared the figures of Human Development Index and Gender Development Index of different districts in order to study the range of inter-district disparities with respect to values of these two different types of index. An attempt has also been made to show how with such values of index, the international rank of each separate district may be determined and to find out the country which is nearly at par with similar rank of each such district. It shows the nature of development of a particular district at an international level separately with respect to each such index.

A 'standard of living index' as a measure of 'modified human development' has been constructed with respect to each district where this index has been constructed as an average of the following different values of index: (i) Index of Availability of Provision of Basic Amenities, i.e., the percentage of population with access to both safe drinking water and electricity, (ii) Index of economic capability, i.e. the percentage of population above poverty line, (iii) Human Development Index, and (iv) Gender Development Index. This type of index is an extension of the standard measure of UNDP. It may be claimed that it is a relatively better measure to indicate the standard of living of a community by including these additional dimensions of human development.

Different dimensions of poverty and deprivation in different districts have also been studied which include percentage figures of the following: (i) total poverty ratio; (ii) capability poverty measure which includes percentage figures of low-birth weight babies, non-institutional deliveries, i.e. birth of babies not attended by skilled health personnel and female illiteracy; (iii) index of deprivation in knowledge considering the percentage figures of illiteracy and out-of-school children; (iv) index of deprivation in health considering the percentage figures of non-institutional deliveries, i.e. birth of babies not attended by skilled health personnel and lack of immunisation of children from principal child diseases; (v) index of deprivation in provision of basic amenities, i.e. percentage figures of population suffering from non-availability of both safe drinking water and electricity; (vi) human poverty index following the measure of UNDP; and (vii) incidence of unemployment. The estimates of rural and urban per capita monthly consumption expenditures and those of rural and urban poverty ratios in the districts have been compared and furthermore, the rural-urban disparity with respect to these estimates in each separate district has also been compared.

All these different statistical data and different measures have been shown in Tables 1 to 22. Kolkata has been excluded from this study mainly for two reasons: (i) It is the capital city of the state, and (ii) There is no rural population and hence there is absence of activities of the primary sector in Kolkata. For the purpose of a rationally comparable study of regional disparity, therefore, Kolkata has been excluded from the construction of index of disparity. The different types of index of disparity are shown in Table 22. The inter-district disparity in industrial development has not been studied as excepting Kolkata, Durgapur, Haldia and a few adjacent areas of Kolkata and Asansol, any significant development of industries did not occur in other areas of the state.

III. ENVIRONMENTAL DISPARITIES

At present, there are 19 districts in West Bengal: (1) Darjeeling, (2) Jalpaiguri, (3) Coochbihar, (4) Uttar Dinajpur, (5) Dakshin Dinajpur, (6) Malda, (7) Murshidabad, (8) Nadia, (9) Kolkata, (10) North 24-Parganas, (11) South 24-Parganas, (12) Howrah, (13) Hooghly, (14) Medinpur (East), (15) Medinpur (West), (16) Burdwan, (17) Birbhum, (18) Bankura, and (19) Purulia.

The physiography and soil characteristics of the state vary widely. Such variations have naturally caused variation in the cropping pattern of different districts. The geo-hydrological classification of the state, as conducted by the Geological Survey of India, also shows regional disparities. On account of such differences, the deposits of groundwater also vary significantly among districts of the state. Accordingly, the degree of utilisation of groundwater for the purposes of operating wells and tubewells as sources of minor irrigation has also varied among districts. It has caused disparity in the production of 'Rabi Crops', such as, Boro variety of paddy, wheat, potato, etc. in different districts of West Bengal. In fact, this state can be clearly classified into different geo-hydrological and agro-climatic regions (*Bulletin of the Geological Survey of India*) as follows:

1. The region 'A' represents the "Northern Hilly Region" comprising Darjeeling district (barring Siliguri Sub-division) and some northernmost parts of Jalpaiguri district. The nature of the soil in this rocky region is mostly of the light sandy loam variety.
2. The "Terai-Bhabar Region" at the Himalayan foothills represents the region 'B'. This region consists of those parts of the districts of Darjeeling and Jalpaiguri which are not included in the region 'A'. This region is characterised by the existence of mostly sandy soil.
3. The Region 'C' consists of the Rocky plateau region in Western part of the state, including coalfield areas. This Archaean terrain includes the regions like the entire district of Purulia, the Asansol sub-division of Burdwan district, coal field areas of Birbhum and Bankura districts and the western fringe areas of Jhargram sub-division of Medinpur district. This entire region is characterised by the existence of laterite soil.
4. The Region 'D' is called the "Barind Tract" of North Bengal comprising entirely of the districts of West Dinajpur (both Uttar Dinajpur and Dakshin Dinajpur combined) and Malda. This region is called the 'Barind Tract of Older Alluvium Area'. The entire original district of West Dinajpur has mostly light sandy loam and partly clay soil while the district of Malda has mostly clay soil.
5. The Region 'E' consists of laterite soil region including the major parts of Birbhum and Bankura districts, Durgapur sub-division of Burdwan district and major parts of the Sadar Sub-division of Medinpur district.
6. The Region 'F' consists of the Valley Flat region of the entire district of Coochbihar with the characteristic of mostly sandy soil.
7. The Region 'G' consists of the New Alluvium Region. It includes the Gangetic plains of major parts of the southern parts of West Bengal, such as, Sadar, Kalna and Katwa sub-divisions of Burdwan district, Tamluk and Ghatal sub-divisions of the original Medinpur district, entire

districts of Murshidabad, Nadia, Hooghly. Howrah, Kolkata and major parts of the districts of North and South 24-Parganas. This entire region is characterised by the existence of mostly clay soil and partly sandy soil.

8. The Region 'H' consists of the 'Coastal Region.' It includes the entire Contai Sub-division of the district of Medinpur (East) and the blocks of the Sundarban Biosphere Reserve Region and its adjacent blocks of the districts of North and South 24-Parganas. Partly sandy loam and mostly saline sandy varieties of soil are observed in this region.

West Bengal is thus characterised by wide environmental disparities among its different regions. Besides such agro-climatic and geo-hydrological disparities, the patterns of rainfall and temperature also vary considerably among different districts. while the districts of Medinpur (West), Bankura, Purulia, Birbhum and Asansol sub-division of Burdwan district are traditional drought-prone areas, most of the remaining parts of West Bengal are traditional flood-prone areas on account of heavy rainfall and inadequate as well as inefficient management of flood control. Deforestation, soil erosion, destruction of embankments of all the rivers in many areas, etc. are regular incidents in this state. Even coastal areas are also not free from these dangers of environmental degradation. While variation in the nature of physical environment of the districts of West Bengal has caused regional disparity in the cropping pattern as well as in the amount of value-added by the agricultural sector in Net District Domestic Product, environmental degradation has more or less uniformly taken place in all the districts of West Bengal. The degree of different types of such environmental degradation is shown in Table 1. It shows the regional disparities in environmental degradation of non-forest areas. In the entire state of West Bengal, 29.07 percent of total non-forest area suffers from such a degradation. These figures are at 84.93, 65.86 and 63.16 percentages of non-forest area in the districts of South 24-Parganas, Medinpur (East) and Howrah—the three leading districts suffering mainly on account of the incidence of 'Saline Alkaline' type of degradation. These different types of environmental degradation act as severe obstacles in the way of increasing agricultural production in different districts of West Bengal. However, it is also observed that there is a wide range of

TABLE 1

Degraded Land of the Districts of West Bengal, 2003-04

District	*Percentage of Degraded Land to Total Non-Forest Land*	*Ravinous Gullied Rill (Percent)*	*Water Logged (Percent)*	*Saline Alkaline (Percent)*	*Mixing (Percent)*	*Land Slip/ Slide (Percent)*	*Sea Coastal (Percent)*	*Stream Bank and Sand Laden (Percent)*
(1)	(2)	(3)	(4)	(5)	(6)	(7)	(8)	(9)
Darjeeling	35.26	18.40	-	-	1.05	15.76	-	0.05
Jalpaiguri	18.93	11.27	2.25	-	0.90	1.13	-	3.38
Coochbihar	18.79	10.61	3.64	-	-	-	-	4.55
Uttar Dinajpur	4.38	3.17	0.95	-	-	-	-	0.25
Dakshin Dinajpur	4.33	3.65	0.45	-	-	-	-	0.23
Malda	7.53	1.35	5.37	-	-	-	-	0.81
Murshidabad	20.37	3.39	11.65	-	-	-	-	5.32
Nadia	13.85	-	13.52	-	-	-	-	0.33
Kolkata	-	-	-	-	-	-	-	-
North 24-Parganas	45.92	-	8.80	36.99	-	-	-	0.13
South 24-Parganas	84.93	-	23.74	59.46	-	-	1.70	0.03
Howrah	63.16	-	23.86	39.27	-	-	-	0.03
Hooghly	15.97	-	15.91	-	-	-		0.06
Medinpur (East)	65.86	0.96	13.48	51.00	-	-	0.38	0.04

(Contd.)

TABLE 1 (*Contd.*)

(1)	(2)	(3)	(4)	(5)	(6)	(7)	(8)	(9)
Medinpur (West)	20.45	16.73	3.62		0.07	-	-	0.03
Burdwan	19.74	9.65	7.13	-	0.74	-	-	2.22
Birbhum	23.67	19.34	2.05	-		-	-	2.28
Bankura	19.86	15.75	3.70	-	0.37	-	-	0.04
Purulia	27.16	26.94	0.01	-	0.19	-	-	0.02
West Bengal	29.07	8.67	7.73	10.68	0.19	0.46	0.16	1.18

Sources: (i) Soil Conservation Wing, Dept. of Agriculture, Govt. of West Bengal.
(ii) *Economic Review, 2004-05*, Govt. of West Bengal.

disparity with respect to the degradation of land among these districts. It has been measured by the index of disparity, i.e., the coefficient of variation which is found to be abnormally high at 78.08 per cent as shown in Table 22.

IV. DEMOGRAPHIC DISPARITIES

It may quite reasonably be stated that the regional disparities are also quite evident in the social and demographic features of West Bengal. Tables 2, 3, 4 and 5 indicate such features. It is observed in Table 2, that the annual rate of growth of population during 1991-2000 was at 1.8 percent in West Bengal, the total

TABLE 2

Principal Demographic Features of West Bengal, 2001

District	*Total Population (in Lakhs) 2001*	*Annual growth rate of population (percent)*	*Sex-Ratio: Female per thousand Male, 2001*	*Density of Population per Sq.km. 2001*	*Literacy Rate (percent) 2001*
(1)	*(2)*	*(3)*	*(4)*	*(5)*	*(6)*
Darjeeling	16.09	2.4	943	511	71.79
Jalpaiguri	34.01	2.2	941	546	62.85
Coochbihar	24.79	1.4	949	732	66.30
Uttar Dinajpur	24.42	2.2	937	778	47.89
Dakshin Dinajpur	15.03	2.9	950	677	63.59
Malda	32.90	2.5	948	881	50.28
Murshidabad	58.67	2.4	952	1,102	54.35
Nadia	46.05	2.0	947	1,173	66.14
Kolkata	45.73	0.4	828	24,718	80.86
North 24-Parganas	89.34	2.3	927	2,182	78.07
South 24-Parganas	69.07	2.1	938	693	69.45
Howrah	42.73	1.5	906	2,913	77.01
Hooghly	50.42	1.6	947	1,601	75.11
Medinpur (Original Combined)	96.11	1.6	955	683	74.90
Burdwan	68.96	1.4	921	982	70.18
Birbhum	30.15	1.8	949	663	61.48
Bankura	31.93	1.4	953	464	63.44
Purulia	25.37	1.4	953	405	55.57
West Bengal	801.76	1.8	934	903	68.64

Source: Census Report, 2001.

TABLE 3

Percentage Decadal Variation of Population in the Districts of West Bengal (Excluding Kolkata) 1951-2001

District	*1951-1961*	*1961-1971*	*1971-1981*	*1981-1991*	*1991-2001*
(1)	(2)	(3)	(4)	(5)	(6)
Darjeeling	35.90	25.16	31.02	26.91	23.79
Jalpaiguri	48.27	28.76	26.55	25.44	21.45
Coochbihar	52.45	38.67	25.28	22.55	14.19
Uttar Dinajpur	-	-	30.20	34.00	28.72
Dakshin Dinajpur	-	-	28.04	24.39	22.15
West Dinajpur (Original Combined)	35.51	40.50	29.31	30.05	26.13
Malda	30.33	31.98	26.00	29.78	24.78
Murshidabad	33.47	28.39	25.49	28.20	23.76
Nadia	49.78	30.14	33.29	29.95	19.54
North 24-Parganas	-	-	31.42	31.69	22.69
South 24-Parganas	-	-	19.77	30.24	20.85
24-Parganas (Original Combined)	40.84	23.53	27.10	21.02	21.88
Howrah	26.61	18.58	22.74	25.71	14.57
Hooghly	39.02	28.72	23.86	22.43	15.77
Medinpur (Original Combined)	29.26	26.89	22.39	23.57	15.35
Burdwan	40.65	27.04	23.47	25.13	13.96
Birbhum	35.55	22.80	18.01	21.94	17.99
Bankura	26.17	22.02	16.93	18.12	13.82
Purulia	16.33	17.86	15.65	20.00	14.02
West Bengal	32.80	26.87	23.17	24.73	17.77

Source: Statistical Abstract, Govt. of West Bengal (Volumes from 1978 to 2003).

population being at 801.76 lakhs in 2001. The highest annual rate of growth of population was at 2.9 percent in Dakshin Dinajpur district while the lowest rate was observed at 0.4 percent in the district of Kolkata. But the sex-ratio, i.e., female per thousand male is the lowest in Kolkata (828) and the highest in Medinpur (955). The density of population per square kilometre is the highest in Kolkata (24,718), being followed by 2,182 in the North 24-Parganas

TABLE 4

Density of Population per Sq. Km. in the Districts of West Bengal (Excluding Kolkata), 1951-2001

District	1951	1961	1971	1981	1991	2001
(1)	(2)	(3)	(4)	(5)	(6)	(7)
Darjeeling	149	203	254	325	413	511
Jalpaiguri	147	218	280	356	450	546
Coochbihar	196	299	414	523	641	732
Uttar Dinajpur	-	-	-	-	604	778
Dakshin Dinajpur	-	-	-	-	595	677
West Dinajpur (Original Combined)	188	254	357	449	-	-
Malda	253	329	434	544	706	881
Murshidabad	321	429	550	695	890	1,102
Nadia	291	436	568	755	981	1,173
North 24-Parganas	-	-	-	-	1,779	2,182
South 24-Parganas	-	-	-	-	574	693
24-Parganas (Original Combined)	323	455	612	760	-	-
Howrah	1.093	1,383	1,640	2,022	2,542	2,913
Hooghly	510	709	913	1,130	1,383	1,601
Medinpur (Original Combined)	245	316	401	479	592	683
Burdwan	312	439	557	688	861	982
Birbhum	236	320	393	461	562	663
Bankura	192	242	295	345	408	464
Purulia	187	217	256	296	355	405
West Bengal	299	398	504	615	767	903

Source: Statistical Abstract, Govt. of West Bengal (Volumes from 1978 to 2003).

district. The literacy rate is the highest in Kolkata (80.66 percent), being followed by North 24-Parganas (78.07 percent). The lowest literacy rate is observed in the district of Uttar Dinajpur (47.89 percent). The literacy rate in the entire state is at 68.64 percent. The problem of high density of population has become very serious in all the districts and naturally also at the State level (903). Figures in Table 3 show the percentage rates of decadal variation of population in the districts of West Bengal. This rate is gradually falling. But the density of population has been rapidly rising as

TABLE 5

Classification of Population in West Bengal, 2001

District	*Male Population (percent) 2001*	*Female Population (percent) 2001*	*Rural Population (percent) 2001*	*Urban Population (percent) 2001*	*Scheduled Caste Population (percent) 2001*	*Scheduled Tribe Population (percent) 2001*
(1)	(2)	(3)	(4)	(5)	(6)	(7)
Darjeeling	51.65	48.35	67.66	32.34	16.09	12.69
Jalpaiguri	51.48	48.52	82.16	17.84	36.71	18.87
Coochbihar	51.31	48.69	90.90	9.10	50.11	0.57
Uttar Dinajpur	51.60	48.40	87.94	12.06	27.71	5.11
Dakshin Dinajpur	51.23	48.77	86.90	13.10	28.78	16.12
West Dinajpur (Original Combined)	51.46	48.54	87.55	12.45	28.12	9.31
Malda	51.34	48.66	92.68	7.32	16.84	6.90
Murshidabad	51.22	48.78	87.51	12.49	12.00	1.29
Nadia	51.40	48.60	78.73	21.27	29.66	2.47
Kolkata	54.67	45.33	0.00	100.00	6.01	0.21
North 24-Parganas	51.93	48.07	45.70	54.30	20.60	2.23
South 24-Parganas	51.61	48.39	84.27	15.73	32.12	1.23
Howrah	52.47	47.53	49.64	50.36	15.42	0.45
Hooghly	51.37	48.63	66.53	33.47	23.58	4.21
Medinpur (Original Combined)	51.15	48.85	89.76	10.24	16.40	8.31
Burdwan	52.03	47.97	63.06	36.94	26.98	6.41
Birbhum	51.31	48.69	91.43	8.57	29.51	6.74
Bankura	51.24	48.76	92.63	7.37	31.24	10.36
Purulia	51.16	48.84	89.93	10.07	18.29	18.27
West Bengal	51.72	48.28	72.03	27.97	23.02	5.50

Source: Census Report, 2001.

is evident from figures in Table 4. It has been regularly reported in all the daily newspapers of the state that there has been a rapid and regular 'cross-border migration' of population from Bangladesh along all the border districts of the state and from Nepal in the districts of Darjeeling and Jalpaiguri. This is creating ethnic problems, secessionist movements and communal tensions in the state. It has created excesive pressure of population on land, acute shortages of essential goods and services, rapidly rising unemployment and several other problems. "All the border districts together account for 44.5 percent of the 13.4 million population that were added to 1981 census aggregate to make the state population size stands at 68 million in 1991. . . Given the moderate levels of vital rates, this implies that the reported increase in immigration over the decade was not confined to a few border districts, but has possibly undergone a spatial diffusion to other parts of the state." (*West Bengal Human Development Report*, 2004, p. 11). Besides, there is always an increasing flow of population from other states to West Bengal. All these have now reached such a stage that the linguistic population group of Bengalees has turned out to be a minority in Kolkata. The abnormal rise in immigration has also intensified a rapid rise in crime rates and other social problems in the state. This type of disequilibrium in the society has been impeding the process of development of the state, specially, along the border districts and within the city of Kolkata and its adjacent areas. The acquisition of land for the purposes of industrialisation and provision of different facilities of infrastructure has also become increasingly difficult. The prospect of any development through acquisition of land is regularly thwarted by the problem of displacement of population who are mostly immigrants in the city of Kolkata and its adjacent areas. The acquisition of agricultural land for the said purpose has also become difficult as the state government could not yet been able to evolve any suitable justified policy to compensate and arrange appropriate economic and social rehabilitation to the possible victims of such measures of development. The failure to create adequate facilities of physical, social and financial types of infrastructure in the districts has always encouraged the state government to have a 'bias' for development measures mainly in and around the city of Kolkata. This has further encouraged migration of population to Kolkata in search of 'expected higher income.' In Table 5, we observe the inter-district variations with respect to the classification of population into groups, such as Male, Female, Rural, Urban, Scheduled Caste and Scheduled Tribe. If we exclude Kolkata, we find that there is a very low percentage of urban population in all the districts indicating a very limited urbanisation.

V. SOCIAL SECTOR DISPARITIES

The inter-district disparity in the development of Social Sector of West Bengal is observed from the figures mentioned in Tables 6,7 and 8.

Figures in Table 6 show the inter-district disparity in terms of the values of Human Development Index. It is observed that at the top, the ranks 1 and 2 are occupied by Kolkata (0.78) and North 24-Parganas (0.66) districts respectively while at the bottom,

TABLE 6

Human Development Index for the Districts of West Bengal, 2001-02

District	*Health Index*	*Per Capita Income Index*	*Education Index*	*Human Development Index*
(1)	*(2)*	*(3)*	*(4)*	*(5)*
Darjeeling	0.73 (4)	0.49 (3)	0.72 (5)	0.65 (4)
Jalpaiguri	0.61 (11)	0.38 (10)	0.60 (13)	0.53 (10)
Coochbihar	0.50 (14)	0.41 (7)	0.65 (10)	0.52 (11)
West Dinajpur (Original Combined)	0.62 (10)	0.39 (9)	0.53 (15)	0.51 (13)
Malda	0.49 (15)	0.36 (21)	0.48 (17)	0.44 (17)
Murshidabad	0.57 (12)	0.29 (12)	0.52 (16)	0.46 (15)
Nadia	0.65 (9)	0.41 (7)	0.66 (9)	0.57 (9)
Kolkata	0.82 (1)	0.73 (1)	0.80 (1)	0.78 (1)
North 24-Parganas	0.72 (5)	0.49 (3)	0.76 (2)	0.66 (3)
South 24-Parganas	0.71 (6)	0.40 (8)	0.68 (7)	0.60 (8)
Howrah	0.77 (2)	0.53 (2)	0.75 (3)	0.68 (2)
Hooghly	0.77 (2)	0.46 (5)	0.67 (8)	0.63 (6)
Medinpur (Original Combined)	0.68 (7)	0.45 (6)	0.74 (4)	0.62 (7)
Burdwan	0.74 (3)	0.47 (4)	0.71 (6)	0.64 (5)
Birbhum	0.53 (13)	0.27 (13)	0.61 (12)	0.47 (14)
Bankura	0.67 (8)	0.26 (14)	0.62 (11)	0.52 (ID
Purulia	0.61 (11)	0.18 (15)	0.55 (14)	0.45 (16)
West Bengal	0.70	0.43	0.69	0.61

Note: Ranks of each separate index are shown in parentheses.

Source: West Bengal Human Development Report, 2004 (p. 13), Govt. of West Bengal.

the ranks 16 and 17 are occupied by Purulia (0.45) and Malda (0.44) districts respectively. The inter-district disparity index of Human Development as measured by the coefficient of variation is found at 13.96 percent in 2001-02. It is shown in Table 22.

The figures of inter-district disparity in terms of the values of Gender Development Index are shown in Table 7. It is observed that at the top, the ranks 1 and 2 are occupied by Kolkata (0.642) and Darjeeling (0.600) districts respectively while at the bottom the ranks 16 and 17 are occupied by Murshidabad (0.423) and Malda (0.416) districts respectively. The inter-district disparity index of Gender Development as measured by the coefficient of variation is found at 11.92 percent in 2001-02 (Table 22).

Kolkata occupied the highest rank while Malda occupied the lowest rank in Tables 6 and 7. The ranks of other districts differ in these two tables. So, a significant gender disparity exists in West Bengal and the level of human development is also low in all the districts as is evident from these data.

In Table 6, respective ranks of districts in Health Index, Per Capita Income Index, Education Index and Human Development Index have been mentioned. The Health Index varies from the lowest value, 0.49, in Malda to the highest value, 0.82, in Kolkata. The Per Capita Income Index varies from the lowest value, 0.18, in Purulia to the highest value, 0.73, in Kolkata. The Education Index varies from the lowest value, 0.48, in Malda to the highest value, 0.80, in Kolkata. The Human Development Index varies from the lowest value, 0.44, in Malda to the highest value, 0.78 in Kolkata. If Kolkata is excluded from the study, then the next highest values of Health Index, Per Capita Income Index and Education Index are observed at 0.77 in both Howrah and Hooghly districts, 0.53 in Howrah district and 0.76 in North 24-Parganas district respectively.

The level of gender development has been primarily reflected in the Equally Distributed Index Numbers for Health, Income and Education and finally, in the level of Gender development respectively in Table 7. The Gender Development Index varies from the lowest value, 0.416, in Malda to the highest value, 0.642, in Kolkata which is followed by the next highest value, 0.600, in Darjeeling district.

In both Tables 6 and 7, the index-wise ranks have been mentioned. It is observed that three districts, such as, Malda,

TABLE 7

Gender Development Index for the Districts of West Bengal, 2001-02

District	*Equally distributed Index for*			*Gender Development Index*
	Health	*Income*	*Education*	
(1)	*(2)*	*(3)*	*(4)*	*(5)*
Darjeeling	0.731 (5)	0.356 (1)	0.714 (6)	0.600 (2)
Jalpaiguri	0.614 (12)	0.281 (6)	0.581 (13)	0.492 (11)
Coochbihar	0.497 (16)	0.287 (5)	0.628 (10)	0.471 (13)
West Dinajpur (Original Combined)	0.616 (11)	0.291 (4)	0.527 (14)	0.478 (12)
Malda	0.491 (17)	0.291 (4)	0.465 (16)	0.416 (17)
Murshidabad	0.566 (14)	0.176 (14)	0.527 (14)	0.423 (16)
Nadia	0.649 (10)	0.215 (10)	0.653 (9)	0.506 (9)
Kolkata	0.824 (1)	0.320 (3)	0.783 (1)	0.642 (1)
North 24-Parganas	0.721 (6)	0.219 (9)	0.752 (2)	0.564 (6)
South 24-Parganas	0.705 (7)	0.192 (12)	0.666 (8)	0.521 (8)
Howrah	0.773 (2)	0.194 (11)	0.742 (3)	0.570 (5)
Hooghly	0.764 (3)	0.259 (8)	0.720 (5)	0.581 (3)
Medinpur (Original Combined)	0.683 (8)	0.323 (2)	0.728 (4)	0.578 (4)
Burdwan	0.740 (4)	0.270 (7)	0.669 (7)	0.560 (7)
Birbhum	0.533 (15)	0.178 (13)	0.595 (12)	0.435 (14)
Bankura	0.662 (9)	0.215 (10)	0.605 (11)	0.494 (10)
Purulia	0.606 (13)	0.161 (15)	0.506 (15)	0.424 (15)
West Bengal	0.697	0.270	0.681	0.549

Note: Ranks of each separate index are shown in parentheses.
Source: *West Bengal Human Development Report, 2004* (p. 14), Govt. of West Bengal.

Murshidabad and Purulia are in abnormally deplorable condition in their performance in the social sector if the values of different types of index in these districts and also their separate index-wise ranks are observed. These three districts have consistently occupied three ranks in the bottom, i.e., within the range of the ranks from 15 to 17. In case of Human Development Index, the ranks 15, 16 and 17 are respectively occupied by Murshidabad, Purulia and Malda districts. In case of reducing gender discrimination in education, health and in earning income, i.e., in the field of achieving gender development, the ranks 15, 16 and 17 are respectively occupied by Purulia, Murshidabad and Malda. So, Malda district's performance has been the worst in the social sector. On the other hand, Kolkata district, also the capital city, has occupied the highest rank in both Human Development Index and Gender Development Index.

The figures of Human Development Index and Gender Development Index of the districts of West Bengal have been considered in the international context in Table 8. The comparable, i.e., nearly at par international ranks according to the values of Human Development Index (HDI) and Gender Development Index (GDI) have been mentioned and the country with the approximate value of any such index and accordingly its rank at the international level have also been mentioned. For example, the value of HDI in case of Kolkata is 0.78 and with an approximate value, Albania's international rank is 65. Hence, it may be stated that Kolkata's international rank in HDI is 65. Similarly, the value of GDI in case of Kolkata is 0.642 and with an approximate value, Egypt's international rank is 99. Hence, it may be stated that Kolkata's international rank in GDI is 99. It is observed that the range of disparity in HDI in terms of international rank is such that it varies from 65 in case of Kolkata at par with Albania to as low as 156 in case of Malda at par with Eritrea as estimated by the UNDP. Also, the range of disparity in GDI in terms of internatioal rank is such that it varies from 99 in case of Kolkata at par with Egypt to as low as 129 in case of Malda, Murshidabad and Purulia (with values of GDI at 0.416, 0.423 and 0.424 respectively) approximately at par with Rwanda. The UNDP in it's *Human Development Report*, 2004, has considered a study of 176 countries of the world and it classified the levels of both human development and gender development as follows:

(i) High Human Development and High Gender Development: Values of Index lying above 0.800;
(ii) Medium Human Development and Medium Gender Development: Values of Index lying between 0.500 and 0.800; and
(iii) Low Human Development and Low Gender Development: Values of Index lying below 0.500.

TABLE 8

Assessment of HDI and GDI of Districts of West Bengal in the International Context (2001-02)

District	*Human Development Index*	*Comparable International level at the nearest rank and the country concerned*		*Gender Development Index*	*Comparable international level at the nearest rank and the country concerned*	
		Rank	*Country*		*Rank*	*Country*
(1)	*(2)*	*(3)*	*(4)*	*(5)*	*(6)*	*(7)*
Darjeeling	0.65 (1)	121	Guatemala	0.600 (3)	101	Namibia
Jalpaiguri	0.53 (1)	136	Comoros	0.492 (4)	111	Cameroon
Coochbihar	0.52 (1)	137	Swaziland	0.471 (4)	120	Pakistan
West Dinajpur (Original Combined)	0.51 (1)	138	Bangladesh	0.478 (4)	119	Togo
Malda	0.44 (2)	156	Eritrea	0.416 (4)	129	Rwanda
Murshidabad	0.46 (2)	153	Haiti	0.423 (4)	129	Rwanda
Nadia	0.57(1)	129	Vanuatu	0.506 (3)	109	Swaziland
Kolkata	0.78 (1)	65	Albania	0.642 (3)	99	Egypt
North 24-Parganas	0.66 (1)	119	South Africa	0.564 (3)	104	Ghana
South 24-Parganas	0.60 (1)	127	India	0.521 (3)	107	Lao Paople's Dem. Rep.
Howrah	0.68 (1)	114	Bolivia	0.570 (3)	103	India
Hooghly	0.63 (1)	124	Solomon Islands	0.581 (3)	102	Botswana

(Contd.)

TABLE 8 (*Contd.*)

(1)	(2)	(3)	(4)	(5)	(6)	(7)
Medinpur (Original Combined)	0.62 (1)	125	Mexico	0.578 (3)	102	Botswana
Burdwan	0.64 (1)	123	Sao Tome and Principe	0.560 (3)	104	Ghana
Birbhum	0.47 (2)	150	Madagascar	0.435 (4)	126	Yemen
Bankura	0.52(1)	137	Swaziland	0.494 (4)	111	Cameroon
Purulia	0.45 (2)	155	Gambia	0.424 (4)	129	Rwanda
West Bengal	0.61 (1)	127	India	0.549 (3)	105	Cambodia

Notes: (1) MHD = Medium Human Development, (2) LHD = Low Human Development
(3) MGD = Medium Gender Development, (4) LGD = Low Gender Development

Sources: (1) *West Bengal Human Development Repot, 2004*, Govt. of West Bengal.
(2) *Human Development Report, 2004*, UNDP.

Considering this classification, we can classify the districts of West Bengal in terms of human development and gender development as follows:

(i) There are 13 districts which have attained 'medium human development'. These districts are Darjeeling, Jalpaiguri, Coochbihar, original West Dinajpur (Uttar and Dakshin combined), Nadia, Kolkata, North 24-Parganas, South 24-Parganas, Howrah, Hooghly, Original Medinpur (East and West combined), Burdwan and Bankura as their values of HDI lie between 0.500 and 0.800.

(ii) There are 4 districts which still belong to the stage of 'low human development', such as Malda, Murshidabad, Birbhum and Purulia as their values of HDI are below 0.500.

(iii) There are 9 districts which have attained 'medium gender development', such as Darjeeling, Nadia, Kolkata, North 24-Parganas, South 24-Parganas, Howrah, Hooghly, Original Medinpur and Burdwan as their values of GDI lie between 0.500 and 0.800.

(iv) There are 8 districts which still belong to the stage of 'low gender development', such as Jalpaiguri, Coochbihar, Original West Dinajpur, Malda, Murshidabad, Birbhum, Bankura and Purulia as their values of GDI are below 0.500.

It is observed that there is a high positive rank correlation and hence a close association of human development and gender development with urbanisation and industrialisation as observed in Table 21(B). For this reason, few districts closely located near Kolkata and other districts like Darjeeling and Burdwan could attain relatively higher values in terms of both these types of index. Also, on account of absence of the similar factor, 4 districts such as Jalpaiguri, Coochbihar, Original West Dinajpur and Bankura could not attain 'medium gender development' in spite of attaining medium human development on account of low percentage of urban population in these districts (Table 5). The rank correlation between urbanisation and different indicators of standard of living has been examined and shown in Tables 21(A) and 21(B). For this similar reason, 4 other districts belong to the stages of both 'low human development' and 'low gender development'. These districts are Malda, Murshidabad, Bankura and Purulia. It is quite deplorable to observe that the status of performance in the social sector with respect to both human development and gender development, few districts of West Bengal are still at par with the 'poorest section of countries' of Africa as revealed in Table 8. The low level of economic development of these districts is thus quite reasonably associated with the low level of their social sector development.

VI. STANDARD OF LIVING DISPARITIES

Figures in Table 8 show an average low standard of living in all the districts while being compared to Kolkata. Some districts have a significantly high rural poverty ratio, such as, Purulia (78.22 percent), Bankura (59.62 percent), Birbhum (49.37 percent), Jalpaiguri (35.73 percent) and Malda (35.40 per cent). Significantly high urban poverty ratio is observed in the districts of Jalpaiguri (61.53 percent), Bankura (52.83 percent) and Murshidabad (49.58 percent)

The daily news papers have frequently reported about high incidence of poverty and abnormally low standard of living in a few districts, such as Medinpur (West), Uttar Dinajpur, Dakshin Dinajpur, Bankura and Purulia. A few incidents of death caused by starvation in a village called 'Amlashole' in Medinpur (West) were reported. But the estimates of per capita monthly consumption expenditure and poverty as prepared by the National Sample Survey Organisation (NSSO) in its 55th round of survey in 1999-2000 as shown in Table 9 do not reveal the segregated estimates in this context with respect to the districts of Uttar Dinajpur and Dakshin Dinajpur and also those of the districts of Medinpur (East) and Medinpur (West). Instead, this report of the NSSO mentioned these figures in a combined form, i.e., the figures of original districts of West Dinajpur and of Medinpur. So, the study of this paper suffers from an important limitation as the separate estimates of per capita monthly consumption expenditures and poverty of Uttar Dinajpur, Dakshin Dinajpur, Medinpur (East) and Medinpur (West) could not be obtained from the report of the NSSO. At an All India level, the NSSO estimated the per capita monthly consumption

TABLE 9

Economic Capability and Poverty in the Districts of West Bengal (1999-2000)

District	Per Capita Monthly Consumption Expenditure (in Rs.)		Poverty Ratio (percent)			Population above Poverty Line (percent)
	Rural	Urban	Rural	Urban	Total	
(1)	(2)	(3)	(4)	(5)	(6)	(7)
Darjeeling	465.42	744.90	19.66	15.21	18.22	81.78 (5)
Jalpaiguri	416.43	465.23	35.73	61.53	40.44	59.66 (13)
Coochbihar	466.43	797.92	25.62	15.44	24.70	75.30 (9)
West Dinajpur (Original Combined)	484.56	843.27	27.61	19.29	26.57	73.43 (11)
Malda	428.67	655.18	35.40	6.60	33.29	66.71 (12)
Murshidabad	385.69	522.27	46.12	49.56	46.55	53.45 (14)
Nadia	458.29	774.12	28.35	15.51	25.62	74.38 (10)
Kolkata	-	992.53	-	11.17	11.17	88.83 (2)
North 24-Parganas	550.84	839.81	14.41	9.99	12.01	87.99 (3)
South 24-Parganas	453.20	828.60	26.86	8.50	23.97	76.03 (8)
Howrah	590.19	839.81	7.63	1.33	4.46	95.54 (1)
Hooghly	486.90	723.03	20.43	11.43	17.42	82.58 (4)
Medinpur (Original Combined)	490.20	864.26	19.83	19.25	19.77	80.23 (7)
Burdwan	501.58	707.92	18.99	17.00	18.26	81.74 (6)
Birbhum	382.81	669.37	49.37	21.83	47.01	52.99 (15)
Bankura	353.28	500.40	59.62	52.38	59.09	40.91 (16)
Purulia	280.15	603.00	78.72	6.47	71.44	28.56 (17)

Note: Ranks in Col. (7) are shown in parentheses.

Sources: (1) West Bengal *Human Development Report*, 2004, (p. 80), Govt. of West Bengal.
(2) *National Sample Survey*, 55th Round, 1999-2000, NSSO.

expenditures at poverty line of rural and urban population at Rs. 327.56 and Rs. 454.11 respectively. It is observed that only in Purulia, the rural per capita monthly consumption expenditure is at Rs. 280.15, i.e., below the level of Rs. 327.56 as estimated by the NSSO while in all the districts, the urban per capita monthly consumption expenditure is above the level of Rs. 454.11. The estimates of rural and urban per capita monthly consumption expenditures and rural and urban poverty ratios are with respect to the year 1999-2000 which are till now the latest estimates made by any organisation of the government. The figures of rural per capita monthly consumption expenditures vary from the lowest figure, Rs. 280.15, in Purulia to the highest figure, Rs. 590.19 in Howrah being followed by the figure, Rs. 550.84, in North 24-Parganas. Since there is no rural area in Kolkata, it is excluded from the study of rural per capita monthly consumption expenditure and that of rural poverty ratio. The urban per capita monthly consumption expenditures vary from the lowest figure, Rs. 465.23, in Jalpaiguri to the highest figure, Rs. 992.53 in Kolkata being followed by Rs. 864.26 in Medinpur. The figures of rural poverty ratio vary from the lowest percentage figure, 7.63 in Howrah to the highest percentage figures, 78.72, in Purulia being followed by 59.62 in Bankura. The figures of urban poverty ratio vary from the lowest percentage figure, 1.33, in Howrah to the highest percentage figure, 61.53, in Jalpaiguri being followed by 52.38 in Bankura. The figures of total poverty ratio (i.e., rural and urban poverty ratios combined) vary from the lowest percentage figure, 4.46, in Howrah to the highest percentage figure, 71.44, in Purulia being followed by 59.09 in Bankura. The inter-district disparity index of poverty ratios as measured by the coefficients of variation are found to be abnormally high at Rural (55.78 percent), Urban (82.14 percent) and total (55.87 percent) in 1999-2000. These are shown in Table 22. So, alternatively, it may be stated that the percentage of population living above the poverty line have 'economic capability', as the percentage of population living below the poverty line suffers from 'economic deprivation' while the percentage of population living above the poverty line does not have this suffering in a relative sense. Hence, it has 'ecoomic capability'. So, the percentage figure of the population living above the poverty line can be used to consider the 'Economic Capability Index' (*Haq*, 1997, pp. 114-15).

The percentage figures of this economic capability vary from the lowest figure, 28.56, in Purulia to the highest figure, 95.54, in Howrah being followed by 88.83 in Kolkata and thereafter 87.99 in North 24-Parganas. There are two interesting points to note as follows:

(i) In two districts, urban poverty ratio is higher than rural poverty ratio. In Jalpaiguri, the percentage figures of rural and urban poverty ratios are 35.73 and 61.53 respectively and in Murshidabad, these ratios are 46.12 and 49.56 respectively.

(ii) The total poverty ratio in Kolkata (11.17 percent) is higher than the same in Howrah (4.46).

There may be different factors behind it. But one important factor must be the high rate of rural-urban migration in Jalpaiguri, Murshidabad and Kolkata districts. The scale of urban development in Kolkata is much higher than the districts of Jalpaiguri, Murshidabad and also Howrah. It may be stated that these poor people of Kolkata consist of all pavement-dwellers, a considerable section of slum-dwellers, domestic servants and a considerable section of workers in different activities of the unorganised sector in the district of Kolkata. They have a low monthly income on an average. So all these sections of population live below poverty line and hence they suffer from a low standard of living. In the districts of Murshidabad and Jalpaiguri, the factors like increase in cross-border migration from Bangladesh, continuous sub-division and fragmentation of agricultural land holdings, sharp fall in the percentage figures of both landowner cultivators and land-less agricultural labourers (Table 14), sharp rise in the percentage figure of non-agricultural labourers (Table 14), etc. have caused high rates of rural-urban migration as well as the incidence of relatively higher poverty in urban areas.

The figures of incidence of rural poverty and total poverty in at least two districts, such as Bankura and Purulia are found to be either nearly at par or even higher if we refer to the cases of a few countries like Bolivia, Colombia, Guatemala, Nicaragua, Kyrgiz Republic, Malawi and Zambia and also the states of Orissa and Bihar in India. This is shown in Table 10. A comparison is also made with the similar figures of India and West Bengal along with the states of Orissa and Bihar (i.e., the states having the first and second ranks respectively in terms of the incidence of state-wise poverty ratios in India).

Figures in Table 11 show that there is not only inter-district disparity, but also a high degree of rural-urban disparity in the districts with respect to both per capita monthly consumption

TABLE 10

Comparison of Incidence of Rural Poverty and Total Poverty in Bankura and Purulia with other Selected States and Countries

District/State/Country	*Incidence of Poverty Ratio (Per cent)*	
	Rural	*Total*
(1)	*(2)*	*(3)*
Bankura	59.62	59.09
Purulia	78.72	71.44
West Bengal	31.85	27.02
Bihar	44.30	42.60
Orissa	48.01	47.15
India	27.09	26.10
Bolivia	81.70	62.7
Colombia	79.0	64.0
Guatemala	74.5	56.2
Nicaragua	68.5	47.9
Kyrgiz Republic	69.7	64.1
Malawi	66.5	65.3
Zambia	83.1	72.9

Sources: (1) National Sample Survey, 55th Round, 1999-2000, NSSO.
(2) Human Development Report, 2004, UNDP.
(3) World Development Report, 2004, World Bank.

expenditures and poverty ratio. The ratio of urban to rural monthly per capita consumption expenditure varies from the minimum figures of 1.12 in Jalpaiguri to the maximum figure of 2.15 in Purulia. The ratio of rural to urban poverty ratio varies from the minimum figure of 0.58 in Jalpaiguri to the maximum figure of 12.17 in Purulia.

Different dimensions of poverty and deprivation in percentage figures are shown in Table 12. The total poverty ratio varies from 4.46 in Howrah to 71.44 in Purulia. The capability poverty varies from 19.41 in Kolkata to 52.40 in Malda. The deprivation in knowledge varies from 12.95 in Kolkata to 49.77 in Uttar Dinajpur. The deprivation in Health varies from 8.55 in Kolkata to 68.66 in Malda. The deprivation in the provision of basic amenities varies from 5.90 in Kolkata to 65.56 in Purulia. The Human Poverty Index varies from 12.23 in Kolkata to 75.08 in Purulia. The incidence of unemployment varies from 1.23 in Bankura to 2.08 in South

TABLE 11

Rural-Urban Disparity in Per Capita Monthly Consumption Expenditures and Poverty Ratio in the Districts of West Bengal (1999-2000).

District	*Difference in Urban and Rural Per Capita Monthly Consumption Expenditures in Rs. (Urban-Rural)*	*Difference in Rural and Urban Poverty Ratios in percentage (Rural -Urban)*	*Ratio of Urban to Rural Per Capita Monthly Consumption Expenditure*	*Ratio of Rural to Urban Poverty*
(1)	*(2)*	*(3)*	*(4)*	*(5)*
Darjeeling	279.48 (9)	4.45 (11)	1.60 (8)	1.29 (11)
Jalpaiguri	48.80 (10)	-25.80 (16)	1.12 (15)	0.58 (16)
Coochbihar	331.49 (4)	10.18 (6)	1.71 (6)	1.66 (8)
West Dinajpur (Original Combined)	358.71 (3)	8.32 (8)	1.74 (5)	1.43 (10)
Malda	226.51 (12)	28.80 (2)	1.53 (9)	5.36 (3)
Murshidabad	136.58 (15)	-3.44 (15)	1.35 (14)	0.93 (15)
Nadia	315.83 (6)	12.84 (5)	1.69 (7)	1.83 (6)
North 24-Parganas	288.97 (7)	4.42 (12)	1.52 (10)	1.44 (9)
South 24-Parganas	375.40 (1)	18.36 (4)	1.83 (2)	3.16 (4)
Howrah	249.62 (10)	6.30 (10)	1.42 (12)	5.74 (2)
Hooghly	236.13 (11)	9.00 (7)	1.48 (11)	1.79 (7)
Medinpur (Original Combined)	374.06 (2)	0.58 (14)	1.76 (3)	1.03 (14)
Burdwan	206.34 (13)	1.99 (13)	1.41 (13)	1.12 (13)
Birbhum	286.56 (8)	27.54 (3)	1.75 (4)	2.26 (5)
Bankura	147.12 (14)	7.24 (9)	1.42 (12)	1.14 (12)
Purulia	322.85 (5)	72.25 (1)	2.15 (1)	12.17 (1)

Note: Ranks of each separate item are shown in parentheses.
Source: Calculated from the data of *NSS 55th Round Survey Report*, 1999-2000, NSSO.

24-Parganas. Here the 'incidence of unemployment' is defined as the percentage of persons unemployed in the age group of 15 years and above on the usual principal and subsidiary status to the total number of persons in the labour force" according to the NSSO (*Chatterjee and Ghosh*, 2003, p. 47).

In Table 13, the 'Index of standard of living—A Modified Measure of Human Development' has been constructed as a

TABLE 12

Different Dimensions of Poverty and Deprivation in the Districts of West Bengal (1999-2002)

District	*Total Poverty Ratio (percent)*	*Capability Poverty Measure (percent)*	*Index of Deprivation (percent) in:*			*Human Poverty Index (percent)*	*Incidence of unemployment (percent)*
			Knowledge	*Health Services*	*Provision of Basic Amenities*		
(1)	*(2)*	*(3)*	*(4)*	*(5)*	*(6)*	*(7)*	*(8)*
Darjeeling	18.22	48.08	31.14	35.90	43.94	51.85	1.83
Jalpaiguri	40.34	44.73	32.77	43.27	51.53	59.06	1.60
Coochbihar	24.70	45.54	32.27	59.42	55.03	61.79	1.56
Uttar Dinajpur	-	51.70	49.77	68.05	56.90	73.60	1.61
Dakshin Dinajpur	-	42.59	32.75	57.81	50.03	57.80	1.45
West Dinajpur (Original Combined)	26.57	-	-	-	-	-	-
Malda	33.29	52.40	45.25	68.66	58.14	71.67	1.45
Murshidabad	46.55	49.35	41.70	65.89	53.81	66.08	1.93
Nadia	25.62	34.52	32.05	36.97	36.45	46.53	1.85
Kolkata	11.17	19.41	12.95	8.55	5.90	12.23	1.65
North 24-Parganas	12.01	31.69	29.99	41.75	32.45	42.18	1.99
South 24-Parganas	23.97	44.96	33.30	56.60	46.56	55.24	2.08
Howrah	4.46	30.15	30.18	40.38	32.03	42.01	1.97
Hooghly	17.42	28.98	27.91	31.82	26.86	36.74	1.71

(Contd.)

TABLE 12 (*Contd.*)

(1)	*(2)*	*(3)*	*(4)*	*(5)*	*(6)*	*(7)*	*(8)*
Medinpur (Original Combined)	19.77	37.87	28.77	54.92	51.07	56.61	1.56
Burdwan	18.26	32.41	32.78	43.67	38.63	48.66	1.82
Birbhum	47.01	40.60	35.09	57.20	50.01	59.09	1.67
Bankura	59.09	34.30	35.93	33.57	42.07	53.32	1.23
Purulia	71.44	52.00	40.53	62.97	65.56	75.08	1.25
West Bengal	29.41	39.02	32.40	51.05	44.03	52.67	1.72

Note: Incidence of Unemployment refers to the percentage of labour force that is not in participation of work.

Sources: (1) *National Sample Survey*, 55th Round, 1999-2000, NSSO.

(2) *Towards a District Development Report for West Bengal*, 2005, SIPRD, Govt. of West Bengal.

TABLE 13

Index of Standard of Living—A Modified Measure of Human Development in the Districts of West Bengal (1999-2002)

District	*Index of Availability of Provision of Basic Amenities*	*Economic Capability Index*	*Human Development Index*	*Gender Development Index*	*Standard of living Index—A modified Measure of Human Development*
(1)	*(2)*	*(3)*	*(4)*	*(5)*	*(6)*
Darjeeling	0.56 (8)	0.83 (5)	0.65 (4)	0.600 (2)	0.66 (5)
Jalpaiguri	0.48 (12)	0.60 (13)	0.53 (10)	0.492 (11)	0.53 (9)
Coochbihar	0.44 (14)	0.75 (9)	0.52 (11)	0.471 (13)	0.55 (8)
West Dinajpur (Original Combined)	0.34 (16)	0.73 (11)	0.51 (13)	0.478 (12)	0.52 (10)
Malda	0.42 (15)	0.67 (12)	0.44 (17)	0.416 (17)	0.49 (12)
Murshidabad	0.46 (13)	0.54 (14)	0.46 (15)	0.423 (16)	0.47 (13)
Nadia	0.64 (5)	0.74 (10)	0.57 (9)	0.506 (9)	0.62 (6)
Kolkata	0.94 (1)	0.89 (2)	0.78 (1)	0.642 (1)	0.81 (1)
North 24-Parganas	0.67 (4)	0.88 (3)	0.66 (3)	0.564 (6)	0.70 (3)
South 24-Parganas	0.53 (9)	0.76 (8)	0.60 (8)	0.521 (8)	0.60 (7)
Howrah	0.68 (3)	0.96 (1)	0.68 (2)	0.570 (5)	0.72 (2)
Hooghly	0.73 (2)	0.83 (4)	0.63 (6)	0.581 (3)	0.69 (4)
Medinpur (Original Combined)	0.49 (11)	0.80 (7)	0.62 (7)	0.578 (4)	0.62 (6)
Burdwan	0.61 (6)	0.82 (6)	0.64 (5)	0.560 (7)	0.66 (5)
Birbhum	0.50 (10)	0.53 (15)	0.47 (14)	0.435 (14)	0.49 (12)
Bankura	0.58 (7)	0.41 (16)	0.52 (11)	0.494 (10)	0.50 (11)
Purulia	0.34 (16)	0.29 (17)	0.45 (16)	0.424 (15)	0.38 (14)

Notes: Ranks of each separate index are shown in parentheses.

Sources: (1) *National Sample Survey*, 55th Round, 1999-2000, NSSO.
(2) Towards a *District Development Report for West Bengal*, 2003, SIPRD, Govt. of West Bengal.
(3) Calculation of Standard of living Index is on the basis of two reports (1) and (2) as mentioned above.

simple average of figures of the following different types of index: (i) Index of Availability of Provision of Basic Amenities, (ii) Index of Economic Capability, (iii) Human Development Index; and (iv) Gender Development Index. The level of standard of living of people is reflected in this type of index that varies from the lowest figure of 0.38 in Purulia to the highest figure of 0.81 in Kolkata. The inter-district disparity index of standard of living as measured by the coefficient of variation is found at 17.24 percent. It is shown in Table 22.

In is observed in Table 14 that during 1971 to 2001, the percentage figures of landowner cultivators decreased by 15.88, 30.48, 26.81 and 13.67 respectively and the percentage figures of landless agricultural labourers increased by 1.08, 13.90, 9.72 and 2.38 respectively in four districts like Darjeeling, Coochbihar, West Dinajpur and Purulia. In all other districts, the percentage figures of both landowner cultivators and landless agricultural labourers decreased. So, there has also occurred occupational shifts. It is also observed that despite of the claim of remarkable progress in land reforms in the state of West Bengal, there has occurred loss of possession of land of *pattadars* and eviction of *bargadars* by significant percentages in most of the districts. In the state of West Bengal, the data related to the year 2002 show that 13.23 percent of *pattadars* have lost their possession of land and 14.37 per cent of *bargadars* have been evicted from their land. It is quite natural that all these factors have adversely affected the economic condition and standards of living of a significant percentage of rural households in the districts of West Bengal. However, the percentage figures of Non-Agricultural workers have increased in all the districts. If we consider the state of West Bengal as a whole we find that the percentage figures of both landowner cultivators and landless agricultural labourers have decreased from 31.97 to 19.03 and from 26.46 to 24.92 respectively, but the percentage figures of Non-Agricultural workers has increased from 41.57 to 56.05. So, it may be concluded that there has occurred a uniform process of occupational shift from agriculture to both organised and unorgansied segments of secondary and tertiary sectors in all the districts of West Bengal and hence accordingly, also at the state level.

VII. REGIONAL ECONOMIC DISPARITIES

Since 1981-82, the districts of West Bengal have been gradually able to improve the condition of their economies. This has been largely aided by land reforms and decentralised development

TABLE 14

Changes in the Composition of Working Population in the Districts of West Bengal (1971, 2001, 2002)

District	*Landowner Cultivators as percentage of Main Workers*		*Landless Agricultural Labourers as percentage of Main Workers*		*Non-Agricultural Workers as percentage of Main Workers*		*Percent of Pattadars who have lost possession of land 2002*	*Percent of Bargadars who have been evicted 2002*
	1971	*2001*	*1971*	*2001*	*1971*	*2001*		
(1)	*(2)*	*(3)*	*(4)*	*(5)*	*(6)*	*(7)*	*(8)*	*(9)*
Darjeeling	30.47	14.59	9.13	10.21	60.40	75.20	14.71	16.00
Jalpaiguri	39.79	20.30	18.22	17.64	42.99	62.06	16.72	31.60
Coochbihar	67.95	37.47	15.60	29.50	16.45	33.03	12.33	30.90
Uttar Dinajpur	-	29.54	-	39.63	-	30.83	22.35	31.49
Dakshin Dinajpur	-	30.94	-	36.26	-	32.80	19.17	30.73
West Dinajpur (Original Combined)	57.05	30.24	28.23	37.95	14.72	31.82	-	-
Malda	45.58	20.71	32.94	30.68	20.48	48.61	10.41	5.66
Murshidabad	39.46	18.48	36.12	27.99	24.42	53.53	15.87	19.06
Nadia	37.74	19.66	27.56	23.21	34.70	57.13	11.27	9.74
Kolkata	*	*	*	*	99.93	99.85	*	*
North 24-Parganas	-	9.87	-	13.51	-	76.62	16.99	16.65

(Contd.)

TABLE 14 (*Contd.*)

(1)	(2)	(3)	(4)	(5)	(6)	(7)	(8)	(9)
South 24-Parganas	-	15.96	-	25.99	-	58.05	22.07	10.31
24-Parganas (Original Combined)	24.33	12.92	27.64	19.75	48.03	67.33	-	-
Howrah	12.07	4.98	20.45	10.13	67.48	84.89	9.34	15.90
Hooghly	24.83	14.79	30.15	24.29	45.02	60.92	14.63	10.48
Medinpur (Original Combined)	45.98	28.16	34.43	31.66	19.59	40.18	5.62	9.29
Burdwan	24.23	14.59	30.58	29.88	45.19	55.53	11.93	14.50
Birbhum	37.03	23.10	42.27	36.95	20.71	39.95	16.62	9.83
Bankura	41.62	30.88	39.75	35.18	18.63	33.94	15.45	11.09
Purulia	44.91	31.24	33.71	36.09	21.38	32.67	16.11	6.7
West Bengal	31.97	19.03	26.46	24.92	41.57	56.05	13.23	14.37

Note: *Figures are negligible being 0.1 or less.

Sources: (1) *Census Reports*, 1971 and 2001, Govt. of India.
(2) *West Bengal Human Development Report*, 2004 (p. 41), Govt. of West Bengal.

through Panchayats. Figures in Table 15 show that compared to the base year, 1981-82, the index of agricultural production has remarkably increased in all the districts. Moreover, the adoption of the modern farm technology and the consequent practice of multiple cropping have also significantly increased the intensity of cropping in all the districts.

Table 15 show the figures of Net Cropped Area, Gross Cropped Area, Area under Multiple Cropping and Intensity of Cropping in different districts of West Bengal in 2002-03. It is observed that

TABLE 15

Net Cropped and Gross Cropped Area, Area under Multiple Cropping and Intensity of Cropping in the Districts of West Bengal, 2002-03

District	*Net Cropped Area (in thousand hectares)*	*Gross Cropped Area (in thousand hectares)*	*Intensity of Cropping (percent)*	*Area sown more than once (i.e., Area under multiple cropping) in thousand hectares*
(1)	(2)	(3)	(4)	(5)
Darjeeling	143.11	176.71	123.48 (16)	33.60
Jalpaiguri	329.84	577.64	175.13 (10)	247.80
Coochbihar	253.54	474.91	187.31 (7)	221.37
Uttar Dinajpur	275.21	513.78	186.69 (8)	238.57
Dakshin Dinajpur	194.61	298.50	153.38 (14)	103.89
Malda	228.48	445.69	195 (5)	217.21
Murshidabad	406.46	927.37	228 (3)	520.91
Nadia	310.80	858.40	276 (1)	547.60
North 24-Parganas	264.38	506.80	192 (6)	242.42
South 24-Parganas	380.10	539.76	142 (15)	159.66
Howrah	83.13	176.50	212 (4)	93.37
Hooghly	223.96	517.58	231 (2)	293.62
Medinpur (East)	304.64	486.06	160 (13)	181.42
Medinpur (West)	545.26	900.84	165(11)	355.58
Burdwan	469.75	859.77	183 (9)	390.02
Birbhum	326.85	537.28	164 (12)	210.43
Bankura	357.14	427.46	120 (17)	70.32
Purulia	256.94	285.37	111 (18)	28.43
West Bengal	5,354.20	9,510.42	178	4,156.22

Note: Ranks in Col. (4) are shown in parentheses.
Source: *Economic Review*, 2004-05, Govt. of West Bengal.

the intensity of cropping has varied from the minimum figure of 111 per cent in Purulia to the maximum figure of 276 per cent in Nadia. The inter-district disparity with respect to the intensity of cropping as measured by the coefficient of variation is found at 23.03 per cent in 2002-03. It is shown in Table 22.

Figures in Table 16 show that for similar reasons, compared to the base year, 1981-82, the index of agricultural production has remarkably increased in all the districts. During the period 1981-82 (the base year) to 2003-04, index of agricultural production in all the districts reveals a significant increase in agricultural production. These index numbers vary from the minimum figure of 191.62 in Darjeeling to the maximum figure of 294.30 in Medinpur. The percentage of net area shown to cultivable area in 2003-04 varied from the minimum figure of 41.65 in South 24-Parganas to the maximum figure of 88.66 in Uttar Dinajpur. In 2003-04, the net area sown per agricultural worker varied from the minimum figure of 0.31 hectare in Hooghly to the maximum figure of 0.98 hectare in Darjeeling. It shows excessive pressure and dependence of agricultural workers on land in all the districts of West Bengal.

In Table 17, we can observe the trend of production of rice and total food grains in different districts of West Bengal during the period of 1980-81 to 2003-04. These data relate to the figures of area under production in hectares, quantity of production in thousand tonnes and the yield rate in Kg. per hectare. At present, West Bengal has become the leading producer of rice in India and the production of rice has increased from 7,465.1 thousand tonnes in 1980-81 to 14,662.2 thousand tonnes in 2003-04 and the yield rate per hectare has increased from 1,442 Kg. to 2,504 Kg. during this period. It is quite natural that on account of agro-climatic differences, there has occurred inter-district variations in the production of rice and that of foodgrains.

An account of the progress of land reforms in different districts of West Bengal upto November, 2004 is shown in Table 18. In this Table, we find the data related to the area of vested land to landless agriculturists and also the recording of *bargadars* according to the scheme called 'Operation Barga'. It is observed that 16.50 percent of the net cropped area in the state has been benefited by land reforms which is an important factor behind the remarkable rise in the production of rice. However, inter-district

TABLE 16

Agricultural Production, Utilisation of Land for Agriculture and Intensity of Cropping in the Districts of West Bengal, 2003-04

District	*Percentage of Net Area sown in Cultivable Area, 2003-04*	*Net Area sown per Agricultural Worker (Hectare), 2003-04*	*Intensity of Cropping (percent), 2002-03*	*Index of Agricultural Production, 2003-04 (Base: Triennium ending crop year 1981-82=100)*
(1)	(2)	(3)	(4)	(5)
Darjeeling	47.36	0.98	123	191.62
Jalpaiguri	57.64	0.67	175	228.31
Coochbihar	77.94	0.40	187	227.02
Uttar Dinajpur	88.66	0.42	187	-
Dakshin Dinajpur	88.59	0.47	153	-
West Dinajpur (Original Combined)	-	-	173	284.08
Malda	75.98	0.34	195	220.97
Murshidabad	76.18	0.43	228	252.20
Nadia	79.65	0.44	276	256.95
North 24-Parganas	67.23	0.36	192	194.20
South 24-Parganas	41.65	0.40	142	259.72
24-Parganas (Original Combined)	-	-	162	-
Howrah	66.36	0.39	212	213.00
Hooghly	72.39	0.31	231	247.27
Medinpur (East)	75.16	-	160	-
Medinpur (West)	64.10	-	165	-
Medinpur (Original Combined)	-	0.38	163	294.30
Burdwan	67.93	0.43	183	226.47
Birbhum	74.81	0.46	164	203.56
Bankura	56.57	0.37	120	213.01
Purulia	71.92	0.45	111	259.04
West Bengal	66.31	0.42	178	236.87

Source: Economic Review, 2004-05, Govt. of West Bengal.

variations in the progress of land reforms is also observed. The minimum and maximum percentages of net cropped area being directly benefited by land reforms are 8.96 in Nadia and 23.17 in

TABLE 17

Trend of Production of Rice and Total Foodgrains in the Districts of West Bengal (1980-81 to 2003-04)

District	Trend of Production of Rice						Trend of Production of Total Foodgrains					
	Area in thousand hectares		Production in thousand tonnes		Yield rate in Kgs per hectare		Area in thousand hectares		Production in thousand tonnes		Yield rate in Kgs per hectare	
	1980-81	2003-04	1980-81	2003-04	1980-81	2003-04	1980-81	2003-04	1980-81	2003-04	1980-81	2003-04
(1)	(2)	(3)	(4)	(5)	(6)	(7)	(8)	(9)	(10)	(11)	(12)	(13)
Darjeeling	43.1	35.3	52.8	64.8	1225	1835	86.1	66.7	98.8	113.9	1148	1708
Jatpaiguri	264.7	240.2	294.7	397.6	1113	1655	286.8	277.5	319.7	455.8	1115	1643
Coochbihar	272.7	276.2	277.7	515.4	1018	1866	295.3	307.2	303.8	559.7	1029	1822
Uttar Dinajpur	457.3	295.6	486.4	700.0	1064	2368	542.0	356.9	602.4	821.2	1111	2301
Dakshin Dinajpur	*	212.3	*	519.4	*	2447	*	227.2	*	544.6	*	239.7
Malda	202.9	208.6	287.4	572.6	1416	2745	309.4	300.9	386.9	756.1	1249	2490
Murshidabad	302.6	403.5	421.8	1113.6	1394	2760	513.3	607.1	600.0	1530.1	1169	2520
Nadia	208.4	309.7	280.7	840.1	1347	2713	356.1	432.2	398.6	1034.1	1119	2393
Kolkata	-	-	-	-	-	-	-	-	-	-	-	-
North 24-Parganas	265.5	267.5	444.4	701.6	1674	2623	299.6	285.2	467.8	732.5	1561	2568
South 24-Parganas	374.3	447.5	479.2	969.6	1280	2167	399.8	460.0	495.5	981.5	1239	2134
Howrah	90.3	141.4	151.4	332.5	167.7	2351	106.7	142.1	159.6	333.7	1496	2348
Hooghly	253.2	298.2	509.3	793.2	2011	2660	268.0	299.3	524.7	794.7	1958	2655
Medinpur (East)	903.3	422.3	1255.5	1008.4	1390	2388	969.3	428.0	1289.2	1017.1	1330	2376

Medinpur (West)	*	651.4	*	1508.2	*	2315	*	673.1	*	1538.9	*	2286
Burdwan	549.4	655.5	1002.7	2008.1	1825	3063	577.9	664.3	1028.4	2023.6	1780	3046
Birbhum	356.6	585.8	1643	376.3	1110.3	2951	407.7	423.4	634.9	1208.3	1557	2854
Bankura	380.9	320.5	592.5	867.0	1556	2705	401.8	332.0	6138	888.3	1528	2675
Purulia	251.0	294.6	343.3	639.7	1368	2172	279.5	326.0	357.9	675.1	1281	2071
West Bengal	5176.2	5856.6	7465.6	14662.2	1422	2504	6099.3	6611.8	8281.4	16009.2	1253	2421

Note: * Data are not available.

Sources: (1) Directorate of Agriculture, Evaluation Wing, Govt. of West Bengal.
(2) *Economic Review*, 2004-05, Govt. of West Bengal.

TABLE 18

Progress of Land Reforms in the Districts of West Bengal (upto November, 2004)

District	Net Cropped Area in Hectares	Distribution of Vested Agricultural land (Area in Hectares)	Area of land covered by Operation Barga (Area in Hectares)	Net Cropped Area and its percentage directly benefited by land reforms	Number of Beneficiaries of land reform through:	
					Distribution of Vested Agricultural land	Recording of Bargadars
(1)	(2)	(3)	(4)	(5)	(6)	(7)
Darjeeling	1,43,003	12,586	7,012	19,598 (13.70)	52,061	12,879
Jalpaiguri	3,37,460	40,299	39,096	79,395 (23.53)	1,30,186	61,346
Coochbihar	2,57,004	25,746	33,793	59,539 (23.17)	1,28,560	84,856
Uttar Dinajpur	2,72,577	29,080	9,040	38,120 (13.99)	1,47,512	31,960
Dakshin Dinajpur	1,93,224	19,300	21,634	40,934 (21.18)	76,467	71,836
Malda	2,32,257	31,139	32,024	63,163 (27.20)	1,54,139	81,859
Murshidabad	4,03,818	18,104	26,968	45,072 (11.16)	1,53,531	85,473
Nadia	3,07,216	8,675	18,864	27,539 (8.96)	96,291	64,283
North 24-Parganas	2,57,453	10,348	19,513	29,861 (11.60)	1,22,797	74,129
South 24-Parganas	3,83,454	29,347	34,371	63,718 (16.62)	1,63,050	1,13,696
Howrah	87,106	1,872	10,062	11,934 (13.70)	25,632	42,754
Hooghly	2,25,174	5,170	25,299	30,469 (13.53)	68,834	1,13,894
Medinpur (East)	2,97,293	19,915	21,280	41,195 (13.86)	2,06,698	1,67,785

Medinpur (West)	5,65,283	91,936	31,131	1,23,067 (21.77)	6,32,575	1,50,435
Burdwan	4,66,630	24,738	46,884	71,622 (15.35)	2,09,050	1,33,503
Birbhum	3,11,447	18,880	46,220	65,100 (20.90)	1,50,715	1,13,012
Bankura	3,48,129	25,077	27,109	52,186 (14.99)	1,66,031	1,16,631
Purulia	3,39,144	29,452	3,404	32,856 (9.69)	91,032	9,226
West Bengal	54,27,672	4,41,664	4,53,704	8,95,368 (16.50)	27,75,161	15,29,557

Note: Percentage figures of districts in Col. (5) are shown in parentheses.

Sources: (1) Directorate of Agriculture, Evaluation Wing, Govt. of West Bengal.

(2) Land and Land Reforms Department, Govt. of West Bengal.

(3) *Economic Review*, 2004-05, Govt. of West Bengal.

Coochbihar respectively. The index of inter-district disparity with respect to the percentage of net cropped area being directly benefited by land reform as measured by the coefficient of variation is 30 percent in 2004. It is shown in Table 22.

Figures in Table 19 show a comparative study of inter-district disparity in Net District Domestic Product and Per Capita Income, measured at constant prices with respect to years 1981-82, 1993-94 and 2001-02. Figures in Table 20 show the Annual Compound Rates of·Growth of Per Capita Income of the districts of West Bengal during the period 1993-94 to 2001-02. It is a measure of the nature of their economic development. These growth rates have a trend towards convergence. The inter-district disparity index with respect to the net district domestic product as measured by the coefficient of variation reduced from 92.19 per cent in 1981-82 to 67.29 per cent in 2001-02. Also, the inter-district disparity index with respect to the per capita income as measured by the coefficient of variation reduced from 29.36 per cent in 1981-82 to 14.60 per cent in 2001-02. These show the signs of gradual convergence of those figures among the districts. These are shown in Table 22.

In Table 21(A), the index of urbanisation has been estimated on the basis of the percentage figures of urban population in Table 5. Using the figures of Table 21(A), the Rank Correlation Coefficients have been calculated and shown in Table 21(B). It is observed that there is a high positive rank correlation between the following items: (i) Urbanisation and Human Development (+0.86), (ii) Urbanisation and Gender Development (+0.75), (iii) Urbanisation and Standard of living (+0.81), and (iv) Human Development and Gender Development (+0.94). But it is observed that with an average low standard of living in districts, the inter-district disparity in the standard of living and in its indicators show relatively low percentage figures (Table 22).

VIII. CONCLUDING OBSERVATION

It is worth mentioning that the state government of West Bengal should pay special attention towards reduction of these different types of inter-district disparities in the context of planning for decentralised development. The problems of population explosion and cross-border migration should also be

TABLE 19

Net District Domestic Product and Per Capita Income in the Districts of West Bengal

District	*Net District Domestic Product (Rs. Crore) at Constant Prices*			*Per Capita Income (Rs.) at Constant Prices*		
	1981-82 (1980-81 = 100)	*1993-94 (1993-94 = 100)*	*2001-02 (1993-94 = 100)*	*1981-82 (1980-81 = 100)*	*1993-94 (1993-94 = 100)*	*2001-02 (1993-94 = 100)*
(1)	*(2)*	*(3)*	*(4)*	*(5)*	*(6)*	*(7)*
Darjeeling	184.98	1,059.20	1,879.75	1,750	7,715.18	11,156.18
Jalpaiguri	271.78	1,917.99	3,152.11	1,193	6,512.35	9,157.49
Coochbihar	172.38	1,250.09	1,923.61	947	5,564.27	7,702.19
West Dinajpur (Original Combined)	252.96	1,675.35	3,022.60	1,021	5,107.20	7,828.91
Malda	191.18	1,533.75	2,886.22	949	5,493.04	8,659.76
Murshidabad	463.00	2,898.92	5,199.01	1,219	5,788.67	8,757.07
Nadia	373.69	2,619.44	4,956.43	1,220	6,494.00	10,654.68
Kolkata	1,121.57	4,652.49	9,439.94	3,274	10,464.88	20,560.41
24-Parganas (Original Combined)	2,088.92	8,749.62	13,968.63	1,860	6,378.67	8,706.63
Howrah	660.71	2,669.72	4,821.53	2,173	6,910.56	11,191.74
Hooghly	701.66	3,530.80	5,953.41	1,923	7,806.88	11,712.02
Medinpur (Original Combined)	674.44	5,873.78	9,966.28	962	6,789.38	10,252.62
Burdwan	996.28	5,466.06	8,637.33	2,009	8,726.05	12,384.89
Birbhum	314.76	1,511.45	2,589.82	1,472	5,668.10	8,514.69
Bank ura	276.98	1,778.00	3,167.51	1,144	6,130.52	9,649.34
Purulia	243.91	1,210.97	2,250.63	1,292	5,262.84	8,809.96
West Bengal	8,996.20	48,397.63	83,814.81	1,597	6,755.95	10,375.82

Sources: *Statistical Abstract*, Volumes of (i) 1978-79 to 1989, and (ii) 2003, Govt. of West Bengal.

TABLE 20

Annual Compound Rate of Growth of Per Capita Income in the Districts of West Bengal (Excluding Kolkata), 1993-94 to 2001-02

District	*Annual Compound Rate of Growth of Per Capita Income (percent)*
(1)	*(2)*
Darjeeling	4.72
Jalpaiguri	4.35
Coochbihar	4.15
Uttar Dinajpur	4.20
Dakshin Dinajpur	6.48
Malda	5.85
Murshidabad	5.31
Nadia	6.38
North 24-Parganas	3.79
South 24-Parganas	4.14
Howrah	6.21
Hooghly	5.20
Medinpur (Original Combined)	5.29
Burdwan	4.47
Birbhum	5.22
Bankura	5.83
Purulia	6.65

Source: Calculated on the basis of the data in *Statistical Abstract*, Volume of 2003, Govt. of West Bengal.

TABLE 21(A)

Urbanisation and Standard of Living in the Districts of West Bengal (including Kolkata), 2001-02

District	*Index of Urbanisation*	*Index of Human Development*	*Index of Gender Development*	*Index of Standard of Living*
(1)	*(2)*	*(3)*	*(4)*	*(5)*
Darjeeling	0.323 (6)	0.65 (4)	0.600 (2)	0.66 (5)
Jalpaiguri	0.178 (8)	0.53 (10)	0.492 (11)	0.53 (9)
Coochbihar	0.091 (14)	0.52 (11)	0.471 (13)	0.55 (8)
West Dinajpur (Original Combined)	0.124 (11)	0.51 (13)	0.478 (12)	0.52 (10)

(1)	(2)	(3)	(4)	(5)
Malda	0.073 (17)	0.44 (17)	0.416 (17)	0.49 (12)
Murshidabad	0.125 (10)	0.46 (15)	0.423 (16)	0.47 (13)
Nadia	0.213 (7)	0.57 (9)	0.506 (9)	0.62 (6)
Kolkata	100.00 (1)	0.78 (1)	0.642 (1)	0.81 (1)
North 24-Parganas	0.543 (2)	0.66 (3)	0.564 (6)	0.70 (3)
South 24-Parganas	0.157 (9)	0.60 (8)	0.521 (8)	0.60 (7)
Howrah	0.504 (3)	0.68 (2)	0.570 (5)	0.72 (2)
Hooghly	0.335 (5)	0.63 (6)	0.581 (3)	0.69 (4)
Medinpur (Original Combined)	0.102 (12)	0.62 (7)	0.578 (4)	0.62 (6)
Burdwan	0.369 (4)	0.64 (5)	0.560 (7)	0.66 (5)
Birbhum	0.086 (15)	0.47 (14)	0.435 (14)	0.49 (12)
Bankura	0.074 (16)	0.52 (11)	0.494 (10)	0.50 (11)
Purulia	0.101 (13)	0.45 (16)	0.424 (15)	0.38 (14)

Sources: (i) *Census Report*, 2001, Govt. of India.
(ii) *West Bengal Human Development Report*, 2004, Govt. of West Bengal.

TABLE 21(B)

Analysis of Rank Correlation between Urbanisation and Different Indicators of Standard of Living in West Bengal (including Kolkata), 2001-02

Rank Correlation between the items:	*Size of the Rank Correlation Coefficient*
(1)	(2)
Urbanisation and Human Development	+0.86
Urbanisation and Gender Development	+0.75
Urbanisation and Standard of Living	+0.81
Human Development and Gender Development	+0.94

Source: Calculated on the basis of the figures of Table 21(A).

seriously considered. The attitude of 'bias' towards development of Kolkata and its adjacent areas must change. The unfinished tasks towards land reforms and rural development should be taken up for completion. Attention should also be given towards development of agro-based industries and suitable change of cropping pattern while considering the typical agro-climatic and geo-hydrological features of each region of the State of West

TABLE 22

Analysis of Index of Regional Disparity in West Bengal (Excluding Kolkata)

Item	*Year*	*Index of Disparity: Coefficient of Variation (Percent)*
(1)	*(2)*	*(3)*
Inter-District Disparity in degradation of land	2003-04	78.08
Inter -District Disparity in Poverty Ratio	1999-2000	Rural: 55.78
		Urban: 82.14
		Total: 55.87
Inter-District Disparity in Human Development Index	2001-02	13.96
Inter-District Disparity in Gender Development Index	2001-02	11.92
Inter-District Disparity in Standard of Living Index	2001-02	17.24
Inter-District Disparity in Intensity of Cropping	2002-03	23.03
Inter-District Disparity in the Progress of land reform with respect to the area directly benefited by it	November 2004	30.00
Inter-District Disparity in Net District Domestic Product	1981-82 2001-02	92.19 67.29
Inter-District Disparity in Per Capita Income	1981-82 2001-02	29.36 14.60

Source: Calculated on the basis of figures used in Tables 1, 9, 13, 16, 19 and 28.

Bengal since it is alleged that in different areas, the problem of severe shortage of groundwater has already emerged.

The State Government of West Bengal should pay special attention towards encouraging production of low water intensive crops. The drought-prone areas of the state should be developed by a series of different suitable types of measures. The different types of human deprivation, as observed in Table 12 should be eradicated by adopting suitable measures for human development and welfare activities. Besides Kolkata, all other districts need urbainsation and industrialisation. Finally, the programme for regional development is needed to be implemented on a priority basis, specially, in the districts of North Bengal, Malda and Murshidabad and the western region of the state consisting of the districts, such as Purulia, Bankura, Birbhum and Medinpur (West).

REFERENCES

Bureau of Applied Economics and Statistics, Govt. of West Bengal: *Economic Review*, 2004-05.

Bureau of Applied Economics and Statistics, Govt. of West Bengal: *Statistical Abstract*: Volumes of (i) 1978-79 to 1989, (ii) 2003.

Census Report, 2001, Govt. of India.

Chatterjee, Biswajit and Ghosh, Dilip Kumar (2003), *Towards A District Development Report for West Bengal*, SIPRD, Govt. of West Bengal.

Development and Planning Department, Govt. of West Bengal, *West Bengal Human Development Report*, 2004.

Geological Survey of India, Govt. of India: Bulletin, Series 'B', No. 34.

Haq, Mahbub Ul (1997), *Human Development in South Asia*, Human Development Centre, Pakistan, Oxford University Press.

National Sample Survey Organisation, Govt. if India, *55th Round Survey*, 1999-2000.

Planning Commission, Govt. of India, *National Human Development Report*, 2001.

Roy, Ranajit (1972), *The Agony of West Bengal*, New Age Publishers.

UNDP, *Human Development Report*, 2004.

World Bank, *World Development Report*, 2004.

An Enquiry into the Sub-State Level Disparities

DEBENDRA NARAYAN BHATTACHARYYA

Regional disparity in income and other important indicators of well-being is often a source of serious public concern and dissatisfaction in a federal system like India. This concern is partly reflected in the high priorities, both Planning Commission and serveral Finance Commissions assigned in matters of deciding allocation of resources among Indian states. While volumes of researches have been conducted with standard and non-standard measures of regional disparities at state or regional level, but the study of disparity in various forms within a state still remains largely elusive.

Specifically, the paper tries to explore the extent of inter-district disparities since the beginning of economic reforms in: (i) per capita income, (ii) yield rates of major food crops, (iii) HDI, (iv) percentage of urban population. In each of these four cases the paper examines whether convergence has been taking place. Besides, the study examines the linkage between infrastructural facilities available in various districts and their respective per capita income.

Our empirical analysis shows no significant inequality in PCI among the districts. But, it differs significantly when districts are clustered into four groups. Second, there is tolerable difference within southern districts but differ significantly between north-south division.

I. INTRODUCTION

Regional disparity in income and other important indicators of well-being is often a source of serious public concern and dissatisfaction in a federal system like India. This concern is partly reflected in the high priorities both Planning Commission and several Finance Commissions assigned in matters of deciding allocation of resources among Indian states and in political tensions that pervades in inter-state relationships in India. An important cause of regional tensions which led to popular agitation and at times militant activities is such regional disparities in economic and social development which exist within some of the states. Such agitations led to the creation of some new states like Chhattisgarh and Jharkhand. While volumes of researches have been conducted with standard and non-standard measures of regional disparities at state or regional level, but the study of disparity in various forms within a state, i.e. sub-state level, or what might be called intra-state variations still remains largely elusive. Undoubtedly, measuring intra-regional disparity meets with various problems and challenges. Therefore, it requires cautious attempts in developing required concepts and handling with data and overcoming the theoretical gaps in this field. However, from methodological point of view, study of intra-regional disparity does not drastically differ from the inter-regional disparity. Normally, it differs on the ground that openness of movement of goods and services within the sub-state level far exceeds from those of inter-regional movements.

The major objectives of the paper are to investigate the nature of some aspects of disparities or inequalities among the different districts of West Bengal since the beginning of economic reforms. Some recently grown political events (e.g. Kamtapuri movements, Amiashole events, etc.) point out outburst of increased regional inequalities possibly. Some statistical analysis also support this popular view. It then becomes imperative to go into the details of the intricacies of this phenomenon to draw valid conclusions about what are going on in the districts level, particularly in the economic front. Broadly speaking, variation in the economic outcomes of different districts ought to be due to differences in physical geography, human capital, culture and other initial conditions. These are reflected upon the spatial differences in a wide variety of development indictors, like per capita income, rates of growth of industrialization, trade and employment levels, labour migration, capital movements, etc. Evidently, these warrant explorations to cover the unexplained grounds.

In this context it seems relevant to mention that the inverted U-shaped hypothesis predicts its reduction through factor mobility. Neo-classical growth theory emphasizes supply side factors, like capital stock, technological change and labour which can be relied upon to eliminate regional inequality. Contrasting theories like dependency and structuralist theories, however, predict their inevitable presence as an outcome of capital accumulation and profit maximization. Again, study of convergence has been found of much relevance in the context of developed countries and attempts have also been made to examine its applicability in developing countries. In this context, two process of catching up and convergence have been examined: β-convergence, where poor regions will tend, to grow faster than the more developed regions (because of diminishing marginal returns of capital in developed regions) and α-convergence concerning cross regional dispersion/inequalities which would tend to decrease over time. Literature depicts strong empirical support of this convergence for couple of developed countries, and the opposite picture in majority of developing and transitional countries. The *National Human Development Report* of 2004 reveals vast differences in human development and poverty in 1991 and noted that over a decade and half there has been little reduction of such disparities even with improvements in HDI and HPI during this period in many such regions and also the interstate disparities persisted almost at the same level.

The study, however, is less ambitious and just concentrates efforts largely on the influence of district specific economic activities in studying the level of inter-district disparity in the state of West Bengal.

Specifically, the paper tries to explore the extent of inter-district disparities in: (i) per capita income, (ii) yield rates of major food crops, and irrigation, and (iii) the extent of inequality in the distribution of income. In each of these three cases the paper examines in a very elementary way whether convergence of any type has been taking place over time.

II. REVIEW OF LITERATURE

In fact, there is not much research evidence available exclusively addressing the question of inter-district disparities in the overall growth process in the state of West Bengal. Three principal contributors' viz. Mukherjee (2002), Mukherjee and Bardhan (2003) and Ghatak (2003) brought the issue in the forefront by making extremely careful empirical analysis supported by theoretical arguments. But their central focus lies elsewhere. Marjit *et. al.* (2004) surveyed at length on regional disparities as follows: The principal motivation behind the study of regional disparities/inequality started with the works of Myrdal (1957) and Hirschman (1958). Subsequently, a large volume of studies followed namely, Willamson (1965), Krugman (1996), Sala-I-Martin (1996), Fujita, Krugman and Venables (2003), etc. These studies mostly concentrated to explore the theoretical basis underlying the regional disparities mainly in terms of per capita income. One underlying message of many of such studies is that divergence is not monotonic and should and inter-regional convergence with the passage of time. Moreover, there are abundant empirical research on regional disparities both on India and others, and cross-country levels. Such studies have revealed a number of factors ranging from institutional differences, degree of centralization and decentralization, maketization, market failures, centre-state relationships and the behaviour of global investors, etc. that shape the extent of regional inequality.

Volumes of insightful researches on regional disparities have been conducted on India in the last two decades. K.L. Krishna (2004) provided with an exhaustive survey of these studies. Here we provide a few of them, mainly to draw some insights which will be used subsequently in studying and developing inter-district disparities in West Bengal.

Dholakia (1994) analyses 20 Indian states over the period 1960-90 and finds tendencies of convergence of long-term state domestic product (SDP) growth rates. He identifies 1980 as the year from when several of the lagging states started growing and the leading states beginning to stagnate. In a later study (2003) he re-examines the trends in regional disparity in India's economic and human development over the past two decades, and the direction of their causality. This study shows that while PCI does not show any significant trend in regional disparity over the last two decades, seven out of nine human development indicators show a marked decline in regional disparity during 1981-91. The paper therefore concludes that regional disparity in terms of human development has been decreasing but it is the income or economic development where the regional disparity has been stubborn and almost constant over the past two decades.

Cashin and Sahay (1996) also reached similar conclusions as Dholakia, finding absolute convergence in a study of 20 states over the period 1961-91.

Marjit and Mitra (1996) have examined the issues of regional convergence in 24 Indian states over the period 1961-62 to 1989-90. On the basis of real per capita net state domestic product (PCNSDP), the authors have concluded that there is no prima facie evidence in favour of convergence of PCNSDP among Indian states.

Subsequently, Ghosh, Marjit and Neogi (1997) have tried to link the relationship between growth in PCNSDP and related explanatory variables across states. Their observations also support the findings of divergence among the Indian states.

Nirvikar Singh *et al.* takes 14 Indian states for the time period 1983-2000. They take consumption inequality as a measure of regional inequality, standard of living and five other variables. The paper comes to the conclusion that looking at the broad measure of well-being there is no evidence of absolute divergence that shows in output and consumption measures at the inter-state level. The reform process has helped some states to improve their HDI ranking in the post-liberalisation era.

Dasgupta, Maiti, Mukherjee, Sarkar, Chakravorty (2000) also offer an analytical description of the economic performance of Indian states. The paper takes 1960-61 to 1995-96 as the reference period and shows clear tendency for Indian states to diverge in terms of per capita SDP but converge by sectoral shares of SDP. In other words, the structural parameters show convergence, though per capita SDP does not. The authors further comment that a detailed analysis of the effects of education, human capital formation, health care, nutrition, etc. may need to be studied carefully. The paper stresses on the need to study the sectoral allocations keeping in mind the positive trends displayed by agriculture and manufacturing in the analysis of convergence.

Finally, K.L. Krishna (2004) provides an elegant survey of the literature devoted to exploring the patterns of growth and income disparity in India. It also discusses at length the literature on the determinants of growth at both the aggregative and state levels for India. The paper asserts that during the period 1980-81 to 1990-91, the all-India growth rate accelerated steeply to 3.4 per cent from 1.2 per cent in the previous decade. All 14 states achieved growth rates above 1.9 per cent and improved their performance compared to the previous decade. The performances of Rajasthan (4.6 per cent), Andhra Pradesh (4.4 per cent), Gujarat (4.3 per cent), Tamil Nadu (4.0 per cent) were impressive. Haryana (3.8 per cent), Maharashtra (3.9 per cent), Punjab (3.8 per cent) and Karnataka (3.6 per cent) too surpassed the all-India average. Bihar, Kerala, Madhya Pradesh, Uttar Pradesh and West Bengal registered growth rates far below the all-India average. The coefficient of variation of growth rates was the least (29 per cent) in this decade. Our study is somewhat different from the above-cited approaches and analysis. One limitation of the above-cited literature is that none of them made highly disaggregate analysis. Sample based analysis is sometimes misleading. This is why in order to understand the economic process acting at disaggregative level, we have chosen to view the state of West Bengal as a collection of districts and conducted our analysis on district levels.

III. DATA AND METHODOLOGY

One of the most serious problems in the study of regional economic development is the non-availability of a consistent and reliable set of data on various economic and social outcomes. The major source of data is contained in district census handbooks. Detailed information has been incorporated since 1991. Further details are also available from the same source from 2001 onward and also in the publications of Bureau of Economics and Statistics.

For example, per capita district income originating within the geographical boundaries of the districts and accruing to normal residents of the districts, is less accurate in the sense that there are huge differences between income accruing and income originating in the districts because of movements of capital and labour across districts and also because of the presence of transfer payments, foreign remittances, interest on public debt, etc. Besides, there are several problems associated with measurements when it comes to data on the districts, as well as problems arising out of differences in prices across different districts in a given year. Moreover, relevant data based on sample survey on different districts of West Bengal needed to carry out such studies are rare. In this paper, therefore, only secondary data have been used. The area under specific crop varieties were not available before 1998-99 and for that purpose we had to use and compile such data from unpublished records with West Bengal's Department of Agriculture which maintains district-wise variety, area and yield of major crops since mid-1980s. Moreover, All India Coordinated Rice Improvement Project (AICRIP) maintains different types of data across the country particularly on the practices of modern varieties of rice. Two sources of such data that have been used in this study were taken from (1) *Statistical Handbook of West Bengal* 2004, and (2) *Towards a District Development Report for West Bengal* written by Chatterjee and Ghosh (2003), and some relevant data published by the Planning Commission time to time. In this context, it should be mentioned that the districts of West Bengal did not have any HDI ranking previously, as it had been made available now. So for the said period we had to collect from different sources the estimates of HDI for the different districts since 1991. Chatterjee made an attempt (see Biswajit Chatterjee—'Social Sector in West Bengal; B. Bhattachary in a book edited by Debes Mukherjee; and from All-India district level HDI, Planning Commission, GOI 2004). These measures adopted somewhat different methodologists and their estimates differ from each other. For this purpose we have relied much upon the estimates of Planning Commission. Surprisingly, rank correlation of these three estimates are very high-showing a possibility for substituting one by other. However, for our purpose we have chosen area (both gross cropped area and net sown area), its per capita availability, production and yield rates for four principal crops of West Bengal viz. rice (Aman, Aus and Boro) and wheat. Moreover, some relevant data relating to the practices of modern varieties for paddy and wheat and related to irrigation have been used. There are altogether 19 districts. The number has increased from 17 to 19 because of the bifurcation of two districts—West Dinajpur and Medinpur. Kolkata is obviously excluded for any kind of agricultural production analysis. Now all types of data on these two bifurcated districts are not separately available since its creation. Accordingly we reduced the number of districts into 18 by leaving Calcutta. Since we are conducting disaggregated analysis the first thing that appears to be done is the alternative classifications of these districts. As it is well understood that the aggregate effect on agriculture comes from what individual district performs. For this reason attention has been paid to look into the details of each district with reference to the relevant data. Our first computational requirements therefore are to see the mean and variability of production of different varieties across different districts across different crops, irrigation facilities, etc. Tables below report these.

Here in this paper we employ two kinds of measures to analyze the changes in district level inequality between two periods 1991-98, covering the first phase of reforms and 1998-2004 covering the second phase of economic reforms, the measures appearing in the table are the familiar CV and GiniC, where Coefficient of Variation is the ratio of the standard deviation to the mean of the distribution. The GiniC coefficient has been computed as follows:

$$Gini\ C' = 2cov\ (y, ry)\ y/Ny$$

where cov (,) / y yr is the covariance of indicator y and ranks of all districts according to y and y is the mean of y (see Pyatt *et. al.*, 1980). It must be pointed out that this in fact is a measure of the concentration of indicator y, hence we called it GiniC in order to distinguish it with the population weighted Gini coefficient which we will employ later in the paper. Milnovic (1997) demonstrates that the Gini coefficient is approximately equal to the product of three elements: a constant, the coefficient of variation (CV) and the correlation coefficient between the attribute and its rank.

TABLE 1

District-wise Land Use Statistics of West Bengal (2003-04)

(in hectares)

Sl. No.	*District*	*Reporting Area*	*Net Area Sown*	*Estimated Population 2001***
1	*2*	*3*	*4*	*5*
1.	Burdwan	698736	466630	6895514
2.	Birbhum	451118	311447	3015422
3.	Bankura	688096	348129	3192695
4.	Medinpur (East)	396594	297293	9610788
5.	Medinpur (West)	928581	565283	
6.	Howrah	138676	87106	4273099
7.	Hooghly	312224	225174	5041976
8.	24-Parganas (N)	386524	257453	8934286
9.	24-Parganas (S)	953368	383454	6906689
10.	Nadia	390656	307216	4604827
11.	Murshidabad	532499	403818	5866569
12.	Dinajpur (North)	312466	272577	2441794
13.	Dinajpur (South)	221907	193224	1503178
14.	Malda	371048	232257	3290468
15.	Jalpaiguri	622700	337460	3401173
16.	Darjeeling	325469	143003	1609172
17.	Coochbihar	331376	257004	2479155
18.	Purulia	625483	339144	2536516
	West Bengal*	8687521	5427672	75603321

* Excluding Kolkata Metropolitan.

** Census Figures.

Sources: (1) Census Report.

(2) Directorate of Agriculture, Evaluation Wing, Govt. of West Bengal.

(3) Bureau of Applied Economics & Statistics, Govt. of West Bengal.

Based on the district-wise data on percent gross-cropped area irrigated, ground water availability together with the level of groundwater utilization and source-wise irrigation status. Tables 5 and 6 identify the following districts in the state of West Bengal where the position of irrigation is very grim (net irrigated area less than 25% of the net cropped area). The stylized facts with respect to development of irrigation and watershed in this region are as follows:

TABLE 2

Index Number of Agricultural Area, Production, Productivity, Cropping Pattern, Cropping Intensity, Productivity per Hectare of Net Area Sown of Selected Crops and Net Area Sown in West Bengal (Base: Triennium Ending Crop Year 1981-82 = 100)

Year	*Index of*						
	Area	*Production*	*Productivity*	*Cropping Pattern*	*Cropping Intensity*	*Productivity per hectare of Net Area Sown*	*Net Area Sown*
1	2	3	4	5	6	7	8
1985-86	102.2	129.9	127.1	105.7	108.1	137.5	94.5
1990-91	109.8	162.7	148.2	114.2	111.8	165.7	98.2
1995-96	111.8	187.2	167.4	121.8	114	190.8	98.1
1998-99	113.9	209.9	184.3	130.1	116.6	214.8	97.7
2000-01	110.3	210.2	190.6	128.8	113.4	216	97.3
2001-02 (P)	119.4	240.6	201.5	126.8	120.4	242.5	99.2
2002-03 (P)	115.6	225.4	195	130.1	120.2	234.3	96.2
2003-04 (P)	117.5	236.9	201.6	126.8	120.5	242.9	97.5

P = Provisional Source: Bureau of Applied Economics and Statistics, Govt. of West Bengal.

TABLE 3

Categorization of Districts of West Bengal in terms of Yield, Instability of Yield and Allocation of GCA on Paddy (All varieties: Aus, Aman and Boro)

Districts with % of GCA Allotted	
A. High	*B. Low*
High yield, low C.V. Bankura, Birbhum, Burdwan, Malda, Medinpur, Murshidabad, 24-Parganas	Low yield, low C.V. Coochbihar, W. Dinajpur, Darjeeling
High yield, high C.V. Howrah, Hooghly, Purulia Nadia	Low yield, high C.V.

Notes: Yield >= 13.75 qt/ha (mid-value of range is high, low otherwise.
C.V. >= 20 is high, low otherwise.
Land allocation >= 50 percent of GCA is high, low otherwise.

TABLE 4

Categorization of Districts in the West Bengal in terms of Yield, Instability of Yield and Allocation of GCA on Wheat

	Districts with % of GCA Allotted	
	A. High	*B. Low*
High yield, low C.V.	Murshidabad, Nadia	Birbhum, Howrah, Hooghly, Cooch Behar, Medinpur
High yield, high C.V.		Bankura, Burdwan, Malda, Purulia, W. Dinajpur
Low yield, low C.V.		Jalpaiguri
Low yield, high C.V.		Darjeeling

Note: Yield >= 18.5 qt/ha (mid-value of range) is high, low otherwise.
C.V. >= 20 is high, low otherwise.
Land allocation >= 10 percent of GCA is high, low otherwise.

(i) In West Bengal, mostly the alluvial plains having a flat topography and growing mainly rice during all the three seasons are under irrigation by the major river valley projects which has caused alarmingly high water-logged conditions in the absence of proper drainage arrangements.

(ii) About 20-30 percent of available ground water potential has been utilized in West Bengal against 70-80 percent in Haryana and Punjab (*Ministry of Irrigation*, 1982).

(iii) Two types of factors have been identified for the failure of Deep Tube Wells and River Lift Irrigation: (i) The internal factors which include mechanical inefficiency lead to gradual decline in water discharge rate over time, and the lack of timely maintenance and repair which reduces the life span of the machine, (ii) The external factors include (a) erratic supply of electricity, (b) theft of transformer and machine parts, and (c) political influence on the operator to irregularise the distribution of water.

(iv) Given the imbalance between demand and supply of irrigation water, there exists a scope for making enormous profit by water sellers through selling excess water to the small and marginal farmers and even to sharecroppers.

(v) The impact of irrigation in West Bengal is comparatively lower since kharif paddy is the major crop of the state where there is no absolute necessity of irrigation, given the high rainfall, except in the years of drought. Moreover, the consumption of fertilizer and HYV seeds is quite low in West Bengal, which further brings down the impact of irrigation on crop yield.

TABLE 5

Classification of Districts in Terms of Ground Water Availability and its Use

	Low Utilization < 20%	*High Utilization > 20%*
Low availability (>2cm/year/ha)	Purulia, 24-Parganas (S)	Howrah, Medinpur (E), Dinajpur, Malda, Nadia, 24-Parganas (N)
High Availability (<2 cm/year/ha)	Jalpaiguri, Darjeeling, Coochbihar, Birbhum, Bankura	Burdwan, Hooghly, Murshidabad

TABLE 6

Districts having Critically Low Levels of Irrigation

District	*% GCA Irrigation*	*Level GW Utilization*	*Major Source of Irrigation*
Jalpaiguri	11.93	1.10	Canals
Coochbihar	8.64	4.30	Underground
West Dinajpur	23.13	23.70	Underground

Source: ARPU, Ahmedabad.

Non-availability of data for constructing measures of inequality in the distribution of income created the most difficult problem. Since no district-wise data on income distribution are available, we had to undertake an indirect method to estimate the inequality measures in the distribution of per capita income of the various districts of West Bengal. This is done on the basis of a strong assumption which of course can be justified on theoretical grounds. First, data on the size distribution of land holdings for different districts of West Bengal have become available in 2001 district census reports for West Bengal.

Now, the assumptions we make is that earnings from farming land constitute the basic source of income of the households in villages. In other words, a household's income is assumed to be proportional to the farm size, i.e. Y_iKZ_i where Z_i represents the operational size of land and K is a constant, $0<K<1$. Since productivity across districts differs, size distributions have been normalized by using average state level productivity indices for various crops. It is assumed that both upward and downward biases of the estimate would cancel out in this normalizing process. Here at this point we use an estimate of CSO (and also Planning Commission). It says that of the total income generated in the various districts of West Bengal, roughly 76% arise directly from agricultural practices. Income consumed by the households are also included in it. The rest is accounted for other types of activities such as trade, transport, etc. These mean the value of K in our equation is 76 or income of an average households arising from direct agricultural prices is 76% of the households in total income. Following this procedure we have constructed a set of data as a proxy for income distribution of various districts of West Bengal. These date have then been used to measure the extent of inequality in the distribution of households income by using Gini Coefficient and other statistical measures. Further, to examine the sensitivity of the estimates we have parameterized the Gini Coefficient measure formulae. This reflects upon the reliability of the estimate. To note that the effort made in measuring inequality is just a preliminary one and further researches are required to arrive at more reliable results. Our results can just be taken as indicative ones.

TABLE 7
Descriptive Statistics

	N	*Minimum*	*Maximum*	*Mean*	*Standard Deviation*
Aus Rice	19	1366	2811	2130.158	413.5832
Aman Rice	19	1663	2981	2285.368	363.5405
Boro Rice	19	1913	3544	2890.632	440.7098
Wheat	19	1683	2630	2201.842	287.864
Valid Number (listwise)	19				

TABLE 8

Measures of Inequality for NDDP at Current Prices of the Districts of West Bengal for the Period 1991-98 and 1998-2004

Districts	*CV: 1991-98*	*CV: 1998-2004*	*GiniC: 1991-98*	*GiniC: 1998-2004*
Burdwan	0.428	0.460	0.198	0.232
Birbhum	0.210	0.237	0.105	0.107
Bankura	1.790	1.915	0.559	0.620
Medinpur	0.449	0.346	0.214	0.190
Howrah	0.524	0.282	0.272	0.153
Hooghly	0.536	0.427	0.284	0.245
24-Parganas (N)	0.299	0.261	0.150	0.140
24-Parganas (S)	0.105	0.093	0.056	0.050
Kolkata	0.332	0.255	0.172	0.147
Nadia	0.152	0.317	0.080	0.172
Murshidabad	0.509	0.436	0.247	0.230
Uttar Dinajpur	0.153	0.121	0.082	0.067
Dakshin Dinajpur	0.520	0.363	0.264	0.206
Malda	0.036	0.027	0.019	0.015
Jalpaiguri	0.244	0.164	0.206	0.200
Darjeeling	0.158	0.213	0.334	0.310
Coochbihar	0.282	0.301	0.303	0.344
Purulia	0.251	0.371	0.356	0.398

For example, per capita district income originating within the geographical boundaries as reported in the first two columns in Table 8 show the coefficients of variation (CV) for all NDDP of the districts of West Bengal. Over a decade this measure has worsened in most cases for the two periods. It also shows man irregularity in behaviour. However, other indicators show some improvement which, given the length of the period—a decade—is trivial, (cv of other variables are not reported here)

The GiniC coefficient has worsened for the first two indicators, but some marginal improvement in HDI (which may be due to data-related problems), and significant improvement in PUP For some other variables (like roads and transport, some improvement is observable which is again trivial for a decade, and is not reported here.

However, the above measures do not take into account the

TABLE 9

Measures of inequality for the selected indicators for the Districts of West Bengal for the Period 1991-98 and 1998-2004

Districts	*Gini of NDDP*		*GE: c=0*		*GE: c=1*		*GE: c=2*		*Gini YRFP*		*GE: c=0*		*GE: c=1*		*GE: c=2*	
	91-98	*98-04*	*91-98*	*98-04*	*91-98*	*98-04*	*91-98*	*98-04*	*91-98*	*98-04*	*91-98*	*98-04*	*91-98*	*98-04*	*91-98*	*98-04*
Burdwan	0.271	0.324	0.194	0.219	0.085	0.073	0.175	0.153	0.552	0.215	0.122	0.119	0.865	0.464	0.3b2	.42
Birbhum	0.130	0.129	0.111	0.101	0.082	0.072	0.165	0.144	0.142	0.389	0.339	0.247	0.402	0.164	0.145	.15
Bankura	0.358	0.366	0.829	0.909	0.097	0.058	0.042	0.001	0.813	0.616	0.488	0.343	0.384	0.205	0.202	.16
Medinpur	0.275	0.267	0.209	0.159	0.092	0.068	0.192	0.144	0.101	0.220	0.103	0.150	0.111	0.572	0.404	.70
Howrah	0.404	0.210	0.212	0.070	0.022	0.010	0.054	0.028	0.543	0.212	0.120	0.104	0.513	0.321	0.195	.31
Hooghly	0.434	0.431	0.430	0.342	0.108	0.073	0.264	0.191	0.654	0.176	0.704	0.100	0.585	0.383	0.198	.41
24-Parganas (N)	0.269	0.239	0.122	0.114	0.044	0.050	0.088	0.101	0.605	0.383	0.778	0.130	0.872	0.503	0.314	.44
24-Parganas (S)	0.106	0.095	0.048	0.048	0.037	0.038	0.074	0.076	0.223	0.295	0.430	0.115	0.543	0.361	0.222	.27
Kolkata	0.273	0.248	0.151	0.143	0.064	0.070	0.132	0.147	0.684	0.919	0.540	0.527	0.229	0.1495	0.1224	.81
Nadia	0.142	0.359	0.051	0.134	0.030	0.009	0.060	0.019	0.179	0.973	0.364	0.672	0.416	0.246	0.262	.30
Murshidabad	0.430	0.388	0.268	0.233	0.035	0.048	0.077	0.104	0.901	0.121	0.443	0.856	0.504	0.265	0.207	.22
Uttar Dinajpur	0.145	0.120	0.071	0.062	0.048	0.046	0.098	0.093	0.972	0.291	0.177	0.160	0.191	0.107	0.939	.18
Dakshin Dinajpur	0.430	0.346	0.295	0.229	0.056	0.078	0.126	0.172	0.621	0.195	0.147	0.144	0.147	0.833	0.665	.13
Malda	0.038	0.032	0.012	0.007	0.011	0.006	0.022	0.013	0.243	0.603	0.255	0.364	0.335	0.158	0.115	.16
Jalpaiguri	0.218	0.164	0.120	0.078	0.066	0.048	0.136	0.099	0.223	0.720	0.374	0.359	0.314	0.212	0.173	.22
Darjeeling	0.255	0.339	0.368	0.377	0.290	0.178	0.614	0.292	0.102	0.607	0.484	0.169	0.257	0.110	0.202	.19
Coochbihar	0.131	0.150	0.202	0.250	0.220	0.114	0.424	0.177	0.384	0.477	0.277	0.204	0.254	0.143	0.119	.77
Purulia	0.126	0.251	0.276	0.302	0.237	0.119	0.525	0.164	0.213	0.425	0.364	0.281	0.259	0.131	0.147	.11

TABLE 10

Measures of Inequality for the Selected Indicators for the Districts of West Bengal for the Period 1991-98 and 1998-2004

Districts	*Gini of NDDP*		*GE: c=0*		*GE: c=1*		*GE: c=2*		*Gini YRFP*		*GE: c=0*		*GE: c=1*		*GE: c=2*	
	91-98	*98-04*	*91-98*	*98-04*	*91-98*	*98-04*	*91-98*	*98-04*	*91-98*	*98-04*	*91-98*	*98-04*	*91-98*	*98-04*	*91-98*	*98-04*
Burdwan	0.549	0.205	0.108	0.109	0.768	0.445	0.320	0.407	0.798	0.116	0.404	0.791	0.992	0.692	0.267	.103
Birbhum	0.138	0.361	0.300	0.216	0.358	0.158	0.132	0.148	0.230	0.771	0.237	0.296	0.385	0.282	0.982	.503
Bankura	0.787	0.590	0.432	0.318	0.341	0.197	0.184	0.165	0.295	0.929	0.350	0.427	0.540	0.347	0.153	.531
Medinpur	0.981	0.212	0.918	0.142	0.988	0.550	0.367	0.673	0.949	0.991	0.550	0.884	0.116	0.767	0.283	.102
Howrah	0.539	0.205	0.106	0.985	0.452	0.307	0.177	0.309	0.455	0.107	0.177	0.349	0.683	0.395	0.148	.489
Hooghly	0.619	0.168	0.623	0.921	0.519	0.367	0.180	0.399	0.545	0.108	0.206	0.405	0.511	0.400	0.211	.629
24-Parganas (N)	0.591	0.372	0.689	0.120	0.772	0.484	0.285	0.450	0.739	0.835	0.338	0.635	0.102	0.588	0.231	.803
24-Parganas (S)	0.217	0.282	0.381	0.108	0.483	0.348	0.202	0.270	0.567	0.828	0.236	0.427	0.687	0.464	0.185	.620
Kolkata	0.662	0.868	0.478	0.501	0.203	0.140	0.111	0.790	0.875	0.191	0.181	0.245	0.351	0.173	0.108	.367
Nadia	0.176	0.916	0.322	0.611	0.370	0.238	0.238	0.291	0.449	0.984	0.323	0.572	0.750	0.461	0.249	.666
Murshidabad	0.897	0.114	0.392	0.783	0.455	0.256	0.188	0.215	0.468	0.806	0.260	0.465	0.565	0.427	0.146	.708
Uttar Dinajpur	0.841	0.285	0.156	0.158	0.171	0.103	0.853	0.168	0.164	0.682	0.113	0.228	0.279	0.173	0.568	.236
Dakshin Dinajpur	0.537	0.191	0.130	0.139	0.132	0.805	0.604	0.121	0.132	0.890	0.673	0.142	0.194	0.139	0.516	.260
Malda	0.226	0.570	0.225	0.329	0.300	0.153	0.105	0.153	0.263	0.808	0.133	0.246	0.339	0.228	0.896	.397
Jalpaiguri	0.224	0.687	0.331	0.337	0.279	0.204	0.158	0.205	0.297	0.882	0.276	0.382	0.528	0.276	0.112	.436
Darjeeling	0.102	0.574	0.428	0.158	0.224	0.106	0.184	0.186	0.176	0.110	0.292	0.423	0.615	0.329	0.154	.584
Coochbihar	0.386	0.464	0.245	0.195	0.226	0.138	0.108	0.777	0.186	0.756	0.182	0.250	0.337	0.229	0.807	.347
Purulia	0.217	0.396	0.322	0.252	0.230	0.126	0.133	0.114	0.201	0.798	0.215	0.384	0.421	0.228	0.862	.393

population share of each district despite that they are either in per capita form or ratios. Below we employ a set of measures, which take into account the population share of each district. These measures are the Lorenz-consistent Gini coefficient (Gini) and the Generalized Entropy (GE) set of measures which are also Lorenz-consistent (*Cowell*, 1995, *Shorroks*, 1980, 1984 and *Fedoroy*, 2002). The first one measuring inequality amongst the districts can be presented as:

$$Gini = \frac{1}{\mu} \sum_{i=1}^{R} \sum_{j=1}^{R} f(y_i) f(y_j) \mid y_i - y_j \mid \qquad \text{... (1)}$$

where y_i is the value of the indicator district i, $f(y_i)$ is the population share of the district i in total population and μ is the state mean value for indicator under consideration. The GE set of measures are sensitive to various parts of the distribution. This measure is given by:

$$\Sigma f(y_i)\, [(y_i / \mu)\hat{}\, c - 1], \text{ where } c \neq 0, 1$$

$$GE = \sum_{i=1}^{R} f(y_i) \left(\frac{y_i}{\mu}\right) \log \left(\frac{y_i}{\mu}\right), c = 1 \qquad \text{... (2)}$$

$$\sum_{i=1}^{R} f(y_i) \log \left(\frac{\mu}{y_i}\right), c = 0$$

where all variables are as defined above and c is a sensitivity parameter. For $c = 0$ we will have the mean logarithm deviation which is more sensitive to lower values of the index, i.e. the bottom part of the distribution. For $c = 1$ this measure (the Theil Entropy measure) in sensitive to all parts of the distribution and setting $c \neq 0, 1$ makes the measure sensitive to the middle part of the distribution. Table 9 presents the results for these measures for the selected indicators. The last two columns of Table 9 show the results for Gini coefficient (for early 1991-98 and 1998-2004) which takes into account the population share of each district. The distribution in the latter period as compared to the earlier period shows inequality has become worse for NDDP, YRFC but less worse in the case of PUP. The improvement for HDI is notable while the improvement in other indicators is practically trivial. GE, for $c = 0$, shows that once we take into account the population shares in each district the situation has worsened with respect to NDPP, YRFC and PUP. Improvements in HDI are notable while all other indicators register small improvements after almost a decade. It should be reiterated that this measure is sensitive to the bottom part of the distribution. GE, for $c = 1$ (Theil index), shows that the distribution overall as we compare early 90s with 1998-2004 the situation has worsened further for YRFC. There seems to be notable improvements in NDDP and HDI while the remaining indicators register trivial changes. It should be noted that the Theil measure is sensitive to the entire range of distribution. For GE with $c \neq 0, 1$, sensitive to the middle part of distribution, we used $c = 2$. For this value NNDP; YRFC, HDI and PUP show that the distribution has worsened in the period 1998-2004. However, some improvements could be noted in PUP and the rest of the indicators have trifle improvements. While the situations have worsened with these indicators but there are distinct areas of improvements too. Another phenomenon is noteworthy what is called regional polarization. Polarization in the context of districts may be described as a situation where there are groups of districts at the extremes of the distributions with high intra-group heterogeneity. This reflects a different feature of the distribution than that of inequality. Technically speaking, an equalizing transfer of welfare of the Pigou-Dalton type, from a district above the median of the distribution of a district below the median would reduce inequality and polarization. A common measure of polarization is given by Esteban and Ray (ER), (*Estaben and Ray*, 1994 in *Econometrica*, 62(4), pp. 819-51).

This has been ascertained by making alternating clustering of districts and treating each cluster as a unit. It has been found that first no significant inequality NNDP at 10% level of significance when the districts are compared individually. But disparity widens when the districts are clustered into four groups. It is found that there is tolerable difference within the southern districts but differ significantly between north-south division as well as east-west division. In each cluster smallest inequality is observed with respect to percentage of urban population, the correlation coefficient between infrastructure particularly road length and transport services found to be highly correlated with HDI rank.

Another special feature is that structure of governance measured by the number of high salaried government officials has very high correlation with respect to all indicators.

IV. CONCLUSION

Our study as such provides little evidence in favour of convergence of 'α' or 'β' type. On the contrary, the result shows some divergence particularly in the second phase of reform that is during 1998-2004. One possible explanation may be the divergence between urban and rural income share and infrastructural availability. Moreover, the extent of polarization (the four values of ER : 0.137, 0.211, 0.103, 0.241 for the four clusters) that is visualized could partly be explained in terms of governance or political manoeuvering. On the whole, it can be. said that inter-districts disparities with reference to certain important economic indicators instead of being reduced have rather widened.

REFERENCES

Barro, R.J. and X, Sala-I-Martin (1992), "Convergence," *Journal of Political Economy*, 100, 2, 223-51.

—— (1995), *Economic Growth*, New York: McGraw Hill.

Basant, K.P., P.K. Roy, M.R. Saluja, and S. Venkatram (2000), "Rural-Urban Disparities, Income Distribution, Expenditure Pattern and Social Sector", *Economic and Political Weekly*, 35, 28, 2527-39.

Cashin, P. and R. Sahay (1996), "Internal Migration, Centre-States Grants and Economic Growth in the States of India", *IMF Working Paper*, WP/ 95/66.

Datta, S. *et al* (2004) "Land Use Planning in Eastern States in India," W.P., IIM, Ahmedabad.

Dasgupta, D., P. Maity, R. Mukherjee, S. Sarkar, and S. Chakraborty (2000), "Growth and Inter-State Disparities in India", *Economic and Political Weekly*, 35, 27, 2413-22.

Dholakia, R.H. (1994), "Spatial Dimension of Acceleration of Economic Growth in India", *Economic and Political Weekly*, 29, 35, 2303-09.

—— (2003), "Regional Disparity in Economic and Human Development in India", *Economic and Political Weekly*, 37, 39, 4166-72.

Fujita, M.P. Krugman, and A. Venables (1999), *The Spatial Economy: Cities, Regions, and International Trade*, Cambridge, MA: MIT Press.

Ghosh, B., S. Marjit and C. Neogi (1998), "Economic Growth and Regional

Divergence in India: 1960 to 1995", *Economic and Political Weekly*, 27, 83-116.

Hirschman, A. (1958), *The Strategy of Economic Development*, New Haven: Yale University Press.

Krishna, K.L. (2004), "Patterns and Determinants of Economic Growth in Indian States", *Working Paper No. 144*, ICRIER.

Marjit, S. and A. Mitra (1996), "Convergence in Regional Growth Rates, Indian Research Agenda", *Economic and Political Weekly*, 31, 33, 2239-42.

Pyatt, G.C.N. Chen and J. Fei (1980), 'The Distribution of Income by Factor Components', *Quarterly Journal of Economics*, November, 451-73.

Sing, N., L. Bhandari, A. Chen and A. Khare (2003), "Regional Economic Growth in India: A Fresh Look", *Economic and Political Weekly*, 37, 11, 1069-73.

Shorroks, A. (1980), "The Class of Additively Decomposable Inequality Measures," 48(3), 613-25.

Shorroks, A. (1984), 'Inequality Decomposition by Population Subgroups', *Econometrica*, 52(6), 1369-85.

Willamson, J.G. (1965), "Regional Inequality and the Process of National Development: A Description of the Pattern, *Economic Development and Cultural Change*, 13, 4, 13-45.

Inter-district Income Disparity

Dhires Bhattacharya, Puspa Tarafdar and Abhijit Dutta

The Section I of this paper has focused on the inequality across different states based on the analysis of the National Sample Survey Data and related Sources. It has been shown that there has been marked increase in inequality. The Section II of this paper has taken up the West Bengal and its districts as its main concern. The inter-district inequality has been discussed with the help of regression equations for per capita income as a function of several other variables. The results have identified the variables for inter-district disparities in per capita income. The last section of this paper has given some policy suggestions for reducing the current inter-district income disparities.

I

About one-fifth of the world's population live on less than $ 1 per day, and this is unacceptable in a world of such plenty. The twentieth century was of remarkable average income growth, but it is also quite obvious that progress was not evenly dispersed. The gaps between the rich and poor countries, and between different regions within countries have grown. The richest quarter of world's population saw its per capita GDP increases nearly six-fold during the century, while the poorest countries experienced less than three-fold increase.

Recent studies of the World Bank Development Report (1999-2000) contains the best data on the extent of income inequality (Gini ratios) covering around 50 economies. Few countries in South Asia have data on income distribution. But with poverty levels (that is percentage of people in poverty) in the high 30s or more in most countries, the low expenditure Ginis are merely a reflection of considerable income inequality prevailing in these countries.

None of the South Asian economies have had the pervasive land reforms of the type implemented in China or Taiwan. In the South Asian economies in general and India in particular, there are a wide variety of subsidies on fertilizers, food, electricity, road and rail transport and education and health. In addition, trade unions are powerful in the organized sector. Despite subsidies and unionism, the overall impact is negligible and hence inequality must be relatively high and it is unlikely that the inequality among the different regions will decline significantly in the near future in the absence of rapid economic growth and institutional changes.

In India inequality across different states is a matter of deep concern both for the economists and the policy-makers. The evidence of inequality is discussed in this section when we focus mainly on the period between 1993-94 and 1999-2000. Based on the analysis of the National Sample Survey data and related sources, we argue that there has been marked increase in inequality in the nineties in several forms. *First,* there has been strong divergence of per capita expenditures across the states, with the relatively better-off states (Southern and Western regions) growing more rapidly than the poorer states. *Second,* rural-urban discrepancies of per capita expenditure have risen. *Third,* inequality has increased within urban areas in most states. The combined effect of these different forms of rising inequality is quite large. In rural areas of some of the poorest states, there has been virtually no increase in per capita expenditure between 1993-94 and 1999-2000. Meanwhile, the urban population of most of the better-off states has experienced an increase in per capita expenditure within a range of 20 to 30 percent.

State-specific estimates of average per capita expenditure (APCE) growth between 1993-94 and 1999-2000 are shown in the

Table 1, where states are ranked in the ascending order of APCE growth for rural and urban areas combined. Except for Jammu and Kashmir a striking regional pattern emerges here. The low growth states form one contiguous region made up of the eastern states (Assam, West Bengal and Orissa) and the so-called BIMARU states (Bihar, Madhya Pradesh, Andhra Pradesh, Rajasthan and Uttar Pradesh). The high growth states consist of the southern states (excluding Andhra Pradesh), the western states (Gujarat, Maharashtra) and north-western states (Punjab, Haryana and Himachal Pradesh). It is interesting to note that this pattern is reasonably consistent with separately estimated data on per capita state domestic product (SDP) which is shown in the last column of the Table 1. All the states in low APCE growth set had

TABLE 1

Six Year Growth of APCE (Adjusted) 1993-94 to 1999-2000

States	*Rural*	*Urban*	*Combined*	*Annual Growth Rate of per-capita SDP 1993-94 to 1999-2000*
1	2	3	4	5
Assam	0.9	8.8	1.7	0.58
Orissa	1.4	-0.0	3.3	2.34
West Bengal	2.1	11.5	3.3	5.48
Jammu & Kashmir	5.4	8.0	5.3	2.49
Bihar	6.9	4.8	7.1	2.10
Madhya Pradesh	6.6	14.1	7.8	2.78
Andhra Pradesh	2.8	18.6	8.3	3.57
Rajasthan	7.0	15.4	8.6	4.60
Uttar Pradesh	8.3	10.1	9.0	2.99
Karnataka	9.5	26.5	14.1	5.82
Maharashtra	14.1	16.7	15.9	3.53
Gujarat	15.1	20.9	16.8	4.88
Himachal Pradesh	16.2	28.5	17.6	5.06
Tamil Nadu	15.7	25.1	18.9	5.39
Kerala	19.6	18.2	19.6	4.01
Punjab	20.2	17.9	19.9	2.74
Haryana	31.0	23.0	29.2	3.05
Delhi		30.7	30.71	5.69

comparatively low rates of per capita SDP between 1993-94 and 1999-2000 (below 4%), and conversely all the states in high APCE growth set had comparatively high annual growth rates of per capita SDP. Calculation of correlation co-efficient between combined rural and urban APCE growth and growth rate of per capita SDP is shown in Table 2.

TABLE 2

Correlation Coefficient Between Combined Rural and Urban APCE Growth and Growth Rate of per capita SDP

States	*Six-year growth of Rural and Urban Combined APCE (adjusted), 1993-94 to 1999-2000* (x)	*Annual growth rate of per-capita SDP, 1993-94 to 1999-20* (y)
Assam	1.7	0.58
Orissa	33	2.34
West Bengal	3.3	5.48
Jammu & Kashmir	5.3	2.49
Bihar	7.1	2.1
Madhya Pradesh	7.8	2.78
Andhra Pradesh	8.3	3.57
Rajasthan	8.6	4.6
Uttar Pradesh	5	2.99
Karnataka	14	5.82
Maharashtra	15.9	3.53
Gujarat	16.8	4.88
Himachal Pradesh	17.6	5.06
Tamil Nadu	18.9	5.39
Kerala	19.6	4.01
Punjab	19.9	2.74
Haryana	29.2	3.05
Delhi	30.7	5.69
Total	237	67.1

Correlation Coefficient between x and y = 0.45.

Within this context we undertake to examine in this paper inter-district income disparities in West Bengal and their causes with the help of regression analysis.

States are arranged in ascending order of the growth rate of

APCE for rural and urban areas combined.

Calculations based on data for the 55th rounds of NSS. For SDP calculations based on data supplied by Planning Commission (as presented in *EPW*, Sept. 7, 2002).

The correlation coefficient between rural APCE Growth and growth rate of per capita SDP = 0.224798. The correlation coefficient between urban APCE Growth and growth rate of per capita SDP = 0.722811.

The correlation coefficient between combind rural and urban APCE Growth and growth rate of per capita SDP shows a medium correlation coefficient between the two series (0.45).

Combined Rural and Urban APCE and per capita SDP

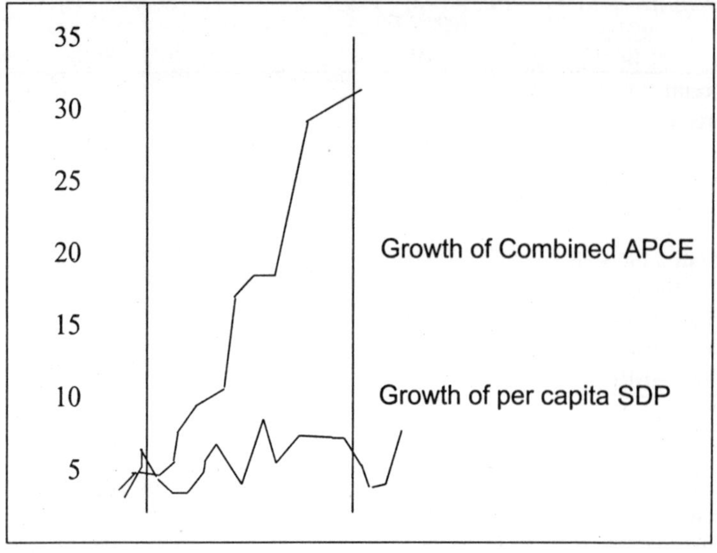

Notes: Correlation Coefficient for Rural is VERY LOW. (=0.224798)
Correlation Coefficient for Urban is HIGH. (=0.722811)
Correlation Coefficient for Combined is MEDIUM (=0.45)

Agricultural wages provide an important source of future information on poverty. Real wages are highly correlated with standard poverty indexes such as head count ratio: where poverty is higher wages tend to be lower, and *vice versa*, It is also possible to think about real wages as a round poverty indicator.

According to recent estimates based on agricultural wages in India (AWI), real agriculture wages were growing at about 5 percent per year in the eighties and 2.5 percent per year in the nineties. But even the reduced growth rate of agricultural wages in the nineties at 2.5 percent per year points to significant growth of per capita expenditure among the poorer section as found earlier.

II

With a population of about 82 million in 2001, according to 2001 census, West Bengal is the fourth most populous state situated in the Eastern region of India. About 72 percent of the people live in rural areas. According to the Planning Commission the proportion of population below the poverty line in 1999-2000 in West Bengal was 31.85 percent. A significant part of the state is relatively more backward economically, and also tends to be less advanced in terms of human development. These include large parts of the six northern districts (Darjeeling, Jalpaiguri, Coochbihar, Malda, Uttar and Dakshin Dinajpur), three western districts (Purulia, Bankura and Birbhum), and the Sundarban area of the South 24-Pargana district in the south of the state.

The aggregate state domestic product in 2000-01 is about Rs. 7860 crores at current prices and per capita SDP was about Rs. 16072. This is higher than the National average. It reflects a compound annual growth rate of 7 per cent and per capita growth of 5.4 per cent over the period 1993-94 to 2000-01, making West Bengal one of the fastest growing states in India in that period.

For a long time food production in West Bengal remained stagnant and the technology of Green Revolution by-passed the state. There has been significant spurt in agricultural production in the early 1980s, and the state is now surplus in foodgrains production. There has also been some diversification in cultivation so that along with jute, West Bengal is now the major producer of vegetables in the country. Tea plantations, a major foreign exchange earner, also occupy a substantial proportion of land in West Bengal. Despite the apparent success in certain sectors, on the whole the process of global economic integration did little to improve the trend rate of GDP growth beyond the levels achieved from the early 1980s, did not cause a dramatic improvement in the material conditions of most of the population and generally added to greater vulnerability and insecurity. The rate of growth of aggregate GDP in constant prices has been between 5.5 per cent and 5.8 per cent each in each five year period since 1980. Moreover, this growth has been marked by significant increases in regional and spatial inequalities. Most significantly, the period since 1990 has been marked by very low rates of employment generation. Rural employment in the period 1993-94 to 1999-2000 grew at a low annual rate of less than 0.6 percent per annum while urban employment growth was 2.3 per cent per annum.

In sum, the economic reforms policy which are typically described as a package of globalization, liberalization and privatization, bore some adverse effects on the economy such as increasing income inequality, worsening trends in per capita food consumption and nutrition and deceleration in employment generation. All these in turn meant that progress in improving human development indicators as a whole has been relatively slow in West Bengal. It is evident that human development in West Bengal presents a mixed picture, and this is further complicated by the variations across the districts in the state. The following Table 3 presents the calculations of HDI for different districts, as well as for the state as a whole. The Table refers to undivided Dinajpur because of the nature of available data. There are very substantial differences across districts, such that HDI ranges from a high of 0.78 per cent for Kolkata to a low of 0.44 per cent for Malda. The Gini coefficient for rural consumption expenditure in West Bengal was 0.224 compared to national average of 0.258 and for urban areas it was 0.328 as compared to the national average 0.341.

The State of West Bengal currently has 19 administrative districts. The metropolitan city, Kolkata (formerly Calcutta) constitutes a district by itself and has, as expected, the highest per capita income among all the districts. Since agricultural incomes have little or no importance in this district, we have decided to leave Kolkata out of account in our regression.

The district of Dinajpur has only recently been bifurcated into North and South Dinajpur. Comparable data not being available for pre-bifurcation and post-bifurcation scenarios, we decided to work out the regression by omitting Dinajpur altogether from our analysis. As for the district of Medinpur, now divided into two

TABLE 3

Human Development Indices by Districts

	Health Index	*Income Index*	*Education Index*	*HDI*	*HDI rank*
Darjeeling	0.73	0.49	0.72	0.65	4
Jalpaiguri	0.61	0.38	0.60	0.53	10
Coochbihar	0.50	0.41	0.65	0.52	11
Dinajpur	0.62	0.39	0.53	0.51	13
Malda	0.49	0.36	0.48	0.44	17
Murshidabad	0.57	0.29	0.52	0.46	15
Birbhum	0.53	0.27	0.61	0.47	14
Burdwan	0.74	0.47	0.71	0.64	5
Nadia	0.65	0.41	0.66	0.57	9-
North 24-Parganas	0.72	0.49	0.76	0.66	3
Hoogly	0.77	0.46	0.67	0.63	6
Bankura	0.67	0.26	0.62	0.52	11
Purulia	0.61	0.18	0.55	0.45	16
Medinpur	0.68	0.45	0.74	0.68	7
Howrah	0.77	0.53	0.75	0.68	2
Kolkata	0.82	0.73	0.80	0.78	1
South 24-Parganas	0.71	0.40	0.68	0.60	8
West Bengal	0.70	0.43	0.69	0.61	

Source: Human Development Report, 2004, p. 13, Govt. of West Bengal.

separate districts, East and West Medinpur, we have made use of available data for the undivided district of Medinpur for all the four years to which our data relate.

As a result, the number of districts included for our analysis in this particular study happens to be 15. Among these 15 districts the highest per capita income (same as per capita State Domestic Product) was generated in Burdwan district in three out of four years that we studied; in the last year of our study, however, (year 2000-01) Howrah district stole the show from Burdwan.

The lowest per capita income fell usually to the lot of Purulia district, but Malda was also a close second. In one particular year out of four (1998-99) Malda's per capita income fell below that of Purulia. The range of per capita income was between Rs. 7857.06 and Rs. 11401.00 in 2000-01, prices of 1993-94 being used for all income calculations. The average per capita income for this particular year (Rs. 9249.84) was over 40 per cent of the corresponding average in 1993-94, thus implying a uniform growth rate of a little less than 5 per cent per year.

We have estimated equations across 15 West Bengal districts for per capita income using a linear specification of the variables in four different years, viz. 1993-94, 1995-96, 1998-99 and 2000-01. Thus both cross-section as well as time series data were used to obtain the results. The multiple regression equation used by us was

$$PCIS = \beta_0 + \beta_1\ INEMS + \beta_2\ AGPYS + \beta_3\ RDPAS + \beta_4\ LTS.$$

Here, PCIS, the dependent variable, is the standardized value of per capita income across districts. The set of independent variables used to explain the variability in PCIS is INEMS (standardized value of number of industrial employees), AGPYS (standardized value of agricultural productivity index), RDPAS (standardized value of total road length, maintained both by Public Works Department and Jila Parishad, per unit of area) and LTS (standardized value of literacy rate). Standardized values are taken to make the different measures free from unit. The β-coefficients measure the impact of the regressors on the regressand, and all are expected to be positive.

The data for a district-wise record of the PCI was collected from the State Domestic Product and District Domestic Product of West Bengal (1993-94 to 2002-03). One advantage for the choice of 1993-94 as the starting point of the analysis is that the measurements of PCI for all succeeding years are calculated with 1993-94 as the base year. The district-wise data on the number of industrial employees, agricultural productivity index and data on road lengths was collected from the Statistical Abstract 1993-94, 1997-98 and 2001-02, published by the Bureau of Applied Economics and Statistics, Government of West Bengal. For the district-wise break-up of the percentage literacy rate, we used the data on Census of India, 1991 and 2001. Here, literacy rate excludes children in the age group 0-6 for both the years. Since we do not have the data on literacy rate for all the intermediate years, the rate of growth over the decade 1990-91 to 2000-01 has been dispersed assuming uniform growth rate over the decade (Table 5).

TABLE 4

	1993-94	1995-96	1998-99	2000-01
INEMS	0.2673 (0.4193)	0.2076 (0.3211)	0.1126 (0.6591)	-0.1663 (0.2287)
AGPYS	0.0069 (0.2797)	0.1189 (0.3010)	-0.3112 (0.4335)	0.1857 (0.4118)
LTS	0.4211 (0.3576)	0.1741 (0.3075)	0.3230 (0.5593)	0.6550 (0.3265)
RD/AS	0.0156 (0.2615)	0.2908 (0.2901)	-0.0867 (0.3595)	0.2143 (0.3791)
HOSPS	0.2283 (0.2637)	0.3251 (0.3062)	0.5327 (0.4882)	-0.31367 (0.2689)
R^2	0.59914	0.46297	0.48178	0.49615

TABLE 5

Literacy Rates in Districts of West Bengal

Dists.	1990-91	1993-94	1995-96	1998-99	2000-01	Per annum
Bankura	52.04	55.58	57.94	62.66	63.84	1.18
Birbhum	48.56	52.64	55.36	60.8	62.16	1.36
Burdwan	61.88	64.62	66.44	70.09	71.00	0.912
Coochbihar	45.78	52.21	56.50	65.07	67.21	2.143
Darjeeling	57.95	62.43	65.41	71.38	72.87	1.492
Hoogly	66.78	69.42	71.19	74.71	75.79	0.881
Howrah	67.62	70.63	72.63	76.64	77.64	1.002
Jalpaiguri	45.09	50.65	54.36	61.77	63.62	1.853
Malda	35.62.	40.15	43.17	49.20	50.71	1.509
Medinpur	69.32	71.08	72.25	74.59	75.17	0.585
Murshidabad	38.28	43.31	46.67	53.37	55.05	1.677
N 24-Parganas	52.53	56.74	59.54	65.15	66.55	1.402
Nadia	66.82	70.32	72.66	77.33	78.49	1.168
Purulia	43.29	47.15	49.72	54.85	56.14	1.285
S 24-Parganas	55.10	59.62	62.63	68.65	70.16	1.506

Our regression equation was fairly successful in identifying the variables responsible for inter-district disparities in per capita income. Some additional explanatory variables (such as weather variations) could have been primarily responsible for the remaining disparities.

Estimated equations for four periods (1993-94, 1995-96, 1998-99 and 2000-01) are as follows:

1993-94: $PC1S = \beta_0 + 0.45\ INEMS + 0.08\ AGPYS - 0.01\ RDPAS + 0.37\ LTS.$
$\qquad\qquad (0.36) \qquad (0.26) \qquad (0.26) \qquad (0.35)$
$R^2 = 0.57$

1995-96: $PCIS = \beta_0 + 0.38\ INEMS + 0.23\ AGPYS + 0.22\ RDPAS + 0.22\ LTS.$
$\qquad\qquad (0.28) \qquad (0.29) \qquad (0.29) \qquad (0.31)$
$R^2 = 0.40$

1998-99: $PCIS = \beta_0 + 0.71\ INEMS + 0.02\ AGPYS + 0.14\ RDPAS - 0.16\ LTS.$
$\qquad\qquad (0.36) \qquad (0.31) \qquad (0.29) \qquad (0.34)$
$R^2 = 0.41$

2000-01: $PCIS = \beta_0 - 0.27\ INEMS + 0.01\ AGPYS + 0.24\ RDPAS + 0.69\ LTS.$
$\qquad\qquad (0.41) \qquad (0.29) \qquad (0.27) \qquad (0.39)$
$R^2 = 0.42$

Industrial employment has positive impact on the PCI but turned out to be negative in the last year of our analysis. As for agricultural productivity index the impact is positive but small except in the period 1995-96. As a proxy for infrastructural development we used total road length per unit of area and the impact is positive except in the first period of our analysis. Literacy rate has positive impact on the PCI except for the year 1998-99.

Our general impression is that industrial employment has been the most important contributing factor in generating income growth, followed by growth in literacy rate and infrastructure (road length per square Km). Agricultural productivity has the least impact among all the four explanatory variables. Here we have not been able to allow for cross effects of literacy on agricultural productivity or industrial employment. As for industrial employment in the districts, the impact in the early years of the decade (1990-2000) does not appear to have been sustained in the later years.

In an alternative specification of the model we used the standardized values of industrial employment, agricultural productivity index, literacy rate, road length per square km. and number of hospitals. The regression result is given below. The coefficients have expected signs in the year 1993-94 and 1995-96.

Literacy rate has expected sign for all the sample years. I lowever. industrial employment in 2000-01, agricultural productivity index in 1998-99, road length per square km. in 1998-99 and number of hospitals in 2000-01 failed to yield expected sign. The coefficient for number of hospitals is not significant (underlined ones) except for the year 1998-99.

Thus we can conclude that no clear picture emerges from the analysis except for the fact that industrial employment has a steadily declining impact on per capita district domestic product. Inclusion of number of hospitals as a proxy for human resource development has not contributed significantly. Agricultural productivity index has irregular impact on PCI.

III

It appears from our regression exercise that the relation between SDP and agricultural production has been relatively less important than other factors like growth in overall literacy, advances in industrialization and last but not the least, improvements in agricultural productivity possibly aided by the emergence of a more literate and better informed farming community. Since the policy of the Government of West Bengal is directed towards higher literacy levels in every district of the State, one can look forward to a time when a literate farming community will by themselves raise district income levels by using more productive techniques of cultivation, as well as by moving away from poorly paid agricultural occupation to better paid non-agricultural activities.

This natural process of narrowing down inter-district income disparities can, however, the quickend through an overhaul of the District Agricultural Extension Services. Mutually re-inforcing activities involving collaboration between "Sarva Shiksha Abhiyan experiment" and the "Agricultural Extension Services" at the district level can be expected to level up incomes in the low-income districts with untapped potential for further intensification of agricultural work.

For districts or 'blocks' where such potential is low or totally absent. State industrial policy has to take over. Types of industry requiring high man-power use at all levels of literacy will have to be encouraged in the low-income districts, with some initial incentive payment and subsidies which are to be gradually withdrawn as income levels and employment generation register an appreciable rise. At the same time, mobility of labour from low-income to high-income districts has to be facilitated as far as practicable, by providing incentive payments initially to entrepreneurs from low-income districts, intending to set-up establishments in vacant occupational fields in the high-income districts. All these will naturally be helped by the development of a travel and transport infrastructure with some cross-subsidization in the fares and charges. In short, further spread of literacy and quicker establishment of non-agricultural workplaces should be the two main pillars of a policy for reducing the current inter-district income disparities.

REFERENCES

Govt. of West Bengal, State Domestic and District Domestic Product of West Bengal, (1993-94 to 2002-03 for PCI).

Govt. of West Bengal, Bureau of Applied Economics and Statistics, *Statistical Abstract, 1993-94, 1997-98, 2001-02, 2002-03*.

Census of India, 1991 and 2001 (literacy exclude children in the age group 0-6 for both the years).

Govt. of West Bengal, *Economic Review* (*2001-02, 2002-03*).

Govt. of West Bengal, Development and Planning Department, *West Bengal Human Development Report, 2004*.

Tarafdar, Puspa (2003), 'Impact of Globalization on Poverty', 86th Conference Volume of Indian Economic Association, Kolhapur.

Tarafdar, Puspa (2001), 'Globalization and its Impact on Developing Countries with Reference to Asia, 84th Conference Volume of IEA, Varanasi.

Growth, Diversification and Instability

Gunendra Prasad Pal

The economy of West Bengal depends on economic development of its constituent districts. Variations in the economic structure of the districts expectedly affect the development pattern of West Bengal. It is expected that there will be a wide variation in the inter-district development pattern if the development policies have not been uniformly implemented everywhere in the state. Periodic variations in the Net District Domestic Product (NDDP) take place specially and occupationally. So it is of importance to examine the nature and extent of diversification in the activity structure of the constituent districts.

The present study concentrates on the inter-district and inter-region performance of different economic activities during the post-reform period, 1993/94—2001/02. The patterns of NDDP among the activities and the nature of NDDP growth are examined district-wise, region-wise and industry-wise. Also examined are the growth divergence and instability of NDDP among the district and the relationship between activity diversification and NDDP of the district.

The occupational patterns of NDDP across districts and across regions are heterogeneous during the post-reforms period. The inter-sector as well as intra-sector heterogeneities are also prominent. West Bengal being a federal state of India has experienced divergent development patterns across its constituent districts and regions. The share of the TS and hence Trade and Commerce has increased at the cost of agriculture: activities have tended to be diversified. But still inter-district and inter-region disparity prevails in the activities performed. The direct relationship between activity diversification and NDDP of the district is indicative of the policies (reforms) should be formulated towards greater diversification of activities in the districts so as to reduce periodic variation in NDDP and hence per capita NDDP.

Interdependence between public and private initiatives has changed in India's economy during the post-reform period. Have changed also the interrelationships among the different types of occupations (sectors): primary, secondary and tertiary. Studies on India's economic performance are numerous at both aggregate and disaggregate levels (*Shetty, Dutta*). The intertemporal study of the sectors performed under both public and private initiatives is also available (*Pal et al.*). As a federal state of India, the economy of West Bengal depends on the economic development of its constituent districts. Variations in the economic structure of the districts expectedly affect the development pattern of West Bengal. It is expected that there will be a wide variation in the inter-district development pattern if the development policies have not been uniformly implemented everywhere in the state. Periodic variations in the Net District Domestic Product (NDDP) have taken place spatially and occupationally. No detailed (disaggregative) study at the district level in West Bengal is, however, available. So it is of importance to examine the nature and extent of diversification actually happened in the activity structure of the constituent districts of West Bengal.

The development pattern in 17 districts of West Bengal has not been uniform. Some districts which are located near the metro city of Kolkata, have been relatively more developed compared to some other districts which are far away from it. The imbalance in development among the districts of West Bengal still persists. 41% of total NDDP have been accounted for jointly by Kolkata, Howrah, Hooghly, 24-Parganas (N) and 24-Parganas (S) in 2001-02. On the contrary, the share is only 15% due to Dakshin Dinajpur, Uttar Dinajpur, Malda, Jalpaiguri, Darjeeling and

Coochbihar in the same year. Per capita income in Kolkata has become more than double of that in Dakshin Dinajpur. Though each district is not endowed with all types of resources, regional imbalance in development should be either reduced or removed so as to maintain the socio-economic integrity of the state and hence of the country.

In order to examine the extent of the regional development in West Bengal, areas of regionalization should be classified. On the basis of geographical factors we have divided the state into three major regions: (i) North Bengal Region (NBR) consisting of Coochbihar, Darjeeling, Jalpaiguri, Dakshin Dinajpur, Uttar Dinajpur and Malda districts; (ii) West Plain Region (WPR) containing Birbhum, Bankura, Medinpur and Purulia districts; and (iii) South Bengal Region (SBR) comprising of Burdwan, Howrah, Hooghly, 24-Parganas (N), 24-Parganas (S), Nadia and Murshidabad districts. The economy of West Bengal is more or less rural-based. Kolkata has metro-infrastructure and performed non-rural activities. So we have excluded the district of Kolkata from our study because of comparison of the three regions in respect of development pattern.

Thirteen economic activities are grouped into three broad sectors: (a) Primary Sector (PS) consisting of agriculture, fishing, forestry and mining and quarrying; (b) Secondary Sector (SS) containing manufacturing, construction, electricity, gas and water supply; and Tertiary Sector (TS) consisting of trade and commerce, transport and communication, banking and insurance, real estate and business services, public administration and other services. Out of thirteen activities, we have studied only four activities in details namely Agriculture (AG), Manufacturing (MF), Trade and Commerce (TC); and Transport and Communication (TRC) because of their prime places in the development pattern of PS, SS and TS respectively during the period 1993/94—2001/02.

Section I deals with the patterns of Net District Domestic Product (NDDP) of the activities performed in 17 districts and three regions of the state while in section II the extent and the nature of NDDP growth and divergence among the districts for the occupations are considered. Periodic variation in NDDP measured in terms of instability index is discussed in section III. Section IV presents the relationship between NDDP and occupational diversification. The last section gives concluding remarks.

I. PATTERN OF NET DISTRICT DOMESTIC PRODUCT

District-wise Pattern

Periodic variations in the shares of different activities in NDDP exhibit the development pattern. The occupational patterns of NDDP across districts are heterogeneous during the post-reforms period. The inter-sector as well as intra-sector heterogeneities in the distribution of NDDP are also prominent. As regards the intra-sector analysis, it is noted that agriculture has contributed more than 83% of NDDP to the primary sector while the share of manufacturing is more than 72% of NDDP to the secondary sector during the period under study. Among the major components of the tertiary sector, the shares of trade and commerce, transport and communication are above 26% and 12% respectively.

Turning to the inter-sector distribution (Table 1) it is found that PS has the prime share in NDDP in most of the districts in 1993-94 and 1997-98 but it has a dominant role in NDDP in Malda and Dakshin Dinajpur during the period. In the state as a whole, its contribution to NDDP has declined overtime: 36% in 1993-94, 34% in 1997-98 and 29% in 2001-02. Across districts, the share ranges from 15% in Howrah to 57% in Coochbihar in 1993-94. These two districts have all through maintained their relative position: 14% and 54% in 1997-98, 11% and 45% in 2001-02. Its share has, however, declined everywhere in the state during the period.

The contribution of SS has declined in the state and in most of the districts all through. Its share is as high as 35% in Howrah being followed by Burdwan, 24-Parganas (N) while Coochbihar has registered the lowest share (less than 9%) all through. Nadia has exhibited its marginal improvement in SS.

TS has become the most important sector everywhere in the state in 2001-02. Its share has considerably increased over time everywhere at the cost of PS. In West Bengal, the share of TS is more than 34% all through.

Among all the activities, agriculture has remained all through dominant almost everywhere in West Bengal. It has recorded its highest share in NDDP in Coochbihar being followed by Malda and Dakshin Dinajpur. Its share has, however, declined overtime everywhere. The place of trade and commerce (TC) is next to agriculture. Its share has considerably increased almost

TABLE 1

Sectoral Distribution (%) of NDDP in West Bengal

District	*1993-94*				*1997-98*				*2001-02*			
	PS	*SS*	*TS*	*All*	*PS*	*SS*	*TS*	*All*	*PS*	*SS*	*TS*	*All*
Burdwan	41.7	23.0	35.3	100.0	39.1	22.2	38.7	100.0	32.7	34.4	42.9	100.0
Birbhum	49.00	12.8	38.2	100.0	49.6	10.4	40.0	100.0	42.9	10.8	46.3	100.0
Bankura	50.0	13.6	36.4	100.0	50.4	12.2	37.4	100.0	40.8	14.2	45.0	100.0
Medinpur	43.4	18.2	38.4	100.0	42.3	16.5	41.2	100.0	35.7	16.8	47.5	100.0
Howrah	15.0	34.4	50.6	100.0	14.2	32.2	53.6	100.0	11.3	31.0	57.7	100.0
Hooghly	34.6	35.4	40.0	100.0	32.0	23.0	45.0	100.0	27.0	24.4	48.6	100.0
24-Parganas (N)	25.0	29.9	45.1	100.0	21.4	35.0	43.6	100.0	20.3	29.8	49.9	100.0
24-Parganas (S)	31.5	28.4	40.1	100.0	28.4	29.2	42.4	100.00	26.1	25.5	48.4	100.0
Nadia	49.2	13.4	37.4	100.0	43.4	18.2	38.4	100.0	39.3	19.2	41.5	100.0
Murshidabad	45.0	34.3	20.7	100.0	42.7	19.9	37.4	100.0	37.8	19.2	43.0	100.0
Uttar Dinajpur	53.0	9.0	38.0	100.0	50.5	8.8	40.7	100.0	42.4	9.9	47.7	100.0
Dakshin Dinajpur	50.6	9.4	40.0	100.0	48.5	9.9	41.6	100.0	45.9	9.0	45.1	100.0
Malda	52.8	10.7	36.5	100.0	52.0	11.2	36.8	100.0	45.6	11.1	43.3	100.0
Jalpaiguri	44.7	19.6	35.7	100.0	41.2	20.9	37.9	100.0	34.5	20.6	35.9	100.0
Darjeeling	37.7	14.1	48.2	100.0	41.8	13.1	45.1	100.0	29.9	13.9	56.2	100.0
Coochbihar	57.4	7.8	34.8	100.0	54.0	8.5	37.5	100.0	45.1	9.2	45.7	100.0
Purulia	44.5	14.9	40.6	100.0	46.1	14.9	39.0	100.0	36.4	17.5	46.1	100.0
West Bengal	35.9	21.3	42.8	100.0	34.0	21.0	45.0	100.0	28.8	20.1	51.1	100.0

Note: PS: Primary Sector; SS: Secondary Sector; TS: Tertiary Sector.
Source: *Statistical Abstract*, Government of West Bengal, 2002-03.

everywhere excepting Darjeeling and Burdwan. TC has contributed as high as 15% in case of Howrah, Hooghly, 24-Parganas (N), 24-Parganas (S) during the period whereas Uttar Dinajpur, Dakshin Dinajpur and Coochbihar have registered as low as 10% of NDDP in TC. MF has occupied its place next to TC. In the State it has shared about 15%. The districts registering less than 7% of NDDP (lowest) are Coochbihar, Uttar Dinajpur, Bankura, Birbhum, Darjeeling and Dakshin Dinajpur. The share of MF is as high as 28% of NDDP in Howrah being followed by 24-Parganas (N), Hooghly, 24-Parganas (S). TRC has contributed more than 8% over time only in Howrah but its share is less than 4% in most of the districts.

Region-wise Pattern

The heterogeneities in the structural composition of NDDP have been found also in different regions. As regards intra-sector analysis, it is noted that agriculture has accounted for more than 93% of NDDP of PS in the NBR during the period under study. On the contrary, manufacturing has shared more than 80% all through in the SBR but its contributions are relatively less in two other regions. The share of trade and commerce is as high as 30% in the SBR being followed by the WPR (28%), the NBR (23%). The SBR is relatively advanced in case of manufacturing while the NBR is relatively backward in case of trade and commerce.

The sector-wise distribution reveals that PS has remained all through dominant (40%) in the NBR. Its share has decreased over time everywhere. SS has contributed 25% in the SBR followed by the WPR. Its share is more or less stagnant everywhere. TS has accounted for more than 41% of NDDP in the SBR followed by the WPR. Its share has increased over time at the cost of PS in all regions.

Activity-wise analysis of NDDP reveals that agriculture has appeared to lead the development pattern irrespective of the regions though its share has decreased over time everywhere. Manufacturing has occupied its place next to trade and commerce, excepting in the SBR. Its share has increased only in the SBR over time. The share of TC is highest in the SBR during the period.

Overall Aspect of NDDP-Pattern

Let us now turn to the analysis of overall characteristics of the

NDDP pattern. To examine its overall aspect we have computed the Activity Diversification Index (DI)[1] based on Theil entropy measure (*Theil*, 1967). Higher the value of DI, higher the degree of diversification in the occupational pattern of NDDP and in turn lower the possibility of the activity-pattern being dominated by a particular activity or a group of activities. Here maximum value of DI is unity. This indicates that all activities are contributing equally to NDDP.

Estimates (Table 2) show that values of DI are less than unity everywhere in the state during the period indicating that the activities so performed have not contributed equally to NDDP: a few activities have assumed higher importance in NDDP. Interestingly, Howrah, Hooghly, 24-Parganas (N), 24-Parganas (S), nearer the capital city of Kolkata, have registered diversification indices more than 0.92. Therefore, the occupational patterns of these districts exhibit a relatively smaller degree of activity dominance. On the other hand, activity dominance is relatively more prominent in case of Birbhum, Bankura, Uttar Dinajpur, Dakshin Dinajpur and Coochbihar (less than 0.80 each). DI has increased only in Bankura during the period: the NDDP-pattern in this district has tended to be more diversified.

Among the regions the activity pattern of the SBR has exhibited a relatively smaller degree of activity dominance: 0.9169 in 1993-94 and 0.9453 in 2001-02. On the contrary, activity dominance is relatively more in the NBR: 0.7831 and 0.8090 in the respective years. It is due to agriculture which has assumed the prime place in NDDP.

II. TIME TRENDS OF NDDP

We have estimated the trend growth rates (Table 3) of NDDP of different activities. The annual compound growth rate has varied across districts, across regions and across sectors. Sector-wise findings are as follow:

Primary Sector: In West Bengal PS has grown at the rate of more than 3% during the period under study. It has been mainly due to agriculture and fishing. The district, Dakshin Dinajpur has recorded the highest rate of growth (7.7%) because of the highest growth in agriculture (8.2%). The lowest rate of growth is found in Hooghly (1.8%) which is also due to agriculture (1.6%)

TABLE 2

Indices of Activity—Diversification in the Economic Structure of West Bengal

Yr./District	*BD*	*BR*	*BA*	*MD*	*HW*	*HG*	*PN*	*PS*	*NA*	*MR*	*UD*	*DD*	*MA*	*JL*	*DJ*	*CB*	*PR*	*WB*
1993-94	0.891	0.768	0.789	0.871	0.939	0.916	0.935	0.921	0.803	0.854	0.728	0.766	0.784	0.810	0.832	0.730	0.819	0.898
1994-95	0.890	0.763	0.769	0.861	0.938	0.912	0.932	0.920	0.800	0.847	0.717	0.756	0.780	0.807	0.824	0.732	0.807	0.894
1995-96	0.878	0.767	0.786	0.869	0.925	0.914	0.927	0.904	0.807	0.857	0.724	0.764	0.781	0.814	0.833	0.747	0.811	0.895
1996-97	0.907	0.768	0.787	0.869	0.942	0.915	0.933	0.922	0.852	0.864	0.736	0.778	0.808	0.895	0.837	0.761	0.832	0.901
1997-98	0.893	0.749	0.783	0.858	0.939	0.919	0.926	0.925	0.858	0.870	0.748	0.768	0.796	0.825	0.831	0.755	0.832	0.903
1998-99	0.881	0.740	0.792	0.859	0.929	0.914	0.929	0.920	0.862	0.869	0.744	0.759	0.812	0.836	0.816	0.759	0.836	0.895
1999-00	0.870	0.752	0.792	0.846	0.910	0.897	0.954	0.930	0.880	0.878	0.751	0.804	0.821	0.757	0.759	0.777	0.824	0.892
2000-01	0.862	0.745	0.794	0.893	0.897	0.896	0.936	0.936	0.868	0.885	0.746	0.761	0.822	0.826	0.771	0.777	0.822	0.886
2001-02	0.877	0.752	0.801	0.872	0.923	0.923	0.930	0.928	0.870	0.884	0.762	0.773	0.821	0.834	0.795	0.786	0.845	0.891

Note: Column Heads: BD: Burdwan; BR: Birbhum; BA: Bankura; MD: Medinpur; HW: Howrah; HG: Hooghly; PN: 24-Parganas (N); PS: 24-Parganas (S); NA: Nadia; MR: Murshidabad; UD: Uttar Dinajpur; DD: Dakshin Dinajpur; MA: Malda; JL: Jalpaiguri, DJ: Darjeeling; CB: Cooch Bihar; PR: Purulia; WB: West Bengal.

Source: As in Table 1.

TABLE 3

Trend Growth Rates (%) of NDDP in West Bengal: 1993/94—2001/02

Districts/ Activities	*AG*	*MF*	*TC*	*TRC*	*PS*	*SS*	*TS*	*ALL*
Burdwan	1.14+	4.92	7.25	4.08	2.53	5.12	8.98	5.65
Birbhum	3.87	2.02*	6.93	7.25	4.29	4.29	9.96	6.71
Bankura	3.66	6.18	8.65	8.87	4.08	7.46	10.74	7.14
Medinpur	2.84	4.18	8.54	6.6	2.94	3.56	10.52	6.18
Howrah	1.91*	6.18	11.18	6.72	2.12*	5.97	9.42	7.78
Hooghly	1.61*	4.08	8.22	7.68	1.82*	4.5	9.42	5.86
24-Pgs (N)	3.56	8.33	8.76	7.46	2.53	8.54	8.65	7.25
24-Pgs (S)	2.84	5.13	9.74	9.3	2.53	5.23	9.53	6.18
Nadia	4.29	16.53	12.3	8.65	4.6	1.31*	10.52	8.22
Murshidabad	4.60	7.89	11.52	10.07	4.29	3.56	14.45	7.36
Uttar Dinajpur	3.46	8.65	9.09	9.85	3.87	8.87	10.41	8.93
Dakshin Dinajpur	8.22	8.76	11.74	5.54	7.68	7.36	11.07	9.09
Malda	5.97	10.29	11.4	9.3	5.44	9.52	11.4	8.33
Jalpaiguri	3.56	8.76	8.22	7.35	3.04	6.93	14.46	6.61
Darjeeling	2.32*	11.07	3.46	5.12	2.02*	9.09	3.25	7.03
Coochbihar	3.04	8.65	8.44	7.04	2.22*	8.00	10.18	5.97
Purulia	2.22*	12.86	10.74	6.28	3.15	9.96	10.74	7.36
West Bengal	3.35	6.29	9.09	7.46	3.87	6.50	9.74	7.14
DVI (%)	48.73	63.42	23.62	22.11	39.02	37.04	24.51	14.27

Note: AG: Agriculture; MF: Manufacturing; TC: Trade & Commerce; TRC: Transport & Communication; PS: Primary Sector; SS: Secondary Sector; TS: Tertiary Sector; ALL: All thirteen activities; DVI: Diversification index; All values are significant excepting + values.
Source: As in Table 1.

Secondary Sector: Its growth rate in West Bengal is 6.5%. Across districts the growth rate has ranged from 1.3% in Nadia to 9.96% in Purulia. MF has displayed the highest rate of growth in both Nadia and Purulia (more than 12%). In case of Nadia, SS has grown at a low rate (1.3%) which is due to construction and electricity *et al.*

Tertiary Sector: Its overall growth rate is highest (9%) compared to PS and SS. Murshidabad and Jalpaiguri (more than 14% each) have registered the highest growth rate in TS in which TC and TRC being its components have displayed the high growth rates (11.5% and 10%) in Murshidabad.

TABLE 4

Regression of NDDP on DI during 1993/94-2001/02

Districts	*Intercept*	*Coefficient*	*t-value*	R^2
Burdwan	5.88	-5.19*	-1.62	0.27
Birbhum	2.57	-9.75*	-3.17	0.59
Bankura	8.24	11.56*	2.48	0.47
Medinpur	6.92	2.05	0.50	0.03
Howrah	5.19	-8.83*	-2.61	0.49
Hoogly	5.94	-2.23*	-3.80	0.02
24-Pargana (N)	6.90	5.83*	0.71	0.07
24-Pargana (S)	7.11	11.71*	2.50	0.46
Nadia	6.80	5.38*	7.10	0.88
Murshidabad	7.67	12.03*	8.44	0.91
Uttar Dinajpur	7.38	8.30*	4.77	0.69
Dakshin Dinajpur	5.85	4.82*	1.07	0.14
Malda	7.32	8.90*	5.57	0.82
Jalpaiguri	5.47	-1.90	-0.13	0.002
Darjeeling	4.22	-3.39**	-2.15	0.40
Coochbihar	6.71	5.93*	9.58	0.93
Purulia	6.89	9.22*	2.43	0.47
West Bengal	6.78	-17.83*	-1.74	0.30

Note: DI: Diversification Index
+: 1% level of Significance
+: 5% level of Significance

Source: As in Table 1.

All Sectors: The overall rate of growth of NDDP is more than 7%. Among districts it is as high as 9.1% in Dakshin Dinajpur followed by Uttar Dinajpur (8.9%), Malda (8.3%), Nadia (8.2). Burdwan has recorded the lowest rate of growth (5.6%).

Let us now turn to the time trends of NDDP in different regions. The annual compound growth rates of activities are statistically significant everywhere. The region-wise study reveals that among the activities, manufacturing of SS has appeared to lead the growth of NDDP in the North Bengal region: the rate is 9.7%. Trade and Commerce of TS has grown at the rate of more than 9% in both the West Plain region and the South Bengal region. The performance of agriculture belonging to PS has not been satisfactory everywhere: the rate is around 3%. All the regions have registered 7% rate of growth in case of transport and communication.

Growth Divergence

We have discussed in section II the inter-district variations in annual compound growth rate of NDDP across the sectors. We shall now make an aggregative analysis of such variations by means of growth divergence index (GDI).[2]

Indices of growth divergence among the districts are remarkably high. GDI of growth rates in cases of MF and AG has been greater than that in cases of TC and TRC. This indicates the districts of West Bengal have been divergent more in AG and MF than in TC and TRC.

III. INSTABILITY OF NDDP

NDDP of the state by industry of origin at constant (1993-94) prices fluctuates over time. Periodic variations in NDDP of West Bengal are due to changes in NDDP of the regions. A region is a composite of some districts. Therefore, a change in NDDP-activity structure of a district can affect NDDP of a region. Variations in shares of an activity in NDDP are mainly due to uncertainty in production. Thus, it is important to examine the degree of variability in NDDP by activities across regions and districts in West Bengal.

Periodic variations in NDDP are measured by an instability index. It may be examined in the alternative contexts of:

(a) State's NDDP/Region's NDDP for an activity,
(b) State's NDDP/Region's NDDP for a group of activities or a sector,
(c) State's NDDP/Region's NDDP for all groups of activities or all sector.

Here we have used Log-Variance Method (Coppok Method) to estimate the periodic instability. The instability index for y is defined as:

$$I = \text{antilog } (V_{\log})^{1/2}$$

where $V_{\log} = \sum_{i=1}^{n-1} [\log (y_{t+1} / y_t) - m]^2 / (n - 1),$

and $m = \sum_{i=1}^{n-1} \log (y_{t+1} / y_t) / (n - 1)$.

m measures the constant percentage trend. The degree of instability is judged by the value of the index (I). Higher the value of I, higher the degree of instability and *vice versa*. Estimates reveal the following:

> Among the activities, instability index for transport and communication is lower in the West Plain region of Bengal (1.0019) indicating that this activity is relatively stable in NDDP during the period. On the contrary, manufacturing has been most unstable in NDDP: I is 1.0145 in the NPR.

It is noted that the instability index is as high as 1.00184 in the NBR, being followed by the WPR (1.00109) and the SBR (1.00023). Across the districts, the index ranges from 1.00029 in Jalpaiguri to 1.01525 in Darjeeling. It is quite high in Purulia, 24-Parganas (N), Hooghly, Dakshin Dinajpur and Howrah. On the contrary, the low values are recorded in Murshidabad, Coochbihar, Uttar Dinajpur, 24-Parganas (S). These districts are relatively more stable in NDDP. The instability index for the state as a whole is low (1.0001).

IV. DIVERSIFICATION AND GROWTH OF NDDP

Diversification may take place at two levels: occupation (sector/industry) and location (district). At the activity level it refers to activity composition while the distribution of NDDP among districts indicates locational (special) diversification. In our study we have taken the former. Larger the number of activities performed, higher the degree of diversification and in effect, lower the degree of uncertainty involved in NDDP and *cetris paribus*, higher the NDDP proceeds. We have hypothesised that activity diversification directly affects NDDP of the districts: higher (lower) the degree of activity diversification, higher (lower) the NDDP proceeds. Activity diversification is conductive to the growth of NDDP of the district economy: the effects of risks and uncertainties are minimized. District NDDP proceeds are regressed on the indices of activity diversification of the districts:

Log NDDP = Log a + b Log DI.

Estimates (Table 4) reveal that Dl has turned out statistically significant in influencing the district's NDDP directly in most of the districts. In the districts such as Burdwan, Birbhum, Howrah, Hooghly, Jalpaiguri and Darjeeling, the relationship has, however, become negative and significant. The overall relation between Dl and NDDP has turned out significantly negative. The direct relationship between Dl and NDDP is indicative of the policies towards increasing diversification of the activities.

V. CONCLUDING REMARKS

The occupational pattern of NDDP across districts and across regions is heterogeneous during the post-reform period (after 1991). Inter-district disparity prevails in the activities performed. The structural changes of NDDP are reflected in the falling contribution of the primary sector. The contribution of the secondary sector has also fallen in most of the districts and the state. The share of the tertiary sector has gradually increased at the cost of the primary and secondary sectors. Trade and commerce being a component of TS has recorded appreciable increase in its share in NDDP.

Divergency in development of the regions is found till now. The South Bengal is relatively advanced in case of manufacturing and trade and commerce due to its high urbanization and better infrastructural facilities. The North Bengal has lagged behind in case of trade and commerce because of the strong dominance of agriculture. A relatively smaller degree of activity dominance is experienced by the South Bengal while the reverse has happened in the North Bengal. Instability in production persists among the activities.

Development policies should be formulated towards greater diversification of activities in the districts so as to reduce periodic variation in NDDP. Information gap between the blocks or districts and the State should be reduced so as to make people more aware of it. Poverty alleviation measures should be strictly implemented for the targeted people so that the suffering districts will be benefited. The allocation of the state resources among the districts should be made on the basis of need and performance of the districts.

NOTES AND REFERENCES

1. $DI = \sum p_i \log (1/p_i) / \log n$,
   where p_i: share of activity i in the total, and n: number of activities
2. $GDI = [1/(n-1) \sum (g_{is} - G_s)^2]^{1/2} / G_s$
   where g_{is} : overall annual compound growth rate of NDDP (sector or activity) in West Bengal,
   G_s: annual compound growth rate of NDDP (sector or activity) of district i,
   and n: number of districts.

REFERENCES

Dutta, R. (1995), "New Economic Reform—Need for some Reth in King", *IEA*, Vol. 42, No. 3.

Sheety, S.L. (1978), "Structural Retrogression in the Indian economy since the Mid-sixties", *EPW, Special Number*.

Pal, P.K., Pal, G.P. and Pal, D.P. (1997), "Indian Economy: A Structural Analysis, 1950-95" (Summary), IEA, Conf. Vol.

Theil, H. (1967), *Economics and Information Theory*, North-Holland, Amsterdam.

Regional Disparity Trends

PAVEL CHAKRABORTY AND DEBASHIS CHAKRABORTY

Regional disparity is a serious concern in the state of West Bengal. As reflected in the West Bengal Human Development Report, 2004, several inequality measures have been used in this paper with the help of Theil Index, Coefficient of Variation, etc. This paper also has drawn attention to the fact of environmental degradation and slow growth of cooperatives in different districts of West Bengal.

THE ISSUES

Poverty reduction has been identified as one of the millennium development goals in developing countries like India. However, apart from boosting economic growth in general, lowering the prevailing level of inequality is one important aspect of economic development, the absence of which might impede the very development process in the long-run. The Central Government in India recently committed to respond to the growing regional imbalances, among States as well as within States, through fiscal, administrative and other means (*NCMP*, 2004). It is worth-noting that regional imbalances have been accentuated by not just historical neglect, but also through distortions in Plan allocations and Central Government assistance (*Chakraborty*, 2005).

Various studies have focused on the poverty, inequality and disparity trends in India, some of which came with conflicting observations. While a Planning Commission (1993) report on poverty shows that percentage of people below the poverty line has decreased steadily in almost every state and union territory over 1973-74 to 1988-89, working on the same dataset Das and Barua (1996) noted a rise in income and consumption inequality across the regions. Sundaram and Tendulkar (2003) noted that the change in the recall period in NSSO 55th round may have led to an underestimation of inequality in expenditure levels. The other recent studies on inequality in India worth mentioning are Bhanumurthy and Mitra (2004), Deaton and Dreze (2002), Kurian (2000), Rao *et al.* (1999), Singh *et al.* (2003), etc. Apart from the all-India trends, the regional inequality within various parts of the country (e.g., North-east region) is also showing an increasing trend (*Barua and Bandyopadhyay*, 2005).

West Bengal is placed at the mid-level among other Indian states in terms of various economic and administrative achievements (*India Today*, 2004). The poverty and inequality scenario in the state is a much-discussed issue. It has been argued that land distribution and panchayat empowerment has been a positive step towards reduction of inequality (*Rogaly et al*, 1999). On the other hand, the industrial slowdown in seventies and eighties had adverse implications on both poverty and inequality scenario. However, Guruswamy *et al* (2005) note that West Bengal has performed reasonably well *vis-a-vis* other Indian states on the economic front. Furthermore, Bhanumurthy and Mitra (2004) noted that inequality has declined in West Bengal in the post-reform period. However, Guha (2005) notes the presence of disparity in West Bengal economy on various counts (e.g., environmental, demographic, economic and social sector indicators, etc.), which is supported by Sen and Pal (2005). Bhowmik (2005) also notes the presence of an inter-district disparity in annual average daily wage rate of male agricultural labourers, which unmistakably has consequences on rural income.

Given this scenario, regional disparity is a serious concern in the state. The *West Bengal Human Development Report* (2004) notes, "The inequality in consumption was lower in the state than for all-India, and for most other states, in both rural and urban areas. However, the difference between rural and urban per capita consumption was higher in West Bengal than the all-India pattern (p. 8)." As noted by the *Statistical Review* of the West Bengal economy (2003-04) and Bagchi and Sarkar (2005), the western and the northern parts of the state are poorer than rest of the parts and there is an urgent need to ensure their economic development. Through an analysis of Bankura district, Hill (2003) notes that the recent government policies could not tackle the underlying conditions perpetuating chronic poverty in the more arid regions of West Bengal. Furthermore, the development programmes (e.g., food security programmes, wage employment, availability of formal credit, etc.) have been wholly insufficient towards poverty alleviation. This view has been supported by the *West Bengal Human Development Report* (2004):

> "The western parts of the state include some of the most backward areas from the point of view of infrastructure and material development, with the lowest levels of per capita income and also relatively poor HDI rankings. The relative inadequacy of transport and communication networks, and the inadequate physical provision of basic public goods and services, has already become apparent in the previous chapters. However, the lack of development in this region is evident not only in terms of the level of basic infrastructure in the region, but also with respect to agricultural development. This is compounded by the fact that this region is relatively speaking the driest in the state; it receives the least amount of annual rainfall and is more prone to drought than other parts of West Bengal (pp. 203-04)."

The effects of these historical factors have accentuated owing to various recent incidents as well. For instance, in the recent period, although several major developmental projects have been set-up or in the process of establishment, they are mostly located in southern part of the state. For instance, the Falta and Manikanchan SEZ, Bakraswar power plant, modernization of Haldia port, Purulia pumped storage programme, the high density of transmission projects in Southern part of the State, etc. could be named. The recent focus on infrastructure upgradation or the FDI inflow in the State has also been concentrated mostly in the Southern region. Stated alternatively, the recent spread of insurgencies in North and West part of the state, however, insignificant they may look for the time being, is open proof of their economic alienation. High inter-district migration in West Bengal is also a major indication of economic dissatisfaction (*Black et al*, 2005). On the other hand, the displacement of a significant number of people in Malda and Murshidabad due to Ganga river erosion has increased poverty in these two districts (*Rudra*, 2004), with obvious consequences on disparity.

In Diagram 1, the sectoral composition of the district income (average over 1993-94 to 2002-03) is noted. It is observed that while the contribution of the service sector is lower in case of districts like Dakshin Dinajpur, in case of southern districts like Kolkata and Howrah it contributes significantly to the total income. The service sector is also quite significant in northern districts like Darjeeling, presumably owing to the importance of travel and tourism services. It is observed that manufacturing sector has a substantial presence in Howrah, the two 24-Parganas, Burdwan, Hooghly and Kolkata. Given the low income generating capacity of traditional agriculture, and the varying presence of manufacturing sector, which has maximum employment-generating potential, the presence of economic disparity in West Bengal looks obvious.

The current analysis is organized along the following line. First the Theil index of inequality and coefficient of variation indices are presented, to be followed by a trend analysis of various sectoral components of inequality. The study also attempts to analyze whether there is any non-linearity in the inequality trends, followed by a brief analysis on the interrelation between inequality and growth. Finally, the findings are summarized with the policy conclusions.

DATA SOURCES

The State Domestic Product and District Domestic Product brought out by the Bureau of Applied Economics and Statistics, Government of West Bengal is the main source of data for various sectoral economic activities considered in the current study. The

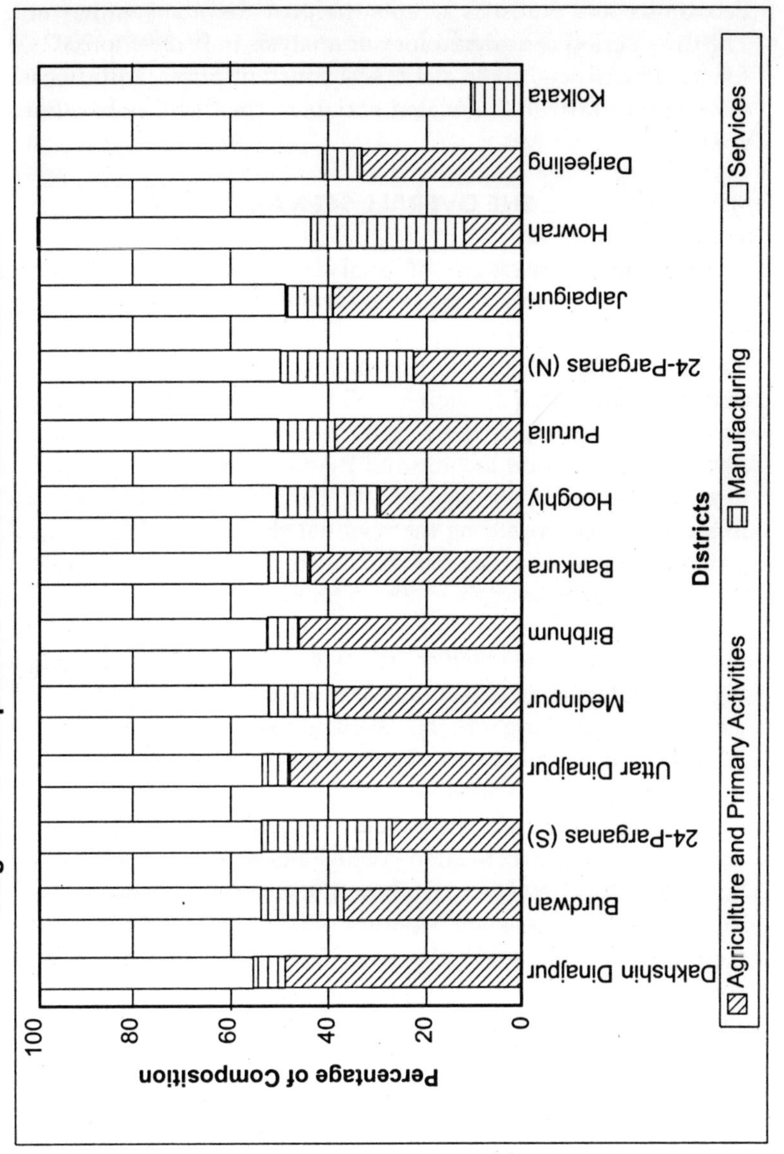

Diagram 1: Composition of Various Sectors in Total GDP

district level income data are, however, compiled by the statistical departments of various districts and the Bureau of Applied Economics and Statistics accepts the provided data as they are. The time period considered for our analysis is 1993-94 to 2002-03 for the 18 districts, taken at 1993-94 constant prices. Also in case of certain infrastructure-related variables, the CMIE publications are used.

THE OVERALL SCENARIO

One simple measure of analyzing cross-region income inequality is to compare the (y_i/p_i) and (q_i/p_i) ratios, where y_i, q_i and p_i are the i-th region's share in total NSDP, total manufacturing output and population respectively. The idea is that the regions that are doing well in these categories will have (y/p) and (q/p) ratios above unity and *vice versa*. Looking at the district-level data on income and manufacturing orientation for three separate time periods (1993-94, 1997-98 and 2002-03), certain interesting facts regarding the regional structure of West Bengal economy could be observed. Burdwan, Howrah, Hooghly and Kolkata quite consistently exhibit high manufacturing orientation $[(q/p) > 1]$, as well as high-income position $[(y/p) > 1]$. The districts characterized by dissimilar features (i.e., characterized by high manufacturing orientation but lower income position and *vice versa*) are 24-Parganas (N), 24-Parganas (S) and Darjeeling for all the three points of time. The rest of the regions show lower manufacturing orientation as well as lower income positions.

Apart from the absolute picture emerging from the earlier analysis, the rank correlation coefficients of the districts for the three reported time periods show the relative stability in their location within the state economy. While the rank correlation coefficient between 1993-95 and 2002-03 for relative income position and manufacturing orientation of the districts are 0.88 and 0.95 respectively, the same between 1997-99 and 2002-03 are 0.84 and 0.96 in that order. In addition, the manufacturing ranking of the districts is positively correlated with their manufacturing orientation (0.61 in 2002-03).

INEQUALITY TRENDS IN WEST BENGAL ECONOMY

Theil Index of Inequality

The current study calculates the regional inequality for West Bengal following Theil (1967). According to the Theil Index relative inequality in any economic indicator among the districts of West Bengal (e.g., income, consumption or degree of industrialization) is best described by a simple ratio, which compares the region's shares in that indicator with their respective shares in population. One advantage of this measure over Gini coefficient or Coefficient of Variation (CV) is that it is independent of size-variations among regions. Azad (1992) shows that Theil index captures all moments of the distribution, whereas CV or disparity ratio is based upon mean and dispersion only. Furthermore, while the CV is an average index of inequality for all the regions, Theil index (or, entropy measure) apart from giving an average index also provides information on the relative position of a region in the sample as described in terms of the ratios. Theil's inequality index can be defined by the following formula:

$$E_x = \Sigma\, x_i \,.\, \log (x_i/p_i)$$

Where

x = Economic indicators such as per capita income, agriculture, manufacturing, services, infrastructure, etc.

i = Districts of West Bengal.

p_i = region i's share in total population.

x_i = region i's share in various economic activities of India like NDDP, Agriculture, Manufacturing, etc.

In the measure, E_x, p_i and x_i can be regarded as prior and posterior probabilities, because $\Sigma\, x_i = \Sigma\, p_i = 1$. Thus E_y, E_{apr}, E_m, E_{infra}, E_{ser} are respectively the entropy measures of inter-district inequality in income, agriculture and primary activities, manufacturing, infrastructure and services in a given year. The inequality measures, E_x, take non-negative values. The zero value of E_x denotes an equal distribution, implying that every region's share in population and a particular economic indicator are equal.

The inequality estimates over 1993-94 to 2002-03 are shown in Table 1, where all values of E_x have been multiplied by 100.

TABLE 1

Theil Estimates at Constant Prices (1993-94=100)

Year	E_y	E_{ag}	E_{pri}	E_{agpri}	E_{rm}	E_{urm}	E_m	E_s	E_{inf}
1993-94	1.8	9.4	21.8	8.6	46.5	8.2	14.6	5.5	19.8
1994-95	1.7	10.1	25.4	9.3	43.8	5.8	13.2	5.3	16.6
1995-96	1.9	10.2	24.5	9.2	43.3	6.1	13.0	5.8	17.6
1996-97	1.9	10.6	25.6	9.8	42.9	5.8	12.5	5.3	16.4
1997-98	1.8	10.6	21.2	9.5	50.6	7.6	14.4	6.7	20.4
1998-99	2.3	10.1	23.7	9.1	50.5	*in*	14.7	7.0	22.0
1999-00	2.6	9.9	23.5	8.8	41.9	7.7	11.5	7.5	22.9
2000-01	3.3	10.4	26.3	9.0	41.5	11.1	17.6	8.6	20.7
2001-02	3.5	10.6	27.8	9.5	41.9	7.9	13.3	9.5	20.6
2002-03	4.1	10.1	25.5	8.8	42.4	7.9	13.5	10.0	20.6

Where the E_{is} denote inequality in—

E_y = Net state domestic product

E_{ag} = agriculture

E_{pri} = primary activities

E_{agpri} = agriculture and primary activities

E_{rm} = registered manufacturing

E_{urm} = unregistered manufacturing

E_m = manufacturing

E_s = services

E_{inf} = infrastructure

The above table shows the overall as well as sectoral inequality trends. While agriculture means only cultivation, primary activities include forestry and logging, fishing, mining and quarrying. The study also focuses on manufacturing (further separated into registered and unregistered in the same table), infrastructure (includes construction, electricity, gas, water supply and transport, storage and communication), and services (includes trade, hotels and restaurants, banking and insurance, real estates, ownership of dwellings and ownership services, public administration and other services) inequalities. The above table indicates that inequality has increased in almost all the heads except for manufacturing. While the service, infrastructure and income inequalities have increased over the years; the primary and agricultural activities have shown a declining trend during the last calculated period.

Coefficient of Variation (CV)

$$CV_x = (\text{Standard Deviation}_x / \text{Mean}_x) \cdot 100$$

Where, x denotes the economic activities like manufacturing, agriculture and primary activities, etc.

The CV trends are reported in Table 2. It is observed that in line with the Theil measure, the inequality is generally increasing over the years, although a cyclical trend is observed in case of agriculture, primary activities and manufacturing. However, income inequality, as well as service and infrastructure inequality is generally on the rise for the entire period under consideration. A separate analysis by the authors with Gini indices of inequality also demonstrates similar trends.

TABLE 2

Coefficient of Variation Estimates at Constant Prices (1993-94=100)

Year	E_y	E_{ag}	E_{agpri}	E_m	E_s	E_{inf}
1993-94	139.29	139.86	156.03	198.89	182.87	246.74
1994-95	139.45	135.56	150.16	184.74	209.96	204.68
1995-96	164.01	146.38	158.30	191.86	248.65	234.98
1996-97	168.84	163.57	179.69	192.32	232.32	225.65
1997-98	169.25	194.91	197.63	254.96	301.88	305.16
1998-99	241.44	173.05	185.58	270.83	363.50	365.24
1999-2000	289.30	177.11	181.60	212.25	420.78	405.13
2000-01	387.25	189.60	189.98	298.40	538.33	399.12
2001-02	443.34	205.91	215.21	261.10	627.65	409.81
2002-03	550.54	190.10	191.85	272.56	751.40	427.34

The inequality trends of the Theil index have further been analysed with the help of Table 3. It is observed that the annual average growth rate of inequality has been highest in case of income (9.99 per cent) followed by services (7.57 per cent) and both are highly significant. A break-up of the sample period in case of manufacturing inequality shows an increasing trend during the period 1994-98, followed by a decreasing trend during 1999-2003, both of which taken together indicates presence of non-linearity in the series. It is observed while the registered manufacturing inequality is negative and non-significant, unregistered manufacturing witnessed a moderately significant increasing trend at the rate of 3.39 per cent. The conflicting trend of inequalities in registered and unregistered manufacturing sectors perhaps originates from the existence of different labour market conditions (and the associated dynamics), namely, unionization of the labour force in the registered manufacturing sector and the lack of it in the unregistered manufacturing segment. Also, while the public sector enterprises, part of registered manufacturing sector, are guided by regional considerations in the allocation of resources, the unregistered industries, mostly small scale and cottage industries, are purely market-oriented. It has already been shown in Table 1 that the level of inequality in unregistered manufacturing is rising but remains at a much lower level as compared to the inequalities in registered manufacturing.

TABLE 3

Inequality Growth Trends in West Bengal

Variable	*Inequality Index*	*Period*	*Average Annual Growth Rate*	*t-value*
NDDP	E_y	1994-2003	9.99	7.40
Agriculture	E_{ag}	1994-2003	0.51	1.23
Primary Activities	E_{pri}	1994-2003	1.34	1.57
Agriculture & Primary activities	E_{agpri}	1994-2003	-0.14	-0.30
Manufacturing (Registered)	E_{rm}	1994-2003	-0.84	-1.02
Manufacturing (Unregistered)	E_{urm}	1994-2003	3.40	1.76
Manufacturing	E_m	1994-2003	0.41	0.31
	E_m	1994-1998	-0.70	-0.29
	E_m	1999-2003	-0.28	-0.05
Services	E_s	1994-2003	7.57	9.15
Infrastructure	E_{inf}	1994-2003	0.43	2.11

The linear trend result, particularly for manufacturing indicates that certain non-linearity may be present in the behaviour of inequality over time. The results of non-linear trend estimation of the relationships between inequality and time are summarized in Table 4 in the following.

TABLE 4

Non-linearity Trends in Inequality

Dependent Variable	*Constant*	*t*	t^2	t^3	R^2
E_y	0.020	-0.003	0.0007	-0.00001	
	(7.20)	(-1.47)	(1.56)	(0.67)	0.979
E_{ag}	0.086	0.009	-0.0016	0.00008	
	(14.23)	(2.13)	(-1.73)	(1.46)	0.577
E_{pri}	0.222	0.011	-0.0025	0.00018	
	(5.54)	(0.39)	(-0.40)	(0.49)	0.302
E_{agpri}	0.079	0.009	-0.0017	0.00009	
	(13.03)	(2.03)	(-1.82)	(1.59)	0.479
E_{rm}	0.442	0.004	0.0001	-0.00010	
	(6.07)	(0.09)	(0.02)	(-0.15)	0.213
E_{urm}	0.112	-0.040	0.0090	-0.00053	
	(5.33)	(-2.56)	(2.78)	(-2.75)	0.673
E_m	0.165	-0.026	0.0058	-0.00034	
	(4.61)	(-0.99)	(1.05)	(-1.04)	0.169
E_{inf}	0.224	-0.044	0.0110	-0.00069	
	(7.98)	(-2.09)	(2.53)	(-2.64)	0.711
E_s	0.060	-0.007	0.0019	-0.00008	
	(9.86)	(-1.56)	(2.05)	(-1.46)	0.977

It is observed from Table 4 that although non-linearities are not significant in all cases, the coefficients of the higher degrees of time are significant for a number of inequality indices. The results show significant polynomial relationship up to third degree and second degree in case of unregistered manufacturing, infrastructure and services respectively. Even though the non-linearity in income and agriculture inequality is not significant for higher degrees of time, a high R-square is reported. The presence of non-linearities suggests a cyclical nature of the growth of inequality indices. In Diagrams 1-5, the inter-district inequality in agriculture, agriculture and primary activities, manufacturing, services and infrastructure are shown.

POLICY PERSPECTIVE

The basic problem is not whether inequality rises with income but whether inequality rises with the rate of growth of income,

Diagram 1: Inequality Trends in Agriculture

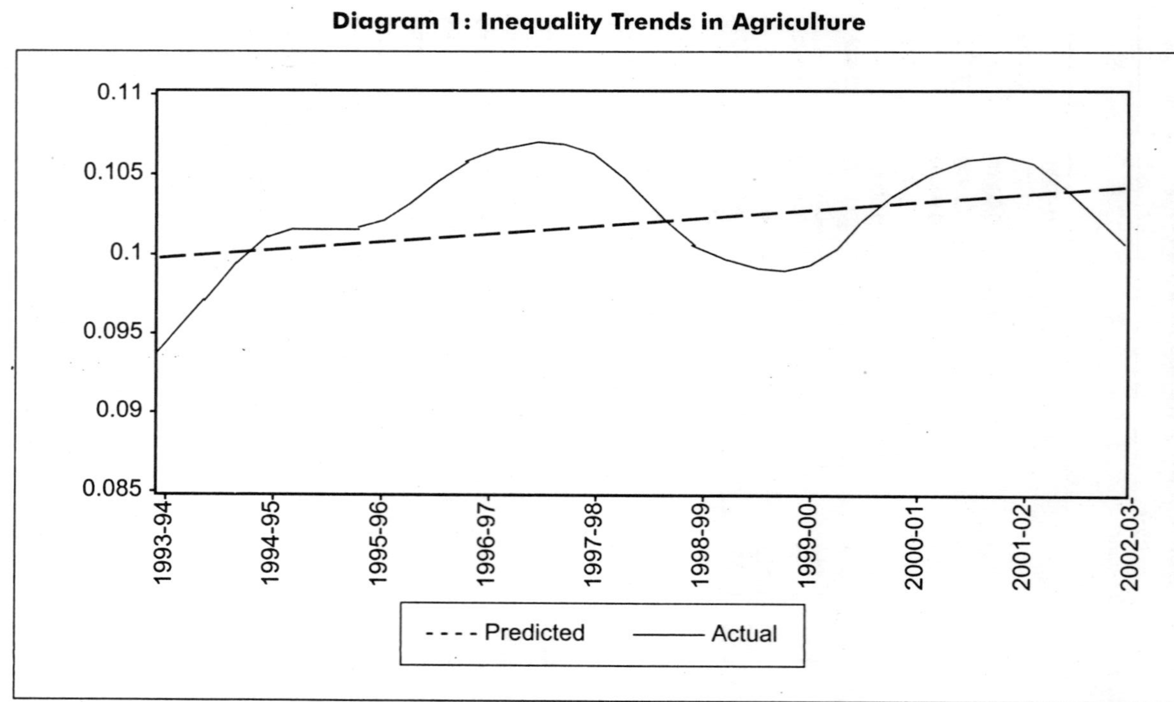

Diagram 2: Inequality Trends in Agriculture and Primary Activities

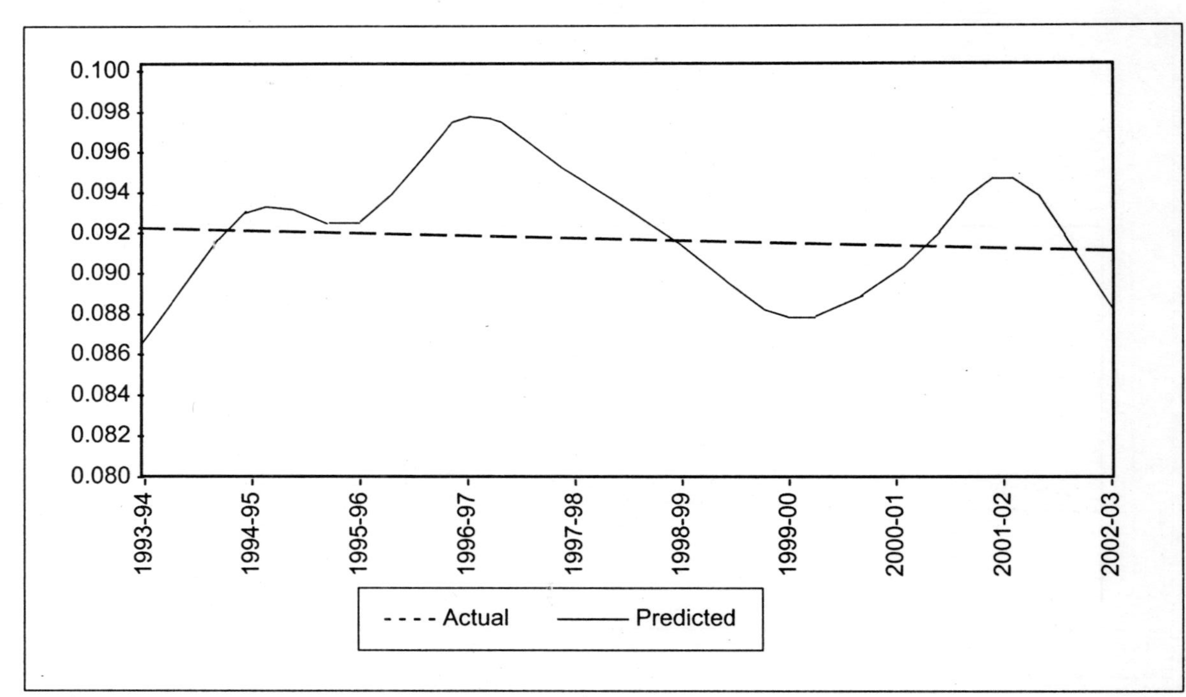

Diagram 3: Inequality Trends in Overall Manufacturing

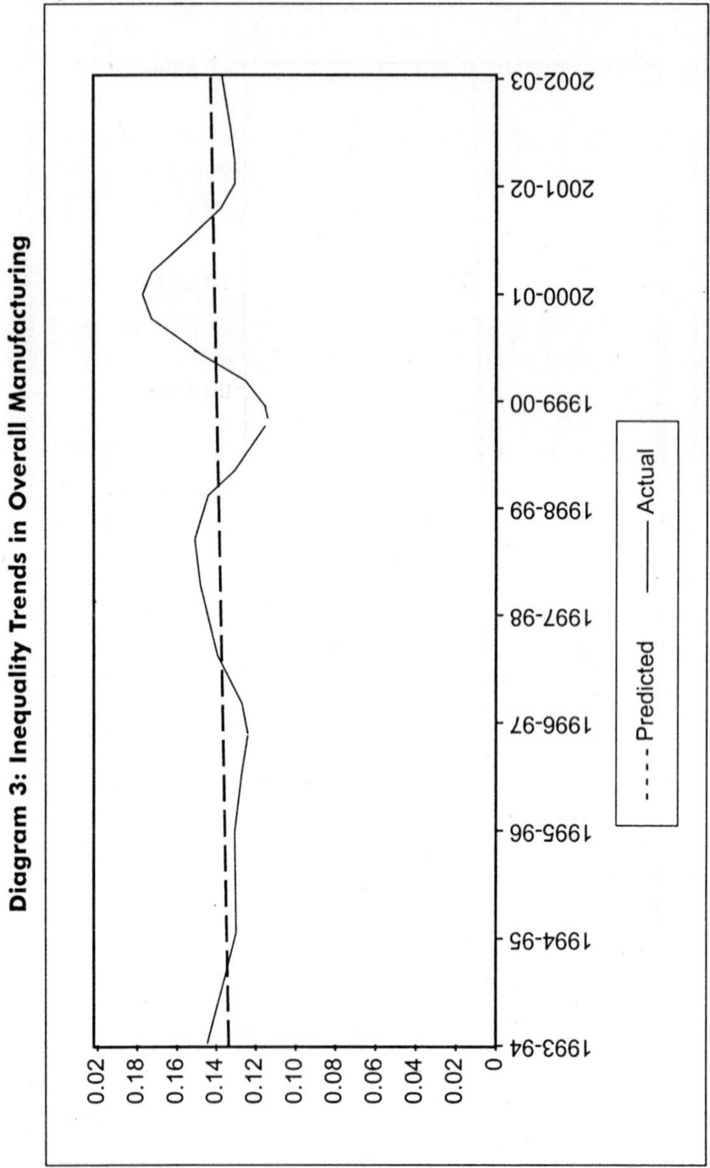

Diagram 4: Inequality Trends in Services

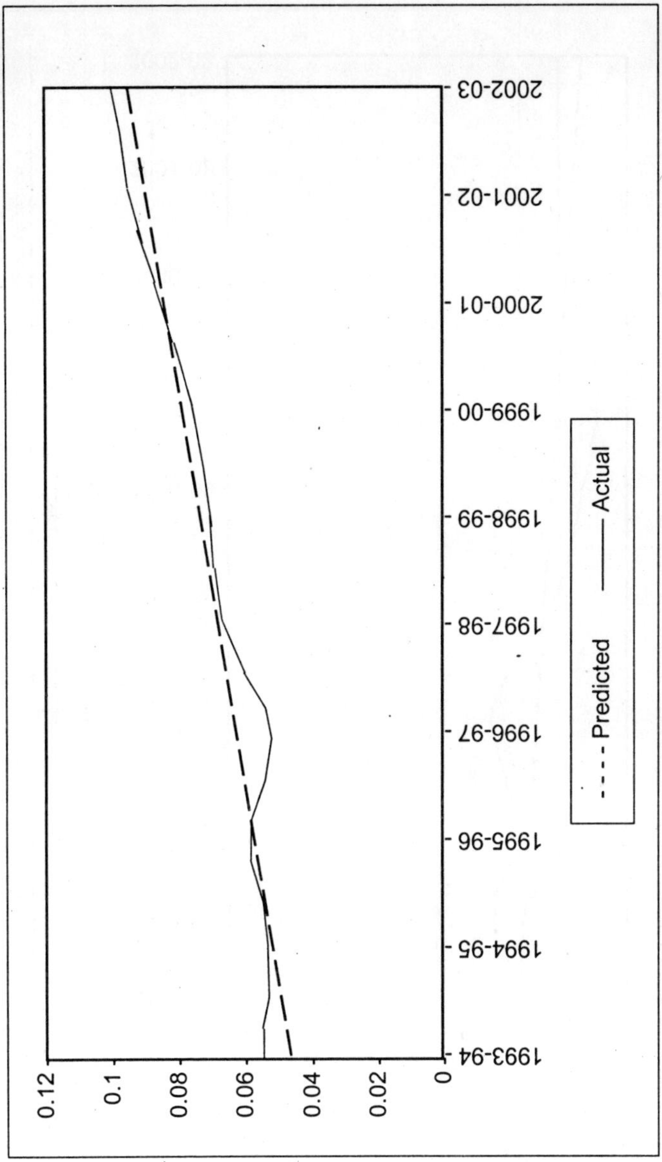

Diagram 5: Inequality Trends in Infrastructure

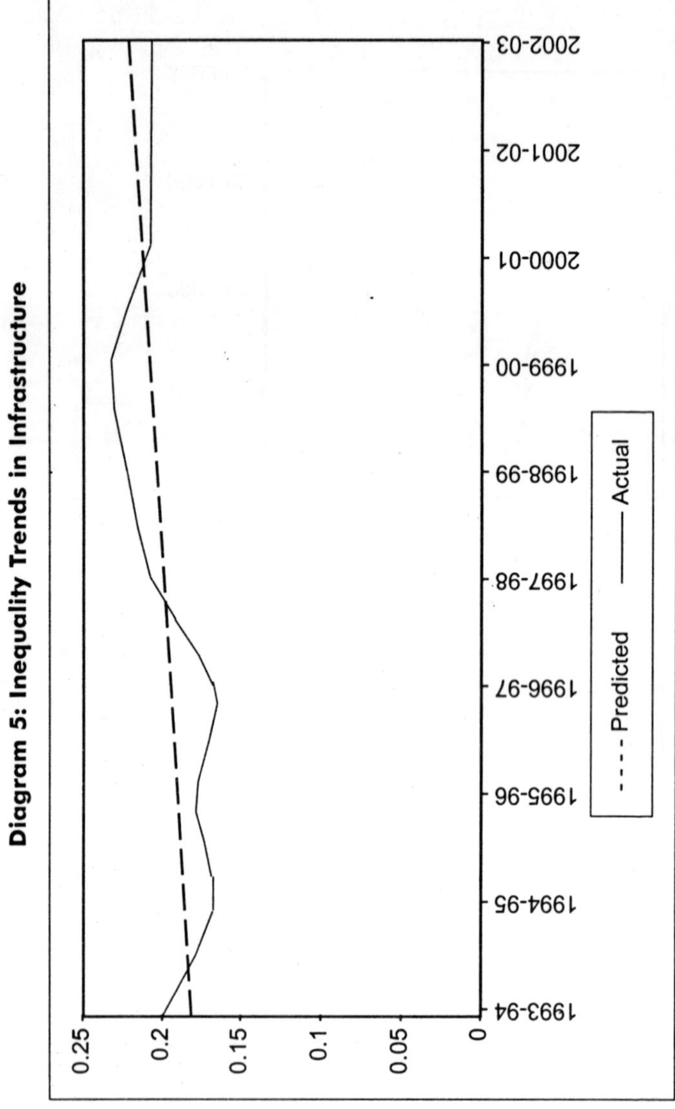

which brings the redistributive aspect in picture. The study focuses on the correlation coefficients between the level of inequality (measured by entropy) and the annual (year to year) growth rates of per capita income. It is worth interest to analyze the summary statistics presented in Table 5 to see whether the West Bengal economy experiences any conflict between growth and regional inequality both at the macro-level and the sectoral-level.

TABLE 5

Correlation Coefficient Between Entropy Measures of Inequality and the Corresponding Annual Growth Rates of per capita Income

Category	*1994-2003*	*1994-1997*	*1998-2003*
Net State Domestic Product	0.494 (2.61)	0.780 (7.97)	-0.569 (-3.36)
Agriculture	0.386 (1.81)	-0.477 (-2.47)	0.730 (6.14)
Primary Activities	0.571 (3.39)	0.883 (16.68)	0.090 (0.36)
Agriculture & Primary Activities	0.647 (4.45)	0.195 (0.81)	0.788 (8.30)
Manufacturing—Registered	0.602 (3.77)	0.953 (41.31)	0.229 (0.96)
Manufacturing—Unregistered	0.651 (4.52)	0.877 (15.23)	0.853 (12.55)
Manufacturing	0.905 (20.11)	0.833 (10.88)	0.935 (29.69)
Services	0.361 (1.66)	0.987 (156.92)	0.191 (0.79)
Infrastructure	0.442 (2.19)	0.941 (32.94)	0.657 (4.63)

Note: Figures in the parenthesis are t-values. The t-values in the above table have been calculated based on the formula: $t = \bar{\rho}\,[\{n-2\}/\{1-(\bar{\rho})^2\}]^{1/2}$

The correlation between growth and inequality has been calculated separately for the entire period (1994-2003) and two sub-periods, 1994-97 and 1998-2003 respectively. In general, no turning point in the relationship between growth and inequality at the aggregate or at the sectoral levels is noticed except agriculture (negative coefficient in 1994-97) and income (negative coefficient in 1998-2003). Elsewhere, growth and inequality are significantly and positively correlated. The result indicates that inequality may rise in the West Bengal economy if the rate of growth is sufficiently high.

The result noted in Table 5 forces one to think about the

determinants of the rising inequality. It could be hypothesized that the overall income inequality is caused by the inequality in the distribution of various components of it. The contribution of the components to income inequality is estimated by a regression analysis where various entropy measures of regional inequalities are regressed on E_y for the study period.

$$E_y = 0.044 - (0.383).\ E_{agpri} - (0.014).\ E_m - (0.107).\ E_{inf} + (0.540).\ E_S \quad \ldots (1)$$

$$(1.83) \quad (-1.87) \quad (-0.36) \quad (-2.50) \quad (11.40)$$

$$(R^2 = 0.972)$$

In the equation, we find that while the service sector is the significant determinant of income inequality, agriculture and primary activities, manufacturing and infrastructure sector contributes negatively to it. In other words, reducing inequality on these counts would contribute in reducing the overall inequality as well. It could further be argued that the result evolves from the low employment-creating characteristic of the service sector. However, if the regression is re-run by keeping inequalities in agriculture and primary activities as separate explanatory variables, we find that primary sector and manufacturing is positively related to overall income inequality, although agriculture continues to contribute negatively to it. This further indicates that there is scope for future research on testing of U-hypothesis in case of West Bengal economy.

One logical inference from the earlier analysis is that the West Bengal economy might continue to develop only at the cost of rising regional disparities. Thus any attempt to reduce regional inequality must focus primarily on services and primary activities. The focus of any development strategy should be on horizontal expansion of primary activities across all areas rather than concentrating efforts only in select regions. Also there is a need to re-formulate the industrial policies for expansion of labour-intensive industries so as to lower the unemployment rate. Finally, regional dispersal of industries cannot be achieved without improving the infrastructural facilities across regions. Haider and Roy (2005) showed that there is a correlation between human poverty index and infrastructure. Herein lies the important role of the government in allocation of public goods. The government responsibility also involves encouraging private sectors to come forward for provision of various areas of infrastructure.

Table 6 shows the level of connectivity of the villages in West Bengal *vis-a-vis* rest of the economy. Given the fact that agricultural inequality is negatively related to overall inequality, there is an urgent need to develop the marketing network by ensuring better connectivity of the villages with rest of the economy. The connectivity here includes both road and electricity. Although currently the villages in states like Gujarat, Haryana, Kerala, etc. are well connected, the same could not be ascertained for several populous states like Madhya Pradesh, Uttar Pradesh, West Bengal, etc. as seen from Table 6. In order to boost production as well as to ensure a steady supply chain to domestic and foreign markets, the connectivity with the nearest town should be enhanced at the earliest, where the produced crops could be brought to the processing units for the necessary value-addition. This would ensure better income to the farmers on one hand with consequences on overall income inequality, and reduce the post-harvest losses on the other.

TABLE 6

Proportion of Villages Connected by Roads

State	*1991-92*		*1994-95*		*1996-97*	
	A	*B*	*A*	*B*	*A*	*B*
India	274088	46.53	281791	47.83	353287	56.55
Better Connected States						
Andhra Pradesh	15927	58.22	16149	59.03	22832	85.88
Gujarat	15445	85.27	16262	89.78	17006	94.33
Haryana	6677	98.99	6697	99.29	6678	98.80
Kerala	1268	100.00	1268	100.00	1718	99.25
Punjab	12075	99.07	12125	99.48	12089	97.27
Poorly Connected States						
Madhya Pradesh	19504	27.52	19745	27.86	18606	28.39
Orissa	16874	35.67	17935	37.91	25047	49.14
Rajasthan	11436	34.34	12023	36.10	19713	52.03
Uttar Pradesh	49268	43.77	50122	44.53	56866	50.41
West Bengal	17506	45.98	17996	47.27	18531	48.67

A—Number of Villages connected; B—As % of total Villages.
Source: CMIE (2004).

While the need for enhancing the infrastructure level is obvious, the required thrust from the state exchequer in that respect is not easily forthcoming. The competitive demand of various sectors of the economy on State Budget is well-known, and barring the exception of states like Gujarat, Haryana, Kerala, Punjab, etc. the proportion of revenue expenditure devoted for this purpose is lower than 2 percent for most of the other states. It is observed from Table 7 that West Bengal is also no exception to this trend. This brings the question of obtaining private funds for enhancing the infrastructure level to the forefront.

TABLE 7

A Cross-State Comparison on Devolution of Funds for Creating Transport and Communication

(Percentage of Revenue Expenditure)

State/Year	*1998-99*	*2000-01*	*2002-03*	*2004-05*	*2005-06*
Andhra Pradesh	1.68	1.60	1.70	1.23	1.25
Gujarat	3.14	2.23	2.44	2.40	2.79
Haryana	6.36	6.31	5.60	5.48	5.75
Karnataka	1.76	2.05	1.64	1.72	1.73
Kerela	2.03	2.13	2.76	2.37	3.94
Maharashtra	0.46	0.11	2.11	0.20	0.23
Orissa	1.24	1.33	1.09	1.10	1.33
Punjab	3.80	3.17	2.78	1.35	3.38
Rajastan	1.26	1.03	1.19	0.92	1.46
Tamil Nadu	1.71	1.09	1.22	1.50	1.67
West Bengal	1.66	2.09	1.49	1.48	1.66
All States	1.92	1.76	1:89	1.38	1.68

2004-05—Revised estimate, 2005-06—budget estimate.
Calculated from CMIE (2005).

The situation could further be explained with the help of Table 8, where the key development pockets and their infrastructural requirements are summarized. While the agro-food processing sector has tremendous potential throughout Bengal, several value-added sectors are concentrated in and around Kolkata. Chemicals and Petrochemicals have a potential in Haldia and Iron and Steel industry could get a boost by locating in the west part of the State.

Similarly, tourism has a huge potential in North and South Bengal as well as places with historical and cultural relevance. However, the potential could not be fully harnessed due to lack of adequate infrastructure so far. Although the scenario has improved in the recent period to some extent, there is enough room for improving the connectivity in the State. The CII (2005) study notes that without expanding the existing network, the minimum expenditure required to simply improve and upgrade approximately 8,000 km of major highways and roads in the state would require an approximate expenditure of Rs. 12,000-Rs. 42,000 crores. Given this need, several unended projects are currently in progress. For instance, the Asian Development Bank (ADB) is funding the mega West Bengal Corridor Development Project and a number of roads, including National Highways, State Highways, and rural roads are being upgraded under this. Japan Bank for International Co-operation (JBIC) in the last 10-15 years has funded 8 major infrastructure projects all over West Bengal but 7 of them are located in the southern region namely, Metro Railways—Phase (II) of the construction has been funded by the organization; Calcutta Infrastructure Development Project—under which 4 flyovers have been constructed; West Bengal Pollution Control Board though its headquarter is in Kolkata, but most of the regional testing centers are also located in southern region, barring a few in the north; Bakreswar Thermal Power Project, etc. In the northern region of West Bengal, JBIC has funded only Teesta Canal Hydroelectric Project, which turned out to be one of the most effective projects for the region given the abysmal power situation in North Bengal and was consistent with the 7th five-year state development plan.

The cluster development approach is a widely acknowledged growth policy. Recently in West Bengal a number of clusters have been proposed or currently under various stages of construction (e.g., toy-park in Salt Lake; Hosiery park in Kashipore; software technology park in Salt Lake, Durgapore, Kharagpore, Shiliguri, Haldia, Rajarhat; tea-park in Khidirpore, etc.). However, it is obvious from the list that most of them are concentrated in and around Kolkata and therefore the repercussions on the West Bengal economy as a whole would be limited. In other words, the consequences on inequality would not be negligible. Creation of better infrastructure throughout the State would facilitate

TABLE 8

Regions with Corresponding Potential Sectors that Need Proper Road Connectivity/Improvements in Existing Road Networks

Region/District/Centre	*Sector*
Hooghly, Burdwan, Medinpur (W), Malda, Murshidabad, N & S 24-Parganas, Jalpaiguri, Darjeeling, Coochbihar, N. Dinajpur, Nadia	Agro & Food Processing
Purulia, Bankura, Burdwan, Birbhum	Iron & Steel
Darjeeling, Digha, Sunderbans, Shantiniketan, Vishnupur	Tourism
Haldia	Chemicals & Petrochemicals
In and around Kolkata	Other Industries (Leather, IT & ITeS, Gems & Jewellery, Real Estate & Housing, Biotechnology, Retail, etc.)

Source: CII (2005).

construction of clusters at any strategic location in the State, and in turn lower income inequality.

Last but not the least, two issues with serious consequences on future disparity trends need to be borne in mind. First, to revitalize the rural economy, ensuring smooth functioning of the producer cooperatives could also play a key role. However, it has been observed that in the all-India scale the cooperatives in West Bengal have not performed too well. The saving grace is that Dutta (2004) noted although government support structure is low in West Bengal, the leadership support structure is high. One possible option for the government to enhance the overall growth potential of the entire economy (i.e., to lower disparity) is to remove the systemic problems on the sector. Second, in various regions of the State the water table is depleting fast due to uneconomic use of the irrigation system. If the trend continues in the next twenty years, the water crisis would reach a new height. Water conservation through traditional methods and reduction in wastage of water through irrigation has to be accorded due priority. Agricultural diversification by focusing on water-saving crops with value-addition opportunities would, apart from solving the primary problem, would also enhance the scope of rural non-farm employment, which would be instrumental in lowering the disparity level.

References

Azad, N.A. (1992), "Trade Performance and Trade Distribution: A Study of North *vs.* South", Unpublished Ph.D. Thesis, JNU, New Delhi.

Bagchi, Kanak Kanti and Satyen Sarkar (2005), "Comparative Backwardness of North Bengal: Strategies for its Development", *Artha Beekshan*, Vol. 14, Nos. 3 & 4, pp. 201-18.

Banerjee, Abhijit *et al* (2002), "Strategy for Economic Reform in West Bengal", *Economic and Political Weekly*, October 12, pp. 4202-18.

Barua, Alokesh and Arindam Bandyopadhyay (2005), "Structural Change, Economic Growth and Regional Disparity in the North-East: Regional and National Perspectives", in Alokesh Barua (Ed.), *India's North-East: Developmental Issues in a Historical Perspective*, Manohar, New Delhi.

Bhanumurthy, N.R. and Arup Mitra (2004), "Economic Growth, Poverty, and Inequality in Indian States in the Pre-reform and Reform Periods", *Asian Development Review*, Vol. 21, No. 2, pp. 79-99, available at http://www.adb.org/Documents/Periodicals/ADR/pdf/ADR-Vol21-2-Bhanumurthy.pdf

Bhowmik, Debesh (2005), "Disparity and Convergence of Daily Wage Rate of Male Agricultural Labour in West Bengal", *Artha Beekshan*, Vol. 14, Nos. 3 & 4, pp. 219-235-

Black, Richard, Claudia Natali and Jessica Skinner (2005), "Migration and Inequality", World Development Report, 2006, 'Equity and Development', Background Papers, 20 January, available at http://siteresources.worldbank.org/INTWD R2oo6/Resources/477383-m8673432Qo8/Migration and Inequality.pdf

Centre for Monitoring Indian Economy Private Limited (2004), *Infrastructure*, Economic Intelligence Service: Mumbai, March.

____, (2005), *Public Finance*, October.

Chakraborty, Debashis (2005), "Evolution of Indian Industry: Key Issues and a Firm Level Analysis", presented at the Workshop on "Impact of Globalization on National Firms", Zhongnan University of Economics and Law, Wuhan, November 25-26.

Confederation of Indian Industry (2005), *West Bengal's Road Network: An Assessment*, Kolkata.

Das, S.K. and Alokesh Barua (1996), "Regional Inequalities, Economic Growth and Liberalization: A Study of the Indian Economy", *Journal of Development Studies*, Vol. 32, No. 3, pp. 364-90.

Deaton, Angus and Jean Dreze (2002), "Poverty and Inequality in India: A Re-examination", *Economic and Political Weekly,* September 7, pp. 3729-48.

Datta, Samar K. (2004), "Co-Operatives in Agriculture", Vol. 24, *State of Indian Farmer,* Academic Foundation, New Delhi.

Government of India, Planning Commission (1993), *Report on Poverty.*

____, "National Common Minimum Programme", available at http://www.nac.nic.in/ncmp.htm. 2004.

Government of West Bengal, Bureau of Applied Economic and Statistics, Various *District Handbooks.*

____, *Economic Review,* 2003-04, Statistical Appendix.

Guha, Biswajit (2005), "Regional Disparity in West Bengal", *Artha Beekshan,* Vol. 14, Nos. 3 & 4, pp. 183-200.

Guruswamy, Mohan *et al* (2005), "Economic Growth and Development in West Bengal: Reality *versus* Perception", *Economic and Political Weekly,* May 21, pp. 2151-57.

Haider, Sushil K. and Kajari Roy (2005), "District Level Disparity of Human Poverty Index in West Bengal: The Role of Infrastructure", *Artha Beekshan,* Vol. 14, Nos. 3 & 4, pp. 279-92.

Hill, Douglas, "Policy, Politics and Chronic Poverty: The experience of Bankura District, West Bengal", South Asia Research Unit, Curtin University of Technology, Paper for the International Conference on "Staying Poor: Chronic Poverty and Development Policy", IDPM, University of Manchester, 7-9 April, 2003.

India Today (2004), "The States of India: India's Best and Worst States", August 16.

Kurian, N.J. (2000), " Widening Regional Inequalities in India: Some Indicators", *Economic and Political Weekly,* February 12, pp. 538-50.

Rao, M. Govinda, Ric Shand and K.P. Kalirajan (1999), "Convergence of Income across Indian States: A Divergent View", *Economic and Political Weekly,* March 27-April 2.

Rogaly, Ben, Barbara Harriss-White and Sugata Bose (1999), *Sonar Bangla? Agricultural Growth and Agrarian Change in West Bengal and Bangladesh,* Sage, New Delhi.

Rudra, Kalyan (2004), "Ganga Bhangan Katha: Malda-Murshidabad", *Swedesh Samakal Granthamala 1, Mreettika,* Second Edition.

Saha, Anamitra and Madura Swaminathan (1994), "Agricultural Growth in West Bengal in the 1980s: A Disaggregation by Districts and Crops", *Economic and Political Weekly,* March 26, pp. A2-A11.

Sen, Jayanta and D.P. Pal (2005), "Economic Development of West Bengal: A Study of Convergence", *Artha Beekshan,* Vol. 14, Nos. 3 & 4, pp. 267-78.

Singh, Nirvikar *et al* (2003), "Regional Inequality in India: A Fresh Look", *Economic and Political Weekly,* March 15, 1069-73.

Sundaram, K. and S. Tendulkar (2003), "Poverty has declined in the 1990s: A Resolution of Comparability Problems in NSS Consumer Expenditure Data", *Economic and Political Weekly,* January 25, pp. 327-37.

Theil, H. (1967), *Economics and Information Theory,* North Holland, Amsterdam.

UNDP (2004), Human Development Resource Centre, *West Bengal Human Development Report* available at http://www.undp.org.rn/hdrc/shdr/WB/dwnld chap wb.htm.

Economic Development: A Study of Centricity

JAYANTA SEN AND D.P. PAL

The structure of West Bengal's economy was mono centric in nature at the time of independence. After independence the same structure has however continued. There are tendency of higher production of goods and services in some historically developed regions. Naturally, in these regions per capita income has been expectedly high. In this paper an attempt has been made to examine whether the West Bengal economy today has revealed any regional convergence in terms of economic development. Concentration of development towards high-income areas has been examined in terms of social development as well as human development in the districts of West Bengal.

During the British rule in West Bengal, colonial administration and trade were concentrated in and around Calcutta. The British Government developed all the sectors for that particular region in order to make their trade balance favourable. The structure of the economy was thus mono centric in nature. After independence the same structure has continued. At present also the centric nature of the West Bengal economy seems to persist (*Bhattacharya,*

1998). There would always be a tendency of higher production of goods and services in some historically developed regions. Naturally, in these regions per capita income is expectedly high. In this paper, an attempt has been made to examine whether the West Bengal economy today reveals any regional convergence in terms of economic development.

Infrastructure and growth are correlated. Various components of infrastructure stimulate growth and social development of an economy (*Pal and Sen*, 2003, *Joshi*, 1990; *Ghosh and De*, 1998). So the question is, are the high-income regions are having high social development? In other words, is there any concentration of social development towards high-income regions? In this paper these issues are also examined in the light of West Bengal economy. Nature of human development in the districts of West Bengal is also discussed. Role of historically inbuilt development is implicitly examined.

I. METHODOLOGY: DEVELOPMENT INDICES

The term 'development' indicates the movement of an economy from one state to another or in other words a movement towards a more desirable state. Sustained and substantial increase in real per capita income is a necessary condition for economic development. Though economic welfare is traditionally viewed as an increase in per capita income, the concept of development has been widened in the 1990s by introducing some non-income variables. Economic development as per this new perception is much broader than was initially comprehend by the economists in the light of growth paradigm. Some social aspects as education, health, sanitation, drinking water, nutrition, etc. are viewed as important constituent of development. These non-income factors are basically social development indicators. In the 1990s the concept of development has turned towards a new concept of human development which includes both economic and social aspects of development. Human development is defined as a process of enhancing the basic capabilities and widening the range of choices of the people to ascertain their own well-being (*UNDP*, 1990). Let X_{ij} be the i-th variable for the j-th locational unit. The variable X is basically divergent and may or may not be comparable across space. At a particular time point in an economy

X_{ij} falls between two boundary values— lower (a_{ij}) and upper (b_{ij}) i.e., $a_{ij} \leq X_{ij} \leq b_{ij}$.

Over time/across space, X_{ij} approaches towards b_{ij} from a_{ij}. The movement towards b_{ij} is judged as the attainment of the economy in terms of the variable in question.

For comparability X_{ij}s are to be scaled using some scaling function. The scaling function may be linear and log-linear depending upon the nature of the variable. In case of linear scaling, the attainment index is:

$$A_{ij} = (X_{ij} - a_{ij})/(b_{ij} - a_{ij}) \quad \text{... (1)}$$

When the scaling function is log-linear then

$$A_{ij} = (\log X_{ij} - \log a_{ij}) \ / \ (\log b_{ij} - \log a_{ij})$$
$$= \log (X_{ij}/a_{ij})/\log (b_{ij}/a_{ij}) \quad \text{... (2)}$$

Log linear scaling function is used when the variable is having declining marginal significance (*Sen and Pa*l, 2004).

The boundary values are normative values which are used to judge the level of attainment in relative terms. One may use either some functional values or actual extreme values depending upon the mode of analysis. To examine the regional disparity in a country or state one should use the system-determined values.

As said earlier, development is measured in terms of both per capita income and some non-income (social) variables. We shall construct attainment indices in terms of income and non-income variables.

I.1 Economic Development Index (EDI)

Goods and services satisfy wants of the people. Income is required to purchase goods and services. It is no doubt the fact that decent standard of living of the people depends on access to goods and services. Income is thus indicative of the purchasing power, i.e., the access. The greater the magnitude of per capita income, the higher the degree of access and consequently the higher the level of welfare. Attainment of the high level of income is naturally an important factor of development. So for the variable per capita income we shall construct an attainment index by using the formula (2), which is a unit free value comparable with other aspects:

$$PCI_j = \log (X_{ij}/a_{ij})/\log (b_{ij}/a_{ij})$$

Log linear scaling function is used here as per capita income is having declining marginal significance. PCI_j reflects the attainment of income for j-th locational unit and we may call it the Economic Development Index (EDI_j).

1.2 Social Development Index (SDI)

It is realised that an increase in per capita income does not *per se* ensure the actual welfare of the people. Actual welfare is dependent on some social aspects like education, health, sanitation, safe drinking water, nutrition, etc. Access to such social services has considerable impact on human capabilities and freedom and enhances in a meaningful way people's well-being (*UNDP*, 1990, *Pal et al*, 1998). Education and health are the two important variables. Education helps the people to think properly, makes them conscious about their rights and duties. Literacy is thus the precondition for attainment in education. Good health is essential to be capable of enjoying what is available. Overall condition of sanitation and safe drinking water is important for the healthy life; and all these are manifest in two important factors—life expectancy and infant mortality. Constructed are thus the attainment indices by using (1) for each of different literacy components—Male literacy, Female literacy and Total literacy, life expectancy and infant survival. Aggregation of individual attainment indices is required to arrive at Social Development Index. Taking the simple arithmetic mean of attainment indices for male literacy, female literacy and infant survival/life expectancy, SDI may be constructed as

$$SDI_j = \sum_{i=1}^{3} A_{ij}/3.$$

In our earlier analysis we found high correlation coefficients between simple mean index and rank weighted indices (*Pal and Sen*, 2003). Therefore, we may choose the simple mean formula to arrive at SDI_j.

II. DATA AND ESTIMATES

Per capita district domestic product (PCDDP) for different districts of West Bengal are used as proxy for per capita income. Data on PCDDP (at 1993-94 constant prices) are collected from Bureau of Applied Economics and Statistics, West Bengal. In case of Social Development Index, data on literacy rate (male, female) are obtained from census reports 1991, 2001. Figures on life expectancy are not available for the districts itself for 1991-92. So only infant survival rate is used and data are collected from census report. Life expectancy is used for 2000-01 and data are collected from Census 2001. Hence in constructing SDI, we have used male literacy rate, female literacy rate and infant survival rate/life expectancy.

II.1 Economic Development: Inter-District Disparity

Table 1 presents the Economic Development Index (EDI) for two time points 1993-94 and 1999-2000 for the districts of West Bengal. With respect to the relative position of the districts we find Kolkata, Darjeeling, Burdwan and Hooghly have occupied first, second, third and fourth positions and have maintained the same positions over time. Uttar Dinajpur continues to be in the lowest position. Malda and Murshidabad have kept their ranks intact. Other 12 districts have changed their relative positions. Birbhum, Medinpur, 24-Parganas (N), Dakshin Dinajpur, Jalpaiguri and Coochbihar have declined, and Bankura, Howrah, 24-Parganas (S), Nadia and Purulia have increased over time in terms of their positions. Relative position of Purulia district has improved substantially whereas in case of Jalpaiguri the position has gone down. During the period under study it appears that the economically backward districts—Uttar Dinajpur, Coochbihar, Malda and Dakshin Dinajpur has remained backward over time.

It thus follows from the above discussion that the districts of West Bengal have exhibited a high disparity level in terms of economic development. We find a very feeble tendency of convergent development. The inter-district disparity is examined in terms of District Disparity Index (DDI) as

$$DDI = \left[\left\{ \sum_{i}^{n} (x_i - x^*)^2 \Big/ n \right\} \Big/ x^* \right] * 100,$$

where x_i = Economic development index in the district i,
x^* = Economic development index in West Bengal as a whole, and
n = number of districts.

Estimates of DDI supports the increase in inter-district disparity in development. This actually provides us with some idea about the inter-temporal behaviour of converging or diverging development trend. District Disparity Index has tended to fall (53% in 1993-94 and 51% in 1999-2000).

II.2 Social Development: Inter-District Disparity

A wide disparity is observed in the districts of West Bengal in terms of Social Development. Two census years have been considered. Data reveal that (Table 2) Kolkata, Howrah, Hooghly, Medinpur and 24-Parganas (N) have occupied the top five positions in 1990-91. Though over time these districts have remained as top five districts in terms of social development, 24-Parganas (N) has occupied the 3rd position. Malda has ranked the lowest position and remained unchanged during the period. Rank of the districts is almost same over time. The rank correlation coefficient for the two years is very high (0.905). Social development greater than the state level is observed in seven districts—the aforesaid top five districts and Burdwan and Darjeeling.

If we look into the attainment index of the components of SDI (Table 2), we find that there are also variations in male literacy rate. Kolkata, Medinpur, Howrah and Hooghly have exhibited the top four in 1990-91. In 1999-2000, Medinpur has occupied the first position. 24-Parganas (S) and Bankura have maintained their positions. Coochbihar, Darjeeling, Jalpaiguri, Murshidabad have improved their positions. Rank correlation coefficient is very high (0.932). It implies that the rank of the districts have remained more or less same over time. Burdwan, 24-Parganas (N) and 24-Parganas (S) including the top four districts are having the attainment level greater than the state level in both 1991 and in 2001.

In case of female literacy rate, Kolkata, 24-Parganas (N), Howrah and Hooghly have been the top four districts and have remained the same over time. The positions of Malda, Medinpur,

Nadia and 24-Parganas (S) have remained unchanged. Ranks of Coochbihar, Darjeeling and Jalpaiguri have declined. Female literacy rate is lowest in Purulia in 1991 but Malda has replaced Purulia in 2001. During the time period the ranks of all the districts not changed substantially. The correlation coefficient of ranks for two years (0.929) proves it. Kolkata, Howrah, Hooghly, 24-Parganas (N), Medinpur, Burdwan and Darjeeling have exhibited the female literacy rate above the state level in 1991 and have remained so in 2001.

There are also inter-district variations in infant survival rate/ life expectancy. Attainment in infant survival is highest in Kolkata and lowest in Malda in 1991 and in 2001. Kolkata, Howrah and Hooghly have ranked first, second and third respectively and remained unchanged over time. In case of 24-Parganas (N) and Purulia infant survival rate has increased highly. A high inter-district variation is observed which is revealed by the value of DDL.

III. ECONOMIC DEVELOPMENT VIS-A-VIS SOCIAL DEVELOPMENT

There is a well marked tendency for the infrastructural facilities to concentrate at the high-income regions. Social development is positively related to social infrastructure. Components of social infrastructure concentrate at the highly developed regions. Moreover, the attitude of the administrative authorities seems to be in favour of the economically developed regions. The districts of West Bengal having high per capita income are the districts having high social development. To verify this hypothesis we have performed the regression analysis. The cross-district regression of SDI on EDI in West Bengal yields:

1991-92

$$SDI = 0.112 + 0.759\ EDI \qquad R^2 = 0.63$$
$$(1.53) \quad (5.16)^* \qquad n = 18$$

2000-01

$$SDI = 0.173 + 0.820\ EDI \qquad R^2 = 0.60$$
$$(1.99) \quad (4.88)^* \qquad n = 18$$

* significant at 5% level.

The regression coefficients have turned out positive and statistically significant. R^2 is also high. Thus the regression results strongly support the hypothesis that the high-income regions are having high social development. In other wards, it reflects the concentration of social development towards high-income regions/districts in West Bengal.

Let us examine the patterns of economic development and social development and their relationship in terms of 2×2 district classification table (Given below). This classification is made in terms of state level values.

2×2 District Classification Table

ED → SD ↓	Developed *(More than the state level)*	Less Developed *(Less than or equal to the state level)*
Developed *(More than the state level)*	I	II
Less Developed *(Less than or equal to the state level)*	III	IV

Cell I shows high social (SD) and high economic development (ED) and cell II both low. It is expected that the districts will fall in cell I and cell IV. Tables 5 and 6 reveal the concentration of social development towards economically developed districts in West Bengal. Most of the districts are concentrated on cell 1 and cell 4. It implies that the districts which are economically developed (less developed) also socially developed (less developed). An interesting point is that there is no district in cell 3 which implies that it is impossible for the districts to be economically more developed as well as socially less developed.

IV. ECONOMIC DEVELOPMENT, SOCIAL DEVELOPMENT AND HUMAN DEVELOPMENT

In the above sections we have calculated attainment indices for economic development and social development. The variables that go into the making of attainment indices are PCDDP, total literacy rate, male literacy rate, female literacy rate, infant survival rate,

TABLE 1

Economic Development Index (EDI), West Bengal: 1993-94 and 1999-2000

Districts	*EDI*	
	1993-94	*1999-2000*
Bankura	0.351 (11)	0.395 (9)
Birbhum	0.254 (13)	0.286 (14)
Burdwan	0.810 (3)	0.715 (3)
Kolkata	1.000 (1)	1.000 (1)
Coochbihar	0.209 (15)	0.154 (17)
Darjeeling	0.911 (2)	0.989 (2)
Hooghly	0.668 (4)	0.605 (4)
Howrah	0.426 (7)	0.557 (5)
Jalpaiguri	0.443 (6)	0.380 (10)
Malda	0.201 (16)	0.245 (16)
Medinpur	0.482 (5)	0.456 (8)
Murshidabad	0.258 (12)	0.290 (13)
Nadia	0.422 (8)	0.470 (7)
Purulia	0.139(17)	0.313 (12)
24-Parganas (N)	0.412(10)	0.373 (11)
24-Parganas (S)	0.418 (9)	0.527 (6)
U. Dinajpur	0000 (18)	0000 (18)
S. Dinajpur	0.216 (14)	0.276 (15)
West Bengal	0.514	0.569
DDI (%)	53	51

( ) Rank of the districts in descending order.
Source: Census 1991 and 2001. Govt. of India, Bureau of Applied Economics and Statistics, Govt. of West Bengal.

etc. Aggregation of these attainment indices yields a set of alternative aggregative indices. These indices are nothing but Human Development Indices (HDI). Their components are:

1. HDI_1: Per capita income, total literacy rate and infant survival rate.
2. HDI_2: Per capita income, male literacy rate and infant survival rate.

TABLE 2

Social Development Index (SDI) and Attainment Indicators: West Bengal, 1990-91 and 2000-01

Districts	*1990-91*					*2000-01*				
	ML	*FL*	*TL*	*IS*	*SDI*	*ML*	*FL*	*TL*	*LE*	*SDI*
Bankura	0.572	0.272	0.391	0.50	0.448 (8)	0.691	0.310	0.465	0.520	0.507 (10)
Birbhum	0.361	0.285	0.308	0.157	0.268 (12)	0.474	0.369	0.414	0.125	0.323 (14)
Burdwan	0.695	0.578	0.625	0.528	0.600 (6)	0.770	0.607	0.684	0.745	0.707 (7)
Kolkata	1.000	1.000	1.000	1.000	1.000 (1)	0.955	1.00	1.000	1.00	0.985 (1)
Coochbihar	0.308	0.206	0.242	0000	0.171 (14)	0.676	0.488	0.568	0.020	0.395 (13)
Darjeeling	0.581	0.504	0.532	0.571	0.552 (7)	0.847	0.656	0.742	0.720	0.741 (6)
Hooghly	0.826	0.689	0.742	0.728	0.748 (3)	0.915	0.749	0.825	0.820	0.828 (4)
Howrah	0.836	0.708	0.762	0.757	0.767 (2)	0.940	0.828	0.888	0.845	0.871 (2)
Jalpaiguri	0.270	0.204	0.225	0.271	0.248 (13)	0.554	0.386	0.459	0.375	0.438 (12)
Malda	0.005	0.034	0000	0.028	0.222 (17)	000	0.111	0.064	000	0.037 (18)
Medinpur	0.981	0.684	0.803	0.357	0.674 (4)	1.00	0.674	0.812	0.575	0.750 (5)
Murshidabad	0000	0.130	0.063	0.300	0.143 (16)	0.083	0.274	0.197	0.225	0.194 (16)
Nadia	0.384	0.434	0.402	0.257	0.358 (10)	0.514	0.562	0.548	0.475	0.518 (9)
Purulia	0.443	0000	0.163	0.614	0.352 (11)	0.574	0000	0.230	0.350	0.307 (15)
24-Parganas (N)	0.797	0.711	0.743	0.300	0.603 (5)	0.965	0.857	0.914	0.695	.839 (3)
24-Parganas (S)	0.620	0.355	0.464	0.314	0.430 (9)	0.794	0.553	0.659	0.645	0.664 (8)
U. Dinajpur	.095	0.094	0.087	0.128	0.106 (15)	0.001	0.0002	000	0.375	0.125 (17)
D. Dinajpur						0.541	0.440	0.484	0.375	0.452 (11)
West Bengal	0.602	0.477	0.526	.514	.531	0.705	0.565	0.630	0.605	0.625
DDI (%)	53	60.4	57	56	48.7	46	50.8	47.1	49.9	45.3

( ) Rank of the districts in descending order.
TL: Total literacy, IS: Infant Survival
ML: Male literacy, FL: Female Literacy.
LE: Life expectancy.
Source: Census 1991 and 2001. Govt. of India; Bureau of Applied Economics and Statistics, Govt. of West Bengal.

3. HDI_3: Per capita income, female literacy rate and infant survival rate.
4. HDI_4: Per capita income, male literacy rate, female literacy rate and infant survival rate.

When infant survival rate serves as a proxy of life expectancy, HDI_1 is UNDP's Human Development Index (HDI_1). Estimates of HDIs (Table 3) for different districts and the rank of the districts are more or less stable. Rank correlation matrices (Table 4) show a high rank correlation (more than 0.96) among the alternative human development indices. This implies that whatever way the HDI is defined, the ranks of the districts is almost unchanged. The low ranking districts are low in everything. The insensitivity of ranking of the districts on the basis of different HDIs makes the choice among HDIs immaterial, i. e., one may statistically examine the pattern of development using any of the four HDIs.

IV.1 Economic Development and Human Development: A Dummy Variable Approach

Human Development (HDI) is as we have said before is a function of attainment in four variables—Per capita district domestic product (PCDDP), Male literacy rate (ML), female literacy rate (FL) and infant survival rate (IS)/life expectancy (LE). Therefore, we may write $HDI_4 = f(EDI, SDI)$. Data on cross-section units are used. But cross-section units are susceptively heterogeneous and have a significant impact on the estimates. We have used the districts of West Bengal as cross-section units. The fact is that the districts of West Bengal are identified with different development levels. There are some historically developed districts. Naturally this historical development as such has an impact on the HD. This can be captured by a district dummy which would explain the convergent pattern of development in West Bengal. The dummy variable defined as

D = 1; for the districts having PCDDP greater than the state level
= 0; for otherwise.

The regression is of the form

$$HDI_4 = \alpha + \beta_1 SDI + \beta_2 D$$

Using cross-section data on districts of West Bengal the OLS

TABLE 3

Alternative Human Development Indices, West Bengal: 1990-91 and 2000-01

Districts	*1990-91*				*2000-01*			
	HDI_1	HDI_2	HDI_3	HDI_4	HDI_1	HDI_2	HDI_3	HDI_4
Bankura	0.414	0.474	0.374	0.424	0.46	0.535	0.408	0.479
Birbhum	0.24	0.257	0.232	0.264	0.275	0.295	0.26	0.314
Burdwan	0.654	0.678	0.639	0.653	0.715	0.743	0.689	0.709
Kolkata	1.000	1.000	1.000	1.000	1.000	0.985	1.000	0.989
Coochbihar	0.15	0.172	0.138	0.181	0.247	0.283	0.221	0.335
Darjeeling	0.671	0.688	0.662	0.642	0.817	0.852	0.788	0.803
Hooghly	0.713	0.741	0.695	0.728	0.75	0.78	0.725	0.772
Howrah	0.648	0.673	0.63	0.682	0.763	0.781	0.743	0.793
Jalpaiguri	0.313	0.328	0.306	0.297	0.405	0.436	0.38	0.424
Malda	0.076	0.078	0.088	0.067	0.103	0.082	0.119	0.089
Medinpur	0.547	0.607	0.508	0.626	0.614	0.677	0.568	0.676
Murshidabad	0.207	0.186	0.229	0.172	0.237	0.199	0.263	0.218
Nadia	0.36	0.354	0.371	0.374	0.498	0.486	0.502	0.505
Purulia	0.305	0.399	0.251	0.299	0.298	0.412	0.221	0.309
24-Parganas (N)	0.445	0.503	0.474	0.555	0.661	0.678	0.642	0.723
24-Parganas (S)	0.452	0.451	0.362	0.427	0.61	0.655	0.575	0.630
U. Dinajpur	0.072	0.074	0.074	0.079	0.125	0.125	0.125	0.094
D. Dinajpur	0.144	0.146	0.146	0.133	0.378	0.397	0.364	0.408
West Bengal	0.467	0.543	0.502	0.527	0.601	0.626	0.580	0.617

TABLE 4

Rank Correlation Matrix of Alternative Human Development Indices, West Bengal: 1990-91 and 2000-01

Period	*1990-91*				*2000-01*			
HDI	HDI_1	HDI_2	HDI_3	HDI_4	HDI_1	HDI_2	HDI_3	HDI_4
HDI_1	1				1			
HDI_2	0.988	1			0.996	1		
HDI_3	0.986	0.988	1		0.982	0.973	1	
HDI_4	0.983	0.983	0.975	1	0.990	0.981	0.980	1

TABLE 5

2x2 District Classification on the Basis of Economic Development (ED) and Social Development (SD): West Bengal, 1990-91

ED → *SD ↓*	*Developed (More than the state level)*	*Less Developed (Less than or equal to the state level)*
Developed (More than the state level)	Kolkata, Darjeeling, Burdwan, Hooghly	Howrah, Medinpur, 24-Parganas (N), 24-Parganas (S)
Less Developed *(Less than or equal to the state level)*		Bankura, Birbhum, Coochbihar, Jalpaiguri, Malda, Murshidabad, Nadia, Purulia, Uttar Dinajpur, Dakshin Dinajpur

estimates are:

1990-91

$$HDI_4 = \underset{(0.729)}{0.018} + \underset{(15.33)^*}{0.885}\,SDI + \underset{(2.74)^*}{0.096}\,D \qquad R^2 = 0.97,\; n=18$$

2000-01

$$HDI_4 = \underset{(1.96)}{0.033} + \underset{(26.61)^*}{0.862}\,SDI + \underset{(3.96)^*}{0.083}\,D \qquad R^2 = 0.99,\; n=18$$

* Significant at 5% level.

TABLE 6

2x2 District Classification on the Basis of Economic Development (ED) and Social Development (SD): West Bengal, 2000-01

ED → *SD ↓*	*Developed* *(More than the state level)*	*Less Developed* *(Less than or equal to the state level)*
Developed *(More than the state level)*	Kolkata, Darjeeling, Burdwan, Hooghly	Howrah, Medinpur, 24-Parganas (N), 24-Parganas (S)
Less Developed *(Less than or equal to the state level)*		Bankura, Birbhum, Coochbihar, Howrah, Jalpaiguri, Malda, Murshidabad, Nadia, Purulia, 24-Parganas (S), Uttar Dinajpur, Dakshin Dinajpur

OLS fitting is very good and R^2 is very high. Both the coefficients β_1 and β_2 are positive and significant. The districts relatively more (less) economically developed have turned out with high (low) level human development. The coefficient of D has been significantly positive. It indicates that the disparity in development in the districts is generated by an inbuilt developmental inequality prevailing among the districts. However, the estimated coefficient of D has declined over time. The effect of inbuilt disparity has marginally fallen, which indicates a tendency of development convergency among the districts of West Bengal. However, one may ignore such tendencies since difference in the estimated values is very small (0.096–0.083 =0.013).

VI. CONCLUSION

From the study it emerges that regional concentration in economic development in West Bengal exists. There is always a tendency of economic development towards Kolkata and its surrounding districts. Kolkata, Hooghly, Howrah, Burdwan and

24-Parganas (N) are economically developed districts and still remain developed. Coochbihar, Uttar Dinajpur and Malda are the less developed districts. Concentration of social development is also revealed. High inter-district disparity in economic development as well as the social development is observed. A wide disparity in human development is observed. Districts with high income (historically developed) have turned out to be with high human development. Disparity in human development or the social development is basically generated through a historically inbuilt development inequality.

The process of development in West Bengal should be made centrifugal. The less developed districts should be emphasized in terms of new industrial projects, new training and educational centres, new health units and above all, the administration should be decentralized to the extent required.

REFERENCES

Guha, B. (1998), 'Human Development in India—A Study of Interstate Disparity', *Conference Volume*, Indian Economic Association, India.

Joshi, B.M. (1990), *Infrastructure and Economic Development in India*, Ashish Publishing House, New Delhi, India.

Pal, D.P. and Sen, J. (2003), 'Economic Development and Infrastructure: An Inter-District Study in West Bengal", *Artha Beekshan*, Vol. 12, No. 1, June 2003.

Pal, D.P. and Sen, J. (2002), "Social Sector Reforms and Relative Income Deprivation in India: A Note", *Conference Volume*, Indian Economic Association, India.

UNDP, Human Development Report, 1995, 1996, 1997.

PART II

AGRICULTURE

Regional Disparity in Productivity of Boro and Aman Paddies in Six Districts

RUMA BHATTACHARYA AND BISWAJIT CHATTERJEE

Boro and Aman paddies are important sources of agricultural production in West Bengal. This paper has considered the inter-district variation of Boro paddy cultivation and the performance of Aman paddy which has been quite the opposite in comparison with that of Boro Paddy. With the help of the features of six districts for which the comparable data are available, the cost functions of these two types of paddies are estimated to explain the inter-district disparities in agricultural productivity. The outline of this paper has been designed as follows:

Section I deals with the source and explanation of data choise and methodology of computation of factor productivity and several elasticities of input. In Section 2 the empirical results are analysed and their implications are discussed. Section 3 presents the conclusion. The appendix contains the estimated parameters and elasticities for the Boro and Aman paddy cultivation for the state as a whole and also for the related districts.

INTRODUCTION

Agricultural production in West Bengal was mired in stagnation during the first three decades of the post-independence period. The state is endowed with rich natural resources and the climatic condition is favourable for agriculture. These include large areas of good alluvial soil, abundant surface and ground water resources and good rainfall. The climate of the region is tropical that is hot and humid. In spite of these favorable conditions for many years agricultural production in the state was low and lagged behind the national average. In his famous book on agricultural growth in West Bengal and Bangladesh, Boyce documented the slow growth of agriculture in the state between 1950 and 1980. He called it an 'agricultural impasse' and attributed it to the failure to effect those institutional changes which would allow better control for plant cultivation. The inequality of distribution of holdings, the lack of access of poor peasants on affordable terms to water which is the basic limitational input and the complementary inputs like fertilizers, credit, etc. led to this impasse. According to his calculations, the simple exponential growth rate of agricultural output in West Bengal over the period 1949-80 was 1.74 percent, far below the rate of population growth causing poverty levels to rise. A dramatic spurt took place in agricultural production in the state in the last two decades and it cannot be attributed merely to favourable weather, and West Bengal has emerged as the largest rice producing state in the country. It appears that Boyce's agricultural impasse had ended. The growth rate which increased from 1.7% per annum to 6% per annum in the 90s has been stable and for some time it appeared that a shift to a higher growth path was underway. By the beginning of the new millenium, however, certain disquieting factors have been observed in the trend of productivity of rice in the state which has once again become a concern for the planners. While *Boro* paddy has not only gained immensely in quantum but also in acreage and yield *Aman* paddy has been loosing ground in terms of both acreage and yield.

The acceleration in the growth of agricultural productivity was also accompanied by high incidence of inter-district variations, which are governed by variations in agro-climatic conditions and in the use and speed of technological adoption. One example of such inter-district variation and the consequent disparity in agricultural performance has been the case of *Boro* paddy cultivation, which is basically water-intensive and requires adequate supply of assured irrigation. Another feature of disparity lies in the fact that the performance of *Aman* paddy in the state has been quite the opposite in comparison to that of *Boro* paddy. In this paper we estimate the cost functions *of Boro* and *Aman* paddy for six districts, to explain that inter-district disparity in agricultural productivity persists along with disparity in the two types of paddy. Our choice of only six districts is conditioned by the availability of requisite comparable data set.

Boro cultivation in West Bengal has perhaps seen the most prominent change in the last two decades. The total area under *Boro* cultivation has gone up from 346.5 thousand hectares in 1980-81 to 1401.8 thousand hectares in 2001-02, the maximum increase taking place in the eighties. The total production of *Boro* paddy has increased from 865.2 thousand tonnes in 1980-81 to 4541.3 thousand tonnes in 2001-02. The per hectare production of *Boro* has taken a quantum leap from 2497 kg per hectare to 3240 kg per hectare. *Boro* is a summer crop and technological accessories like fertiliser, irrigation and other farm machinery are considered essential in its production process. The production of *Aman* paddy, on the other hand, increased from 6024 thousand tonnes in 1980-81 to 7202.28 thousand tonnes in 2001-02 and the yield increased from 1429 kg per hectare to 1979 kg per hectare during the same period. That is, whereas in case of *Boro* paddy the increase in yield was about 5.5 times during the period under consideration, in case of *Aman* paddy the increase was only about 1.3 times approximately.

It is observed from the beginning that the yield in *Boro* paddy is normally higher and that the investment is also higher in comparison to other paddy like *Aus* paddy and *Aman* paddy of both local and HYV varieties in the state. While there has been no doubt that *Boro* paddy has emerged as the most important crop in the state, there has been wide disparity in the degree of use of factor inputs and their productivity in the different districts of West Bengal. It also appears from the cost structure that while the big group of farmers spent the maximum amount it is the Marginal group of farmers who seems to be the more benefited class in respect of *Boro* paddy of high yielding variety. In case of

Aman paddy however all the four classes have participated. The cost of cultivation is much lower for this paddy than that of *Boro* which might have induced the farmers to keep on cultivating *Aman* in spite of a lower yield rate. This inter-class variation in yield per acre for both the crops however can not be explained by inter-class variation in amount of cost only, a detailed itemised cost structure can throw light in this respect. It has been observed that the small and marginal group of farmers spent the maximum amount towards the items like cost of seed, fertilisers, plant protection chemicals and for family labours whereas the big group of farmers are more dependent on hired labour and have invested much more in irrigation. The small group of farmers in fact use more fertiliser per unit of land than the big group of farmers in producing *Boro* paddy in the state whereas the use of fertiliser for *Aman* paddy on the whole has been much lower in general. Along with this the medium group of farmers spent the maximum amount towards the cost of irrigation and seems to be the most benefited class in the early nineties for *Boro* crop. In case of *Aman* paddy on the other hand irrigation costs have been much lower.

A disaggregated study at the district level provides further insight into the diversity of the allocative scenario of the farmers of West Bengal. This paper proposes to perform the task of economic evaluation of the farming system of *Boro and Aman* paddy cultivation of the farmers on the basis of which the agricultural extension workers and the policy-makers might be aware of the underlying economic factors responsible for the level of productivity of the *Boro* and *Aman* paddy crops grown in the different districts of the state.

Data used in this study is for *Boro* and *Aman* paddy cultivated in the state as a whole and Burdwan, Medinpur, Murshidabad, 24-Parganas, Malda and Nadia districts of West Bengal for the Marginal and Small group of farmers. The choice of districts as well as the class is in respect to availability of continuous data for the period under consideration The data reflects that *Boro* cultivation has been carried out mostly by the marginal and small group of farmers in these districts. While all these districts have shown a quantum increase in their level of productivity in *Boro* paddy, the growth rate was highest in Nadia (26.9%), and remarkably high in Murshidabad (26.4%), Medinpur (22.4%) and 24-Parganas (20.4%) and relatively high in Malda (13.8%) and

Burdwan (13.1%). In case of Aman paddy in some of these districts like Burdwan, Murshidabad and Nadia there has in fact been a decrease in total quantum of production implying a shift in choice of crop. For the other three districts the increase has been relatively low, Medinpur ((21%), Malda (19%) and 24-Parganas (9%). However, the yield rates were relatively high for these districts considering the fact that there has been a gradual decline in area under *Aman* paddy especially in the eighties.

The corresponding increase in acreage during the same period for *Boro* paddy was very little, in fact in the nineties area under all foodgrains stagnated in the statistical sense in all the districts. Therefore, the higher rate of growth in the production of *Boro* paddy in these districts of the state once again can be attributed to increase in productivity. Another notable feature is that the rate of growth of *Boro* paddy production was relatively higher in the eighties than in the nineties for all the chosen districts. An accelerated growth rate in agricultural production is more than welcome as it would not only contain widening rural-urban income disparity but also help in achieving a higher reduction in rural poverty. At this juncture therefore it would be interesting to investigate and identify the policy instrument and to formulate a strategy to improve output growth in the agricultural sector in the recent years to come so as to revive the downward trend in the rate of productivity and to ensure the higher growth path.

With this view the outline of this paper has been designed as follows: Section I deals with the source and explanation of data choice and methodology of computation of factor productivity and several elasticities of input using a non-linear iterative seemingly unrelated regression technique. In Section II, the empirical results are analysed and their implications are discussed. Section III presents the conclusions. The estimated parameters and elasticities of *Boro* and *Aman* paddy cultivation are reported first for the state as a whole and then for the selected districts in the Appendix.

I

I.1 Sources of Data

The data set used in this study has been collected by the Directorate of Agriculture, West Bengal under the Farm

Management Study Scheme. It provides data on costs, prices, yield of different crops and farming economics of different districts of West Bengal according to four size classes: (a) marginal with holding size below 1 hectare, (b) small with holding size 1.0-2.0 hectares, (c) medium with holding size 2.0-4.0, and (d) big with holding size more than 4.0 hectares. Despite the fact that there has been apprehension about the reliability of data, the main criticism being over-estimation of area and yield, several past researchers have used these data. As Khasnobis (2003) writes: "It is too much to hold that the data are so contaminated that these cannot be used for a serious analysis of growth rates of agricultural production in West Bengali." Perhaps what can reasonably be said is that it is the nature of bias, rather than the bias itself which is of more importance here. In this context Dasgupta (1995) argues that if the bias in the yield data remained constant over time, then the rate of growth would have remained unaffected. Further, Sen and Sengupta (1995) conducted growth exercises for West Bengal agriculture by using alternative data set and they observe that "the estimates come close to official ones, particularly for the latest years when the two give almost identical figures." Thus, if there has been any upward bias in the official yield it might indeed have remained constant over time. Then the rate of growth or yield per hectare figures need not be rejected outright and a useful study could be attempted to understand agricultural performance in West Bengal using these data.

The Farm Management Studies are being conducted regularly in the State of West Bengal since 1963. The villages under Farm Management Studies are selected through stratified random sampling procedure taking the districts as a first stratum for selecting the blocks and block as the second stratum for selecting the villages. The villages are then selected in pairs from each of the selected blocks. The selection of the farmers is made according to the total strength of the farmers in each operational size classes. It appears from the data that over the period under consideration the number of large farmers have dwindled and in most of the districts there were no large farmers in the blocks taken into consideration. This might be an effect of the land reform measures taken in the early eighties or it might be because of the fact that the block under random sampling did not have large farmers. Further sources of data are Economic Review, Statistical Appendix,

Statistical Abstract, and Fertiliser Statistics. The data for this study spans over a period of 1981-2002. It is not a panel data, different households were surveyed in different years. For this study the data on *Boro* and *Aman* paddy has been used.

I.2 The Explanatory Variables

The survey provides a wide range of information on all the variables used for cultivation. The endogenous variables under consideration here are the quantities of human labour, bullock labour, fertiliser and irrigation. The market variables, interest on working capital cost of implements and rent value of land under cultivation, are also treated as endogenous. In a typical Indian agricultural family a large part of the human labour is supplied by the members of the household. Therefore, it is necessary to make a distinction between family labour and hired labour as the usage of the family labour is independent of the market wage rate and as the amount of working capital available for purchase of inputs from the market is the main constraint in this analysis. Both components of human labour are measured in man-days and market wage rate is used as price for hired labour while the price of family labour is computed from the imputed cost data. The bullock labour is also measured in bullock days that is eight hours per day. The price of bullock is the daily rental price of a pair of bullocks. The data set used here shows considerable variations in these prices not only across the region but also within a particular region amongst the different classes. The fertiliser input represents the combination of chemical fertiliser as well as manure and pesticides used in the cultivation of *Boro* and *Aman* paddy. Its price is measured in rupees per kilogram and has been obtained from the Fertiliser Statistics published by The Fertiliser Association of India, New Delhi. Irrigation price includes actual taxes/charges paid for canal, river lift irrigation and deep tube wells, etc. The data shows that in the nineties where there has been a considerable decline in irrigation by wells and other minor sources the increase in area irrigated by tanks and tubewells have increased substantially. Interest is worked out on the basis of 11% per annum for owned fixed capital as well as the working capital. The rental value of land is computed as 25% of the value of the main produce of the owned land. Interest, cost of implements and rent are clubbed together and treated as market variables. As interest on fixed capital is quite small and interest on working capital is considerably higher and comprises a major portion of the farmer's budget, it is the interest on working capital that is taken into consideration here. Also the small and marginal farmers rent whatever implements they use for cultivation from large landowners and such alike so the cost of machinery is the rent they pay for hiring them.

I.3 Methodology

The literature on production and cost have evolved in several directions. The classic paper by Arrow *et al.* (1961) called into question the inherent restrictions of the Cobb-Douglas model that all elasticities of factor substitution are equal to one. Researchers have since developed numerous flexible functional forms that allow substitution to be unrestricted. The Transcendental logarithmic or translog function is a popular flexible functional form used in empirical work. This function was first developed by Kmenta (1967) as a means of approximating the CES production function and was formally introduced in a series of papers by Brendt, Christensen, Jorgensen and Lau. This study uses the translog cost function. Christensen and Greene (1976) gave the following reasons for preferring cost function to the production function:

(i) In the production function methodology certain arbitrary constraints on production pattern like assumption of additivity and homogeneity are imposed. Since the cost functions are homogenous in prices regardless of the homogeneity properties of the production function, it is not necessary to impose homogeneity of degree one restriction on the production process to arrive at estimation equations.

(ii) The cost function methodology uses input prices as the independent variables rather than the input quantities as in the case of the production function. As prices are exogenous variables this makes the estimation more realistic. Also the inputs here can be treated as endogenous variables.

(iii) As input prices are used as the independent variable

instead of input the problem of multi-colinearity does not arise here.

The translog cost function can be written as:

$$C = \ln\alpha + \Sigma\beta_i \ln P_i + 1/2\Sigma\Sigma\gamma_{ij} \ln P_i \ln P_j$$

where C is the total cost and P_i and P_j input prices. The input share equations are therefore

$$S_i = \beta_i + \gamma_{ii} \ln P_i + \Sigma\gamma_{ij} \ln P_j + \varepsilon_i.$$

The symmetry condition holds for the parameter estimates. The cost shares must sum to 1, therefore:

$$\Sigma\beta_i = 1$$
$$\Sigma\gamma_{ij} = 0$$
$$\Sigma\phi_{iy} = 0$$

The system of share equations provides a seemingly unrelated regressions model that can be used to estimate of the model. To make the model operational, we must impose the restrictions and solve the problem of singularity of the disturbance covariance matrix of the share equations. This is accomplished by dividing the first M-1 prices by the M-th price and thus eliminating the last row and the column of the parameter matrix and by dropping the last share equation.

Here ϕ_{iy} gives the scale bias

If $\phi_{iy} > 0$, this implies that cost share of the corresponding input increases with a change in level of output,

If $\phi_{iy} < 0$, then cost share has decreased, and

If $\phi_{iy} = 0$, scale bias to the corresponding input is zero.

The function is also an increasing function in input prices, that is $\delta C/\delta P_i > 0$. In other words, the estimated cost share equations (S_i) is positive for each input i at every observation and can be tested after the parameters of the model has been estimated. This assures the monotonicity of the function.

Furthermore, because the main purpose here is to estimate the substitution possibilities between the inputs as their relative prices change and the coefficients γ_{ij}'s directly do not explain this, several concepts of elasticities are developed here. The ordinary elasticities of output supply and input demand for a constrained budget situation, known as constant cost elasticities is considered first. For the translog model the expression for these elasticities are

$$e_{yc} = \delta \ln_y / \delta \ln C$$
$$e_{yi} = \delta \ln_y / \delta \ln P_i$$

In general, the sign of e_{yc} is positive, indicating an increase in optimal production as a relaxation of budget constraint. Similarly, e_{yi} is negative in general indicating a fall in output cause by a reduction of the budget in real terms, following an input price hike. For changes in producer's budget the impact on demand for the ith variable input is measured by the following elasticities

$$e_{ic} = \delta \ln X_i / \delta \ln C$$

The concept of elasticity of substitution has been devised to provide more insight. The most widely used measure, Allen Partial Elasticities of Substitution (AES) between inputs i and j, are computed employing the Uzawa (1964) procedure. This elasticity is designed to reflect the curvature properties of an isoquant.

If

$$e_{ij} = [\delta^2 c / \delta P_i \, \delta P_j] / (\delta c / \delta P_i)(\delta c / \delta P_j)$$
$$= [(\gamma_{ij} / \beta_i \beta_j] + 1 \qquad \forall i, j; i \neq j$$
$$= [\gamma_{ii} - \beta_i) / \beta_i^2] + 1 \quad \forall i$$

Then $\eta_{ij} = \beta_j e_{ij}$ and $\eta_{ii} = \beta_i e_{ii}$

Uzawa has derived the Allen Partial Elasticities of Substitution (AES) between the inputs i and j. This measures the percentage change in input ratio following a one percent change in marginal rate of technical substitution (MRTS) along an isoquant. Under perfect competition the MRTS between two is equated to their price ratio. Hence the elasticity is supposed to measure the response of a change in the input use ratio to the change in the price ratio.

However, the Allen-Uzawa elasticity does not allow for optimal adjustment of all inputs to a change in a price ratio. For a meaningful discussion of input substitutability it is necessary to go beyond the simple own and cross price elasticity measures especially in the presence of many inputs. This is because following an input price change, a change in the ratio of constant-output demands for inputs i and j may be brought about in several ways. It may be caused by a change in either of the variables or because of simultaneous change in both the variables. The Allen-Uzawa measure does not capture all these changes. An alternative measure of elasticity of substitution in the multi-factor case is known as Morishima elasticity of substitution and is defined as

$$\varepsilon_{ij}^{M} = \varepsilon_{ji} - \varepsilon_{ii}$$

Morishima's measures is a two-input-one-price elasticity of substitution (TOES). It captures the changes in both the variables as a result of change in the price of one. Morishima measure therefore provides more information than AUES. As it classifies factors somewhat differently from Allen's measure, more specifically, for any two inputs X_i and X_j, it may be that $\varepsilon_{ij}^{M} > 0$ but that $\varepsilon_{ij} < 0$, so that by Morishima measure, the inputs are substitutes, but by Allen measure, the inputs are complements. In general factors that are substitutes by Allen measure will be substitutes by Morishima measure; but factors that are complements by Allen measure may still be substitutes by the Morishima measure. Therefore, the Morishima measure has a bias towards treating inputs as substitutes. This is because AUES simply tells that the constant output demand for input i falls as price of the j-th one rises. But it is also true that the demand for the j-th input falls as its own price rises. If the proportionate fall in the j-th input is more than the proportionate reduction in the i-th input then the ratio of the i-th input to the j-th input will increase and this will indicate that the input i is a substitute for input j.

Thus the classification of inputs as substitutes or complements is not invariant to the choice of elasticity of substitution formula.

The specific form of the Translog cost function used in this study is given below

$$\begin{aligned} C = \; & \alpha + \beta_l L + \beta_h H + \beta_f F + \beta_g G + \beta_r R + \beta_y Y + 1/2\phi_{yy} Y^2 + \phi_l LY + \\ & \phi_h HY + \phi_f FY + \phi_g GY + \phi_r RY + 1/2\gamma_{ll} L^2 + 1/2\gamma_{hh} H^2 + 1/2\gamma_{ff} F^2 + \\ & 1/2\gamma_{gg} G^2 + 1/2\gamma_{rr} R^2 + \gamma_{lh} LH + y_{lf} LF + \gamma_{lg} LG + \gamma_{lr} LR + \gamma_{hf} HF \\ & + \gamma_{hg} HG + \gamma_{hr} HR + \gamma_{fg} FG + \gamma_{fr} FR + \gamma_{gr} GR + \varepsilon \end{aligned}$$

and the share equations are

$$Sl = \beta_l + \gamma_{ll}L + \gamma_{lh}H + \gamma_{lf}F + \gamma_{lg}G + \gamma_{lr}R + \phi_l Y + \varepsilon_l$$

$$Sh = \beta_h + \gamma_{lh}L + \gamma_{hh}H + \gamma_{hf}F + \gamma_{hg}G + \gamma_{hr}R + \phi_h Y + \varepsilon_h$$

$$Sf = \beta_f + \gamma_{lf}L + \gamma_{hf}H + \gamma_{ff}F + \gamma_{fg}G + \gamma_{fr}R + \phi_f Y + \varepsilon_f$$

$$Sg = \beta_g + \gamma_{lg}L + \gamma_{hg}H + \gamma_{fg}F + \gamma_{gg}G + \gamma_{gr}R + \phi_g Y + \varepsilon_g$$

$$Sr = \beta_r + \gamma_{lr}L + \gamma_{hr}H + \gamma_{fr}F + \gamma_{gr}G + \gamma_{rr}R + \phi_r Y + \varepsilon_r$$

Where

L = ln (Pl/Pb), H = ln(Ph/Pb), F = ln(Pf/Pb), G = ln(Pg/Pb), R = ln(Pr/Pb), C = total cost, Y= output, L = family labour, H = hired labour, F = fertilizer, G = irrigation, R = market variable including rent and interest, B = bullock, P = price.

There are a total of 50 parameters in the model, but 25 constraints leave only 25 free parameters to be estimated. It is a standard practice to specify the classical disturbances for cost and share equations and eventually estimate the parameters of the cost function through the multivariate regression using Zellener's (1962) iterative method for seemingly unrelated regression (SUR), commonly known as SURE models with linear constraints.

Three separate models are estimated for the state level data, the pooled model, the small model including the marginal and the small farmers and the big model including the medium and the big farmers and the results are given in the following section. In the next stage six district level data has been estimated using the same functional form.

II

II.1 Analysis of Results—State Level

This section summarises the results obtained from the estimation of the translog cost function. The parameter estimates and their asymptotic standard errors for each model for the state as a whole and the six chosen districts are reported in the Table 1 and Table 3. All the elasticities discussed in Section II are presented in Table 2 for the state as a whole, and in Table 4 for the six districts.

Boro Paddy

The most important observation here are the elasticities of output supply and input demand, e_{yc} and e_{ic}, for a marginal change in the producer's budget. The result indicates that optimal output is expected to rise by 0.24 per cent for a one rise in budget for the entire sample. Farm size-wise estimates show this elasticity to have the value of 0.21 for the small farms and 0.17 for the large ones. With changes in the producer's budget, the demand for family labour rises by 0.83 percent for the entire model and by 1.55 and 0.41 percent respectively for the small and the big farms. The demand for hired labour rises more than proportionately for all the size-classes. For one per cent relaxation in the producer's budget the increase in demand for hired labour are in the order of 1.04 for all farms combined, 1.06 for Small farms and 1.23 for big farms. The corresponding figures for fertiliser are 0.25, 0.35 and 1.04 respectively. For irrigation the respective figures are 0.29, 0.15 and 0.05 and for market variables the figures are 0.27, 0.26 and 0.30 respectively. The small farms have a relatively higher demand for family labour and irrigation as compared to the big farms whose demand for hired labour and fertiliser are higher. These results highlight the importance of cost constraint. It also shows the dependency of the small farmers on family labour. The results also show that for an one percent change in the land size the output change will be considerable.

For each input an increase in price causes a further stringency in the budget situation and consequently lowers output. A doubling of wage of hired labour is expected to bring about an output reduction of 10% for the pooled model, 8% and 6% for the small and the big farmers. The impact on output is strongest for a rise in price of fertiliser, for the pooled model the reduction will be 11% and for the small and the big farms it will be 35% and 33% respectively. Similar effects are observed for increases in price of irrigation and market variables. The small farms once again are worse affected if there is a rise in the imputed wage of the family labour. This is in line with their more restrictive budgetary situation, making them more vulnerable to market price changes. The broad pattern of relationships between the different inputs as observed in the three models does not follow any regular pattern of substitutability. In the pooled model family labour is a substitute for hired labour and fertiliser and complements with the rest. On the other hand, hired labour is a complement with fertiliser and market variables and a substitute for irrigation. In the case of small farms family labour is a substitute for all the variables other than the market variable. Similarly, hired labour is also a substitute for the other variables. Since small farmers are in a worse position regarding availability of cash, an additional demand for a particular input leads to a fall in the demand for the other.

The own price elasticities of demand (ε_{ii}) for all variable inputs are negative, other than that of the market variable in case of the pooled model, reflecting the concavity property of the cost function. The positive sign of the market variable might be attributed to measurement error in the capital price variable as it includes rent of land, interest on working and fixed capital and such factors the cost of which are imputed as a percentage of the total produce. This can also be the result of a very strong budget effect, where for a reduction in either rent or interest, under a cash-strapped situation, the extra amount of real capital is used for some other factor inputs. Farm size-wise comparison reveals that the magnitudes of these elasticities are higher for the small farms in case of hired labour and irrigation. In the nineties the big group of farmers spent highest amount towards paid-out costs like P.P. chemicals and irrigation without actually earning a remarkable gain of net-income. This has dampened their demand for these inputs and irrigation has a positive own price elasticity. This is where the importance of proper allocative decision become prominent. All the other inputs in the three groups have negative own price elasticities, meaning that as the price of these inputs decreases, the quantities demanded of these goods increases. The own price elasticities for all the inputs, family labour, hired labour, fertiliser, irrigation and market variables are inelastic.

In the small and big group fertiliser is a substitute for hired labour and irrigation. Hired labour and irrigation are substitutes in all the models. In case of the small group and the big group family labour is a complement only for the market variable all the rest are substitutes. With the exception of the market variable in both the groups the pairs of inputs turn out to be substitutes of each other. The market variable by its nature is a factor which comprises a major portion of the total cost of the farmers. Any increase in the price of this variable leads to a fall in the demand for the other variables as the farmer is always facing a constrained budget. This is markedly observed in case of hired labour and the market variable in the pooled model. The strongest substitutability of all the inputs is with family labour. The estimate of AES for family labour and hired labour in the small group is 0.81191, which implies that a 1% increase in the factor price ratio (P_l/P_h) will result in. a 0.81 per cent rise in the factor use ratio L/H. On the whole, the degree of substitutability is not very high amongst the different inputs.

Morishima estimates of elasticities provide more insight by measuring the response of the input use ratio to a price change. In the pooled model with the exception of e_{gl} and e_{hr} all the other pair of inputs are substitutes and the substitutability is quite strong. In the small group the Morishima values show that family labour and market variables are actually complements and the rest are substitutes. Substitutability is highest between family labour and hired labour, family labour and fertiliser. Once again family labour and fertiliser have the highest substitutability in the big group also. The small farms exhibit more response to relative price changes in most of the cases. On the whole, the predominant form of relationship among variable inputs is of substitutability, particularly for the small farms.

Aman Paddy

Aman paddy cultivation in the state projects an altogether different scenario. The output demand elasticities indicate that optimal output is expected to rise by 0.13 per cent for a one percent rise in budget for the entire sample which is considerably lower than that of *Boro* paddy. Similarly, the farm-wise estimates show this elasticity to be 0.11 per cent for the small farms and 0.17 per cent for the large farms respectively. Productivity in *Aman* paddy being much lower than that of *Boro* paddy has induced the farmers of the state to actually move out *of Aman* paddy production in between the period 1980-81 to 2001-02 so much so that quantum of output for the state as a whole has sharply declined. Farmers who have opted for *Boro* paddy cultivation in the summer have in winter taken up production of other high valued winter-crops like vegetables, fruits, etc. Although it is hard to specify a cut-off year for this shift, the major decline has taken place in the later nineties when trade in agricultural commodities started being encouraged. In fact, the state as a whole and the marginal farmers specially looked out for diversification in their winter production that would earn them higher positive return over their paid-out cost. With lower returns on the crop the significance of the elasticity values of the inputs do not follow the general specifications. With changes in producer's budget the demand for family labour rises by 1.19 per cent for the entire model and 0.91 per cent for the small farms and 1.04 per cent for the large farms respectively. The demand for hired labour, on the other hand, shows a reverse impact for the entire sample as well as for the small farms and the big farms. The wrong sign of the elasticity of input demand may be because of presence of excess labour in the winter season in rural Bengal. It may also be because of the fact that hired labour is a component of paid-out cost. As the return in *Aman* paddy is relatively lower farmers are unable to increase their paid-out cost component. The corresponding figures for fertiliser are 0.27, 0.01 and 0.02 respectively for the three groups. For irrigation once again the sign of elasticity do not conform to the general practice which is perhaps because *Aman* is a winter crop with lesser need for water control. Finally, the results show that for one percent change in the land size the change in output will be considerable.

An increase in input prices has in general a negative impact on the output as it restricts the already constrained budget situation. A doubling of wage of hired labour is expected to bring about an output reduction of 11% for the pooled model and 32% and 10% for the small and the big farms respectively. For family labour these figures are 6% for the pooled model, 11% for the small farms and 1% for the big farms. The impact on output is strongest for a rise in price of fertiliser as well as irrigation in case of big farms followed by small farms and the pooled model. The effects of market variable also are along the same line.

The own price elasticities have wrong sign for hired labour and irrigation in the pooled model and irrigation in the small farms and big farm model. The substitutability among the factors do not follow any pattern, as usual it is different for different districts. The Morishima values of elasticity once again reports substitutability among most of the factors implying a restrictive budget situation.

II.2 The District Results

In order to understand the regional difference in the agricultural performance a district-wise disaggregation has been done. A similar exercise has been carried out using the translog cost function for *Boro* and *Aman* paddy of the six districts, Burdwan, Medinpur, Malda, 24-Parganas, Nadia and Murshidabad of West Bengal. The results show that the output supply elasticity for *Boro* paddy is highest for Medinpur (0.43) and quite high for the districts 24-Parganas (0.42) and Nadia (0.32) and moderate for the districts Murshidabad (0.29), Burdwan (0.21) and Malda (0.11). On the whole, the optimal output is expected to rise for all the districts for a rise in the budget which is in line with the results for the small and marginal farmers at the state level (0.41). As Burdwan, Medinpur, 24-Parganas and Nadia accounted for 59% of total production during 1980-81 and 2000-02 the values of these elasticities have significant implications. In case of *Aman* paddy the output supply elasticity is highest for the district of Medinpur (0.30) and relatively high for 24-Parganas (0.27), Malda (0.26) and Burdwan (0.21) and relatively low for Nadia (0.12) and Murshidabad (0.01). While Burdwan and Medinpur together had been the largest producer of *Aman* crop in the state the other districts have actually moved away from production of the crop, the sharpest shift has been recorded in Nadia district where the quantum of output fell from 129.1 tonnes in 1980-81 to 44.8 tonnes in 2001-02. *Boro* crop with a higher yield rate has turned out to be the major crop produced by these districts. What is interesting to note that even Malda which has a higher output elasticity for *Aman* paddy records a higher growth for *Boro* paddy.

With changes in the producer's budget the demand for the different inputs rises at a different rate for the different districts for the two different crops. The disparity in these figures is quite substantial. For a one per cent budget relaxation in case of *Boro* paddy Medinpur recorded the highest increase in demand for family labour (1.22 per cent), followed by Burdwan (0.88 per cent), Murshidabad (0.15 per cent), Malda (0.01 per cent) and 24-Parganas (0.01 per cent). For hired labour these figures are 0.45 per cent for Burdwan, 0.07 per cent for Medinpur, 0.66 per cent for Malda 1.18 per cent for 24-Parganas, 1.78 per cent for Nadia and 1.61 per cent for Murshidabad. The demand for hired labour rises at a higher rate than family labour for most of the districts and more than proportionately for Nadia, Murshidabad and 24-Parganas in case of *Boro* paddy. However, the marginal and small farmers of Medinpur are more dependent on family labour than hired labour in case of *Boro* cultivation. Demand for hired labour for *Aman* paddy cultivation increases at a higher rate for 24-Parganas (1.98 per cent), Malda (1.42 per cent) and Burdwan (1.22 per cent) followed by Nadia (0.95 per cent), Murshidabad (0.37 per cent) and Medinpur (0.04 per cent). On the other hand, the increase in demand for family labour for the same crop due to one percent relaxation of budget is felt most strongly in Medinpur (1.95 per cent) followed by Burdwan (0.89 per cent), Nadia (0.72 per cent) and Malda (0.10 per cent). The elasticity values have a negative sign for the districts of 24-Parganas and Murshidabad. The reason behind this negative sign confirms the existence of excess labour whose marginal producivity is either zero or less than zero. In case of fertiliser the figures are high for Medinpur (1.17 per cent), Nadia (1.78 per cent) and Murshidabad (0.80 per cent) and relatively low for Burdwan (0.11 per cent), Malda (0.54 per cent) and 24-Parganas (0.07 per cent) for *Boro* paddy. In case of *Aman* paddy these values are different for different districts having different implications. While for Murshidabad (1.38 per cent), Burdwan (0.81 per cent) and 24-Parganas (0.67 per cent) the demand for fertiliser increases at quite a high rate for the rest of the districts the increase in demand is not so pronounced. In case of Nadia district a one percent relaxation in budget actually leads to a decrease in demand for fertiliser. The figures for irrigation for *Boro* paddy are high for all the districts and highest for Medinpur (1.18 per cent). This is because Boro being a summer crop is always an irrigated crop based fully on high yielding variety of seeds. On the other hand, *Aman* being a winter crop has lesser need for water control and as a result while Malda, Medinpur and Murshidabad registers an increase in demand for irrigation the other three districts have a negative elasticity value. The demand for market variable increases at a higher rate for Murshidabad (0.36 per cent) and Malda (0.21 per cent) and at a relatively lower rate for Burdwan (0.12 per cent), Medinpur (0.09 per cent), Nadia (0.04 per cent) and 24-Parganas (0.03 per cent) for *Boro* crop. Land under *Boro* cultivation has increased from 4.52 per cent of the gross cropped area since the 1980-81 to 16.15 per cent of the gross cropped area in 2001-02. Additional demand for land would involve a significantly high level of investment which is beyond the capacity of the marginal and small farmers considering the fact that it already comprises a major portion of their stringent budget and so the impact on demand is smaller than rest of the inputs. The elasticity value of the market variable is positive for all the districts under consideration in case *of Aman* paddy. During the period from 1980-81 to 2001-02 there has been a substantial decline in the area under *Aman* crop as compared to the gross cropped area in the state from 55 per cent to 39 per cent approximately. Considering the fact that the yield rate is positive in all the districts an increase in land area would definitely lead to increase in quantum production.

For each input an increase in price causes a further stringency in the budget situation and consequently lowers output. A doubling of the wage of hired labour is expected to bring about an output reduction of 56 per cent in Burdwan, 52 per cent in Medinpur, 82 per cent in Malda, 36 per cent in 24-Parganas, 29 per cent in Nadia and 58 per cent in Murshidabad in case of *Boro* crop. A similar increase in the wage of hired labour would result in a decrease in output of 37 per cent in Burdwan and relatively very low in the rest of the districts Malda (0.08), Medinpur (0.08), 24-Parganas (0.05), Nadia and Murshidabad (0.01) respectively. For family labour in *Boro* paddy cultivation the effects are strongest for Malda (69%) and Murshidabad (68%). Similar effects of smaller magnitude are observed in case of fertliser, where the fall in output would be of the order Nadia (31%), Medinpur (31%), Burdwan (21%), Murshidabad (12%), Malda (10%) and 24-Parganas (4%). Once again there is no clear pattern observed here. The impact on output with a rise in price of irrigation is strongest in Burdwan and in Murshidabad. In case of *Aman* paddy on the other hand any change in the price of irrigation does not seem to have any adverse effect on the output. On the whole, all the farmers of all the districts are vulnerable to input price changes but the output effect of the farmers of Malda to market price changes is more pronounced in case of *Boro* paddy in comparison with the other districts.

The demand for an individual input as has been observed, can change in either direction following an increase in amount of any other input. In case of *Boro* paddy Burdwan, Nadia and 24-Parganas family labour is a substitute for all the other inputs with the exception of irrigation in case of Nadia and market variables in case of 24-Parganas. In contrast, the use of hired labour, fertiliser as well as irrigation facility is found to increase with a rise in the number of family labour in Murshidabad. There is once again so similarity in the pattern of change in demand of one input with respect to changes of quantity of another input. In case *of Aman* paddy substitutability of factors do not follow any pattern as in the case of *Boro* paddy, however, there is a higher degree of complementarity in some of the cases.

The own price elasticities are once again negative for all the inputs in all the districts other than that of hired labour in 24-Parganas in case of *Boro* paddy and Burdwan, Malda, Murshidabad and Medinpur. This wrong sign could be the result of declining efficiency of the hired labour which would have important significance in terms of input allocation or it could be the result of the method of collecting data at the stratified level in case of *Boro* paddy. In case of *Aman* paddy a higher cost of labour becomes unprofitable for the farmers as the return over paid-out cost is lower. As compared to the pooled model for the state as a whole for *Boro* paddy the elasticity values are much higher for the family labour in all the districts and considerably lower for hired labour on the whole. On the district level, therefore, the demand for hired labour is relatively less elastic for *Boro* paddy. Demand for fertiliser is also almost inelastic in all the districts except for Murshidabad and Medinpur. Irrigation, on the other hand, has a considerably inelastic demand for all the districts. Both fertiliser and irrigation have wrong signs in different districts for *Aman* paddy. This conforms with the state results.

The Morishima estimates in case of elasticities of *Boro* paddy for Burdwan show that all the inputs are substitutes for each other with the exception of hired labour and irrigation. The degree of substitutability is also quite high in most of the cases. In case of Medinpur fertliser and market variables are complements between themselves and the rest are all substitutes of each other. Substitutability is quite strong among all the inputs in the district of Malda. In 24-Parganas complementarity exists between all the inputs and hired labour, the rest are substitutes. In Nadia hired labour and irrigation are complements so are fertiliser and market variable. Family labour and hired labour, family labour and market variable, hired labour and fertliser, hired labour and irrigation are complements in Musrshidabad. While the factors are quite strong substitutes on the whole they are actually weak complements in all the cases.

III. CONCLUSION

The most important conclusion of this study of the cost structure of the farmers of *Boro* paddy of the state of West Bengal is that in addition to the well known constraint of fixed capital, the limited amount of working capital available for variable input purchase becomes an output limiting factor. This is revealed by the positive elasticities of output supply and input demand for a marginal relaxation of the farmer's budget constraint. The output elasticity is in fact quite high for the districts of Medinpur, 24-Parganas, Nadia and Murshidabad, indicating their greater need for production loans. Most of these farmers are dependent on rental markets in technology and even for the supply of inputs including fertiliser, seeds and diesel, which continues to be largely controlled by large landowners, their dependency has increased. The higher investments in *Boro* cultivation therefore drives the small and marginal farmers to high-interest production and consumption loans and increases their dependency on those with economic and social power. In view of the restrictive effects of these farmers' budget constraint, a change in approach of credit policy increasing their access to formal sector loans and reducing their dependency on the traditional loan sharks would bring about a potential change in the level of output of *Boro* paddy in the state.

Another interesting observation is that the fall in output caused by a reduction of the budget in real terms, following an input price hike, does not follow any definite pattern for the farmers of the different districts. In other words, the needs of the farmers vary from district to district. Therefore, there exists a diversity in the input demand pattern in the different districts despite the fact that the basic geographical structure is quite similar. In order to raise productivity the agricultural extension workers and the policy makers would therefore have to take into consideration the underlying economic factors responsible for the level of productivity of the particular district. This is also reflected through the input demand elasticity values, therefore, reallocation of the available resources might prove to be a potent instrument in raising output of *Boro* paddy in the state.

Finally, under a constrained budget situation most of the inputs become substitutes of each other, but the degree of substitutability between any two inputs are not the same for the different districts implying a clear disparity. In a multiple factor case the values of these elasticities reflects the fluidity of elasticity of substitution which can bear significant implications for cost allocation as well as productivity. In case of *Aman* paddy the results show a definite shifting out in favour of other high-valued winter crops and a preference for diversification in search of higher returns through trade. The main implications of our exercise involving six districts of the state for inter-district disparity are as follows. Since different districts chosen have similar agro-climatic conditions, the effect of uniform policy of green revolution on *Boro* paddy cultivation are different in the districts because of differences in input demand and productivity of this crop, and this is despite the fact that in all the districts chosen *Boro* cultivation is mainly undertaken by small and marginal farmers. The differences between farms and across districts in agricultural productivity calls for district specific interventions and market. The value of output elasticities also indicate that the effect of availability of working capital will have different effects in different districts and that explains this inter-district variation and disparities.

Note: An earlier version of this paper was presented in the 26th Annual Conference of Bangiya Arthaniti Parishad at Viswa Bharati University, Santiniketan during February 10-12, 2006. We have benefited from the comments of the participants. The usual disclaimer applies.

References

Alagh, Y.K. and Sharma, P.S. (1980), 'Growth of Crop Production: 1960-61 to 1978-79, Is it Decelerating? *Indian Journal of Agricultural Economics*, Vol. 35, No. 2, April-June.

Bandopadhyay, Aloke (1989), 'Growth and Instability in the Production of Main Cereal Crops of West Bengal and Punjab-Haryana, 1950-51 to 1984-85—a Note,' *Indian Journal of Agricultural Economics*, Vol. 44, No. 2, April-June,

Bhalla, G.S. and Alagh, Y.K. (1979), "Performance of Indian Agriculture: A District-wise Study", Sterling Publisher Pvt. Ltd., New Delhi.

Blynn, George (1976), 'Measurement of Growth rates in Agriculture', *Indian Journal of Agricultural Economics*, Vol. 22, No. 1, January-March.

Boyce, James K., Agrarian Impasse in Bengal, Oxford University Press (1987).

Brendt, E.R. and L.R. Christensen, "The Translog Function and Substitution of Equipment, Structures and Labour in U.S. Manufacturing 1929-68," *Journal of Econometrics* (1973): 81-113.

Chambers, R.G. (1982), 'Duality, the Output Effect and Applied Comparative Statics', *American Journal of Agricultural Economics*, 64 (152-56).

Chattopadhyay, Arup Kumar and Das, Purnendu Sekhar (2000), 'Estimation of Growth Rate: A Critical Analysis with Reference to West Bengal Agriculture', *Indian Journal of Agricultural Economics*, Vol. 55, No. 2, April-June.

Dandekar, V.M. (1980), 'Seminar on Data Base and Methodology for the Study of Growth Rates in Indian Agriculture: Introduction', *Indian Journal of Agricultural Economics*, Vol. 35, No. 2, April-June.

Dasgupta, B. (1995), "West Bengal's Agriculture since 1977", Paper presented at workshop on Agricultural Growth and Agrarian Structure in Contemporary West Bengal and Bangladesh, Centre for Studies in Social Sciences, Kolkata.

Desai, B.M. and Namboodiri, N.V. (1997), "Determinants of Total Factor Productivity in Indian Agriculture", *Economic and Political Weekly*, December 27.

Dholakia, R.H. and Dholakia, B.H. (1993), "Growth of Total Factor Productivity in Indian Agricultur", *The Indian Economic Review*, Vol. 10, Nos. 25-26.

Harris, John (1993), "What is happening in Rural West Bengal: Agrarian Reform Growth and Distribution," *Economic and Political Weekly*, Vol. 28, No. 24.

Jamal, Harun and Zaman, Asad (1992), 'Decomposition of Growth Trend in Agriculture: Another Approach', *Indian Journal of Agricultural Economics*, Vol. 47, No. 4, October-December.

Johnston, J., Econometric Method, Third Edition, McGraw-Hill, New York.

Kalirajan, K. (1981), "The Economic Efficiency of Farmers Growing High Yielding Irrigated Rice in India", *American Journal of Agricultural Economics*, 63.

Khasnobis, R. (2003), 'Economic Consequences of Land Reforms: West Bengal Agriculture under Left Front Rule', in A.K. Bagchi, M. Chattopadhyay and R. Khasnobis (ed.), Economy and Quality of Life: Essays in Memory of Ashok Rudra, Dasgupta and Co. Pvt. Ltd.

Kumbhakar, S.C., A. Bhattacharyya (1992), "Price Distortion and Resource Use Efficiency in Indian Agriculture: A Restricted Profit Function Approach", *The Review of Economics and Statistics*, 231-39.

Pillai, Renuka (2001), 'An Analysis of Paddy Productivity Growth in West Bengal and Orissa', *Indian Journal of Agricultural Economics*, Vol. 56, Oct.-December.

Rahim, K.M.B. and Hazra, A.K., "Identification of Appropriate Farm Technologies in Lateritic Belt of West Bengal", Economy of West Bengal.

Rawal, V. and M. Swaminathan (1998) , "Changing Trajectories: Agricultural Growth in West Bengal", 1950-96, *Economic and Political Weekly*, Vol. 33: 2595-2602.

Reddy, M.N., Katyal, J.C., Reddy, Y.V.R. and Rama Rao, C.A. (1998), 'Estimating Agricultural Growth—A Piecewise Regression Approach', *Indian Journal of Agricultural Economics*, Vol. 53, April-June.

Rudra, A. (1992), Political Economy of Indian Agriculture, KPB, New Delhi.

Sampath, R.K. (1978), "Economic Efficiency in Indian Agriculture—Theory and Measurement," Macmillan, India.

Sahota, G.S. (1980), 'Efficiency in Resource Allocation in Indian Agriculture," *American Journal of Agricultural Economics* 50: 584-605.

Sen, Abhijit and Ranja Sengupta (1995), 'The Recent Growth in Agricultural Output in Eastern India, with Special Reference to the Case of West Bengal', Paper presented at the Workshop at Centre for Studies in Social Sciences, Kolkata.

TABLE 1A

Parameter Estimates of *Boro* Paddy for the State of West Bengal

Pooled Model			*Small Farms*			*Big Farms*		
α	-2.73044	.8271	α	11.38414	0460	α	-7.34162	.7220
β_1	.60228	.0056	β_1	.70449	.0017	β_1	.23817	.0272
β_h	.37146	.0030	β_h	.30543	.0035	β_h	.48677	.0036
β_f	.20689	.0002	β_f	.18074	.0023	β_f	.38265	.0000
β_g	.19803	.0172	β_g	.23806	.0006	β_g	.01905	.0504
β_r	-.85493	.0054	β_r	-.59922	.0028	β_r	-.32397	.0044
β_ψ	3.85693	.0156	β_y	-4.30286	.0000	β_y	6.99743	.0023
γ_{ll}	-.05491	.0004	γ_{ll}	-.06753	0000	γ_{ll}	-.02378	.0120
γ_{lh}	-.02485	.0040	γ_{lh}	.03281	0011	γ_{lh}	.02679	.0077
γ_{lf}	.04331	.0545	γ_{lf}	.04713	0008	γ_{lf}	.21031	.0012
γ_{lg}	-.01341	.0032	γ_{lg}	-.01283	0501	γ_{lg}	.06781	.0015
γ_{lr}	.02035	.0030	γ_{lr}	-.04526	0077	γ_{lr}	.01976	.0055
γ_{hh}	-.09888	.0000	γ_{hh}	-.06846	0007	γ_{hh}	-.08009	.0003
γ_{hf}	-.03159	.0000	γ_{hf}	.06905	0000	γ_{hf}	-.02336	.0013
γ_{hg}	.01109	.0502	γ_{hg}	-.00818	0017	γ_{hg}	.01468	.0000
γ_{hr}	.00198	.0000	γ_{hr}	.01670	0002	γ_{hr}	-.01911	.0026
γ_{ff}	-.01103	.0000	γ_{ff}	-.01218	0072	γ_{ff}	-.09292	.0521
γ_{fg}	-.04802	.0171	γ_{fg}	-.00642	0098	γ_{fg}	.02207	.0000
γ_{fr}	.08839	.0011	γ_{fr}	.04819	0028	γ_{fr}	.15755	.0062
γ_{gg}	-.12512	.0000	γ_{gg}	-.04884	0000	γ_{gg}	.14178	.0000
γ_{gr}	.10448	.0000	γ_{gr}	-.03976	0000	γ_{gr}	-.13865	.0000
γ_{rr}	-.08404	.0000	γ_{rr}	-.05039	0000	γ_{rr}	-.17775	.0000
γ_{lc}	-.12060	.0108	γ_{lc}	-.46299	0013	γ_{lc}	.02540	.0005
γ_{hc}	-.07003	.0000	γ_{hc}	-.03247	0095	γ_{hc}	-.10465	.0131
γ_{fc}	.01342	.0021	γ_{fc}	.11615	0027	γ_{fc}	-.08576	.0003
γ_{gc}	.00818	.0013	γ_{gc}	.25669	0011	γ_{gc}	.09223	.0040
γ_{rc}	.02296	.0025	γ_{rc}	.09302	0036	γ_{rc}	.08975	.0030
Φ_{cc}	.21596	.0008	Φ_{cc}	.12689	0016	Φ_{cc}	.02502	.0001

Small includes both marginal and small farmers.
Big includes medium and large farmers.

TABLE 1B

Parameter Estimates of *Aman* Paddy for West Bengal

Pooled Model			*Small Farms*			*Big Farms*		
α	13.2783	.0074	α	17.39040	.0874	α	13.07688	.0108
β_l	.07309	.0050	β_l	.27885	.0033	β_l	04065	.0022
β_h	.32751	.0141	β_h	.34450	.0535	β_h	07574	.0035
β_f	.57617	.0000	β_f	.92144	.0000	β_f	38894	.0083
β_g	-.01894	.0154	β_g	-.26272	.0564	β_g	13290	.0585
β_r	.74494	.0154	β_r	.04838	.0052	β_r	06111	.0005
β_ψ	3.85693	.0156	β_y	.75166	.2438	β_y	81118	.0023
γ_{ll}	-.01787	.0002	γ_{ll}	-.03825	.0594	γ_{ll}	24480	.0000
γ_{lh}	.09401	.0000	γ_{lh}	.10513	.0000	γ_{lh}	21659	.0000
γ_{lf}	.09441	.0000	γ_{lf}	.06766	.0000	γ_{lf}	11007	.0000
γ_{lg}	-.09745	.0000	γ_{lg}	-.12978	.0000	γ_{lg}	04619	.0015
γ_{lr}	.08733	.0009	γ_{lr}	.00787	.0550	γ_{lr}	00182	.0055
γ_{hh}	-.01183	.0025	γ_{hh}	-.00762	.0056	γ_{hh}	44577	.0000
γ_{hf}	-.13189	.0000	γ_{hf}	-.12452	.0000	γ_{hf}	15440	.0000
γ_{hg}	-.00540	.0703	γ_{hg}	.01193	.0564	γ_{hg}	08599	.0000
γ_{hr}	.05934	.0217	γ_{hr}	-.00200	.0022	γ_{hr}	00535	.1705
γ_{ff}	-.02965	.0000	γ_{ff}	-.05979	.0000	γ_{ff}	03195	.7522
γ_{fg}	.00274	.4732	γ_{fg}	.00684	.0196	γ_{fg}	00667	.0008
γ_{fr}	-.00518	.0061	γ_{fr}	.01779	.0097	γ_{fr}	00864	.0927
γ_{gg}	-.17505	.0000	γ_{gg}	-.17774	.0000	γ_{gg}	16188	.0000
γ_{gr}	-.04234	.0000	γ_{gr}	-.00526	.0109	γ_{gr}	05891	.0000
γ_{rr}	-.04384	.0000	γ_{rr}	.05039	.0000	γ_{rr}	00833	.0000
γ_{lc}	-.11806	.0338	γ_{lc}	-.16428	.0171	γ_{lc}	09175	.0105
γ_{hc}	.09816	.0057	γ_{hc}	.10459	.0245	γ_{hc}	03952	.0136
γ_{fc}	-.12132	.0016	γ_{fc}	.14321	.0006	γ_{fc}	07419	.0158
γ_{gc}	-.05869	.0177	γ_{gc}	-.09566	.0031	γ_{gc}	05379	.0067
γ_{rc}	-.02013	.0551	γ_{rc}	.01623	.7198	γ_{rc}	06975	.0030
Φ_{cc}	.21884	.0831	Φ_{cc}	.07001	.0495	Φ_{cc}	14862	.0101

TABLE 2A

Elasticity Estimates at the State Level for *Boro* Paddy

Pooled Model		*Small Farms*		*Big Farms*	
e_{ll}	.48889	e_{ll}	-.33458	e_{ll}	-.86167
e_{hh}	.89473	e_{hh}	-. 91871	e_{hh}	-.67776
e_{ff}	.72905	e_{ff}	-.65125	e_{ff}	-.86018
e_{gg}	-1.12179	e_{gg}	-.80641	e_{gg}	.18207
e_{rr}	1.01658	e_{rr}	-.22871	e_{rr}	-.77530
e_{lh}	.33020	e_{lh}	.35200	e_{lh}	.59925
e_{hl}	.53538	e_{hl}	.81191	e_{hl}	.29320
e_{lf}	.41355	e_{lf}	.44767	e_{lf}	1.07679
e_{fl}	.81161	e_{fl}	.82833	e_{fl}	.67022
e_{lg}	.04475	e_{lg}	.31984	e_{lg}	.47526
e_{gl}	.06771	e_{gl}	.66653	e_{gl}	.59412
e_{lr}	.82114	e_{lr}	-.63497	e_{lr}	-.24100
e_{rl}	.57847	e_{rl}	-.63976	e_{rl}	.17717
e_{hf}	.12614	e_{hf}	.60681	e_{hf}	.33466
e_{fh}	.15268	e_{fh}	.48678	e_{fh}	.45272
e_{hg}	.60007	e_{hg}	.31127	e_{hg}	.30161
e_{gh}	.56001	e_{gh}	.28123	e_{gh}	.77060
e_{hr}	4.47538	e_{hr}	-.64454	e_{hr}	-.28471
e_{rh}	-1.94451	e_{rh}	.28154	e_{rh}	.42778
e_{fr}	.42769	e_{fg}	.32119	e_{fg}	.57682
e_{rf}	.15352	e_{gf}	.36174	e_{gf}	1.15853
e_{er}	.32733	e_{tr}	-.57265	e_{tr}	-.32396
e_{re}	.15239	e_{re}	.31182	e_{rf}	.38264
e_{gr}	.32733	e_{gr}	-.81683	e_{gr}	.38698
e_{rg}	.15239	e_{rg}	.39492	e_{rg}	-1.05172
e_{yl}	.25642	e_{yl}	-.03671	e_{yl}	-.06845
e_{yh}	.10353	e_{yh}	-.08764	e_{yh}	-.03216
e_{yf}	.11867	e_{yf}	-.01230	e_{yf}	-.01458
e_{yg}	.12056	e_{yg}	-.07832	e_{yg}	-.10674
e_{yr}	24236	e_{yr}	-.21459	e_{yr}	-.18735
e_{yc}	3413	e_{yc}	.4165	e_{yc}	.2713
e_{lc}	.83657	e_{lc}	1.5579	e_{lc}	.4156
e_{hc}	1.04366	e_{hc}	1.0658	e_{hc}	1.2374

(Contd.)

Pooled Model		*Small Farms*		*Big Farms*	
e_{fc}	25415	e_{fc}	.3599	e_{fc}	1.0448
e_{gc}	.29939	e_{gc}	.1586	e_{gc}	.0589
e_{rc}	.27250	e_{rc}	.2664	e_{rc}	.3076
ρ_{lh}	1.02427	ρ_{lh}	1.73062	ρ_{lh}	1.46092
ρ_{hl}	1.22493	ρ_{hl}	.68658	ρ_{hl}	.97096
ρ_{lf}	1.54066	ρ_{lf}	.78225	ρ_{lf}	1.93846
ρ_{fl}	1.30051	ρ_{fl}	1.74705	ρ_{fl}	1.53040
ρ_{lg}	.42118	ρ_{lg}	.65442	ρ_{lg}	1.33693
ρ_{gl}	-1.06138	ρ_{gl}	1.47294	ρ_{gl}	.77620
ρ_{lr}	1.06736	ρ_{lr}	-.30038	ρ_{lr}	.62067
$\rho_{\rho\lambda}$	.19544	$\rho_{\rho\lambda}$	-.41104	$\rho_{\rho\lambda}$	1.03759
ρ_{hf}	.74205	ρ_{hf}	1.52552	ρ_{hf}	1.01242
ρ_{fh}	.60291	ρ_{fh}	1.13803	ρ_{fh}	1.28590
ρ_{hg}	1.45474	ρ_{hg}	1.22999	ρ_{hg}	.97937
ρ_{gh}	1.72186	ρ_{gh}	1.08764	ρ_{gh}	.95268
ρ_{hr}	-1.04978	ρ_{hr}	.27417	ρ_{hr}	.39305
ρ_{rh}	.45881	ρ_{rh}	.51025	ρ_{rh}	1.20309
ρ_{fg}	.88257	ρ_{fg}	.97244	ρ_{fg}	1.43701
ρ_{gf}	.69411	ρ_{gf}	1.16816	ρ_{gf}	1.34060
ρ_{fr}	.88144	ρ_{fr}	.07860	ρ_{fr}	.53621
ρ_{rf}	1.34391	ρ_{rf}	.54053	ρ_{rf}	1.15795
ρ_{gr}	1.37029	ρ_{gr}	-.01042	ρ_{gr}	.56905
ρ_{rg}	-1.34391	ρ_{rg}	.623636	ρ_{rg}	-.27640

TABLE 2B

Elasticity Estimates at the State Level for *Aman* Paddy

Pooled Model		*Small Farms*		*Big Farms*	
e_{ll}	- 1.20322	e_{ll}	-.85831	e_{ll}	-.66156
e_{hh}	.70816	e_{hh}	-.64419	e_{hh}	-.61281
e_{ff}	- .47528	e_{ff}	-.14344	e_{ff}	-.69043
e_{gg}	.06348	e_{gg}	-.586181	e_{gg}	.08515
e_{rr}	.25287	e_{rr}	-.1.87133	e_{rr}	-.23077
e_{lh}	1.63172	e_{lh}	.72151	e_{lh}	.60855
e_{hl}	.36013	e_{hl}	.58401	e_{hl}	.32665
e_{lf}	1.86786	e_{lf}	1.16407	e_{lf}	3.09661
e_{fl}	.2394	e_{fl}	.35227	e_{fl}	.32364
e_{lg}	2.05038	e_{lg}	.77283	e_{lg}	.38820
e_{gl}	-.49344	e_{gl}	-.72813	e_{gl}	-1.26918
e_{lr}	.14816	e_{lr}	.07660	e_{lr}	.05088
e_{rl}	.37758	e_{rl}	.44159	e_{rl}	.33852
e_{hf}	-.17346	e_{hf}	-.55998	e_{hf}	-1.64961
e_{fh}	-.09860	e_{fh}	-.20936	e_{fh}	-.32123
e_{hg}	.28668	e_{hg}	.29909	e_{hg}	-.57128
e_{gh}	-.016579	e_{gh}	-.22809	e_{gh}	.10024
e_{hr}	.18118	e_{hr}	.05418	e_{hr}	.07674
e_{rh}	2.06903	e_{rh}	.38583	e_{rh}	.95135
e_{fr}	.43150	e_{fg}	.89540	e_{fg}	.89540
e_{rf}	-.01418	e_{gf}	-.25529	e_{gf}	-.25529
e_{er}	-.01500	e_{tr}	-.06772	e_{tr}	-1.87133
e_{re}	-.30267	e_{re}	-1.28992	e_{rf}	-1.02513
e_{gr}	-.07577	e_{gr}	-.371442	e_{gr}	-.37144
e_{rg}	.12045	e_{rg}	0.06840	e_{rg}	.06841
e_{yl}	-.06362	e_{yl}	-0.32453	e_{yl}	-.10224
e_{yh}	-.11156	e_{yh}	-0.21667	e_{yh}	-.05227
e_{yf}	-.08921	e_{yf}	-0.35264	e_{yf}	-.42675
e_{yg}	-.05312	e_{yg}	-0.20566	e_{yg}	-.29641
e_{yr}	-.01576	e_{yr}	-0.11543	e_{yr}	-.49986
e_{yc}	.13214	e_{yc}	0.11834	e_{yc}	.17443
e_{lc}	1.19963	e_{lc}	0.91369	e_{lc}	1.04553
e_{hc}	-1.53648	e_{hc}	-0.07543	e_{hc}	-0.54668

(Contd.)

Pooled Model		*Small Farms*		*Big Farms*	
e_{fc}	.70348	e_{fc}	0.00312	e_{fc}	0.02608
e_{gc}	.44825	e_{gc}	-0.06033	e_{gc}	0.32926
e_{rc}	.62556	e_{rc}	.26409	e_{rc}	0.00874
ρ_{lh}	2.83494	ρ_{lh}	1.44232	ρ_{lh}	0.98821
ρ_{hl}	1.06682	ρ_{hl}	1.36571	ρ_{hl}	1.22136
ρ_{lf}	1.44016	ρ_{lf}	1.21058	ρ_{lf}	0.98523
ρ_{fl}	2.34314	ρ_{fl}	1.30751	ρ_{fl}	3.78704
ρ_{lg}	.70978	ρ_{lg}	.13017	ρ_{lg}	-0.60782
ρ_{gl}	2.11386	ρ_{gl}	1.35901	ρ_{gl}	0.47362
ρ_{lr}	1.58082	ρ_{lr}	1.29999	ρ_{lr}	1.00841
$\rho_{\rho\lambda}$	.40103	$\rho_{\rho\lambda}$	1.94793	$\rho_{\rho\lambda}$	0.28165
ρ_{hf}	.60326	ρ_{hf}	-0.04165	ρ_{hf}	0.29158
ρ_{fh}	.30182	ρ_{fh}	-0.06592	ρ_{fh}	-0.95918
ρ_{hg}	.69158	ρ_{hg}	0.41613	ρ_{hg}	0.71305
ρ_{gh}	1.72186	ρ_{gh}	0.88527	ρ_{gh}	0.47336
ρ_{hr}	-1.04978	ρ_{hr}	1.03002	ρ_{hr}	1.56416
ρ_{rh}	.45881	ρ_{rh}	1.92551	ρ_{rh}	0.30751
ρ_{fg}	.88257	ρ_{fg}	-0.11185	ρ_{fg}	0.57468
ρ_{gf}	.69411	ρ_{gf}	1.48154	ρ_{gf}	0.42390
ρ_{fr}	.88144	ρ_{fr}	-1.14682	ρ_{fr}	-1.18092
ρ_{rf}	1.34391	ρ_{rf}	1.80411	ρ_{rf}	-1.64056
ρ_{gr}	1.37029	ρ_{gr}	0.65468	ρ_{gr}	0.53453
ρ_{rg}	-1.34391	ρ_{rg}	1.49988	ρ_{rg}	-9.54367

TABLE 3A

Parameter Estimates of *Boro* Paddy of the Six Districts of West Bengal

	Burdwan	*Nadia*	*24-Parganas*	*Malda*	*Medinpur*	*Murshidabad*
α	122.0145	-16.4703	-7.09828	6.668534	5.070086	48.78817
	(.0022)	(.2141)	(.0516)	(.0351)	(.3292)	(.0000)
β_l	0.469813	-1.0188	-0.52107	-0.82916	.8501641	-1.43544
	(.0537)	(.0172)	(.0228)	(.0002)	(.0094)	(.0343)
β_h	0.58311	1.859747	1.511826	1.485659	-0.62029	2.285286
	(.0379)	(.0004)	(.0013)	(.0000)	(.0406)	(.0007)
β_f	0.307178	0.018019	-0.04428	0.048994	0.029112	0.029617
	(.0182)	(.0301)	(.0085)	(.0009)	(.0098)	(.0002)
β_g	-0.32947	0.013935	0.006973	0.045647	0.040677	0.002438
	(.0572)	(.0021)	(.0034)	(.0054)	(.0053)	(.1278)
β_r	0.120461	0.040428	-0.07437	0.243669	0.041341	0.064435
	(.1152)	(.0498)	(.0011)	(.0340)	(.0400)	(.0001)
β_y	6.03159	11.86763	8.860734	-0.31765	0.934026	-22.4891
	(.0032)	(.0062)	(.0147)	(.0055)	(.0164)	(.0357)
γ_{ll}	-0.00571	-0.78317	0.451284	0.098782	0.409748	0.535711
	(.0006)	(.0061)	(.0117)	(.0237)	(.0004)	(.0152)
γ_{lh}	0.04033	0.57851	-0.45473	-0.07598	-0.40537	-0.49925
	(.0221)	(.0934)	(.0628)	(.0104)	(.0005)	(.1019)
γ_{lf}	0.030797	0.027004	0.003983	0.006302	-0.00059	-0.00878
	(.0003)	(.0126)	(.0037)	(.0001)	(.3568)	(.0009)
γ_{lg}	-0.0576	0.045309	-0.003	-0.01882	-0.00309	-0.00045
	(.1025)	(.0002)	(.0629)	(.0456)	(.0128)	(.1088)
γ_{lr}	0.021971	0.051963	0.003887	-0.00756	0.000416	-0.02166
	(.0806)	(.0011)	(.0089)	(.0034)	(.0568)	(.0675)
γ_{hh}	-0.04412	-0.37067	-0.69555	-0.75057	-0.40863	-0.45193
	(.0139)	(.0048)	(.0040)	(.0077)	(.0005)	(.0009)
γ_{hf}	0.0242	-0.02628	-0.00164	-0.01034	-0.00033	0.013246
	(.0009)	(.1111)	(.3361)	(.0103)	(.0022)	(.1888)
γ_{hg}	-0.00597	-0.04737	-0.00132	-0.00748	0.000152	0.004652
	(.3709)	(.0000)	(.0000)	(.0002)	(.2997)	(.0669)
γ_{hr}	-0.05382	-0.05033	-0.0082	-0.05489	-0.00225	0.024253
	(.0000)	(.0012)	(.0000)	(.0000)	(.0000)	(.0000)

(*Contd.*)

	Burdwan	*Nadia*	*24-Pargan*	*Malda*	*Medinpur*	*Murshidabad*
γ_{ff}	-0.06214	0.007701	-0.00484	-0.00903	-0.0056	-0.00663
	(.0000)	(.0000)	(.0000)	(.0248)	(.3677)	(.0009)
γ_{fg}	-0.01837	0.000107	-0.00243	0.001755	-.0000452	-0.00076
	(.0000)	(.0009)	(.0019)	(.0000)	(.0000)	(.1083)
γ_{fr}	-0.04414	-0.00761	-0.00449	-0.00749	-0.00447	-0.00796
	(.0012)	(.0000)	(.0037)	(.0000)	(.1446)	(.0000)
γ_{gg}	-0.00661	-0.00094	0.004367	-0.02839	0.001528	-0.00247
	(.0000)	(.1109)	(.0000)	(.0002)	(.0820)	(.0192)
γ_{gr}	0.066916	-0.00072	0.001747	-0.00571	0.000689	-0.00066
	(.0040)	(.0656)	(.0136)	(.0002)	(.2624)	(.0244)
γ_{rr}	0.005954	-0.00769	-0.0068	0.075622	0.00611	-0.00568
	(.0000)	(.0000)	(.0303)	(.0000)	(.0500)	(.0663)
γ_{ly}	-0.1955	0.28028	0.254564	0.312113	-0.30071	0.504171
	(.0469)	(.0380)	(.0101)	(.0179)	(.0261)	(.0821)
γ_{hy}	-0.08369	-0.26015	-0.29228	-0.17368	0.322447	-0.48479
	(.0142)	(.0465)	(.0439)	(.0316)	(.0032)	(.0416)
γ_{fy}	0.092348	0.000456	0.012399	-0.00879	-0.00546	-0.00221
	(.0048)	(.0274)		(.0012)	(.0316)	(.0292)
γ_{gy}	0.047596	-0.00018	0.003833	0.014882	-0.00707	0.001949
	(.0510)	(.0484)	(.0146)	(.0261)	(.0012)	(.0036)
γ_{ry}	0.11771	-0.0049	0.022035	-0.14519	-0.00804	-0.00941
	(.0229)	(.01827)	(.0139)	(.0013)	(.0411)	(.0415)
Φ_{yy}	.1531098	.288334	.255668	0.46168	-0.08925	6.161998
	(.0036)	(.0161)	(.0164)	(.0411)	(.0507)	(.0000)

TABLE 3B

Parameter Estimates of *Aman* Paddy of the Six Districts of West Bengal

	Burdwan	*Nadia*	*24-Parganas*	*Malda*	*Medinpur*	*Murshidabad*
α	55.4744543	33.431377	-10.03538	21.470930	-12.385003	19.5243516
	(.0000)	(.0000)	(.0429)	(.0000)	(.0153)	(.0000)
β_l	0.34740578	.7819483	-0.566176	-0.0521170	0.7926977	-0.6450299
	(.0016)	(.0203)	(.0217)	(.0420)	(.0000)	(.0039)
β_h	0.78584681	-.5563542	1.732185	.64540434	-0.2982840	0.7648718
	(.0000)	(.0017)	(.0000)	(.0000)	(.0309)	(.0036)
β_r	0.21701402	0.4858274	-0.057260	0.0535866	0.6430052	0.3242001
	(.0000)	(.0000)	(.0245)	(.00271)	(.0642)	(.0000)
β_g	0.53248903	0.5334374	0.2926787	0.31962724	-0.0230455	0.4809908
	(.0001)	(.0000)	(.0128)	(.0005)	(.0086)	(.0001)
β_r	-0.8247954	.1222088	-0.1619056	-0.1283969	0.1923408	-.09186293
	(.0000)	(.0000)	(.0011)	(.0057)	(.0143)	(.0066)
β_y	-27.329975	-19.462618	7.8604363	-11.067275	9.9897726	-8.4045667
	(.0001)	(.0000)	(.0347)	(.0000)	(.0103)	(.0000)
γ_{ll}	-.05602977	0.0259796	-0.1841650	0.06221987	-0.2654658	-0.0814268
	(.0006)	(.0000)	(.0028)	(.0000)	(.0000)	(.0000)
γ_{lh}	-03159986	-.6686299	0.1717095	-0.0410103	0.0035528	-0.1042380
	(.0054)	(.0769)	(.0023)	(.0009)	(.0002)	(.0015)
γ_{lf}	-0.00829233	0.0262812	-0.0093923	-0.0014833	0.0643436	0.0250309
	(.0000)	(.0270)	(.0017)	(.0034)	(.0133)	(.0002)
γ_{lg}	-0.0299264	0.1167047	0.0357197	-0.0314406	0.0238495	-0.0324652
	(.1025)	(.0000)	(.0032)	(.0055)	(.0013)	(.0019)
γ_{lr}	0.051746	-.05484359	-0.07979405	0.01767593	-0.0746425	0.0647790
	(.0000)	(.0509)	(.0000)	(.0392)	(.0105)	(.0023)
γ_{hh}	.2502437	.170648541	-0.04793636	0.3252899	0.0038219	-0.1613775
	(.0000)	(.0048)	(.0000)	(.0019)	(.0019)	(.0019)
γ_{hf}	0.010202	-0.0316625	0.00480461	-0.0192830	-0.0330558	-0.02264496
	(.0001)	(.0135)	(.0031)	(.0000)	(.0000)	(.0085)
γ_{hg}	-0.039588	-0.083405	-0.06122548	0.0213149	-0.0432162	0.02446906
	(.0012)	(.0094)	(.0000)	(.0142)	(.0003)	(.0008)
γ_{hr}	-0.098872	0.07788142	-0.0797940	0.0107369	0.00408603	-0.04178689
	(.0000)	(.0018)	(.0000)	(.0000)	(.0000)	(.0076)
γ_{ff}	-0.010481	0.0361405	0.0038891	0.0120586	-0.0082150	0.2630369
	(.0000)	(.0000)	(.0017)	(.0000)	(.0096)	(.0000)

(*Contd.*)

	Burdwan	*Nadia*	*24-Pargan*	*Malda*	*Medinpur*	*Murshidabad*
γ_{fg}	.0050675	-0.0077262	0.0049916	0.0164735	-0.00104137	-0.00127073
	(.0006)	(.0000)	(.0071)	(.0000)	(.0000)	(.0064)
γ_{fr}	-0.0202337	-0.0634007	-0.00558944	-0.0105988	-0.10203234	-0.03587522
	(.0000)	(.0000)	(.0000)	(.0000)	(.0001)	(.0000)
γ_{gg}	.35562119	.1209462	-0.0140763	0.0100979	0.1636119	-0.00731868
	(.0000)	(.0000)	(.0000)	(.0608)	(.0098)	(.0063)
γ_{gr}	0.0048608	-0.0076376	0.0018609	-0.0102138	0.0266032	-0.0491915
	(.0048)	(.0351)	(.0298)	(.0333)	(.0278)	(.0000)
γ_{rr}	0.0537279	0.021079	0.0962978	-0.020489	-0.106537	0.06377518
	(.0000)	(.0000)	(.0000)	(.0000)	(.0000)	(.0020)
γ_{ly}	.5777092	-0.05326261	0.0434915	0.056188	0.202997	0.00111493
	(.0101)	(.0049)	(.0501)	(.0111)	(.0070)	(.0188)
γ_{hy}	-0.212714	0.03192765	-0.3773525	-0.0838870	0.0662087	-0.00591822
	(.0022)	(.0171)	(.0003)	(.0000)	(.0000)	(.0054)
γ_{fy}	0.0306984	-0.674688	-0.0019666	0.01334025	-0.0417846	-0.05117967
	(.0028)	(.0002)	(0000)	(.0019)	(.0089)	(.0118)
γ_{gy}	0.094336	-0.1452933	0.10669246	-0.0388403	-0.00707	-0.00314599
	(.0093)	(.0000)	(.0195)	(.0169)	(.0012)	(.0000)
γ_{ry}	-.1629742	-0.2443481	0.0138446	0.1500940	0.0055084	0.001202131
	(.0000)	(.0000)	(.0000)	(.0000)	(.0411)	(.0014)
Φ_{yy}	.0131299	.0630075	-0.1117747	0.1452517	0.31090310	0.04719280
	(.0000)	(.0100)	(.0011)	(.0001)	(.0079)	(.0001)

TABLE 4A

Estimates of Elasticities of *Boro* Paddy at the District Level

	Burdwan	*Nadia*	*24-Parganas*	*Medinpur*	*Malda*	*Murshidabad*
e_{ll}	-0.6517	-0.8523	-2.3871	-0.6215	-1.7571	-2.8085
e_{hh}	-0.2872	-0.6646	0.2207	-1.6587	-0.0195	-0.0614
e_{ff}	-0.2749	-0.0382	-0.1650	-1.1631	-0.0694	-2.7791
e_{gg}	-1.2272	-0.1532	-0.0929	-0.0205	-0.0735	-0.0857
e_{rr}	-0.3852	-0.0404	-0.0347	0.0731	-0.4458	-0.0443
e_{lh}	0.6689	0.2114	0.2630	-0.1434	1.5772	-1.8238
e_{hl}	0.3142	-0.2459	-0.1370	-0.1219	-1.3078	0.9885
e_{lf}	0.3727	-0.0113	0.0360	0.2221	-0.0565	-1.7310
e_{fl}	0.1751	0.0104	-0.0188	0.1888	0.0682	0.0357
e_{lg}	0.6157	-0.0353	0.0754	0.4307	0.0691	-1.6217
e_{gl}	-0.2430	0.0325	0.5210	0.3662	-0.0573	0.0275
e_{lr}	0.0739	-0.0162	-0.0818	0.5417	0.2527	-1.7715
e_{rl}	0.0346	0.0148	-0.2715	0.4605	-0.2096	0.0795
e_{hf}	0.3486	-0.0125	-0.0453	0.3451	0.0420	1.7325
e_{fh}	0.2033	-0.0108	-0.0685	-0.2140	0.0624	0.0513
e_{hg}	-0.0497	-0.0411	0.0118	0.0444	0.0406	1.4760
e_{gh}	-0.2895	-0.0353	0.1086	0.0275	1.3217	0.0359
e_{hr}	0.0281	-0.0181	-0.7978	0.0529	0.2067	1.6616
e_{rh}	0.0164	-0.0155	0.1206	-0.0328	0.3071	0.1070
e_{fg}	-0.4545	0.0198	-0.0147	0.0636	0.0808	-0.2810
e_{gf}	-0.1396	0.0003	0.0618	0.0018	0.0039	-0.0068
e_{ft}	-0.0232	-0.3821	0.0270	-0.1042	0.0044	0.1531
e_{rf}	-0.0071	-0.0068	-0.0160	-0.0030	0.0182	0.0098
e_{gr}	-0.0490	-0.0115	0.1761	0.0641	0.1185	-0.0784
e_{rg}	0.0193	-0.0001	0.0673	0.0606	0.0054	-0.0050
e_{yc}	0.3186	0.3216	0.4124	0.4382	0.1136	0.2915
e_{yl}	-0.3207	-0.3504	-0.6856	-0.5631	-0.6989	-0.6872
e_{yh}	-0.5665	-0.2958	-0.3622	-0.5247	-0.8231	-0.5891
e_{yf}	-0.2108	-0.3167	-0.0415	-0.3179	-0.1027	-0.1232
e_{yg}	-0.2643	-0.0178	-0.0765	-0.0368	-0.0965	-0.0685
e_{yr}	-0.1294	-0.0434	-0.0399	-0.0923	-0.2136	-0.3621
e_{lc}	0.8860	0.1104	0.0141	1.3304	0.0104	0.1568
e_{hc}	0.4558	1.7896	1.1869	0.1818	0.6680	1.6115

(*Contd.*)

	Burdwan	*Nadia*	*24-Parganas*	*Medinpur*	*Malda*	*Murshidabad*
e_{fc}	0.1134	0.8958	0.0797	0.8138	0.5426	0.8065
e_{gc}	0.0963	1.0096	0.3299	1.1829	0.3028	0.7601
e_{rc}	0.3385	1.0221	-0.1713	0.9492	1.1367	0.7626
ρ_{lh}	0.9660	0.4996	2.2500	0.4996	0.4492	3.7970
ρ_{hl}	0.9561	0.8854	0.0422	0.8854	1.1929	-1.7623
ρ_{lf}	0.8268	0.8107	0.1462	0.8109	1.8253	2.8442
ρ_{fl}	0.6467	1.3852	2.4232	1.3852	0.0128	1.0481
ρ_{lg}	0.4087	0.9878	2.9082	.9.878	1.6997	2.8360
ρ_{gl}	1.84297	0.4513	0.1683	0.4513	0.1426	-1.5393
ρ_{lr}	0.6863	1.0821	2.1156	1.0821	1.5475	-1.5359
ρ_{rl}	0.4589	0.6149	-0.0470	0.6149	0.6986	2.8880
ρ_{hf}	0.4905	0.8148	-0.2893	0.8148	0.0820	-1.7271
ρ_{fh}	0.6236	1.5082	0.1193	1.5082	0.1116	4.5116
ρ_{hg}	-0.0023	1.0565	-0.1121	1.0565	1.3412	0.0974
ρ_{gh}	1.1775	0.0650	0.0104	0.0650	0.1141	1.5618
ρ_{hr}	0.3036	0.9960	-0.1001	0.9960	0.3266	0.1685
ρ_{rh}	0.4134	0.1261	-0.0450	0.1261	0.6525	1.7060
ρ_{fg}	0.1353	1.1649	0.1836	1.1649	0.0734	2.7723
ρ_{gf}	0.7724	0.0842	0.0781	0.8242	0.1543	-0.1952
ρ_{fr}	0.2678	1.1600	0.0041	1.1600	0.0313	2.7890
ρ_{rf}	0.3169	-0.0310	0.0618	-0.0310	-0.3035	0.1975
ρ_{gr}	1.2466	0.0812	0.1620	0.0812	0.0161	0.0908
ρ_{rg}	0.3361	0.1372	0.2194	0.1372	0.5644	-0.0340

TABLE 4B

Estimates of Elasticities of *Aman* Paddy at the District Level

	Burdwan	*Nadia*	*24-Parganas*	*Medinpur*	*Malda*	*Murshidabad*
e_{ll}	-1.7560	0.7253	-1.2405	-0.5421	-0.5982	-1.7712
e_{hh}	0.1042	0.9529	-1.1035	1.2987	0.2832	0.2373
e_{ff}	-0.8312	-0.0907	-0.3594	-0.2934	-0.4416	-0.5946
e_{gg}	-0.4007	-0.3127	-0.0797	-0.7877	-0.6487	-0.5038
e_{rr}	-1.8899	0.8723	-1.7216	0.5754	-0.9688	-1.8293
e_{lh}	-0.3876	0.9021	-0.4670	0.2312	-0.4576	-0.7813
e_{hl}	0.8768	-0.6418	1.4288	-0.0870	0.5667	0.9264
e_{lf}	0.3091	-0.5948	-0.7302	0.7982	-0.0548	-0.5678
e_{fl}	0.1931	0.8360	0.0736	0.6474	0.5564	0.2853
e_{lg}	0.5323	0.0768	-0.6882	1.0718	-0.6195	-0.7125
e_{gl}	0.8160	1.0008	-0.3557	-0.3116	0.3799	0.5313
e_{lr}	0.2846	0.3331	-0.5488	0.9166	-0.3835	-1.3502
e_{rl}	-0.6758	0.0520	-0.1569	0.2224	0.0944	0.1922
e_{hf}	0.8325	-0.6215	1.8160	-0.2923	0.2855	1.2964
e_{fh}	0.2300	0.5427	0.0600	0.6301	0.0238	0.5495
e_{hg}	0.7112	-0.7127	1.9413	-0.2295	0.7120	0.8157
e_{gh}	0.4820	0.6833	-0.3280	-0.1773	0.3526	0.5129
e_{hr}	0.9054	0.0809	2.2250	-0.5229	0.3610	1.2197
e_{rh}	-0.9506	0.0177	-0.2079	0.3372	0.1450	-0.0784
e_{fg}	0.2265	0.4713	0.0402	0.6786	0.1051	0.0583
e_{gf}	0.5558	0.5175	-0.2055	-0.2432	0.6270	0.0865
e_{fr}	0.2415	-0.0329	0.091	0.6375	-0.0289	0.7147
e_{rf}	-0.9180	-0.0082	-0.2595	0.1907	-0.0694	-0.2025
e_{gr}	0.5265	0.4709	-0.3041	-0.2219	0.2400	1.0164
e_{rg}	-0.8156	0.1078	-0.1682	0.1852	0.0964	-0.1941
e_{yc}	0.2135	0.1217	0.2727	0.3054	0.2641	0.0164
e_{yl}	-0.2434	-0.0180	-0.0502	-0.0810	-0.1643	-0.0013
e_{yh}	-0.3773	-0.0357	0.0130	-0.0236	-0.0859	-0.0026
e_{yf}	-0.1966	-0.0058	-0.0106	-0.0148	-.0.0318	-0.0004
e_{yg}	0.1066	-0.0016	0.0038	-0.0311	-0.0266	-0.0012
e_{yr}	-0.5584	-0.0141	-0.0389	-0.0081	-0.0541	-0.0010
e_{lc}	0.8941	0.7253	-0.2669	1.9571	0.1080	0.3465
e_{hc}	1.2250	0.9529	1.9828	0.0414	1.4265	-0.3787
e_{fc}	0.8179	-0.0907	0.6712	0.1968	0.0310	1.3819
e_{gc}	-0.2281	-0.3127	-1.1482	1.9839	1.9068	0.7241
e_{rc}	0.9486	0.8723	0.0389	-0.0353	-0.4757	1.2583
ρ_{lh}	2.6328	0.4996	2.2500	0.4996	0.2786	0.6874
ρ_{hl}	0.2833	0.8854	0.0422	0.8854	-0.6708	0.9899
ρ_{lf}	0.08864	0.8107	0.1462	0.8109	-0.4051	2.0566

(*Contd.*)

	Burdwan	*Nadia*	*24-Parganas*	*Medinpur*	*Malda*	*Murshidabad*
ρ_{fl}	1.1404	1.3852	2.4232	1.3852	0.7507	0.0268
ρ_{lg}	2.5720	0.9878	2.9082	.9878	0.2178	2.3028
ρ_{gl}	0.9331	0.4513	0.1683	0.4513	1.1872	-0.2087
ρ_{lr}	1.0801	1.0821	2.1156	1.0821	-1.2742	1.5789
ρ_{rl}	2.1745	0.6149	-0.0470	0.6149	1.2534	0.4791
ρ_{hf}	0.1257	0.8148	-0.2893	0.8148	-0.0532	0.3121
ρ_{fh}	1.6647	1.5082	0.1193	1.5082	1.2741	1.8911
ρ_{hg}	0.3778	1.0565	-0.1121	1.0565	0.1988	0.5784
ρ_{gh}	1.1119	0.0650	0.0104	0.0650	1.6834	1.3195
ρ_{hr}	-1.0549	0.9960	-0.1001	0.9960	-1.2338	-0.3157
ρ_{rh}	2.8053	0.1261	-0.0450	0.1261	0.6534	0.9824
ρ_{fg}	0.8492	1.1649	0.1836	1.1649	1.2045	0.5903
ρ_{gf}	1.0142	0.0842	0.0781	0.8242	0.6681	0.6530
ρ_{fr}	-0.6246	1.1600	0.0041	1.1600	-0.4764	1.6268
ρ_{rf}	2.1314	-0.0310	0.0618	-0 0310	1.2103	2.5442
ρ_{gr}	0.9272	0.0812	0.1620	0.0812	-0.1669	0.3096
ρ_{rg}	0.2416	0.1372	0.2194	0.1372	1.4953	1.5202

An Analysis of Inter-district Disparity in Foodgrains Production*

ARPITA GHOSE (NEE DHAR) AND DIPYAMAN PAL

This paper analyses the inter-district disparity regarding growth and instability in foodgrains production for 13 major districts of West Bengal, for the period 1960-61 to 1999-2000. We have calculated the magnitude of shift of growth rate as well as the degree of instability taking 1982-83 and 1991-92 as break point separately. The reasons for taking 1982-83 as a break point is that certain favourable events like land reforms, introduction of panchayat system and irrigation strategies were undertaken in West Bengal agricultural system during this period. The reason for taking 1991-92 as a break point is that it is the year when different liberalization policies were introduced in the Indian economy. We have also tried to find out the factors determining the yield of foodgrains for these 13 districts. Our results support strong evidence of inter-district disparity. The functional form of growth

*An earlier version was presented in the 26th Annual Conference of Bangiya Arthaniti Parisad, held at Department of Economics, Visva Bharati, Santinikatan, during February 9-10, 2006.
We are indebted to the participants of the conference. We are also indebted to Professors S.K. Bhoumik and Manabendu Chattopadhyay for helpful suggestions and comments. The general disclaimer applies.

rate, the magnitude and also the extent of instability vary among different districts. This inter-district disparity becomes more prominent if we combine the results of growth rate with the results of instability. None of the districts performs well after 1982-83 and also after 1991-92 and the West Bengal economy performs badly after 1991-92. Inter-district disparity also get reflected in the sense that the function specifying the relationship between yield of foodgrains and the factor inputs, as well as the significant factors determining the yield of foodgrains varies across different districts of West Bengal. We have made some policy prescriptions for boosting up of yield of foodgrains for different districts of West Bengal, and to reduce the existing level of disparity across different districts emphasizing the significant explanatory variables determining the yield of foodgrains production, which are also different for different districts.

1. INTRODUCTION

Foodgrains crops play a vital role in Indian agriculture providing our staple foods and many other processed food products. Foodgrains from agricultural farm may also act as raw materials in food processing industries in the country. Thus to maintain a balance between foodgrains supply and industrial demand and also for human consumption production of foodgrains in all districts of a particular state and all the states of the country must be balanced, so that the income of the rural people who are engaged in production would be increased. The states and the country will get the benefit from the production of these agricultural commodities. At the same time, the question of equality regarding agricultural production and or income across different states of the country or across different districts of a particular state can be ensured. Agricultural growth in West Bengal, as in other part of the eastern and the north-eastern part of India was slow for many years and much behind the all India average. In a pioneering study of agricultural performance in West Bengal, James Boyce (1987) estimated the growth rate of agricultural output and showed that "between" 1949 to 1980 it was only 1.74% per annum. From 1969-70 to 1981-82 the food-grains production grew at a rate of 0.06%. In the 1980s the situation changed. Agricultural growth accelerated, the state domestic product originating from this sector increased at constant

1980-81 prices from Rs. 2477.64 crore in 1980-81 to Rs. 3948.8 crore in 1990-91. The study by CMIE (1993), Saha and Swaminathan (1994), Sen and Sengupta (1995), Rawal and Swaminathan (1998), Chattopadhya and Das (2000) have also confirmed the increase in agricultural production after 1980.

A perusal of the literature on the studies relating to agricultural performance of the West Bengal economy suggests that although some attempts have been done to find out the growth of agricultural output using district level data, but very little work has been attempted to explain the determinants of foodgrains production for different districts of West Bengal. Most of the studies are related either to total agricultural production or to foodgrains or to individual crops using the data of total West Bengal economy. Some of the studies like Raychaudhuri and Sen (1996), Saha (1996), used district level data to carry out their analysis, but while estimating the relation they pooled these district level data together to arrive at a single value of the parameters for the West Bengal economy as a whole. But given the fact that West Bengal agricultural production shows a great variability due to variability in land capacity, climate, fertilizer uses, and irrigated area among other factors, across different districts it is expected that the growth of foodgrains production will also vary from district to district. No single explanation for each and every district will be suitable.

In the present paper an attempt has been made to fill this existing gap in the present literature. In our study the objective is to understand the process of decadal and overall growth of agriculture of West Bengal economy through the examination of growth of total foodgrains production for 13 districts of West Bengal. Specifically, we have considered following aspects of the problem. First of all, we have estimated the overall growth rate of foodgrains production for the entire period 1960-61 to 1999-2000 and also for the two sub-periods 1960-61 to 1980-81 and 1981-82 to 1999-2000. Secondly, we have examined the degree of instability of foodgrains production. Thirdly, we have applied dummy variable analysis to measure shift in the growth rate and the degree of instability of foodgrains production for the period after 1982-83 and also after 1991-92. We have taken 1982-83 as break point because when we plot the level of foodgrains production we find that there exists a break in the path of foodgrains production in all districts as well as for the aggregate West Bengal economy as a whole around the time period 1982-83. The other reason for taking 1982-83 as a break point is that three major changes that have taken place in the rural economy since 1979-80, was the implementation of land reform policies, implementation of the three tier new domestic institution named panchayat system and the introduction of irrigation strategies, and we want to find out the impact of these policies on the growth of output of foodgrains. The reason for taking 1991-92 as break point is that this is a year when different liberalization policies were introduced in the Indian economy and we want to test the impact of such liberalization policies on growth and instability of foodgrains production. Finally, we have tried to find out the major determinants of the yield of foodgrains production for different districts of West Bengal for the period 1960-61 to 1999-2000. Based on the results of estimation we have tried to put some policy prescriptions regarding the enhancement of yield of foodgrains production for different districts of West Bengal. Appropriate or relevant policies may be framed giving emphasis on the variables that are significant for the specific district of the state for boosting up of the yield of foodgrains.

The rest of the present paper is organized as follows. In section II we have analyzed the growth rate of foodgrains production for 13 major districts of West Bengal. We have estimated the growth rate of foodgrains production for the entire period of analysis, i.e., 1960-61 to 1999-2000 and also for the two sub-periods 1960-61 to 1980-81 and 1981-82 to 1999-2000. In section III we have performed a dummy variable analysis to see whether there is an acceleration in growth rate of foodgrains production for different districts of West Bengal or not, in the eighties and nineties. Section IV is concerned with the analysis of instability. In section V we have tried to find out the determinants of the yield of foodgrains production for different districts of West Bengal. Some concluding observations as well as some policy suggestions are made in the final section VI.

II. GROWTH RATE OF FOODGRAINS PRODUCTION IN DIFFERENT DISTRICTS OF WEST BENGAL

The measurement of growth of agricultural production

involves a number of issues like the choice of period, the selection of cut-off points for different sub-periods, estimation of growth parameters and proper interpretation of results. These points have been taken up in a number of studies made earlier (Sen, 1967; Narain, 1977; Rudra, 1982; Reddy, 1978; Das, 1978; Bhalla and Singh, 1979; Srinivasan, 1979; Vidyyanathan, 1980; Dandekar, 1980; Ray, 1983; Sawant, 1983; Dev, 1887; Boyce, 1987; Saha and Swaminathan, 1994; Sawant and Achuthan, 1995; Bhalla and Singh, 1997, among others). Mukhopadhyay and Sarkar (2001) on the other hand used modern time series technique to test for acceleration or deceleration in the growth of foodgrains, rice and wheat production taking aggregate data for West Bengal agricultural sector.

We are first concerned with the basic question, what is the trend equation of growth? For this purpose we have estimated the two types of trend equation: linear and exponential trend, for the period 1960-61-2000-01, and also for the two sub-periods 1960-61 to 1980-81 and 1981-82 to 1999-2000 respectively.

The linear specification of the growth rate can be estimated from the equation

$$Y = A + Bt + \text{error term} \qquad \text{... (1)}$$

where, Y = Level of foodgrain production, and t = Time period.

A denotes the intercept parameter. B is the slope coefficient and measures the increase in the level of production due to the change in the time period. In this model the rate of growth is measured as the multiplication between inverse of the average value of level of foodgrains production and the rate of change in the level of production due to the change in time period.

The exponential growth rate can be measured from the equation $Y= ab^t$. Taking logarithmic value on both sides this non-linear equation is transformed into a linear equation with the functional form given as:

$$\text{Log }(Y) = \text{Log }(a) + \text{Log }(b)\, t + \text{error term} \qquad \text{... (2)}$$

Growth of foodgrains can be calculated by taking antilog of Log (b) and then subtracting one from the resulting value. Now since one specification of growth rate is linear and other is non-linear, R^2 or Adjusted R^2 of these two are not directly comparable.

So for finding out which one is the best fitted model we have compared the simple correlation coefficient (Pearson's) between the actual value and the estimated value of the foodgrain production. We choose that functional form as the best fitted one, which has higher value of correlation.

All the data have been collected from the different issues of the Statistical Abstract published by the Government of West Bengal. Due to the unavailability of data here we do not include the districts like Darjeeling and Purulia. We have put together two districts—North 24-Paraganas and South 24-Paraganas under a single district named 24-Paraganas. We again have combined Uttar Dinajpur and Dakshin Dinajpur districts into a single district named West Dinajpur.

The results of estimation of linear and the exponential trend equation for output of foodgrains taking districts level data of West Bengal, as well as the simple correlation between predicted and actual value of output are presented in Tables 1, 2 and 3 respectively.

Table 1 represents the results on growth rate for the time period 1960-61 to 1999-2000. Table 2 and Table 3 represents the same for the time period 1960-61 to 1980-81 and 1981-82 to 1999-2000 respectively. The overall goodness of fit of the model is quite satisfactory. The results of estimation suggest that for the entire period 1960-61 to 1999-2000, a linear growth model is the best fitted one only for the districts Malda, Nadia and Burdwan. The correlation coefficient between the estimated and actual value of the level of foodgrains production is high for the linear specification and is statistically significant at 1% level of significance. Apart from these three districts all other districts have shown an exponential trend as the best fitted model. The growth rate of foodgrains production varies from lowest value 1.28% (for Jalpaiguri) to highest value 3.47% (for Nadia). The same figure for the West Bengal economy as a whole turns out to be 1.16% for this period. When we consider the decadal growth rate, we find that the growth rate in foodgrains production varied from highest value 10.13% (for Murshidabad) to lowest value 1.4% (for Bankura) for the period 1960-61 to 1980-81 and from 9.75% (for Murshidabad) to 2.018% (for 24-Parganas) for the period 1981-82 to 1999-2000. The same figure for the West Bengal economy as a whole for the two sub-periods was 1.3% and 3.69% respectively.

TABLE 1

Trend Equation for Output of Foodgrains for Different Districts of West Bengal for the Period 1960-61 to 1999-2000

Districts	Estimation of Linear trend $Y=A+Bt$					Estimation of Exponential trend $LogY=LogA+(Log\ b)t$					Chosen Growih Rate
	A	B	Adj R^2	$R_{yy\wedge}$	DW	Log A	Log b	Adj R^2	$R_{yy\wedge}$	DW	
1	2	3	4	5	6	7	8	9	10	11	12
24-Paraganas	474.99* (9.273)	26.196* (12.321)	.791	.891*	1.274	6347* (128.645)	.02521* (12.31)	.792	892*	1.534	.0255 E
Bankura	286.589* (7.440)	17.657* (11.049)	.752	.847*	.934	5.877* (94.384)	.02597* (10.05)	.768	.849*	1.250	.0263 E
Birbhum	383.367* (10.463)	14.402* (9.352)	.674	.832*	1.134	6.060* (112.311)	.02068* (9.240)	.678	.839*	1.364	.0284 E
Burdwan	442.693* (8.365)	32.262* (14.693)	.843	.960*	.729	6.361* (160.423)	.02836* (17.23)	.831	.940*	1.076	.0285 L
Nadia	147.851* (6.308)	19.062* (19.604)	.921	.963*	.794	5.446* * (130.977)	.0363* (25.06)	.917	.959*	1.252	.0347 L
Coochbihar	183.442* (14.333)	7.238* (13.631)	.818	.904*	1.076	5.298* (130.864)	.0275* (13.55)	.820	.908*	.970	.0229 E

(Contd.)

TABLE 1 (*Contd.*)

1	2	3	4	5	6	7	8	9	10	11	12
Hooghly	220.266* (9.598)	12.228* (12.843)	.804	.894*	1.313	5.532* (105.319)	.02732* (12.54)	.796	.895*	1.143	.0277 E
Howrah	70.545* (5.968)	4.623* (9.427)	.687	.824*	1.060	4.445* (60.769)	.02845* (9.394)	.690	.832*	1.127	.0288 E
Malda	163.956* (11.100)	13.118* (21.407)	.920	.942*	1.074	5.366* (176.167)	.03094* (24.48)	.937	.920*	.947	.0501 L
Medinpur	612.461* (7.788)	40.833* (12.512)	.796	.895*	.871	6.664* (128.678)	.02688* (12.51)	.795	.896*	1.110	.0272 E
Murshidabad	329.516* (9.710)	20.594* (14.627)	.842	.92**	1.243	5.978* (130.339)	.02830* (14.87)	.864	.922*	1.258	.0287 E
West Dinajpur	277.105* (9.209)	17.931* (14.364)	.837	.917*	.749	5.861* (151.356)	.02681* (16.69)	.874	.937*	1.350	0271 E
Jalpaiguri	221.731* (16.538)	3.778* (6.793)	.542	.736*	.974	5.418* (122.382)	.01280* (6.970)	.543	.745*	1.011	.0128 E
West Bengal	16046.43* (9.191)	1018.201* (14.057)	.853	.914*	.802	4.304* (220.273)	.01157* (14.27)	.835	.916*	1.087	.0116 E

The absolute values of t-ratio are given in the parenthesis.
* Significant at 1% level of significance.
$R_{y\hat{y}}$ is the simple correlation coefficient between actual and predicted value of Y.
L and E stands for linear and exponential trend respectively.

TABLE 2

Trend Equation for Output of Foodgrains for Different Districts of West Bengal for the Period 1960-61 to 1980-81

Districts	*Estimation of Linear trend* $Y=A+Bt$					*Estimation of Exponential trend* $Log\ Y=Log\ A+(Log\ b)t$					*Chosen Growih Rate*
	A	*B*	*Adj* R^2	$R_{yy\wedge}$	*DW*	*Log A*	*Log b*	*Adj* R^2	$R_{yy\wedge}$	*DW*	
1	*2*	*3*	*4*	*5*	*6*	*7*	*8*	*9*	*10*	*11*	*12*
24-Paraganas	604.003* (12.521)	15.475* (3.843)	.420	.671	1.74	6.4187* (100.980)	.01989* (3.749)	.439	.662	1.34	2.018% L
Bankura	411.461* (11.460)	6.825* (2.277)	.181	.473	.937	6.025* (81.591)	.01337* (2.170)	.163	.455	1.750	1.412% L
Burbhum	410.519* (10.026)	14.781* (4.324)	.482	.714	1.234	6.039* (91.478)	.0264* (4.796)	.537	.749	1.664	6.267 E
Burdwan	589.327* (17.474)	20.843* (7.403)	.739	.868	.729	6.412* (161.870)	.0255* (7..735)	.756	.877	1.089	6.047% E
Nadia	228.156* (10.488)	11.624* (6.401)	.678	.834	.784	5.473* (86.924)	.03415* (6.498)	.684	.837	1.152	7.497% E
Cooch-Behar	174.842* (10.951)	8.602* (6.454)	.682	.836	1.06	5.196* (85.645)	.03410* (6.733)	.700	.846	.940	7.48% E

(Contd.)

TABLE 2 (*Contd.*)

1	2	3	4	5	6	7	8	9	10	11	12
Hooghly	214.742* (7.693)	13.646* (5.857)	.637	.810	1.33	3.419* (69.350)	.04032* (6.181)	.662	.824	1.243	9.728% E
Howrah	100.066* (8.134)	1.493 (1.454)	.055	.324	1.060	4.572* (40.507)	.0143 (1.522)	.065	.338	1.927	3.347% E
Malda	198.229* (14.846)	10.449* (9.373)	.820	.911	1.225	5.337* (122.822)	.0351* (9.684)	.830	.917	.847	8.417% E
Medinpur	893.711* (15.810)	16.447* (3.483)	.370	.635	.881	6.796* (125.079)	.01579* (3.480)	.369	.634	1.122	1.0542 L
Murshidabad	328.361* (9.154)	23.121* (7.721)	.755	.876	1.253	5.872* (97.201)	.0418* (8.295)	.781	.890	1.358	10.103% E
West Dinajpur	376.033* (12.977)	9.856* (4.075)	.451	.693	.769	5.938* (102.308)	.0298* (4.329)	.483	.714	1.850	7.102% E
Julpaiguri	204.117* (11.15)	6.212* (4.056)	.450	.692	.874	15.337* (85.91)	.02298* (4.431)	.495	.722	1.11	5.433% E
West Bengal	21919.04* (16.452)	525.564* (4.725)	.529	.799	.892	4.344* (201.401)	.0084* (4.712)	.527	.743	1.997	1.915% L

The absolute values of t-ratio are given in the parenthesis.

* Significant at 1% level of significance.

$R_{yy\wedge}$ is the simple correlation coefficient between actual and predicted value of Y.

L and E stands for linear and exponential trend respectively.

TABLE 3

Trend Equation for Output of Foodgrains for Different Districts of West Bengal for the Period 1981-82 to 1999-2000

Districts	*Estimation of Linear trend* $Y=A+Bt$					*Estimation of Exponential trend* $Log\ Y=Log\ A+(Log\ b)t$					*Chosen Growih Rate*
	A	*B*	*Adj* R^2	$R_{yy\wedge}$	*DW*	*Log A*	*Log b*	*Adj* R^2	$R_{yy\wedge}$	*DW*	
1	*2*	*3*	*4*	*5*	*6*	*7*	*8*	*9*	*10*	*11*	*12*
24-Puraganas	767.905* (10.419)	46.557* (7.567)	.748	.872	1.258	6.68* (93.705)	.04017* (6.751)	.717	.847	1.54	3.704% L
Bankura	460.991* (9.494)	32.942* (8.887)	.796	.898	.859	6.17* (74.37)	.0452* (6.841)	.696 L	.843	1.478	4%
Birbhum	502.103* (17.474)	27.843* (7.103)	.717	.855	1.446	6.258* (87.569)	.03684* (6.472)	.672	.892	1.542	5.278% E
Burdwan	797.397* (11.816)	565.36* (10.486)	.845	.923	.895	6.715* (119.234)	.0427* (9.417)	.814	.907	1.695	5.178% L
Nadia	4453.419* (14,179)	26.679* (10.704)	.850	.926	.658	6.124* (104.426)	.04036* (8.641)	.786	.893	1.247	7.18% L
Cooch-Behar	302.119* (15.206)	9.107* (5.754)	.616	.797	1.256	5.725* (116.776)	.02336* (5.982)	.635	.808	.842	5.526% E

(Contd.)

TABLE 3 (*Contd.*)

1	2	3	4	5	6	7	8	9	10	11	12
Hooghly	414.497* (11.416)	15.992* (5.532)	.597	.785	1.569	6.045* (89.840)	.02836* (5.291)	.574	.772	1.342	9.527% L
Howrah	156.062* (8.2)	5.544* (3.658)	.382	.643	1.478	5.023* (52.428)	.02948* (3.864)	.411	.663	1.741	7.023% E
Malda	358.178* (17.625)	18.768* (11.596)	.870	.936	1.985	5.921* (141.001)	.03544* (10.599)	.848	.925	.967	8.147% L
Medinpur	1025.51* (11.191)	75.339* (10323)	.841	.921	.975	6.989* (100.653)	.04484* (8.107)	.764	.881	1.288	4.063% L
Murshidabad	592.625* (12.510)	31.923* (8.465)	.779	.889	1.347	6.426* (115.161)	.03589* (8.076)	.763	.880	1.476	9.756% L
West Dinajpur	462.683* (17.4025)	32.437* (15.319)	.921	.962	.856	6.232* (172.624)	.04044* (14.065)	.908	.955	1.643	8.172% L
Julpaiguri	266.344* (14.473)	5.905* (4.029)	.432	.679	1.024	5.592* (95.684)	.01796* (3.859)	.410	.663	1.247	2.68% L
West Bengal	26964.29* (13.779)	1816.34* (11.655)	.871	.937	.920	4.453* (169.972)	.01840* (8.819)	.793	.896	1.885	3.869% L

The absolute values of t-ratio are given in the parenthesis.
* Significant at 1% level of significance.
$R_{yy^\wedge}$ is the simple correlation coefficient between actual and predicted value of Y.
L and E stands for linear and exponential trend respectively.

In case of the districts 24-Paraganas, Bankura and Medinpur linear trend is the best-fitted model for both 1960-61 to 1980-81 and 1981-82 to 1999-2000. But the growth rate for the period 1960-61 to 1980-81 is very low as compared with the growth rate for the period 1981-82 to 1999-2000. For this cause we get an exponential trend for these three districts when we consider the overall time span 1960-61 to 1999-2000. In case of Coochbihar exponential curve is the best fitted model for two sub-periods as well as for the entire period. For the remaining districts exponential is the best fitted model for the period 1960-61 to 1980-81 whereas linear is the best fitted model for the period 1981-82 to 1999-2000. That is for these districts growth rate increases at an increasing rate for first two decades but became constant thereafter indicating deterioration in the performance level for the growth of foodgrains production for these districts. So not only the functional form of the growth path of output of foodgrains varies among different districts, the magnitude of the growth of output varies as well.

III. MEASUREMENT OF THE CHANGE IN THE FOODGRAINS PRODUCTION

In this section we will try to find out whether there occurred any shift in the growth path of the foodgrains production after 1982-83 and also after 1991-92 taking districts level data of West Bengal.

In order to find out shift in the growth path of foodgrains production we will use dummy variable model. The regression equation with intercept and slope dummy can be specified as follows:

$$\text{Log}(Y) = A_0 + A_1 D + B_0\, t + B_1\, Dt + \text{error term} \qquad \text{... (3)}$$

D is the dummy variable with a value is equal to zero for the period up to 1982-83 (or, 1991-92) and is equal to one thereafter, i.e.,

D = 0 for the period 1960-61–1982-83
= 1 for the period 1983-84–2000-01

or,

D = 0 for the period 1960-61–1991-92
= 1 for the period 1992-93–2000-01

A_0 represents the intercept term. The growth rate for the first period, i.e. 1960-61–1982-83 (or, 1960-61–1991-92) is B_0. And the growth rate of the second period, i.e. for the period 1983-84–2000-01 (or, 1992-93–2000-01) is $B_0 + B_1$ if B_1 is statistically significant. The growth rate for the second period is greater or less than the first period according as B_1 is positive or negative.

The results of estimation of the dummy variable model taking 1982-83 and 1991-92 as the break point are presented in Tables 4 and 5 respectively.

Case-I: Results of estimation taking 1982-83 as break point

Table 4 reveals that, over all goodness of fit of the model is satisfactory. It suggests that there has been acceleration in growth rate for the period after 1982-83 in case of the districts 24-Paraganas, Bankura, Birbhum, Burdwan, Malda, Nadia, Medinpur and West Dinajpur. These results are significant at 10%, 1%, 5%, 5%, 1%, 1%, 1%, and 1% level of significance respectively. In case of Coochbihar, Hooghly and Murshidabad although there is a negative effect of slope dummy but this is not statistically significant. For the districts Howrah and Jalpaiguri there is a positive effect of slope dummy but this is not statistically significant. In case of the West Bengal economy as a whole we can conclude that there has been an acceleration in growth which is statistically significant at 1% level of significance.

Case-II: Results of estimation taking 1991-92 as break point

Table 5 suggests that, if we take 1991-92 as the break point, there exists a negative effect of the slope dummy for most of the districts (24-Paraganas, Bankura, Nadia, Coochbihar, Hooghly, Howrah, Medinpur, and Murshidabad). But among these districts only in case of Hooghly and Howrah the negative effect is statistically significant at 10% level of significance. For all other districts the slope dummy is not statistically significant. In case of Birbhum, Burdwan, Malda, West Dinajpur, and Jalpaigury there exists a positive effect of the slope dummy, but is not statistically significant.

Performance of any district is different depending on whether we take 1982-83 or 1991-92 as break point. This is true for most

TABLE 4

Estimation of Dummy Variable Model to Findout Shift in Growth Path of Food Grains Production in West Bengal taking 1982-83 as the Break Point

Districts	*Constant term*	*Coefficient of Intercept dummy*	*Coefficient of time*	*Coefficient of time dummy*	*DW*	*Degrees of Freedom*	*Adj.* R^2
24-Paraganas	6.447* (99.476)	-.438*** (2.087)	.0160* (3.216)	.0198** (2.515)	1.854	36	.812
Bankura	6.044* (79.768)	.765* (3.117)	.019*** (1.906)	.033* (3.674)	1.682	36	.780
Birbhum	6.087* (86.816)	.600*** (2.641)	.0210* (3.766)	.017*** (2.078)	1.526	36	.718
Burdwan	6.447* (130.14)	-.492* (3.064)	.0209* (5.555)	.02*** (2.078)	1.464	36	.903
Nadia	238.45* (9.400)	-241.616* (2.941)	10.23* (5.301)	13.936* (4.515)	1.376	36	.942
Cooch-Behar	5.233* (94.028)	-.088 (.490)	.029* (6.879)	-.0075 (1.121)	1.021	36	.823
Hooghly	5.449* (76.324)	-.016 (.073)	.036* (6.640)	-.006 (.762)	1.225	36	.804
Howrah	4.574* (47.281)	.106 (.338)	.013** (1.849)	.0086 (.735)	1.310	36	.713
Malda	209.01* (12.178)	-196.228* (3.529)	9.028* (6.098)	2.088* (4.255)	1.500	36	.944
Medinpur	6.823* (112.53)	-.6546* (3.339)	.0122*** (2.661)	.0304* (4.125)	1.604	36	.854
Murshidabad	5.928* (94.961)	-.164 (.813)	.034* (7.219)	-.00002 (.003)	1.311	36	.852
West Dinajpur	5.954* (128.58)	-.549* (3.661)	.018* (5.349)	.022* (3.923)	1.819	36	.906
Jalpaiguri	5.362* (91.626)	-.226 (.1.192)	.019** (4.422)	.00104 (.147)	1.624	36	.585
West Bengal	4.357* (184.31)	-.243* (3.176)	.0067* (3.772)	.0107* (3.750)	1.465	36	.875

Absolute values of the 't' ratios are given in the parenthesis.

* Significant at 1% level of significance.

** Significant at 10% level of significance.

*** Significant at 5% level of significance.

TABLE 5

Estimation of Dummy Variable Model to Findout Shift in Growth Path of Foodgrains Production in West Bengal taking 1991-92 as the Break Point

Districts	*Constant term*	*Coefficient of Intercept dummy*	*Coefficient of time*	*Coefficient of time dummy*	*DW*	*Degrees of Freedom*	*Adj.* R^2
24-Paraganas	4.333* (208.51)	.183 (.803)	.00916* (8.086)	-.00255 (.403)	1.727	36	.805
Bankura	6.397* (116.25)	.586 (.969)	.0209* (6.973)	-.0115 (.690)	1.521	36	.748
Birbhum	6.096* (97.213)	-.535 (.776)	.0178* (5.218)	.01728 (.906)	1.431	36	.675
Burdwan	6.412* (146.68)	.139 (.290)	.024* (10.099)	.000512 (.039)	1.261	36	.892
Nadia	176.91* (6.911)	242.307 (.861)	16.589* (11.879)	-4.076 (.523)	1.047	36	.916
Cooch-Behar	5.257* (113.43)	.196 (.358)	.0259* (10.251)	-.00846 (.600)	1.047	36	.824
Hooghly	5.515* (92.348)	1.198** (1.824)	.02839* (8.714)	-.0334** (1.839)	1.212	36	.803
Howrah	4.439* (53.323)	1.658** (1.811)	.02855* (6.277)	-.0448** (1.772)	1.164	36	.695
Malda	187.51* (12.219)	143.469 (.850)	11.128* (13.292)	1.885 (.404)	1.547	36	.935
Medinpur	6.746* (124.47)	.444 (.746)	.02001* (6.769)	-.00513 (.311)	1.276	36	.833
Murshidabad	5.978* (110.65)	.465 (.783)	.02819* (9.565)	-.0124 (.757)	1.288	36	.841
West Dinajpur	5.924* (144.76)	-.422 (.938)	.0216* (9.705)	.0165 (1.33)	1.745	36	.895
Jalpaiguri	5.427* (103.4)	-.109 (.189)	.01207* (4.214)	.00368 (.231)	1.510	36	.520
West Bengal	4.333* (208.50)	.183 (.803)	.00916* (8.086)	-.0025 (.403)	1.238	36	.861

Absolute values of the 't' ratios are given in the parenthesis.

* Significant at 1% level of significance.

** Significant at 10% level of significance.

*** Significant at 5% level of significance.

of the districts. For example in the district 24-Paraganas, Bankura, Nadia, Medinpur, there was acceleration in the growth if we take 1982-83 as a break point, and the result is significant, whereas if we take 1991-92 as break point, for these districts there was deceleration in growth rate but the results are not statistically significant. Similarly, for the district Howrah there was an increase in growth rate and the result is not significant, if we take 1982-83 as break point, whereas there was decline in growth rate and the results is significant if we take 1991-92 as break point. For the district Birbhum, Burdwan, and Malda there was acceleration in growth rate if we take either 1982-83 or 1991-92 as break point. The result is significant if we take 1982-83 as break point but not according 1991-92 as a break point. For the district Hooghly, there was a decline in output of foodgrains if we take either 1982-83 or 1991-92 as break point, the result is not significant in case of 1982-83 and is significant at 10% level of significance in case of 1991-92. For the West Bengal economy as a whole there was acceleration in the growth rate if we consider 1982-83 as a break point, and the result is also significant at 1% level of significance. In case of 1991-92 as break point, we can observe that there was a deceleration in growth rate, but this result is not significant.

IV. GROWTH OF INSTABILITY INDEX IN FOODGRAINS PRODUCTION AND ITS CHANGE IN WEST BENGAL

In this section we will try to find out the growth pattern for the instability index and whether there occurred any change in the extent of instability in foodgrains production after 1982-83 and 1991-92.

For the measurement of growth of instability of the foodgrains production we take only linear trend. Because there exist so many negative values for large number of years and exponential trend will not be defined in those cases. The index of instability in a period t is defined as:

$$INS_t = (Yt\text{-}estYt)/estYt. \qquad \dots (4)$$

where Yt and estYt are the actual and estimated value of output of foodgrains in a period t. The linear specification of the growth rate can be estimated from the equation

$$INS_t = A + Bt + \text{error term} \quad \text{... (5)}$$

where A denotes the intercept parameter and B is the slope coefficient. Here B measures the increase in the index of instability due to the change in the time period. In this model the rate of growth is measured as the multiplication between inverse of the average level of instability index and the rate of change in the index of instability due to the change in time period. In order to find out change in instability index the following regression equation is used:

$$INS_t = A_o + A_1D + B_o\, t + B_1\, Dt \quad \text{... (6)}$$

Where A_o is the intercept term and D is the dummy variable with a value which is equal to zero for the period up to 1982-83 (or, 1991-92) and is equal to one thereafter, i.e.,

D = 0 for the period 1960-61-1982-83 (or 1960-61-1991-92)
= 1 for the period 1983-84-2000-01 (or, 1992-93-2000-01)

The methodology of determining growth rate for the two periods is same as in section 3. The comparison of the growth rate and the degree of instability index helps us to draw some conclusions regarding the performance of any districts. The performance of those districts are satisfactory for which growth rate have increased and instability have declined significantly. If the growth rate as well as the index of instability has increased then the performance of that district is not quite satisfactory, because in that case rate of growth becomes very fluctuating. The performance of those districts are also not quite satisfactory for which growth rate have declined along with a decrease in the instability index. This is because although there is a decrease in the instability the growth rate also decreased. Lastly, the performance of those districts are very poor for which there is a decline in the growth rate and there is an increase in the instability.

Tables 6 and 7 represent the results of estimation of Dummy variable analysis regarding the shift in the degree of instability index after the period 1982-83 and 1991-92 respectively. The results suggests that taking 1982-83 as break point, in case of 24-Paraganas, Bankura, Birbhum, Burdwan, Nadia, Malda, Medinpur and West Dinajpur the coefficient of the slope dummy is statistically significant at 5%, 1%, 10%, 1%, 1%, 1%, 1% and 1%

TABLE 6

Estimation of Dummy Variable Model to Findout Instability in Growth Path of Foodgrains Production in West Bengal taking 1982-83 as Break Point

Districts	*Constant term*	*Coefficient of Intercept dummy*	*Coefficient of time*	*Coefficient of time dummy*	*DW*	*Degrees of Freedom*	*Adj.* R^2
24-Paraganas	.101** (1.875)	-.357*** (2.043)	-.0149* (3.628)	.01668*** (2.544)	1.901	36	.349
Bankura	.165*** (2.520)	-.649* (3.054)	-.0134* (2.676)	.0292* (3.661)	1.672	36	.211
Birbhum	.03 (.437)	-.521*** (2.342)	.000317 (.061)	.0147** (1.761)	1.573	36	-.072
Burdwan	.0845** (1.841)	-.460* (3.093)	-.0066** (1.907)	.0147* (3.323)	1.402	36	.168
Nadia	.347* (5.501)	-.592* (2.897)	-.0277* (5.770)	.035* (4.651)	1.432	36	.446
Cooch-Behar	-.0523 (.923)	.0824 (.449)	.00613** (1.921)	-.0073 (1.069)	1.030	36	-.011
Hooghly	-.068 (.973)	-.034 (.152)	.0009** (1.705)	-.0063 (.747)	1.255	36	.028
Howrah	.195* (1.909)	.0828** (.256)	-.0217** (2.238)	.0104 (.855)	1.315	36	.078
Malda	.02* (.382)	-.439* (2.592)	-.0011* (.279)	.0141* (2.218)	1.370	36	.091
Medinpur	.164* (2.959)	-.585* (3.251)	-.014* (3.318)	.0278* (4.123)	1.693	36	.274
Murshidabad	-.0409 (.647)	-.147 (.720)	.00629* (1.308)	-.000893 (.116)	1.346	36	.015
West Dinajpur	0959* (2.056)	-.534* (3.533)	-.744* (2.096)	.0212* (3.736)	1.879	36	.217
Jalpaiguri	-.0507 (.843)	-.206 (.1.057)	.00736** (1.607)	.000074 (.010)	1.586	36	.066
West Bengal	5646.9* (14.566)	-6712.90* (5.356)	83.177* (2.818)	295.822* (6.272)	1.696	36	.903

The absolute values of t-ratio are given in the parenthesis.

* Significant at 1% level of significance.

** Significant at 10% level of significance.

*** Significant at 5% level of significance.

TABLE 7

Estimation of Dummy Variable Model to Findout Instability in Growth Path of Foodgrains Production in West Bengal taking 1991-92 as Break Point

Districts	*Constant term*	*Coefficient of Intercept dummy*	*Coefficient of time*	*Coefficient of time dummy*	*DW*	*Degrees of Freedom*	*Adj. R^2*
24-Paraganas	5.561 (1.213)	.461 (.914)	-.0104* (4.173)	-.0087 (.630)	1.758	36	.322
Bankura	.09219 (1.594)	-.562 (.883)	-.00633* (2.007)	-.00889 (.506)	1.542	36	.118
Birbhum	.04511 (.744)	-.577 (.865)	-.00242 (.730)	.0179 (.973)	1.465	36	-.039
Burdwan	.05428 (1.344)	.09418 (.212)	-.00401** (1.819)	.0015 (.124)	1.285	36	.074
Nadia	.188* (2.883)	.157 (.218)	-.0109* (3.065)	.00256 (.129)	.947	36	.144
Cooch-Behar	-.0292 (.618)	.157 (.303)	.002947 (1.144)	-.0073 (.515)	1.048	36	-.009
Hooghly	.00252 (.042)	1.064 (1.630)	.000667 (.206)	-.0296 (1.640)	1.195	36	-.008
Howrah	.04415 (.515)	1.849** (1.963)	-.00142 (.304)	-.0494** (1.895)	1.136	36	.026
Malda	.04118 (.939)	-.0113 (.023)	-.00347 (1.564)	.00479 (.360)	1.352	36	.080
Medinpur	.0909** (1.853)	.510 (.945)	-.00661* (2.470)	-.00725 (.486)	1.329	36	.185
Murshidabad	.01269 (.231)	.402 (.667)	-.0000204 (.070)	-.0109 (.650)	1.286	36	-.068
West Dinajpur	.0693** (1.694)	-.466 (1.034)	-.005* (2.238)	-.0175 (1.406)	1.740	36	.132
Jalpaiguri	.01775 (.329)	-.124 (.239)	-.0006 (.205)	.00439 (.268)	1.451	36	-.078
West Bengal	5067.4* (14.032)	1793.73 (.452)	140.63* (7.139)	23.7131 (.216)	1.167	36	.879

The absolute values of t-ratio are given in the parenthesis
* Significant at 1% level of significance.
** Significant at 10% level of significance.
*** Significant at 5% level of significance.

level of significance respectively, and are positive. It reflects that after the period 1982-83 the degree of instability in foodgrains production has increased for these districts. In case of Coochbihar, Hooghly, and Murshidabad the coefficient of the slope dummy are negative. However, these coefficients are not statistically significant. For the data on West Bengal economy as a whole the coefficient of the slope dummy is statistically significant at 1% level of significance, and is positive, reflecting the fact that degree of instability has increased after the period 1982-83.

The dummy variable analysis taking 1991-92 as the break point suggests that in case of Birbhum, Burdwan, Nadia, Malda and Jalpaigury, the coefficient of the slope dummy is insignificant and are positive. In case of 24-Paraganas, Bankura, Coochbihar, Hooghly, Medinpur, Murshidabad and West Dinajpur the coefficient of the slope dummy are negative. But these coefficients are not statistically significant. Only in case of Howrah there exists a negative effect that is statistically significant at 10% level of significance. For the data on West Bengal economy as a whole the coefficient of the slope dummy is positive and insignificant.

Comparison between growth and instability for different districts of West Bengal after 1982-83 and after 1991-92 are presented in Table 8 and Table 9 respectively. From Table 8 we find that the performance of the districts 24-Paraganas, Bankura, Birbhum, Burdwan, Howrah, Nadia, Malda, Medinpur, West Dinajpur, Jalpaiguri, and West Bengal economy as a whole are not satisfactory. This is because although there are significant increase in growth rate for all these districts except Jalpaiguri, there are also an increase in the index of instability of foodgrains production, which is significant. For Jalpaiguri, either the increase in growth rate or increase in instability is not statistically significant. For Cooch-Behar, Hooghly and Murshidabad the index of instability as well as growth rate have declined. The decline for the growth rate is not statistically significant for all these three districts. For instability index it is significant for Hooghly but not for Coochbihar and Murshidabad. Thus, performance of these districts are not also satisfactory. The analysis therefore suggests that none of the districts perform well after 1982-83.

From Table 9, we find that after 1991-92, for the districts 24-Paraganas, Bankura, Coochbihar, Hooghly, Medinpur and Murshidabad both the instability index, the growth rate have

TABLE 8

Comparison Between Growth and Instability for Different Districts of West Bengal after 1982-83

Districts	*Growth After 1982-83*	*Instability After 1982-83*
24-Paraganas	Increased and Significant	Increased and Significant
Bankura	Increased and Significant	Increased and Significant
Birbhum	Increased and Significant	Increased and Significant
Burdwan	Increased and Significant	Increased and Significant
Nadia	Increased and Significant	Increased and Significant
Cooch-Behar	Decreased but Insignificant	Decreased but Insignificant
Hooghly	Decreased but Insignificant	Decreased and Significant
Howrah	Increased and Insignificant	Increased and Insignificant
Malda	Increased and Significant	Increased and Significant
Medinpur	Increased and Significant	Increased and Significant
Murshidabad	Decreased but Insignificant	Decreased but Insignificant
West Dinajpur	Increased and Significant	Increased and Significant
Jalpaiguri	Increased and Insignificant	Increased and Insignificant
West Bengal	Increased and Significant	Increased and Significant

TABLE 9

Comparison Between Growth and Instability for Different Districts of West Bengal after 1991-92

Districts	*Growth After 1991-92*	*Instability After 1991-92*
24-Paraganas	Decreased but not Significant	Decreased but not Significant
Bankura	Decreased but not Significant	Decreased but not Significant
Birbhum	Increased and Insignificant	Increased and Significant
Burdwan	Increased but not Significant	Increased and Insignificant
Nadia	Decreased but not Significant	Increased and Insignificant
Cooch-Behar	Decreased but Insignificant	Decreased but Insignificant
Hooghly	Decreased but Insignificant	Decreased but Insignificant
Howrah	Increased and Significant	Increased and Significant
Malda	Increased and Insignificant	Increased and Insignificant
Medinpur	Decreased and Insignificant	Decreased and Insignificant
Murshidabad	Decreased but Insignificant	Decreased but Insignificant
West Dinajpur	Increased and Insignificant	Increased and Insignificant
Jalpaiguri	Increased and Insignificant	Increased and Insignificant
West Bengal	Decreased and Insignificant	Increased and Insignificant

declined. However, the decline in the growth rate and instability index are not statistically significant. Therefore, performance of these districts are not satisfactory after 1991-92. Performance of West Bengal economy as a whole and the district Nadia are bad in the sense that there were a decline in the growth rate and increase in instability index. However, either the increase in growth rate or increase in instability index is not statistically significant. For the districts Birbhum, Burdwan, West Dinajpur, Malda, and Jalpaiguri increase in growth rate are associated with the increase in instability index. However, both the increase in growth rate and the increase in instability index are not statistically significant for all these five districts except Birbhum. For Birbhum the increase in growth rate is not statistically significant, but the increase in instability index is statistically significant. For the district Howrah, increase in growth rate is associated with the increase in instability index and both the increase in growth rate and increase in instability index are statistically significant. Thus, the performance of this district is not satisfactory. The analysis therefore, indicates a great deal of inter-district disparity regarding growth and instability of foodgrains production. None of the district performs satisfactorily and the West Bengal economy as a whole performs badly after 1991-92.

V. DETERMINANTS OF YIELD OF FOODGRAINS FOR DIFFERENT DISTRICTS OF WEST BENGAL

The factors determining the yield of foodgrains production is not very easy for the case of West Bengal economy. For this state the fertility of land shows a great variability, whereas the implementation of the new agricultural strategy is not uniform in all districts. So the functional form between the yield of foodgrains and the factors of inputs in the agriculture varies from district to district.

For the determination of yield of foodgrains we simply run the step-wise regression equation taking the yield of foodgrains as the dependent variable and the factors of production as the independent variables. We run the following regression equation:

$$Y = f(X)$$

where Y is the yield of foodgrains production as represented by YFC. We have taken either YFC or Log value of YFC, i.e., DNYFC as the dependent variable. Under X we have the following components:

RF = Rainfall
FC = Total fertilizer consumption
IA = Irrigated Area
ALB = Agricultural labour.

We have also tried the regression with the log value of the factor inputs as represented by,

LNFC = Log value of total fertilizer consumption
LNRF = Log value of Rainfall
LNIA = Log value of Irrigated area
LNALB = Log value of Agricultural labour

However, to start with we do not assume *apriori* any particular type of functional specification. After the stepwise regression we have taken only the significant explanatory variables as the factors of determination of yield of foodgrains and choose that functional form which gives the most statistical significant result.

The results of estimation are presented in Table 10. The results of our analysis suggest that overall goodness of the fit of the model is satisfactory. The results also highlight the existence of inter-districts disparity regarding the factors determining the yield of foodgrains. The functional forms as well as the factors determining the yield of foodgrains are different for different districts of West Bengal. In the best-fitted model the dependent variable turns out to be log value of yield of foodgrains for all the districts except Burdwan, Malda and Nadia. For Burdwan, Malda and Nadia it is absolute value of yield of foodgrains. Fertilizer consumption is significant explanatory variable and appeared in absolute value for the districts Bankura, Birbhum, and Burdwan and in log value for the districts Nadia, Howrah and Medinpur. Agricultural labour is significant explanatory variable and appeared in absolute value for the districts 24-Paraganas, Burdwan, Coochbihar, Hooghly, Murshidabad, West Dinajpur and Jalpaiguri and it appeared in log value for the districts Nadia, Howrah and Malda. Irrigated area turns out to be a significant

TABLE 10

The Determination of Yields of Foodgrains for Different Districts of West Bengal

Districts	*Dependent Variables*	*Explanatory Variables*								
		Constant	*ALB*	*RF*	*IA*	*FC*	*LN IA*	*LN FC*	*LN ALB*	*Adj* R^2
1	2	3	4	5	6	7	8	9	10	11
24-Parganas	LNYFC	-.730* (8.531)	9.87E-8** (13.139)							.827
Bankura	LNYFC			1.9E-4** (1.656)	1.7E-3** (1.95)	1.7E-5* (3.91)				.796
Birbhum	LNYFC	-.797* (3.14)			6.9E-3* (4.342)	1.1 E-5* (3.756)				.842
Burdwan	YFC	-.577* (4.106)	1.01E-7** (1.803)		2.3E-3* (3.759)	4.8E-6* (3.05)				.944
Nadia	YFC	-23.623* (3.407)						.334** (1.531)	1.488* (2.455)	.896
Coochbihar	LNYFC	-.846* (11.464)	5.778E-7* (14.564)							.852
Hooghly	LNYFC	-.976* (4.756)	3.74E-7* (3.874)		3.5E-3* (2.98)					.877

(*Contd.*)

TABLE 10 (*Contd.*)

1	2	3	4	5	6	7	8	9	10	11
Howrah	LNYFC	-7.415* (7.42)						1.029* (22.88)	.186* (2.35)	.981
Malda	YFC	-22.956* (4.985)							1.642* (4.263)	.868
Medinpur	LNYFC							.178* (2.671)	.222* (2.921)	.844
Murshidabad	LNYFC	-.829* (3.011)	1.42E-7* (2.196)		1.6E-2* (2.905)					.800
West Dinajpur	LNYFC	-.607* (4.528)	3.25E-7* (4.374)							.901
Jalpaiguri	LNYFC	-721* (4.048)	3.3E-7* (3.377)							.396

The absolute values of t-ratio are given in the parenthesis.
*Significant at 1% level of significance.
***Significant at 5% level of significance.
We have not included LNRF as explanatory variable because this is not significant for any district.

variable in absolute value for the districts Bankura, Birbhum, Burdwan, Hooghly and Murshidabad. It is significant in log value for the district Medinpur only. Rainfall is significant only for the district Bankura and in absolute value. For the districts like 24-Paraganas and Coochbihar only significant explanatory variable is agricultural labour. In the best fitted model, for the districts Howrah, and Medinpur since both dependent variable and explanatory variables are in log linear form, it suggests that growth of yield of foodgrains of these districts are dependent on the growth rate of input uses. For the districts Malda and Nadia the dependent variable turns out to be the absolute value of yield of food grains and it is expressed as a function of the log value of the explanatory variables, suggesting that the level of yield of food-grains production of these districts are basically dependent on the rate of growth of input uses. In case of Burdwan the dependent variable turns out to be the absolute value of yield of foodgrains and it is expressed as a function of the absolute value of the explanatory variables. It reflects the fact that the level of yield of foodgrains production of this district depends upon the level of input uses. For the remaining districts the dependent variable turns out to be log value of the yield of foodgrains production and it is expressed as a function of the absolute value of the explanatory variables. It suggests that for these districts growth rate in yield of foodgrains are dependent on the level of inputs uses. These relationships between yield of foodgrains production and input uses basically support the adoption of HYV technology for different districts of West Bengal and also the input intensity of the HYV technology. However, the extent of effectiveness of HYV policies varies among the districts.

VI. CONCLUSION

West Bengal agricultural economy shows a great variability due to the variability in land capacity, irrigated areas, fertilizer consumption, etc. from district to district. The impact of this inter-district variability is reflected in our paper. So we do not get any specific functional form for the trend equation when we tried to calculate the growth of foodgrains production. In the best/fitted model for the growth of foodgrains production, in case of Malda, Nadia and Burdwan a linear trend are chosen and exponential trend are adopted for the remaining districts. Not only the functional specification of the growth but also the magnitude of growth varied between the districts. Now if we compare the decadal growth, for the districts 24-Paraganas, Bankura, Howrah, Medinpur, West Dinajpur, and for the West Bengal economy as a whole foodgrains production grew at a higher rate in second phase, i.e. for the period 1981-82 to 1999-2000. For rest of the districts foodgrains production increased but at a lower rate between 1981-82 to 1999-2000. We have also calculated the magnitude of the shift in the production after 1982-83, the years after land reform policies, the panchayat system and the irrigation strategies were introduced in West Bengal and also after 1991-92, the years after the introduction of different liberalization policies in Indian economy. Our results also support the evidence of strong inter-district disparity on growth rate after the period 1982-83 and also after 1991-92, for the West Bengal. In case of the growth of instability index of foodgrains production we take only linear trend because of negative values of instability index. We have also reported the behaviour of the degree of instability in the period after 1982-83 and 1991-92. The comparison between the analysis of growth and instability suggests that none of a district performs very well. This is true if we take either break point 1982-83 or 1991-92. In respect of determinants of the yield this inter-district disparity also get prominent. Not only the explanatory variables for the yield of foodgrains, but also its functional form specifying the relationship between yield of foodgrains and the explanatory variables vary among districts. Further, our results also have an interesting implication. For the districts Howrah and Medinpur, growth rate of yield of foodgrains depend on the growth rate of inputs uses. For the districts Malda and Nadia, the level of yield foodgrains production are basically dependent on the rate of growth of input uses. For the remaining districts growth rate in yield of foodgrains depend on the level of input uses. These results also supports that the introduction of HYV technologies are effective for most of the districts of West Bengal, but the extent of effectiveness varies.

In order to enhance yield of foodgrains in all districts in an equitable framework, appropriate or relevant policies may be framed giving emphasis on the variables that are significant for the specific districts of the states. But the question may come, what should be the appropriate or relevant policies for different districts?

Let us open a discussion. For example, our analysis suggest that for the districts Bankura and Birbhum the growth of yield of foodgrains are dependent on irrigation and fertilizer consumption. Thus, appropriate policies towards availability of irrigation facilities and fertilizer can help in boosting up the growth of yield of foodgrains for these districts. Similarly, agricultural labour and irrigation facilities are the two major factors determining the growth of yield of foodgrains for the districts Hooghly and Murshidabad. Thus, for these two districts attention should be paid to employ and engage agricultural labour more effectively and to provide irrigation facilities. An important point can be noted here is that although there exists positive influence of fertilizer consumption and irrigation facilities on the growth of yield of foodgrains for the two districts *Bankura and Birbhum* but an increase in either fertilizer consumption or irrigation facilities by an equal amount will not positively affect the growth of yield of food grains by an *equal magnitude,* because of the existence of variation in the responsiveness of growth of yield of foodgrains with respect to input uses among these two districts. With the same logic, an increase in agricultural labour by an equal amount will not increase the growth of yield of foodgrains by an equal magnitude for two districts Hooghly and Murshidabad. In a similar fashion, appropriate policies can be formed for boosting up of yield of foodgrains for other districts also by looking into significant explanatory variables and keeping in mind that responsiveness of any factor input may be different across different districts.

REFERENCES

Banerjee, A. and M. Ghatak (1996): "Empowerment and Efficiency: The Economics of Tenancy Reforms" *(unpublished manuscript).*

Bhaumik, S.K. (1993): *Tenancy Relations And Agrarian Development: A Study of West Bengal,* Sage Publication, New Delhi.

Bhaduri, K., Amit (1984): *Economic Structure of Backward Agriculture,* Macmillan.

Bhalla, G.S. and G. Singh (1997): "Recent Development In Indian Agriculture: A State Level Analysis", *Economic and Political Weekly,* 13, March 29.

Bhalla, G.S. and Y.K. Alaug (1979): *Performance of Indian Agriculture: A Districts-wise Study*, Sterling Publishers Pvt. Ltd., New Delhi.

Boyce, J.K. (1987): *Agrarian Impasse in Bengal: Institutional Constraints to Technological Change*, Oxford University Press, Oxford.

Centre for Monitoring Indian Economy (CMIE) (1993): *Performance of Agriculture in Major States, 1967-68 to 1991-92*, Bombay.

Chattopadhyay, M., C. Neogi, and S.K. Maity (1993): "Growth and Instability of Crop Production in Eastern India", *Asian Economic Review*, 35.61-94.

Chattopadhyay, B. and Bose, B.L. *et al* (1993): *Food System and Human Environment in India*, Vols. I and II, K.P. Bagchi & Co., Calcutta.

Chattopadhaya, A.K. and P.S. Das (2000): "Estimation of Growth Rate: A Critical Analysis with Reference to West Bengal Agriculture", *Indian Journal of Agricultural Economics*, Vol. 55, No. 2, April June.

Christiano, L.J. (1992): "Searching for Structural Break in GNP", *Journal of Business Economic Statistics*, 10, 237-50.

Dandekar, V.M. (1980): "Introduction," *Indian Journal of Agricultural Economics*, Vol. 35, No. 2, April-June.

Das, P.S. (1978): "Growth and Instability in Crop Output in Eastern India", *Economic and Political Weekly*, Vol. 13, No. 41, October 14.

Dev, S. Mahandra (1987): "Growth and Instability in Foodgrains Production: An Inter-State Analysis," *Economic and Political Weekly*, Vol. 22, No. 39, September 26.

Dhar, Arpita and Dipyaman Pal (2005): "Inter District Disparity of Foodgrains Production in West Bengal Growth, Instability, and Determinants of Yield", *Artha Beekshan*, Vol. 14, Nos. 3&4.

Dhar, Arpita and Dipyaman Pal (2005): "Test for Acceleration in the Growth of Agriculture for Different Districts in West Bengal Using Structural Break Analysis", *(unpublished manuscript)*.

Ghatak, M. (1995): "Reforms Incentives and Growth in West Bengal Agriculture", Paper presented in Workshop Agricultural Growth and Agrarian Structure in Contemporary West Bengal and Bangladesh, Center for Studies in Social Sciences, Calcutta, January 9-12.

Kohli, A. (1987): "The State and Poverty in India: The Politics of Reforms", Cambridge, Cambridge University Press.

Mukhopadhyay, D. and Sarkar N. (2001): "Has there been Acceleration in the Growth of Agriculture in West Bengal?: A Fresh Look Using Modern Time Series Technique", *Sankhya*, 63, Series B, Pt. I, pp. 89-107.

Narain, D. (1977): "Growth and Productivity in Indian Agriculture", *Indian Journal of Agricultural Economics*, Vol. 32, No. 1, January-March.

Pal, Dipyaman (2005): *Food Grains in West Bengal: An Econometric Analysis Using District Level Data for the Period 1960-2000*, M.Phil Dissertation submitted to the Department of Economics, Jadavpur University.

Pal, Suresh, Sirohi, A.S. (1988): "Sources of Growth and Instability of

Production of Commercial Crops in India," *Indian Journal of Agricultural Economics*, 43(3), 456-63.

Rao, C.H.H. and Subrata Ray (1988): *Unstable Agriculture and Droughts*, Vikas Publishing House.

Reserve Bank of India (1984): *Report of the Committee on Agricultural Productivity in Eastern India*, Vol. I, Bombay Publishing House, New Delhi.

Rawal, V. and M. Swaminathan (1998): "Changing Trajectory, Agricultural Growth in West Bengal; 1950 to 1996", *Economic and Political Weekly*, 33, Oct. 3.

Ray, S.K. (1983): "Growth and Instability of Indian Agriculture", Institute of Economic Growth, June, Delhi.

Raychaudhuri, A. and D. Sarkar (1996): *Economy of West Bengal: Problems and Prospects.* Allied Publishers and D.S.A. Center For Regional Economic Studies, Jadavpur University, Calcutta.

Raychaudhuri, A. and Asis K. Sen (1996): "Agricultural Reforms And Productivity: Some Important Lessons to be Learnt From West Bengal's Operation Barga", in Raychaudhuri, A. and D. Sarkar (Ed.) *Economy of West Bengal: Problems and Prospects.* Allied Publishers and D.S.A. Center For Regional Economic Studies, Jadavpur University, Calcutta.

Reddy, V.N. (1977): "Statistical Findings of Growth Curves with Illustration from Data on Indian Economy", IIM.

Rudra, A. (1982): *Indian Agricultural Economics: Myths and Realities*, Allied Publishers, New Delhi.

Saha, A. and Swaminathan, M. (1994): "Agricultural Growth in West Bengal in the 1980s: A Disaggregation by Districts and Crops". *Economic and Political Weekly*, Vol. 29, No. 13, March 26.

Saha, A. (1996): "Adoption of Modern Technology in Rice Cultivation in West Bengal", in Raychaudhuri, A. and D. Sarkar (Ed.) *Economy of West Bengal: Problems and Prospects.* Allied Publishers and D.S.A. Center For Regional Economic Studies, Jadavpur University, Calcutta.

Sawant, S.D. (1983): "Investigation of the Hypothesis of Deceleration in Indian Agriculture," *Indian Journal of Agricultural Economics*, Vol. 38, No. 4, October-December.

Sawant, S.D. and C.V. Achuthan (1995): "Agricultural Growth Across Crops and Region: Emerging Trends and Patterns", *Economic and Political Weekly*, Vol. 30, No. 20, March 25.

Sen, S.R. (1967): "Growth and Instability in Indian Agriculture", *Journal of the Indian Society of Agricultural Statistics*, June.

Sen, A. and R. Sengupta (1995): "The Recent Growth in Agricultural Output in Eastern India with the Special Reference to West Bengal", Paper presented at a Workshop on 'Agricultural Growth and Agricultural Structure in Contemporary West Bengal and Bangladesh', Center for Studies in Social Sciences, Calcutta, January 9-12.

Srinivasan, T.N. (1979): "Trends in Agriculture in India, 1949-50 to 1977-78", *Economic and Political Weekly,* Vol. 14, Nos. 30-32 Special Number, August 28.

Vaidyanathan, A. (1980): "On Analyzing Agricultural Growth", *Journal of the Indian Society of Agricultural Statistics,* Vol. 32, No. 1, April.

Vaidyanathan, A. (1987): "Agricultural Development in Eastern India", *Economic and Political Weekly,* Vol. 22, No. 52, December 26.

Disparity and Convergence of Daily Wage Rate of Male Agricultural Labour since 1990-91

DEBESH BHOWMIK

Inequality in income distribution and regional disparities are the phenomena of process of unequal development in a dynamic economy. There are micro and macro-economic factors behind these ill effects in which disparities in wage structure produce the unequal income distribution.

In the Indian economic context, inter-state disparities in the state domestic product, consumption and saving expenditure patterns, social sectors, gender development, human development employment generation, infrastructure development, trade and commerce are the areas of research.

In the similar jurgon, inter-district disparities in income, health and education, electricity, roads, transportation, small scale industries, agricultural production, agricultural wages, gender development are the central economic sectors of West Bengal economy which are to be explored in the new dimensions of sustainability and growth. Under balanced regional development process, poor and backward districts should not remain underdeveloped in the longer-run. Regional wage rate inequalities should be controlled in the long-term growth path because it may boost unequal development where poverty and gender disparity are the two main obstacles that an economy has been facing since the evolution of the civilized society whether local, regional, national or international.

In this paper, we will endeavour to study the nature of disparity in inter-district annual average daily wage rate of male agricultural labour in West Bengal during 1990-91–2003-04. We will also study the convergence analysis of inter-district disparity in daily wage rate and also emphasis on some policies for future.

I. INTRODUCTION

If we look at a glance in the West Bengal economy, we find that the state domestic product has been growing at the rate of 18.584% per year during 1990-91–2003-04, in which the agriculture sector grew at the rate of 14.702% per year during the same period. The per capita income of West Bengal rose by 17.05% per year. But the income share of agriculture in state domestic product has been declining at the rate of 2.45% per year from 1990-91–2003-04 i.e. share was 29.727% in 1990-91 which fell to 21.563% in 2003-04. Among the 58 lakh agriculturists in West Bengal economy, the agricultural labour comprises only 50 lakh as registered in the 1991 census. In other words, the agricultural labour is only 25% of the principal workers of the state. Hence, the daily wage of agricultural labour is partially a determining factor of income share of agriculture or to a greater extent of state domestic product of West Bengal. For example, the agricultural wage earners' share was 9.544% of state domestic product in 2003-04 in comparison to 9.954% in 2002-03.

Therefore, it is very much important to explain the nature of the inter-district disparity in daily wage rate of male agricultural labour in West Bengal economy. The convergence or divergence analysis of daily wage rate of male agricultural labour in West Bengal will show the behaviour of inter-district wage rate inequality and the interaction between aggregate demand and supply of male agricultural labour.

Again, if daily wage rate of male agricultural labour influence growth rate of West Bengal economy or agricultural share, then appropriate wage policy is needed for improving sustainable agricultural development.

According to the endogenous growth theory, per capita income of nations tends to be inversely related to the starting level of output or income per person in the economy or poor economies grow faster than rich ones. There is a force that promotes convergence in levels of per capita product or income. These propositions were nicely done by Barro and Sala-i-Martin, (1992, 1996), Nagaraj, Varaudakis and Veganzones (1997). Cashin and Sahay (1995) addressed the issue of regional convergence including conditional convergence. Marjit and Mitra (1936) reported significant divergence across Indian states and asked how far the predictions of the convergence hypothesis are valid. Sarker (1994) discovered a strong link between development and per capita plan outlays for the Indian states. Dholakia (1994) concluded a marked tendencies of convergence of long-term economic growth rates for the states during 1960-61 to 1989-90. Ghosh, Marjit and Neogi (1998) showed divergence of growth rates over last 35 years in India. Dasgupta, Maity, Mukherjee, Sarker and Chakraborty (2000) verified inter-state disparity in income with a tendency of convergence during 1960-61–1995-96. P.K. Pal (2003) studied that inter-state disparity has widened more in urban areas than in rural areas during the period of 1973-74–1999-2000. Also he (2005) indicated the existence of inter-state disparity in livestock products such that disparity index of milk has risen overtime while the reverse has happened in cases of eggs and wool. Again, P.K. Pal (2005) showed that there exists inter-state disparity in labour force participation rate in both rural and urban areas. Debesh Bhowmik (2004) analysed the divergence behaviour of inter-state fiscal deficit in India during 1970-71–2000-01 and this divergence was shown statistically stable through the degree of consistency.

In this paper, we wish to study the inequality in inter-district daily wage rate of agricultural male labourers in West Bengal economy and also verify convergence criteria of inter-district disparity in an analogous manner of the above literature.

To construct β convergence model, we followed Sala-i-Martin (1996) where we first found out the linear trend line taking the semi-log model as $\log(y) = \alpha + \beta t + U_i$ where y is the annual average of daily wage rate of male agricultural labour in the districts of West Bengal, α is a constant and β is the slope of log (y) or the growth rate of y or rate of increase in daily wage rate per year, u_i is the stochastic variable. We then relate the initial values of daily wage rates of each district with respect to growth rates of daily wage rate which gives the nature of convergence or divergence of β. If β convergence occurs then there will be an inverse relation between initial values of daily wage rate and the growth rates of daily wage rates. Again, we have constructed a figure relating to growth rate of daily wage rate of all the districts and the averages of first five years of initial values of daily wage rate of male agricultural labour and also found out a negative correlation, which showed the more reliable β convergence analysis.

Then we studied for σ convergence and followed Sala-i-Martin (1996) model where we found out inter-district co-efficient of variation of daily wage rate of male agricultural labour of West Bengal during the successive periods, then calculated the trend line of the coefficient of variations as $\log(c.v.) = a + bt + u_i$ where a is constant, b is the slope, t is the time and u is the random error, σ convergence is said to occur when the relevant measure declines through time i.e., when $b < 0$.

Next, we calculated the ranks of the districts in different years in order of highest daily wage rate to the lowest and found out their dispersion of relevant position. To test the degree of consistency or concordance (W), we used the following formula,

$$W = 12Sw / m^2 (n^2 - n)$$

where m= number of periods, n= number of districts, Sw= sum of squares deviations from the mean of the daily wage rate of each district corresponding to the years. Then, we found out the t-test of the degree of consistency of W for acceptance or rejection for stability.

In the second phase, we try to show the inter-district disparity in daily wage rate by using the disparity index as,

$$D.I. = 100[\Sigma (x_i - \overline{x})^2 / (n-1)]^{1/2} / \overline{x}$$

where x_i is the daily wage rate of male agricultural labour in West Bengal for $i = 1, 2, 3, \ldots n$, $\overline{x}$ is is the mean of daily wage rate, n is the number of years. In this case, the higher the index, the higher is the inter-district disparity in daily wage rate of male agricultural labour. Also, we have shown the trend line of disparity index in the graph by calculating $\log(D.I.) = a + bt + u_i$.

To justify the disparity in daily wage rate among the districts of West Bengal, we calculated the Theil Index of inequality in daily wage rate of male agricultural labourers during 1990-91–2003-04 through the following equation,

$$\text{Theil Index} = 1+ [\Sigma\, x_i \ln(x_i)]/\ln(x_i)$$

where x_i, $\forall_i = 1, 2, 3. \ldots N$ reveals the shares of ith daily wage earners. Also, we showed the fitted line of Theil Index for predicting the nature of inequality by the equation log (Theil Index) = a + bt + u, where a is constant, b is the slope, t is time and u is a random error.

We have collected data on annual average of daily wage rate of male agricultural labour of West Bengal during 1990-91–2003-04 from the various issues of *Economic Review*, West Bengal.

II. BEHAVIOUR OF GROWTH RATES OF DAILY WAGE RATE OF MAIE AGRICULTURAL LABOUR IN WEST BENGAL

We have estimated semi log linear trend line of the daily wage rate of male agricultural labourers during 1990-91–2003-04 for all the districts of West Bengal to calculate growth rate of daily wage rate. We found that all the districts achieved positive growth rates but the relatively lower income districts grew higher growth rates. The districts are Paschim Medinpur, West Dinajpur, Murshidabad and Coochbihar whose growth rates of daily wage rate were computed as 9.74%, 9.42%, 9.30% and 9.19% per year respectively during the specified period. The relatively richer districts like Burdwan, Hooghly and South 24-Parganas registered lower growth rates of daily wage rate namely 7.34%, 7.91% and 7.43% per year respectively. The medium income districts like Nadia, Jalpaiguri and Bankura showed medium growth rates of daily wage rate like 8.88%, 8.89% and 7.95% per year respectively during 1990-91–2003-04.

All the growth rates of wage rate computed from semilog linear model are highly significant with high value of R^2. Although, some districts like North and South 24-Parganas, Howrah, Darjeeling did not follow neo-classical growth theory. (Table 1)

TABLE 1

Growth Rate or Trend Line of Daily Wages Rate of Male Agricultural Labour in the Districts of West Bengal during 1990-91–03-04

$\text{Log } a_1 = 3.031 + 0.0993t$
(32.74)* (9.13)*
$R^2 = 0.87$, DW = 0.518

$\log a_2 = 3.0088 + 0.0889t + u_i$
(48.05)* (12.099)*
$R^2 = 0.92$, DW = 0.56

$\text{Log } a_3 = 2.8509 + 0.0919t + u_i$
(51.137)* (14.048)*
$R^2 = 0.94$, DW = 0.615

$\text{Log } a_4 = 2.8319 + 0.0942t + u_i$
(44.08)* + (12.49)*
$R^2 = 0.92$, DW = 0.73

$\text{Log } a_5 = 2.9107 + 0.0880t + u_i$
(59.09)* (15.22)*
$R^2 = 0.95$, DW = 0.78

$\text{Log } a_6 = 2.9199 + 0.09306t + u_i$
(54.92)* (14.90)*
$R^2 = 0.948$, DW = 0.77

$\text{Log } a_7 = 2.9760 + 0.0888t + u_i$
(61.2)* (15.55)*
$R^2 = 0.952$, DW = 0.52

$\text{Log } a_8 = 3.026 + 0.0878t + u_i$
(72.66)* (17.96)*
$R^2 = 0.96$, DW = 0.57

$\text{Log } a_9 = 3.313 + 0.0743t + u_i$
(70.33)* (13.439)*
$R^2 = 0.93$, DW = 0.75

$\text{Log } a_{10} = 3.075\ 1 + 0.0889t + u_i$
(66.35)* (16.34)*
$R^2 = 0.95$, DW = 0.61

$\text{Log } a_{11} = 3.156 + 0.0791t + u_i$
(81.61)* (17.42)*
$R^2 = 0.96$, DW = 0.92

$\text{Log } a_{12} = 3.213 + 0.0734t + u_i$
(76.51)* (14.89)*
$R^2 = 0.94$, DW = 0.83

$\text{Log } a_{13} = 2.8208 + 0.0945t + u_i$
(45.66)* (13.039)*
$R^2 = 0.93$, DW = 0.56

$\text{Log } a_{14} = 3.047 + 0.0795t + u_i$
(61.055)* (13.57)*
$R^2 = 0.93$, DW = 0.56

$\text{Log } a_{15} = 2.745 + 0.0936t + u_i$
(56.25)* (16.33)*
$R^2 = 0.956$, DW = 0.957

$\text{Log } a_{16} = 2.8305 + 0.09474t + u_i$
(49.37)* (14.47)*
$R^2 = 0.94$, DW = 0.48

$\text{Log } a_{17} = 3.184 + 0.0764t + u_i$
(74.87)* (15.3)*
$R^2 = 0.95$, DW = 0.66,

$\text{Log } a_{18} = 3.0185 + 0.0858t + u_i$
(66.82)* (16.17)*
$R^2 = 0.95$, DW – 0.64

Where, daily wage rates of:
a_1 = Darjeeling, a_2 = Jalpaiguri,
a_3 = Coochbihar, a_4 = West Dinajpur ,
a_5 = Malda, a_6 = Murshidabad, a_7 = Nadia,
a_8 = North 24-Pgs, a_9 = South 24-Pgs,
a_{10} = Howrah, a_{11} Hoogly, a_{12} = Burdwan,
a_{13} = Birbhum, a_{14} = Bankura, a_{15} = Purulia,
a_{16} = Paschim Medinpur, a_{17} = Purba Medinpur, a_{18} = West Bengal
* = significant at least 10% level.

II.1 Analysis of β-Convergence

We have already stated that the neo-classical growth theory suggests that at low levels of per capita output, an economy grows at a higher rate and *vice versa*. It leads to the hypothesis of absolute or β-convergence that predicts a negative relationship between the rates of growth enjoyed by a cross-section of economies and the levels of their per capita output at a given initial point of time.

In our paper, we will fit the convergence hypothesis in the annual average of daily wage rate of male agricultural labour in West Bengal during 1990-91–2003-04. Therefore, we have plotted the best fit of estimates of semi-log linear model of growth rates of annual average of daily wage rate of male agricultural labourers of all districts of West Bengal and their initial daily wage rates (i.e. in 1990-91). The phenomenon of β-convergence occurs if the later regression line yields a negative coefficient for wage rate in 1990-91. In the Table 2, the growth rates of daily wage rates of districts and their initial daily wage rates are given. In Figure 1, the initial daily wage rate and the corresponding growth rates of daily wage rates have been scattered. A fitted trend line is seen in the Figure 1, which states that the growth rates of daily wage rate of the districts of West Bengal reveal inverse relation with their initial daily wage rate. Thus, the β-convergence of inter-district daily wage rate of agricultural labour in West Bengal during 1990-91-2003-04 is confirmed. However, the initial condition of the daily wage rate of male agricultural labour may be a weak indicator for initial conditions. Hence, an alternative indicator was chosen. We have calculated the average of annual average of daily wage rate of male agricultural labour in each district of West Bengal of the first five years from 1990-91. Then plotted the growth rates of daily wage rate corresponding to those initial values and fitted the scatter points which is shown in Figure 2. (data seen in Table 2). It is seen in the figure that there is an inverse relation between the initial values of daily wage rate and the daily wage rate of male agricultural labour during 1990-91–2003-04. Hence β-convergence of inter-district daily wage rate of male/agricultural labour in West Bengal from 1990-91 to 2003-04 is found more accurate and perfect.

II.2 Analysis of β-Convergence

The economic literature confirmed that the concept of α

TABLE 2

Indicators of Inter-district Disparity of Daily Wage Rate of Male Agricultural Field Labourers in West Bengal

Year	*Disparity Index*	*Theil Index*	*Inter-district Co-efficient of variation of dally wage rate*
1990-91	13.867	0.01058	19.5711
1991-92	13.255	0.00530	12.857
1992-93	16.8334	0.01375	16.3315
1993-94	18.3869	0.005151	17.8264
1994-95	17.7264	0.005161	17.1971
1995-96	17.0174	0.001334	15.5151
1996-97	12.2717	0.002440	11.8931
1997-98	11.6210	0.001912	10.3866
1998-99	11.1034	0.0020%	10.77197
1999-00	9.3662	0.001597	9.0737
2000-01	8.9384	0.001590	8.65972
2001-02	8.5852	0.001835	8.2839
2002-03	8.4631	0.002278	8.19249
2003-04	8.2778	0.002065	7.97127

Growth rates and Standard Deviation of District-wise annual average daily wage rate of male agricultural field labourers in W.B. (1990-91–2003-04)

	Growth rate of daily wage	*Standard deviation of wage rate*	*Initial wage (in Rs.)*	*1st Five year average of wages*
Darjeeling	9.93	16.80549	18.0	28.084
Jalpaiguri	8.89	14.02748	21.0	25.614
Coochbihar	9.19	12.83192	17.0	22.358
W. Dinajpur	9.42	13.27938	17.4	21.908
Malda	8.80	13.08723	20.0	23.444
Murshidabad	9.30	14.36262	20.20	23.826
Nadia	8.88	14.10355	21.85	24.848
North 24-Pgs	8.78	14.28564	21.15	26.684
South 24-Pgs	7.43	14.24485	27.10	34.094
Howrah	8.89	15.25425	22.65	27.798
Hoooly	7.91	13.98206	24.55	30.168
Burdwan	7.34	12.83733	24.15	31.286
Birbhum	9.45	13.69870	20.25	21.662
Bankura	7.95	12.86936	23.53	26.25
Purulia	9.36	12.52532	17.35	20.504
Paschim Medinpur	9.74	14.58875	20.0	22.208
Purba Medinpur	7.64	13.7784	25.40	30.24
West Bengal	8.58	13.71412		26.07

Source : Economic Review, Various Issues, Computed by Author.

Fig. 1: Beta Convergence

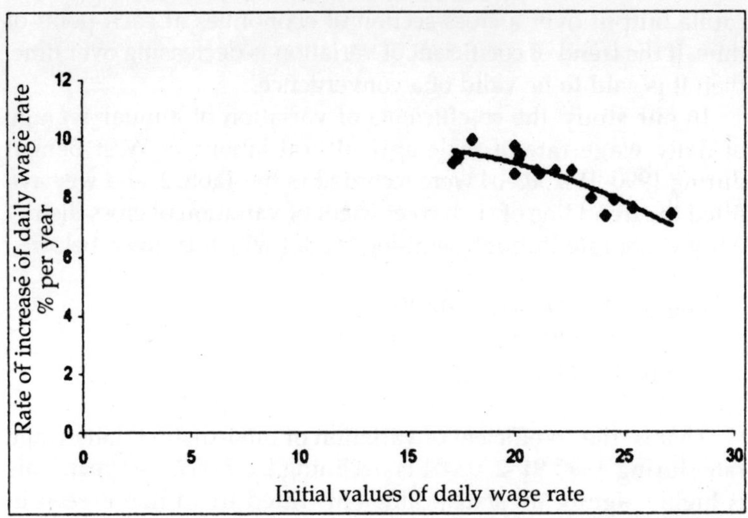

Fig. 2: Beta Convergence

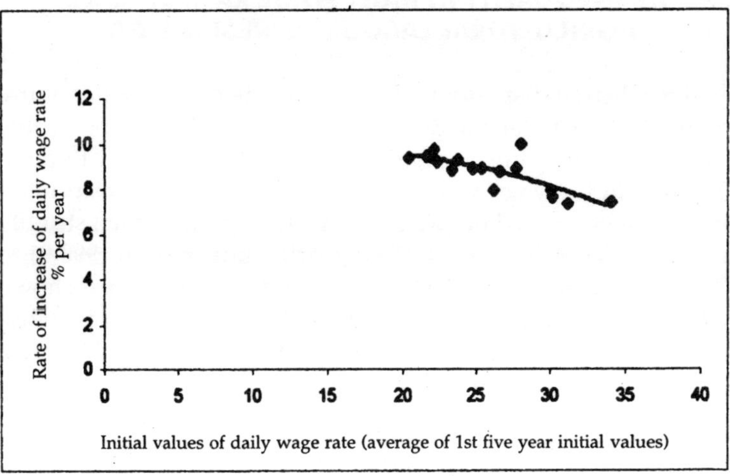

convergence does not relate directly to the growth rates of economies. Instead, it focuses attention on the dispersion of per capita output over a cross-section of economies at each point of time. If the trend of coefficient of variation is decreasing over time, then it is said to be valid of a convergence.

In our study, the co-efficients of variation of annual average of daily wage rate of male agricultural labour in West Bengal during 1990-91–2003-04 were recorded in the Table 2, and we have fitted the trend line of such co-efficient of variation of cross district daily wage rate through semi-log model which is given below:

$$\text{Log (c.v.)} = \underset{(39.68)^*}{3.0054} - \underset{(-7.96)^*}{0.0708176t} + u_i$$

$R^2 = 0.84$, DW= 1.465

That is, the co-efficient of variation of inter-district daily wage rate during 1990-91–2003-04 is declining by 7.08% per year. This is highly significant statistically. This fitted trend line is seen in the Figure 3 which follows that a convergence ensures in inter-district daily wage rate of male agricultural labour in West Bengal during 1990-91-2003-04.

III. INEQUALITY IN DAILY WAGE RATE OF MALE AGRICULTURAL LABOUR IN WEST BENGAL

Inter-district disparity in daily wage rate of male agricultural labour in West Bengal during 1990-91–2003-04 were visible prominently and thus, we have calculated this disparity through Disparity Index which reveals that during the first four years inter-district disparity in daily wage rate increased, then it fell steadily uptil 2003-04. In the Table 2, the disparity indices from 1990-91 to 2003-04 were given and the trend line of disparity index is shown in Figure 4 which confirmed that it is downward sloping i.e. inter-district disparity in daily wage rate in West Bengal is declining. The trend line is found a good fit with high value of R^2.

$$\text{Log (D.I.)} = \underset{(32.33)^*}{2.9401} - \underset{(-5.633)^*}{0.0601576t} + u_i$$

$R^2 = 0.725$, DW=0.64

That is inter-district disparity index in daily wage rate is

Fig. 3: Sigma Convergence

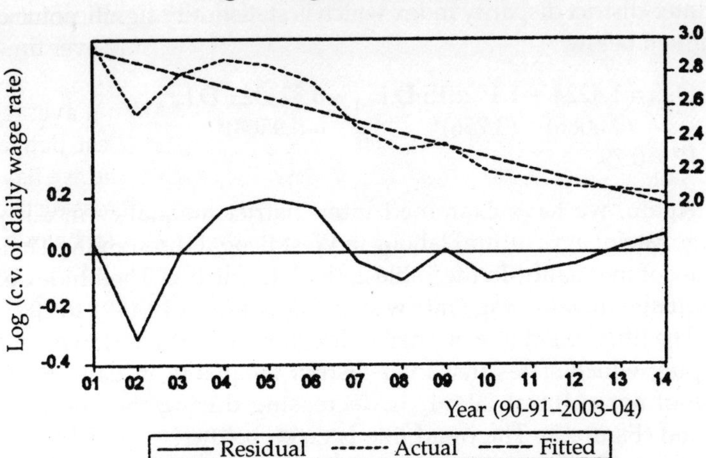

Fig. 4: Trend Line of Disparity Index

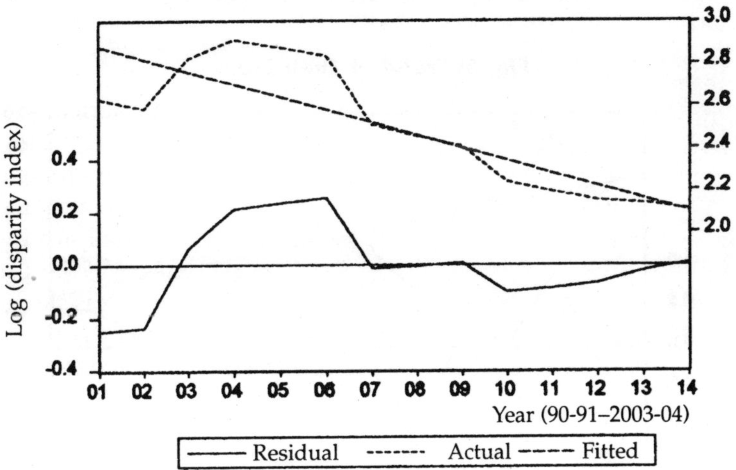

declining at the rate of 6.015% per year during 1990-91–2003-04. Moreover, we have constructed vector auto-regression estimates of inter-district disparity index which is statistically significant and is given below.

$$D.I._t = 1.4224 + 1.192815\ D.I._{t-1} - 0.325323\ D.I._{t-2}$$
$$(0.6066) \quad (3.756)^* \qquad (-0.9568)^*$$
$$R^2 = 0.79$$

Again, we have examined inter-district inequality in daily wage rate of agricultural labour in West Bengal through the Theil Index of inequality. In the Table 2, the inter-district Theil Index of inequality in daily wage rate was computed from 1990-91 to 2003-04. The fitted trend line of Theil index showed that it is downward sloping which states that inter-district inequality in daily wage rate of agricultural labour is decreasing during the specified period (Figure 5). The trend line is given below.

$$\text{Log (T.I.)} = -4.77866 - 0.1345t + u_i$$
$$(-17.138)^* \quad (-4.1366)^*$$
$$R^2 = 0.587, \quad DW = 1.55$$

That is, inter-district inequality in terms of Theil index of daily wage rate is decreasing at the rate 13.54% per year during 1990-

Fig. 5: Trend of Theil Index

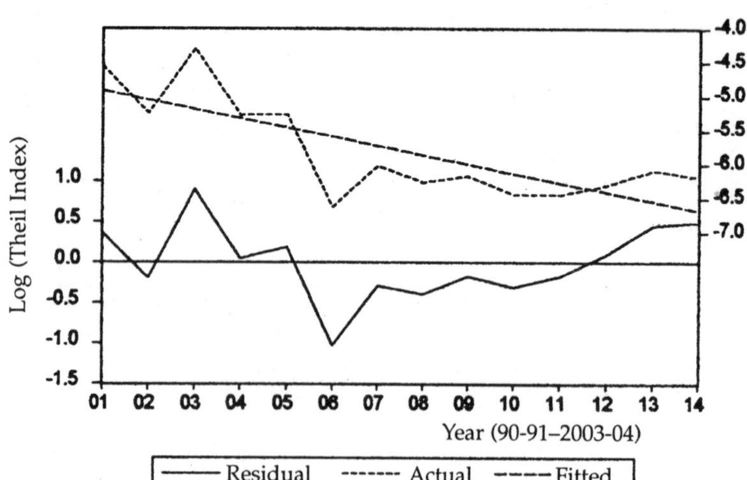

Fig. 6: Theil Indices

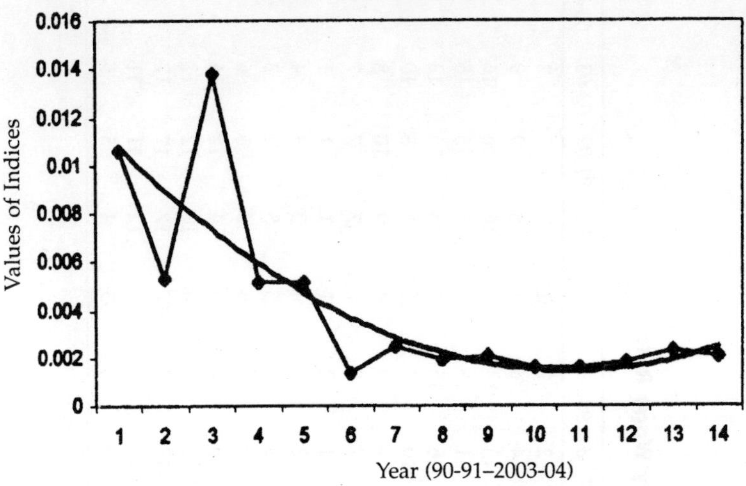

91–2003-04. In Figure 6, Theil Index of inequality is also plotted and is fitted by polynomial function and so far it is the best fit and is found highly significant.

III.1 Rank Analysis

We, then proceed to study the behaviour of the daily wage rate of the districts in terms of ranking over time. The districts are ranked in descending order of the daily wage rate. It is seen in the Table 3. A quick glance at the Table 3 reaveals that some districts have stable pattern of ranking like Darjeeling, South 24-Parganas, North 24-Parganas, Nadia, Purulia and Jalpaiguri. But, the rest of the districts did not show stable pattern of ranking overtime. Besides, the rankings have changed marginally during 1990-91–2003-04, and the rank correlation matrix is shown in the Table 4 which ensured that all the correlation coefficients are highly significant. But, the correlation coefficients tell us that variability of ranks are visible.

Now, in order to test the stability of the degree of consistency or concordance between the rankings of the districts in the different years taken as a whole, we calculated the co-efficients of concordance which was computed as 1.2672 and is found

TABLE 3

Ranks of the Inter-district Daily Wage Rate

	90-91	91-92	92-93	93-94	94-95	95-96	96-97	97-98	98-99	99-00	00-01	01-02	02-03	03-04
Darjeeling	13	14	5	2	2	2	2	2	2	2	2	2	2	2
Jalpaiguri	10	8	9	8	8	8	3	4	6	8	8	9	9	9
Coochbihar	16	15	11	13	12	12	14	13	14	15	16	16	16	15
W. Dinajpur	14	16	12	12	15	15	12	11	13	16	15	15	15	16
Malda	12	10	13	14	13	13	13	16	15	14	13	13	13	13
Murshidabad	9	11	14	11	11	11	7	10	11	11	11	8	10	10
Nadia	7	7	10	10	10	9	9	9	9	9	9	10	8	8
N. 24-Pgs.	8	9	7	7	7	7	10	7	8	7	7	7	7	7
S. 24-Pgs.	1	2	1	1	1	1	1	1	2	1	1	1	1	1
Howrah	6	6	6	6	5	6	4	3	3	4	3	3	4	3
Hooghly	3	3	3	4	4	4	8	8	7	5	5	4	3	4
Burdwan	4	4	2	3	3	3	5	6	4	6	6	6	6	6
Birbhum	11	13	16	17	16	16	15	15	16	13	14	14	14	14
Bankura	5	5	8	9	9	10	11	12	10	10	10	12	12	12
Purulia	15	14	17	16	17	17	17	17	17	17	17	17	17	17
Paschim Mid.	12	12	15	15	14	14	16	13	12	12	12	11	11	11
Purba Mid.	2	1	4	5	6	5	6	5	5	3	4	5	5	5

TABLE 4

Correlation Coefficients of Ranks

	90-91	*91-92*	*92-93*	*93-94*	*94-95*	*95-96*	*96-97*	*97-98*	*98-99*	*99-00*	*00-01*	*01-02*	*02-03*	*03-04'*
90-91	1.0	0.964	0.760	0.702	0.708	0.713	0.597	0.584	0.647	0.755	0.747	0.713	0.7314	0.7182
91-92	0.964	1.0	0.751	0.671	0.689	0.696	0,567	0.542	0.619	0.719	0.712	0.655	0.6835	0.6788
92-93	0.761	0.751	1.0	0.963	0.953	0.953	0.797	0.830	0.885	0.877	0.877	0.826	0.8529	0.848
93-94	0.702	0.671	0.963	1.0	0.980	0.980	0.892	0.907	0.949	0.919	0.927	0.899	0.9093	0.902
94-95	0.708	0.689	0.953	0,980	1.0	0.995	0,885	0.895	0.951	0.544	0.946	0.924	0.9314	0.9363
95-96	0.713	0.696	0.953	0.980	0.995	1.0	0.885	0.897	0.949	0.949	0.946	0.924	0.9387	0.9412
96-97	0.597	0.567	0.797	0.892	0.885	0.885	1.0	0.947	0.929	0.868	0.882	0.870	0.8505	0.8554
97-98	0.584	0.542	0.830	0.907	0.895	0.897	0.947	1.0	0.969	0.909	0.917	0.895	0.8874	0.8948
98-99	0.647	0.619	0.885	0.949	0.951	0.949	0.929	0.969	1.0	0.951	0.961	0.931	0.9314	0.9387
99-00	0.755	0.719	0.878	0.919	0.944	0.949	0.868	0.909	0.951	1.0	0.993	0.968	0.9755	0.9804
00-01	0.747	0.712	0.879	0.926	0.946	0.946	0.882	0.917	0.961	0.993	1.0	0.978	0.9828	0.9853
01-02	0.713	0.656	0.826	0.899	0.924	0.924	0.870	0.895	0.931	O.%8	0.978	1.0	0.9877	0.9877
02-03	0.731	0.684	0.853	0.909	0.931	0.939	0.851	0.887	0.931	0.976	0.983	0.988	1.0	0.9951
03-04	0.718	0.678	0.848	0.902	0.936	0.941	0.855	0.895	0.939	0.980	0.985	0.988	0.9951	1.0

All coefficients are significant at least 10% level of significance.

TABLE 5

District-wise Annual Average Daily Wage Rate of Male Agricultural Field Labour in West Bengal

(*in Rs.*)

	90-91	*91-92*	*92-93*	*93-94*	*94-95*	*95-96*	*96-97*	*97-98*	*98-99*	*99-00*	*00-01*	*01-02*	*02-03*	*03-04'*
Darjeeling	18.0	20.0	28.0	36.67	37.75	39.59	48.07	49.27	62.75	63.17	63.67	64.14	65.02	66.10
Jalpaiguri	21.0	23.74	26.0	28.33	29.0	32.0	45.66	46.10	51.59	55.09	56.56	57.2	57.75	58.85
Coochbihar	17.10	19.86	23.%	24.40	26.47	28.12	36.22	39.21	46.16	49.48	50.23	50.70	51.68	53.54
W. Dinajpur	17.40	19.48	23.81	24.48	24.37	26.44	37.22	40.82	47.09	49.36	50.37	51.63	52.62	53.43
Malda	20.0	23.28	23.68	24.28	25.98	27.78	36.32	38.40	46.01	49.96	52.02	53.27	54.29	55.60
Murshidabad	20.20	23.08	23.25	25.42	27.18	29.25	39.58	42.0	48.06	53.21	54.46	58.89	57.22	58.18
Nadia	21.85	23.93	25.28	25.72	27.46	31.04	38.92	42.5	48.71	54.25	56.0	56.97	58.25	59.58
N. 24-Pgs	21.15	23.45	27.91	30.07	30.84	32.92	38.68	43.96	49.99	55.92	57.52	59.04	60.41	61.75
S. 24-Pgs	27.10	28.05	36.63	38.13	40.56	42.65	48.43	51.84	59.93	64.17	64.98	65.62	66.70	67.97
Howrah	22.65	24.45	27.97	31.0	32.92	34.89	43.77	46.16	54.80	59.21	61.35	62.47	63.35	64.79
Hoogly	24.55	27.16	32.37	32.51	34.25	36.0	39.55	43.43	50.99	58.77	60.17	61.47	63.60	64.6
Burdwan	24.15	26.50	33.98	35.58	36.22	38.14	41.12	44.11	51.79	57.44	59.21	60.27	60.89	62.08
Birbhum	20.25	20.90	21.18	21.68	24.30	25.66	34.09	38.69	44.96	50.46	51.79	53.22	53.66	54.25
Bankura	23.53	25.93	26.43	27.05	28.31	30.32	37.33	40.68	48.50	53.96	55.02	55.52	55.79	56.60
Purulia	17.35	20.0	21.0	22.00	22.17	23.37	31.50	32.69	39.08	45.52	47.48	48.75	50.37	52.00
Paschim Mid.	20.00	21.00	22.30	23.07	24.67	26.90	33.48	38.93	47.27	52.59	54.10	55.68	56.33	57.20
Purba Mid.	25.40	29.80	31.34	32.04	32.62	34.94	40.11	44.43	51.60	59.94	60.87	61.33	62.06	63.25
West Bengal	21.50	23.63	27.15	28.36	29.71	31.47	39.41	42.54	49.96	54.86	55.97	56.93	57.92	59.48

Source: *Economic Review*, Government of West Bengal, 1990-91-2003-04.

insignificant at least 10% level of significance i.e. concordance is insignificant statistically.

$$W = 12S_w/[m^2(n^2 - n)] = 1.2672$$

where $S_w = 5629.8775$, m = 14 and n = 17.

So, the instability of degree of consistency between the rankings of daily wage rate of the districts in West Bengal through time was observed significantly..

III.2 Additional Relevant Findings

(1) As the state domestic product of West Bengal from 1990-91 to 2003-04 increases, the Theil Index of inter-district inequality in daily wage rate of male agricultural labour decreases. The estimated equation is given below:

Theil Index = 0.0055 – 0.00020 (State domestic product of W.B.)
(2.591) (–0.7817)
$R^2 = 0.048$, DW=1.25

(2) If the value of agricultural produce in state domestic product increases, then Theil index of inter-district inequality in daily wage rate declines during the study period. This is shown below,

Log (T.I.) = –0.5802 – 0.57022 log (agricultural produce in SDP)
(–0.247) (–2.2269)*
$R^2 = 0.292$, DW= 1.4565

This double log estimation states that one percent increase in agricultural produce in SDP of W.B. reveals 0.57% decrease in inter-district Theil index of inequality in daily wage rate of male agricultural labour in W.B. during 1990-91–2003-04. This is statistically significant with a low value of R^2.

(3) As the SDP of West Bengal rises through time the inter-district disparity index of wage rate of male agricultural labour also increases. It showed an exceptional observation although it is statistically insignificant with a very low value of R^2.

(4) But, if the values of agricultural produce in SDP increases, the value of inter-district disparity index of daily wage rate in agricultural labour in West Bengal, decreases from 1990-91 to

2003-04. It is given below,

$$\text{Log (D.I.)} = 5.6744 - 0.3483 \log \text{(Agricultural produce in SDP)}$$
$$(9.0355)^{*} \quad (-5.0386)^{*}$$
$$R^2 = 0.683, \quad DW = 1.474$$

This finding reveals that 1% increase in agricultural produce in SDP in West Bengal reduces 0.348% inter-district disparity index of daily wage rate of male agricultural labour in West Bengal during 1990-91–2003-04. This is statistically significant with a high value of R^2.

(5) To note that if mean daily wage rate of agricultural labour enhances, the SDP of West Bengal increases too. This is shown below,

$$\text{Log (SDP of West Bengal)} = 2.6049 + 2.131 \log \text{(mean daily wage rate)}$$
$$(3.579)^{*} \quad (10.778)^{*}$$
$$R^2 = 0.906, \quad DW = 1.05$$

The estimated equation states that 1% increase in mean daily wage rate of male agricultural labour in West Bengal implies 2.13% increase in SDP of West Bengal per year during 1990-91–2003-04.

(6) The relation between the value of agricultural produce of West Bengal and the mean daily wage rate of agricultural labour is positive during 1990-91–2003-04. The estimated equation is given below.

$$\text{Log (agricultural produce)} = 2.8057 + 1.7308 \log \text{(mean daily wage rate)}$$
$$(3.27)^{*} \quad (7.438)^{*}$$
$$R^2 = 0.821, \quad DW = 1.602$$

It states that one percent increase in daily wage rate produces 1.73% increase in the value of agricultural produce in West Bengal during the study period. It is statistically significant with high value of R^2.

(7) The share of agriculture in SDP of West Bengal declines steadily at the rate of 2.45% per year during 1990-91–2003-04. Also, the increase in mean daily wage rate of agricultural labour does not prevent from falling the tendency. This can be verified

as below.

Log (Agricultural share in SDP) = 4.2127 – 0.253 (mean daily wage rate)

(22.44)* (–4.968)*

$R^2 = 0.67$, DW= 1.09

This finding states that 1% increase in mean daily wage rate of agricultural labour produces 0.253% decrease in agricultural share in SDP per year during 1990-91–2003-04.

III.3 Policies

We can formulate some important and feasible policies that would make inter-district daily wage rate for male agricultural labour in more equitable manner. Policies are given below.

(1) Minimum wage act should be strictly enacted uniformly to all districts of West Bengal.
(2) Wage rate should be given in terms of real wage rate so that inflationary situation cannot deteriorate the standard of living of the wage earners.
(3) In Agriculture, there are evidences of contract labour and bonded labour that must be stopped by the enforcement of law.
(4) Wage determination by the big riots or by big bargadars should be prohibited socially and legislatively.
(5) Agricultural child labour must be banned and stopped immediately and low rate offered to them should be halted now.
(6) Social security should be maintained in determining the minimum wage rate in every district of West Bengal and even in India.
(7) Local governance should have control over inequality of minimum wage rate.
(8) Daily wage rate of agricultural labour should be increased.
(9) Gender disparity of daily wage rate must be eliminated.
(10) Government should collect data on daily wage rate of both male and female agricultural labourers in a disaggregate manner.

IV. CONCLUSION

This paper concludes that there is inter-district disparity in annual average daily wage rate of male agricultural labour in West Bengal during 1990-91–2003-04 which follows β and σ-convergences. The trend lines of Disparity Index and Theil Index confirmed that the inter-district inequality in daily wage rate declines gradually since 1990-91. But, the stability of the consistency of the rankings of daily wage rate of the districts is found statistically insignificant. It was verified that the mean daily wage rate of West Bengal is positively associated with the value of agricultural produce, agricultural share in state domestic product of West Bengal and even directly related with the state domestic product of West Bengal during 1990-91–2003-04 which are highly significant statistically. Thus, the paper gave emphasis on enactment of minimum wage rate and its relative increase in future.

REFERENCES

Barro, R.J. and X. Sala-i-Martin (1992): Convergence, *Journal of Political Economy*, Vol. 100, No. 2, pp. 223-51.

—— (1991): Convergence Across States and Regions, *Brookings Papers Econ. Activity*, No. 1, pp. 82-107 (a).

Bhowmik, Debesh (2004): Behaviour of fiscal deficit and reform policy in India-in S. Murty (Ed): Fiscal and Monetary State in India: Some Aspects. (RBSA Publishers, Jaipur), pp. 59-94.

Cashin, Paul A. (1995): Economic Growth and Convergence Across the Seven Colonies of Australia: 1861-1991, *Economic Record*, Vol. 1, June, pp. 132-44.

Cashin, Paul A. and Sahay, Ratna (1996): Internal Migration, Centre-State of India, *JMF Staff Papers*, Vol. 43, No. 1, (March), pp. 123-71.

—— (1996): Regional Economic Growth and Convergence in India, *Finance and Development*, March, pp. 49-52.

Das, Tusar Kanti (1998): Convegence Across Indian States, *IEA 81st Conference Volume*, pp. 503-11.

Dasgupta, Dipankar, Pradip Maity, Robin Mukherjee, Subrata Sarker, Subhendu Chakraborty (2000): Growth and Inter-State Disparities in India, *EPW*, July 1, pp. 2413-22.

Dholakia, R. (1994): Spatial Dimension of Acceleration of Economic Growth in India, *EPW*, August 21, No. 35, pp. 2303-09.

Economic Review (1990-91–2003-04), Government of West Bengal.

Garg, Ajay (2005): Labour Laws, One should know (Nabhi Publication, New Delhi).

Ghosh, Buddhadeb, Sugata Marjit, Chiranjib Neogi (1998): Economic Growth and Regional Divergence in India, 1960 to 1995, *EPW*, June 27, pp. 1623-30.

Marjit, S. and S. Mitra (1996): Convergence in Regional Growth Rates: Indian Research Agenda, *EPW*, Vol. XXXI, No. 33, pp. 2239-42.

Nagaraj, R., A. Varaudakis and M.A. Veganzones (1997): Long-run growth trends and convergence across Indian States, Technical Paper, Development Centre.

Pal, P.K. (2003): Dimensions of poverty in India: Measurement and determinants, *IEA 86th Conference Volume*, pp. 126-42.

—— (2005): Livestock Products in India: Growth, Composition and Determinants, *Artha Beekshan*, Vol. 14, No. 1, June, pp. 32-44.

—— (2005): Workforce in India: An Inter-State Analysis, *Artha Beekshan*, Vol. 13, No. 4, March, pp. 49-60.

Raman, J. (1996): Convergence or uneven development: A note on regional development in India, Valparaiso University, US, Mimeographed.

Salai-i-Martin, X. (1996): Regional Cohesion: Evidence and Theories of Regional Growth and Convergence, *European Economic Review*, Vol. 40, pp. 1325-52.

—— (1990): On Growth and States, Ph.D. Dissertation, Harvard University.

Sarkar, Prabirjit (1997): Are Poor Countries Coming Closer to the Rich?, August 2, pp. 1979-84.

Sarker, P.C. (1994): Regional Imbalances in Indian Economy over Plan Periods, *EPW*, March 12, No. 2, pp. 621-33.

Subrahmanyam, S. (1999): Convergence of Income across States, *EPW*, November 20, Nos. 46 and 47, pp. 3327-28.

PART III

HUMAN DEVELOPMENT

10

Disparity of Human Poverty Index: The Role of Infrastructure

SUSHIL K. HALDER AND KAJARI ROY

The paper consists of two parts: the first part relates to the estimation of human poverty index (HPI) and the second part examines the inter-linkages between HPI and supply side factors in relation to education, health and physical and financial infrastructures across the districts in West Bengal with reference to the year 2001. The concept of HPI is multidimensional developed by Sen and Anand (1997), which is introduced by UNDP and reflected in the 8th HDR-1997. Human poverty index measures deprivation in three basic dimensions of human development. These are longevity, knowledge and economic provisioning. The study reveals that there is wide range of inter-district variations of HPI. In order to study the second part, we pose the question that how far and to what extent the supply side factors as mentioned above are responsive in explaining the variations of HPI across the districts in West Bengal. Keeping in view this objective, the district level sectoral (health, education and physical and financial) infrastructure indices are estimated and thereby a composite overall index is formulated with the help of Principal Component Method. It is found that there is no correlation between HPI and health and education infrastructure indices but there is a significant negative association is observed between HPI and physical (including financial) and Overall Composite Indices across the districts in West Bengal.

INTRODUCTION

The multidimensional view of poverty emerged gradually in relation to and as a criticism of mainstream economic development that focused on growth in GNP per capita growth, though a component of economic progress, is insufficient as an objective, since aggregate growth cannot guarantee to ensure economic equality, equity and social justice (*Rannis et. al.*, 2000). Since the literature on poverty is vast and multifaceted, we will concentrate on Sen's contribution towards poverty.

In *Commodities and Capabilities*, Sen (1985) has argued that poverty can be seen as an absolute inability to pursue certain valuable functioning. This is to be associated with relative poverty in the space of incomes or commodities. Deprivation in capabilities is the result of lack of opportunities—signifying that society has not provided people with, access to the means to develop or maintain essential human capabilities. This enables us to build up a relationship between development and deprivation. Human development is defined by the expansion of capabilities and these are ends. Unlike income, capabilities are reflected not in inputs but in human outcomes in the quality of people's lives. Deprivation is reflected in a lack of basic capabilities—when people are unable to reach a certain level of essential human achievement or functioning (*UNDP*, 1996).

The World Bank's 'Voices of the Poor' studies (*Narayan et. al.*, 2000) and *World Development Report*-2002/2003 (on the theme of poverty and refers to the goal of poverty reduction) have emphasized the goal of 'poverty reduction' or to an end of human poverty from the countries in the world. Sen's proposition of individual advantage in the space of capabilities rather than economic growth or primary goods is also highlighted in the UNDP's *Human Development Rerjort*-2003 as 'Millennium Development Goals'. Sen and Anand (1997) have formulated an index in order to measure capability deprivation in basic three dimensions of human life already reflected in the human development index—longevity, knowledge and decent standard of living. The first deprivation relates to survival—the vulnerability to death at a relatively early age. The second relates to knowledge—being excluded from the world of reading and communication. The third relates to a decent standard of living in terms of overall economic provisioning. This is the human poverty index (HPI) comprising three dimensions, which was introduced, in the 8th Human Development Report-1997 in addition to HDI and GDI. The human poverty index combines basic dimensions of poverty and reveals interesting contrasts with income poverty—it is written as the weighted mean of three different proportions. The human development index uses income but the capability poverty measure does not. The human development index measures average achievement whereas the human poverty index measures deprivations in the three basic dimensions of human development captured in the human development index. The HPI takes into account 'Output' (or attainment) and 'Input' (or process) indicators.[1]

HPI AND ITS COMPONENTS: METHODS OF CONSTRUCTION AND DATA

Human Poverty Index (HPI) measures deprivation in three basic dimensions *of* human development. These are longevity, knowledge and economic provisioning. The first two indicators used are: percentage of people not expected to survive to age 40 (P_1) and the percentage of adults who are illiterate (P_2). The third indicator (P_3) is composed of three variables: percentage of people without access to safe water (P_{31}), percentage of people without access to health services (P_{32}) and percentage of moderately and severely underweight children under five (P_{33}).

$$P_3 = (P_{31} + P_{32} + P_{33})/3$$

Human Poverty Index, P (α), is a weighted mean of order α of P_1, P_2 and P_3. Let $w_i > 0$ be the weight on P_1 (≥ 0) for i = 1, 2, 3. For the calculation of HPI, $\alpha = 3$ is, generally taken into consideration.

Therefore,

$$P(\alpha) = [(w_1 P_1^{\alpha} + w_2 P_2^{\alpha} + w_3 P_3^{\alpha}) / (w_1 + w_2 + w_3)]^{1/\alpha}$$

With $w_1 = w_2 = w_3 = 1$, $P(\alpha) = [(P_1^{\alpha} + P_2^{\alpha} + P_3^{\alpha}/3]^{1/\alpha}$

It is to be mentioned here that P (α) cannot be interpreted as a headcount or incidence of poverty with respect to a poverty line (hyper-plane) drawn in the product space of the three variables though P_1, P_2 and P_3 are the headcount or incidence of poverty in each of three separate dimensions. P (α) is an average, albeit of order α, of the three Sub-indices P_1, P_2 and P_3. If the incidence of poverty happened to be the same in every dimension, then P (α) would clearly be equal to this common number, since

$$[\{w_1P(\alpha)^\alpha + w_2P(\alpha)^\alpha + w_3P(\alpha)^\alpha\}/(w_1 + w_2 + w_3)]^{1/\alpha} = P(\alpha) =$$
$$= [\{w_1P_1^\alpha + w_2P_2^\alpha + W_3P_3^\alpha\}/(w_1 + w_2 + w_3)]^{1/\alpha}$$

This observation allows us to interpret P (α) as the degree of overall poverty that is equivalent to having a headcount ratio of P (α)% in every dimension (*HDR*, 1997). This is suggested by UNDP-1997 for measuring HPI for the developing world. However, the criterion used in constructing HPI differs between developed and developing countries. In India, Planning Commission measures Human Poverty Index (HPI). Planning Commission also considers three dimensions, health, education and economic provisioning (*HDRC*, 2004). The health indicator is percentage of people not expected to survive beyond age 40 (P_1). The second indicator (P_2) is comprised of two variables: illiteracy rate for the population in the age group 7 years and above and proportion of children in the age group 6-18 years not enrolled in the schools. The economic deprivation indicator (P_3) is a composite of four parameters: proportion of people below poverty line; proportion of children in the age group 12 to 23 months not fully vaccinated; proportion of people living in kutchha houses; and proportion of people have not been able to get access to safe drinking water, electricity and health facility. It is to be mentioned here that initially the measure of deprivation in a decent standard of living also included an indicator of access to health services but this has been dropped in the HDR-2003 and now reported only by the percentage of population without sustainable access to an improved water sources and percentage of children underweight for age. Following Chelliah and Sudarshan (1999), Chatterjee *et. al.* (2003) has calculated a modified HPI[2] for each district of the state of West Bengal with reference to the year 2001.

Here, we have estimated HPI for West Bengal and its districts using Census-2001 data. The UNDP methodology for the construction of HPI is followed with minor modifications of some components. As discussed earlier, HPI has three dimensions—longevity, education and a decent standard of living. But, living a healthy life is more desirable than living a long life that may be healthy or unhealthy. Therefore, health deprivation is more critical than longevity deprivation. The health indicator (P_1) is a combination of two variables namely percentage of population treated under communicable diseases (P_{11}) and the percentage of low birth weight babies (P_{12}). Moreover, the district level data pertaining to 'probability of people who do not survive up to age 40' is not available. This is why the health deprivation rather than deprivation of longevity is used.

The second indicator (P_2), that is the education indicator is also comprised of only one variable: illiteracy rate of the female (P_{21}). Women are generally considered as 'vulnerable group' in our patriarchal Indian society. Thus, instead of simple illiteracy rate, the present indicator relating to illiteracy of women, obviously, focuses the gender-related deprived section of the Indian society. The indicator for a decent standard of living (P_3) is too a composite of three separate indicators: P_{31}, P_{32} and P_{33}. P_{31} is comprised of two components: percentage of people who do not have the access of safe drinking water and sanitary facility. P_{32} is the percentage of children, in the age group 12 to 23 months, not fully immunized; and P_{33} is the percentage of non-institutional deliveries. It is to be mentioned here that the weights used by UNDP in measuring different dimensions is same i.e., $W_1 = W_2 = W_3 = 1$; here, in our present exercise we have used the same weights in each dimension.

The data source pertaining to the variables included in the construction of HPI are drawn from Census of India 2001.

District level variations of HDI, HPI and its Components: Deprivations of Health, Knowledge, and Economic Provisioning

The HPI (and its component) is constructed at the district level considering the UNDP methodology. This is given in the following Table 1. Human poverty index and its components vary to a large extent across the districts in West Bengal. HPI is maximum in Uttar Dinajpur (56.13) and the lowest in Kolkata (16.28). Deprivation in health is highest in Coochbihar (22.84) and lowest in Uttar Dinajpur (0.61); knowledge deprivation is maximum in Uttar Dinajpur (63.49) whereas it is the lowest value in Kolkata (22.7); deprivation in economic provisioning is maximum in Uttar Dinajpur (65) whereas it is minimum in Kolkata (9.08).

TABLE 1

HPI (with Components) and HDI in the Districts of West Bengal

Districts	*Health Deprivation Index (P_1)*	*Knowledge Deprivation Index (P_2)*	*Deprivation in Economic Provisioning (P_3)*	*HPI*	*HDI*
Darjeeling	13.92	37.06	39.61	33.79	0.65
Jalpaiguri	3.81	47.79	45.72	40.87	0.53
Coochbihar	22.84	43.88	59.61	46.64	0.52
Uttar Dinajpur	0.61	63.49	65	56.13	0.51
Dakshin Dinajpur	8.50	45.72	57.43	45.66	NA
Malda	4.23	58.75	64.82	54.11	0.44
Murshidabad	5.71	52.35	62.69	50.66	0.46
Birbhum	22.45*	48.45	55.83	46.37	0.47
Burdwan	4.58	39.05	42.93	35.90	0.64
Nadia	13.60	40.42	42.92	36.64	0.58
24-Parganas (N)	6.30	28.28	39.64	30.50	0.66
Hooghly	12.34	32.79	33.47	29.19	0.63
Bankura	15.95	51.55	40.61	41.08	0.52
Purulia	18.02	63.5	61.84	54.97	0.45
Medinipur	18.24	35.58	55.6	42.04	0.62
Howrah	6.32	29.89	39.78	31.06	0.68
Kolkata	7.98	22.7	9.08	16.28	0.78
24-Parganas (S)	4.93	40.99	55.69	43.19	0.60

Notes: HDI for Dakshin Dinajpur was not estimated due to lack of data by the Development and Planning Department, Government of West Bengal.

Source: Components of P_1 are low birth weight babies and persons treated under communicable diseases—the data are drawn from Health on the March, SBHI, 2001-02, Govt. of West Bengal. Components of P, and *Py* are drawn from Census India. West Bengal 2001. HDI values are drawn from West Bengal Human Development Report, 2004 prepared by Development and Planning Deptt, Government of West Bengal.

It is to be mentioned here that the rank correlation coefficient between HPI and HDI across the districts in West Bengal is -0.905, which is statistically significant at 1 and 5 percent level. This means that districts with higher values of HPI manifest lower values of HDI. This is because some of the components included in the measurement of HDI already incorporated in the measurement of HPI as their shortfalls of achievement in particular dimension.

Infrastructure and Poverty: A Brief Review of Literature

Infrastructure facilities can be understood largely as public infrastructural inputs from the supply side. It is argued that many of the infrastructure variables are public goods in nature, which provides increasing returns to scale. But, this property may be disrupted due to overstaffing and inadequate maintenance of some of the infrastructure variables (*World Development Report* 1994). Depending on the nature of services delivered, infrastructure can be divided into three broad categories, namely social, physical and financial (*De & Ghosh*, 2005). Social infrastructure includes health and educational facilities. Physical infrastructure has been defined in terms of the physical facilities (roads, airports, utility supply systems, communication systems, water and waste disposal systems, etc.), and the services (water, sanitation, transport, energy) flowing from those facilities. Financial infrastructure provides banking facilities to the society. Fox (1994) defines public infrastructure as those services derived from the set of public works traditionally supported by the public sector to enhance private sector production and to allow for household consumption. The importance of infrastructure as an instrument of economic development and, potentially, poverty reduction, is reflected in the high level of investment that national governments and international donor agencies put into infrastructure development. Also the support of infrastructural facilities is essential for the successful implementation of various development plans.

There has been much debate about whether infrastructure service provision benefits the poor. Some evidence suggests that certain types of infrastructure service provision, e.g. roads and transport, have a potential contribution to agricultural output, and that infrastructure improvements (in electricity supply, transport and telecommunications) in small towns contribute significantly to industrial growth and employment (*Bhakar and Bhargava*, 2003). At a community or individual level, benefits can accrue to the poor if labour-intensive methods of construction are used rather than capital-intensive methods (*Sida*, 1996). Analyses of poverty and infrastructure services show in many developing countries, the poor people's access to infrastructure is limited, and cite numerous examples of self-provided infrastructure, e.g. assembling materials to build shelter, purchasing water from vendors, as a response to the lack of access to publicly provided infrastructure (*WDR*, 1994).

Using infrastructural stock index by way of Principal Component Method, Raychaudhuri (2005) has found a positive close linkage between infrastructure and State Domestic Product in West Bengal. Devas (1991) suggests that a host of factors explain why existing infrastructure interventions fail to serve the poor:

- the inadequacy of provision in relation to the huge scale of need;
- the relatively high standards adopted, which means either that the poor cannot afford what is offered, or else that a substantial subsidy is required which the government cannot afford;
- any subsidy element is likely to accrue either to higher-income groups, or to the public-officials who administer infrastructure services;
- failure to address the fundamental obstacles, which the poor face in gaining access to land and basic infrastructure;
- inappropriate forms of infrastructure and services, together with inadequate resources for operation and maintenance, which means that services do not effectively reach those who need them, or fall into disrepair and disuse; and
- the adoption of policies which discriminate against the poor or impede them from improving their situation, such as regulatory standards which are unaffordable by the poor, and harassment of informal sector providers.

It is evident that if poverty and associated deprivations are resulted from various social, cultural and economic factors, deprivations in basic amenities reflect the inefficiency of the institutions of governance undertaken by the states in the name of public interest and well-being (*Chatterjee*, 2002). The rural health care system has three tiers: rural sub-centre (SC), public health center (PHC) and rural hospital or community health center (CHC). There exists a national norm regarding the distribution of these health service units. In West Bengal, there is large inter-district variation regarding the distribution of health care system; moreover, the distribution is inconsistent with the national norm (*Haldar*, 2005). In addition to this the performance of the rural SCs is very poor. The report made by SBHI (2001/02) is significant in this context: 'the ANM/health workers visited only 15 percent eligible women in rural villages during the last three months prior to survey conducted in 1998-99'. Mandal and Mukherjee (2005) also showed that although there is huge investment in primary education infrastructure and the feedback is quantitatively better, qualitatively it is very poor. But, our main objective of this section is to investigate the role of infrastructure in human deprivation across the districts in West Bengal with reference to the year 2001.

Indicators of Infrastructure

Infrastructure facilities in the present study are classified into three broad categories, viz. health, education and physical and financial infrastructure. At the district level there are different providers of health services, namely, government, voluntary organizations, private sector and informal therapists (*Banerjee*, 2002). Keeping in mind this problem, we have considered the following health indicators:

(1) Number of hospitals per 10000 population
(2) Number of Public health centers (PHCs) per 10000 population
(3) Number of family welfare planning centres per 10000 population
(4) Number of homoeopathic dispensaries per 10000 population
(5) Proportion of villages having health centre within the village
(6) Number of state health vehicles (on road) per 10000 population

Education indicators are:

(1) Number of pre-primary schools per 1 lakh population
(2) Number of primary schools per 1 lakh population
(3) Number of middle schools per 1 lakh population
(4) Number of Higher Secondary schools per 1 lakh population
(5) Number of primary schools with building per 1 lakh population
(6) Number of primary schools with drinking water facility per 1 lakh population
(7) Number of primary schools with toilet facility per 1 lakh population
(8) School-teacher ratio in primary schools
(9) Teacher-pupil ratio in primary schools

Physical and financial indicators are:

(1) Length of roads per square km.
(2) Number of registered vehicles per 1000 population
(3) Number of post offices per lakh population
(4) Number of post and telegraph offices per 1000 population
(5) Number of telephone exchanges per lakh population
(6) Functioning capacity of telephone exchanges
(7) Number of banks per 1000 population
(8) Number of post offices with savings bank per 1000 population
(9) Proportion of villages electrified

District level secondary data of West Bengal for the year 2001 have been used here. Data have been collected from Census of India 2001, Bureau of Applied Economics and Statistics, Department of School Education and State Bureau of Health Intelligence and different government website.

The data source and reference year of the factors included in the analysis are given in Appendix Table 1.

It is well known that the economic development depends on various socio-economic and infrastructural factors. One of the important problems in empirical verification of such claims is that, given a large set of infrastructural variables, one needs a way to reduce the dimensionality, so that an aggregate study is meaningful (*Raychaudhuri*, 2005). Moreover, if someone wants to find out the determinants of human poverty across the districts using multiple regression analysis may also create another problem like multicollinearity. Both of these problems can be tackled with the help of Principal Component Method[3] (*Kendal*, 1957, *Lawley and Maxwell*, 1963, *McCallum*, 1970, *Koutsoyiannis*, 1978).

The "Principal Component Method" has been used here for data reduction. Only the "First Principal Component" is used to construct the infrastructural development index. The first component derived here is based on the correlation matrix of the relevant variables and literally weighted average of underlying variables.

RESULTS AND ANALYSIS

To assess the sectoral infrastructural development, an overall infrastructural index is constructed with the Principal Component Method. The first principal component accounts for more than 70% of variability. That is why we have considered the first principal component only. PCA has been conducted for each of the three broad categories and infrastructural indices for each of them are calculated, as shown in Table 2. Then an overall infrastructural index (OII) is constructed for each district. Rank of Oil from different districts is then compared with that of HPI. On the basis of the correlation matrix, factor loadings for each of the variables are calculated. The equations for each of the categories are as follows:

$$E_i = 0.271X_{i1} + 0.276X_{i2} + 0.144\,X_{i3} + 0.137\,X_{i4} - 0.227\,X_{i5} + 0.192\,X_{i6} + 0.186\,X_{i7} + 0.048\,X_{i8} \quad (1)$$

$$H_i = 0.829X_{i1} + 0.346X_{i2} - 0.162\,X_{i3} + 0.870\,X_{i4} - 0.721\,X_{i5} + 0.697\,X_{i6} + 0.877\,X_{i7} \quad (2)$$

$$P_i = -0.188X_{i1} + 0.286X_{i2} + 0.266X_{i3} + 0.279\,X_{i4} - 0.086\,X_{i5} - 0.149\,X_{i6} - 0.082\,X_{i7} + 0.033\,X_{i8} + 0.041\,X_{i8} \quad (3)$$

where E, H, P represents education, health and physical and financial infrastructure indices respectively, where 'i' represents the ith district. Table 2 shows the education, health and physical and financial infrastructure indices. The Overall Infrastructure Index (OII) is the weighted average of the three, giving equal weights to all.

Health and physical (and financial) infrastructure index is highest in Kolkata; consequently Kolkata occupies the highest position in OII and lowest in Medinipur. It is interesting to note that the EII is highest in Medinipur, but the health, physical and financial infrastructure is very poor in this district. Medinipur, Howrah, Bankura, Purulia, Coochbihar and Birbhum are in relatively good position in respect of EII. But a perplexing result is come out in relation to EII that most of the districts with relatively good educational infrastructure have high HPI. It reflects that the infrastructure is not properly utilized though the supply side is quite adequate relating to education.

From the PCA, it is observed that only two variables namely, number of primary schools and pre-primary schools carry higher factor scores in educational infrastructure index (EII), while number of hospitals and state health vehicles carry higher proportion of factor loading in health infrastructure index (HII). But in case of physical and financial infrastructural index, number of post and telegraph offices carries higher proportion of variation of factor loadings.

Kolkata, Darjeeling, Coochbihar, Nadia and Purulia are in relatively better off position in relation to health infrastructure index. But the output indicator as measured by HPI shows a very weak correlation with the input (or supply side factors) as measured by HII.

However, there is a great need for improving the health care amenities, especially in the rural areas of the districts. All the districts lag behind in respect of Kolkata with reference to health infrastructure index.

The physical and financial infrastructure facilities are too much high in Kolkata. There exists a great inter-district variations of PII and OII.

The value of rank correlation coefficient between HPI and four infrastructure indices are estimated as:

R (HPI, HII) = –0.11
R (HPI, EII) = 0.15
R (HPI, PII) = –0.408

TABLE 2

Overall Infrastructure Index and its Components

Sl. No.	*District*	*Education infrastructure index*	*Rank*	*Health infrastructure index*	*Rank*	*Physical & financial infrastructure index*	*Overall infrastructure index (OII)*	*Rank*
1.	Darjeeling	-1.1808	17	1.556867	2	23.30145	7.892504	2
2.	Jalpaiguri	-1.13797	16	-0.41579	12	-6.94655	-2.83344	12
3.	Coochbihar	0.247093	6	0.759636	3	-19.456	-6.14976	17
4.	Uttar Dinajpur	-0.90181	15	-0.68665	16	-0.45657	-0.68168	6
5.	Dakshin Dinajpur	-0.13885	9	-0.44129	14	3.805868	1.075242	4
6.	Malda	-0.71792	14	-0.28627	11	-1.31348	-0.77255	7
7.	Murshidabad	-0.4996	13	-0.2462	9	-12.213	-4.3197	14
8.	Birbhum	0.26836	5	-0.18298	8	-5.69	-1.86821	8
9.	Burdwan	-0.09171	7	-0.2656	10	-5.84529	-2.06753	9
10.	Nadia	-0.2,0277	11	0.184303	4	-8.21219	-2.74355	11
11.	24-Parganas (N)	-0.1398	10	-0.7421	17	-6.4462	-2.44274	10
12.	Hooghly	-0.13757	8	-0.09052	7	-1.14991	-0.45933	5
13.	Bankura	1.662852	3	-0.0403	6	-14.1746	-4.18402	13
14.	Purulia	1.899135	2	0.149332	5	-19.8586	-5.93671	16
15.	Medinipur	2.087188	1	4.42516	13	-30.0384	-9.4588	18
16.	Howrah	0.403791	4	-1.3258	18	21.47638	6.851456	3
17.	Kolkata	-1.86684	18	1.671961	1	116.2992	38.70145	1
18.	24-Parganas (S)	-0.42363	12	-0.46207	15	-12.9382	-4.60797	15

R (HPI, OII) = –0.453

The above results indicate that there is no correlation between Human Poverty Index (HPI), education (EII) and health (HII) infrastructure indices, but it is to be mentioned here that the physical and financial (PII) and overall (OII) infrastructure index have a negative effects on HPI which implies that districts having higher values of PII and OII manifest lower values of HPI. The value of the rank correlation coefficient is found to be significant at 10 percent level.

CONCLUSIONS

This paper first estimates HPI across the 18 districts of West Bengal with reference to the year 2001 considering the UNDP methodology and then tries to find out the different infrastructure indices using PCA across the districts. It is observed that the HPI, EII, HII, PII and OII vary to a large extent across the districts in West Bengal. HPI and supply side factors (viz. infrastructure) in relation to social sector infrastructure (i.e., health and education) do not have any relationship in the present exercise. A very pertinent question is coming out regarding the efficiency and management of the education and health infrastructure. Moreover, in the present exercise we have taken only those infrastructure which are provided by the government. But, there are lot of schools, nursing homes, dispensaries, etc. running by private initiatives in those districts where the demand for schooling as well as for health care exists. One important aspect which is ignored in this context is that the demand for schooling and health care which are not entirely determined by the supply side factors, rather demand side factors also plays important role here but that is not captured here and that seems to be beyond the scope of the present analysis. Overall Infrastructure Index (OII) has been constructed considering only the First Principal Component. This index accounts for the region (i.e., district) specific differences in infrastructure. High negative coefficient of rank correlation between HPI and OII supports the conditional convergence hypothesis, which suggests that regions with greater infrastructural facilities have less human poverty and *vice-versa*. More importantly, the results indirectly show that infrastructure is positively correlated to regional human development measured in terms of HDI (as the rank correlation between OII and HDI is also highly positive and statistically significant).

It is observed that the HPI though a non-income dimension of poverty measure is highly influenced by the physical and financial infrastructure. Therefore, from the perspective of regional disparity relating to HPI, it can be suggested to provide more physical and financial infrastructure to those districts having high values of HPI in order to reduce regional disparity and to ensure social justice. Moreover, the findings supports that the supply side factors relating to social sector infrastructure index across the districts is incapable in explaining the variations of human poverty index across the districts in West Bengal. This means that opening of schools/hospitals do not necessarily accentuate human development (or reduction of human poverty) unless and until the demand for schooling/health care is generated.

NOTES

1. In the context of development and deprivation perspective, Kamdar and Basak (2005) have made a distinction between output (or attainment) and input (or process) indicator. Output or attainment indicators reflect the status of the population in that particular dimension of development; for example, life expectancy is an outcome indicator of the health status of the population indicating the number of years a person is expected to survive at age one or at birth. Access to health services is an input indicator or a process indicator as it contributes to higher life expectancy.
2. Chatterjee and Ghosh (2003) has made a modified HPI. By taking simple arithmetic mean of health services deprivation and deprivation of safe drinking water and electricity, the percentage of people having provisioning deprivation is calculated. Let the knowledge deprivation be P_1 and provisioning deprivation be P_2, then HPI can be calculated on the basis of the following formula:

   $$HPI = [(P_1^2 + P_2^2)/2]^{1/2}$$

3. Following Kendal (1957) and Koutsoyiannis (1978) the following steps are evolved in the Principal Component Method:
   (a) Let there be a linear relationship between the infrastructure index and the underlying 'p' infrastructure variables: $Y = a_1X_1 + a_2X_2 + \ldots a_pX_p$.
   (b) Work out the eigen values of R, normalized to unity and arrange

them in descending order. Let these values be $\lambda_1 > \lambda_2 > \lambda_3 > \ldots > X_p$.

(c) Take first few values of λs (say r values), find out the proportion $(\lambda_1 + \lambda_2 + \lambda_3 + \ldots + \lambda s)/p$
if this value is satisfactory, say more than 70% (it may vary from problem to problem) find out the eigen vectors corresponding to these eigen values.

(d) Convert the original variables into standard scores and using the elements given in first eigen vectors as weights, get the weighted sum of the standardized scores for each observation. Similarly, using the other eigen vectors the scores of the second, third and r^{th} principal component can be worked out.

(e) Multiply each eigen vector by the square root of their corresponding eigen values and give them as factor loadings.

REFERENCES

Banerjee, S. (2002): Social Sector Development in West Bengal: An Assessment, *Artha Beekshan*, Vol. 11, No. 3, December, pp. 46-60.

Bhakar, R.R. and P. Bhargava (2003): 'Disparities in Infrastructural Development in Rajasthan', *Indian Journal of Regional Science*, 35(1), pp. 57-65.

Chatterjee, B. (2002): Human Development in India: An Analysis of Inter-State Variations, *Artha Beekshan*, Vol. 11, No. 3, December, pp. 113-38.

Chatterjee, B., and D.K. Ghosh (2003): *Towards a District Development Report for West Bengal*, State Institute of Panchayats and Rural Development, Kalyani, West Bengal, pp. 40-45.

Chelliah, R.J. and R. Sudarshan (1999): *Income Poverty and Beyond: Human Development in India*, Social Science Press.

De, Prabir and Buddhadeb Ghosh (2005): Effects of Infrastructure on Regional Income in the Era of Globalization: New Evidence from South Asia, *Asia-Pacific Development Journal*, Vol. 12, No. 1, June 2005, pp. 81-107.

Devas, C. (1991): 'Financing Mechanisms', in ADB/EDI, in "The Urban Poor and Basic Infrastructure Services in Asia and the Pacific: A Regional Seminar," January 22-28, Manila, Philippines.

Fox, W. (1994): Strategic Options for Urban Infrastructure Management, Urban Management Programme Policy, Paper 17, Washington DC: World Bank

Haldar, S.K. (2005): 'Health and Health Care Facilities in Rural West Bengal: Some Issues' in Mandal, Amal (eds.), *Rural Development in West Bengal*, Northern Book Centre, New Delhi, pp. 230-45.

Human Development Report (1996): United Nations Development Programme, New York.

—— (1997): United Nations Development Programme, New York.

—— (2003): United Nations Development Programme, New York.

Kamdar Sangita and Asoke Basak (2005): 'Beyond the Human Development Index: Preliminary Notes on Deprivation and Inequality', *Economic and Political Weekly*, August 20, pp. 3759-65.

Kendal, M.G. (1957): *A Course in Multivariate Analysis*, London: Griffin, pp. 70-74.

Koutsoyiannis, A. (1978): *Theory of Econometrics—An Introductory Exposition of Economic Method*, The Macmillan Company of India Ltd., Delhi.

Lawlcy, D.N. and A.E. Maxwell (1963): *Factor Analysis as a Statistical Method*, Butterworths Mathematical Texts, London, pp. 2-27.

Mandal, A. and Sanjoy Mukherjee (2005): 'Primary Education in West Bengal—More Concerns than Complacency', in Mandal, Amal (eds.), *Rural Development in West Bengal*, Northern Book Centre, New Delhi, pp. 180-229.

McCallum, B.T. (1970): 'Artificial Orthogonalisation in Regression Analysis', *Review of Economic Studies*, 52, pp. 110-13.

Narayan, Deepa, Raj, Patel, Kai Schafft, Anne Rademacher, and Sarah Koch-Schutte (2000): *Voices of the Poor: Can anyone Hear Us*? New York: Oxford University Press for the World Bank.

Ranis, Gustav, Frances Stewart, and Alejandro Ramirez (2000): 'Economic Growth and Human Development', *World Development*. 28/2: pp. 197-219.

Raychaudhuri, A. (2005): 'Role of Infrastructure on Economic Development of West Bengal in the Last Decade' in Raychaudhuri, A. and T.K. Das (eds.), *West Bengal Economy—Some Contemporary Issues*, Allied Publishers Pvt. Ltd. in collaboration with DSA Centre, Department of Economics, Jadavpur University, pp. 12-44.

Sen, Amartya K. (1985): *Commodities and Capabilities*, Amsterdam: Elsevier.

Sen, Amartya K. and Sudhir Anand (1997): 'Concepts of Human Development and Poverty: A Multidimensional Perspective', Background Paper for UNDP.

Sida (1996): *Promoting Sustainable Livelihoods*, Stockholm: Swedish International Co-operation Development Agency.

World Development Report (1994): World Bank, Washington, DC: The World Bank.

—— (2002/03): World Bank, Washington, DC: The World Bank.

APPENDIX

TABLE 1

Variables Included in the Analysis and the Data Source

Variables	*Data Source (Reference Year)*
Number of hospitals per 10000 population.	West Bengal Human Development Report 2004
Number of Public Health Centers (PHCs) per 10000 population	West Bengal Human Development Report 2004
Number of family welfare planning centres per 10000 population	West Bengal Human Development Report 2004
Number of homoeopathic dispensaries per 10000 population	Health on the March 2001-02
Proportion of villages havmg health centre within the village	www.wbccnsus.gov.in
Number of state health vehicles (on road) per 10000 population	www.indiastat.com
Number of pre-primary schools per 1 lakh population	Annual Report 2001-02, Department of School Education, Government of West Bengal.
Number of primary schools per 1 lakh population	Annual Report 2001-02, Department of School Education, Government of West Bengal.
Number of middle schools per 1 lakh population	Annual Report 2001-02, Department of School Education, Government of West Bengal.
Number of Higher Secondary schools per 1 lakh population	Annual Report 2001-02, Department of School Education, Government of West Bengal.
Number of primary schools with building per 1 lakh population	Annual Report 2001-02, Department of School Education. Government of West Bengal.

Number of primary schools with drinking water facility per 1 lakh population	Annual Report 2001-02, Department of School Education, Government of West Bengal.
Number of primary schools with toilet facility per 1 lakh population	Annual Report 2001-02, Department of School Education. Government of West Bengal.
School-teacher ratio in primary schools	Annual Report 2001-02, Department of School Education, Government of West Bengal.
Teacher-pupil ratio in primary schools	West Bengal Human Development Report 2004
Length of roads per square km	www.indiastat.com
Number of registered vehicles per 1000 population	www. ind iasiat.com
Number of post offices per lakh population	www.indiastat.com
Number of post and telegraph offices per thousand population	www.indiastat.com
Number of telephone exchanges per lakh population	www.indiastat.com
Functioning capacity of telephone exchanges	www.indiaStat.com
Number of banks per 1000 population	www.indiastat.com
Number of post offices with savings bank per 1000 population	www.indiastat.com
Proportion of villages electrified	Census of India 2001

11

Regional Disparity in Income and Human Development since 1980s

Prankrishna Pal

Regional disparity of any indicator is a common feature of any economy like India. India's economy is a composite of federal states. Variation of any indicator of the states expectedly affects India's development pattern. It is expected that there will be a wide variation in the inter-state development pattern. Several scholars have analysed regional disparity at the state/district level. Dholakia (2003) has argued that regional disparity in terms of human development has been decreasing, but it is the income or economic development where the said disparity across regions has been almost constant over the last two decades. T.K. Das (1998) has examined disparities from mid-sixties to mid-nineties in terms of three groups, namely, high income, middle income and low income states. On the other hand, the Report of the 10th Finance Commission has suggested that disparities in a large country like India may not always behave in a uniform manner across all groups of states. Inter-state disparities in levels and growth of per capita GSDP indicate disparities in capacity. Estimates by Rangarajan (2005) has revealed that comparing the trend growth rate of GSDP in the 1980s and the 1990s, it is generally seen that the higher income states have grown at higher rates. There are, however, some significant exceptions. In case of Punjab and Haryana, growth has come down, although Punjab has still the highest per capita GSDP. Among the poorer states, states whose growth rate fell in the 1990s as compared to the 1980s were Assam, Bihar, Orissa, Uttar Pradesh and Rajasthan.

Like any state, regional disparities are observed in West Bengal in respect of various indicators at the district level. Per capita State Domestic Product (SDP) is a good indicator of economic development and level of living of a state. Per capita SDP of West Bengal is an average of per capita District Domestic Product (DDP) of all the districts. So variation of per capita DDP reflects variations of per capita SDP of West Bengal. Over time per capita DDP has varied across the district. So also the per capita SDP. SDP or DDP mainly generates from 13 economic activities. These activities are grouped into three broad sectors: (a) Primary Sector (PS) consists of agriculture, fishing, forestry and logging, mining and quarrying; (b) Secondary Sector (SS) containing manufacturing, construction, electricity, gas and water supply; and (c) Tertiary Sector consisting of trade and commerce, transport and communication, banking and insurance, real estates and business services, public administration and other services.

The present study thus concentrates on the extent of disparities among the districts (regions) of West Bengal with respect to the level and growth of the development indicator during 1980/81-2003/04. Section I deals with the nature and extent of West Bengal's SDP sectorally during 1980/81-2003/04, while in Section II regional disparity in per capita DDP during 1980/81-2001/02 is examined. Regional disparity in growth of per capita DDP during 1980/81-2001/02 is examined in section III, while in section IV disparity in district-wise Human Development Index (HDI) of West Bengal is examined. The relationship between district-wise HDI and per capita DDP is examined in section V. Section VI gives the concluding remarks.

I. SECTORAL COMPOSITION OF PER CAPITA SDP

In West Bengal per capita SDP is an indicator of economic development. It indicates the standard of living of the people. It varies over time. Estimates reveal that per capita SDP at 1993-94 prices has continuously increased from Rs. 4951 in 1980-81 to Rs. 5988 in 1990-91 and to Rs. 9320 in 1990-2000. And it has reached at the level of Rs. 11612 in 2003-04. Thus it has increased by more than 100 times during this period. Comparative analysis of India's per capita GDP and West Bengal's per capita SDP reveals that West Bengal economy's per capita SDP falls consistently below the all-India per capita GDP. That is to say, West Bengal economy is lagging far behind the all-India per capita living standards (*Chatterjee*, 2005).

Let us now discuss the sectoral composition of West Bengal's per capita SDP during 1980/81-2003/04 at 1993-94 prices. Sectoral distribution of SDP in West Bengal has changed over time. Estimates (Table 1) reveal that the tertiary sector (TS) was the prime share in SDP during 1980/81-2003/04 excepting 1985/86-1987/88. The share of the TS in SDP has increased marginally from 35.50% in 1980/81 to 35.71% in 1990-91 and to 50.76% in 2000-01. In 2003-04 it has reached at the level of 55.21%. Thus the contribution of the TS to the states' SDP is more during the 1990s as compared to the 1980s. This contribution has been obtained at the costs of both primary and secondary sectors (PS and SS). This is due to the fact that the service sector activities have been generated gradually during the 1990s. At the all India level the TS has also contributed 51% of GDP in 2003-04. This shows that the contribution of the TS is more in W.B. State's SDP compared to the India's GDP. On the other hand, the share of both the PS and SS has continuously decreased during this period. The share of the PS has decreased from 33.83% in 1980-81 to 32.93% in 1990-91 and to 25.74% in 2003-04. The respective figures for the SS are: 30.67%, 31.36% and 19.05%. Thus we see that compared to the 1980s the contribution of the PS and SS to the states' SDP has significantly declined during 1990s and onwards.

Wide disparities in the sectoral distribution of per capita DDP among the districts of West Bengal are also observed during 1993/94-2001/02. Estimates (Table 2) reveal that the contribution of the PS in total per capita DDP was highest in 1993-94 in almost all the districts (12) of West Bengal excepting Howrah, Hooghly, 24-Parganas (N), 24-Parganas (S), Kolkata and Darjeeling while in 2001-02 the share of the TS was the prime in almost all the districts (16) excepting Dakshin Dinajpur and Malda. Thus the tertiary sector activities (services) have been generated gradually in almost all the districts during the 1990s and as a result the sectoral composition of per capita DDP has changed from the PS to the TS.

TABLE 1

Percentage Distribution of West Bengal's NSDP by Sectors at Constant Prices (1993-94)

Year	*Primary Sector*	*Secondary Sector*	*Tertiary Sector*	*Total*
1980-81	33.83	30.67	35.50	100.00
1981-82	31.67	31.86	36.47	100.00
1982-83	29.37	32.44	38.19	100.00
1983-84	34.22	30.06	35.72	100.00
1984-85	35.34	27.31	37.35	100.00
1985-86	36.84	28.57	34.59	100.00
1986-87	36.58	29.41	34.01	100.00
1987-88	37.48	28.58	33.94	100.00
1988-89	34.52	30.74	34.74	100.00
1989-90	34.12	30.73	35.15	100.00
1990-91	32.93	31.36	35.71	100.00
1991-92	32.77	26.73	40.50	100.00
1992-93	32.02	26.80	41.18	100.00
1993-94	35.90	21.31	42.79	100.00
1994-95	36.18	20.95	42.87	100.00
1995-96	34.34	21.96	43.70	100.00
1996-97	37.00	19.66	43.34	100.00
1997-98	38.09	18.70	43.21	100.00
1998-99	31.05	20.81	48.14	100.00
1999-2000	29.75	21.29	48.96	100.00
2000-01	28.73	20.51	50.76	100.00
2001-02	29.62	20.01	50.37	100.00
2002-03	26.46	19.68	50.86	100.00
2003-04	25.74	19.05	55.21	100.00

Source: Statistical Abstract, West Bengal, various issues.

Sector-wise analysis also reveals the following:

(i) **Primary Sector (PS):** Its share in per capita DDP has significantly decreased in West Bengal and its constituent districts during 1993/94-2001/02. The share is too low in Kolkata (1.53% in 1993-94 and 0.69% in 2001-02) too high in Coochbihar (57.35%) in 1993-94 and Dakshin Dinajpur (45.90%) in 2001-02. Thus there exists a high disparity in the contribution of the PS among the districts of West Bengal during the period under study.

(ii) **Secondary Sector (SS):** Like the PS, the share of the SS

TABLE 2

Sectoral Distribution of Per Capita Income of Districts in West Bengal at Constant Prices (1993-94)

Districts	*1993-94*				*2001-02*			
	PS	*SS*	*TS*	*Total*	*PS*	*SS*	*TS*	*Total*
Burdwan	41.70	23.05	35.25	100.00	32.76	24.41	42.83	100.00
Birbhum	48.97	12.85	38.18	100.00	42.87	10.84	46.29	100.00
Bankura	49.96	13.66	36.38	100.00	40.83	14.24	44.93	100.00
Medinpur	43.38	18.25	38.37	100.00	35.68	16.86	47.46	100.00
Howrah	15.04	34.40	50.56	100.00	11.33	31.01	57.66	100.00
Hooghly	34.64	25.38	39.98	100.00	26.90	24.47	48.63	100.00
24-Pgs. (N)	25.04	29.87	45.09	100.00	20.37	29.75	49.88	100.00
24-Pgs. (S)	31.51	28.41	40.08	100.00	26.10	25.47	48.43	100.00
Kolkata	1.53	24.36	74.11	100.00	0.69	15.68	83.63	100.00
Nadia	49.21	13.40	37.39	100.00	39.36	19.23	41.41	100.00
Murshidabad	45.03	19.53	35.44	100.00	37.88	19.23	42.89	100.00
U. Dinajpur	53.02	8.97	38.01	100.00	42.41	9.94	47.65	100.00
D. Dinajpur	50.57	9.43	40.00	100.00	45.90	9.00	45.10	100.00
Malda	52.77	10.66	36.57	100.00	45.66	11.14	43.20	100.00
Jalpaiguri	44.72	19.63	35.65	100.00	34.59	20.59	44.82	100.00
Darjeeling	37.74	14.07	48.19	100.00	29.88	13.90	56.22	100.00
Coochbihar	57.35	7.85	34.80	100.00	45.11	9.21	45.68	100.00
Purulia	44.51	14.93	40.56	100.00	36.43	17.52	46.05	100.00
West Bengal	35.90	21.30	42.80	100.00	28.76	20.16	51.08	100.00

Notes: PS: Primary Sector, SS: Secondary Sector, TS: Tertiary Sector.
Source: Statistical Abstract, West Bengal, various issues.

has also decreased in West Bengal and its almost all the districts excepting Burdwan, Bankura, Nadia, Uttar Dinajpur, Malda, Jalpaiguri, Coochbihar and Purulia during 1993/94-2001/02. The highest share is observed in Howrah (34.40% in 1993-94 and 31.01% in 2001-02) and the lowest one in Coochbihar (7.85% in 1993-94) and Dakshin Dinajpur (9.00%) in 2001-02. Thus there also exists a regional disparity in the contribution of the SS among the districts of West Bengal during the period under study.

(iii) **Tertiary Sector (TS):** The reverse trend is observed in this sector. Its share has significantly increased in West Bengal and its constituent districts at the costs of the PS and SS during the period under study. The lowest share is observed in Coochbihar (34.80% in 1993-94) and Nadia (41.41% in 2001-02) while the highest one in Kolkata (74.11% and 83.63%). Also, we note that this sector has contributed about 50% or more of per capita income in the districts of Howrah, 24-Parganas (N), Kolkata, Hooghly and 24-Parganas (S) in 2001-02. As a result, its contribution to the state of West Bengal is more than 51% during this period under study.

II. DISPARITY IN PER CAPITA INCOME OF THE DISTRICTS

Already we have said that per capita income is a good indicator of a nation/state/district etc. The national/state/district-level, per capita Gross Domestic Product (GDP)/State Domestic Product (SDP)/District Domestic Product (DDP) indicates the average level of living of the nation/state/district. In our analysis we are to examine the nature and extent of disparity in per capita income (SDP or DDP) in West Bengal during the period of 1980/81-2001/02 at constant prices (1993-94).

Over time wide variations in per capita SDP or DDP are observed in West Bengal and its constituent districts during the period under study. Estimates (Table 3) reveal that at the state level, per capita SDP has increased continuously from Rs. 4951 in 1980-81 to Rs. 5988 in 1990-91 and to Rs. 10376 in 2001-02. Thus per capita SDP has increased by more than 2 times during this period. Based on the state level per capita SDP in different years we can classify the districts according to their per capita DDP:

(i) 1980-81

(a) Districts below the state level: Birbhum, Bankura, Medinpur, 24-Parganas, Nadia, Murshidabad, Uttar Dinajpur, Malda, Jalpaiguri, Darjeeling, Coochbihar and Purulia—12 districts.

(b) Districts above the state level: Burdwan, Howrah, Hooghly and Kolkata—4 districts.

(ii) 1990-91

(a) Districts below the state level: Birbhum, Bankura, Medinpur, 24-Parganas (S), Nadia, Murshidabad, Malda, Coochbihar and Purulia—9 districts.

TABLE 3

Per Capita Income (Rs.) in the Districts in West Bengal at Constant (1993-94) Prices

District	*1980-81*	*1981-82*	*1982-83*	*1983-84*	*1984-85*	*1985-86*	*1986-87*	*1987-88*	*1988-89*	*1989-90*	*1990-91*
1	*2*	*3*	*4*	*5*	*6*	*7*	*8*	*9*	*10*	*11*	*12*
Burdwan	6592	6264	6280	6280	5965	6176	6376	6647	7143	7496	8019
Birbhum	3727	3768	3230	4098	3768	3863	4124	4667	4922	5069	4978
Bankura	3437	2974	2690	3486	3406	3749	3770	4090	4412	4648	5627
Medinpur	3093	2722	2827	3308	3096	3396	3390	3948	4152	4265	5741
Howrah	5897	6019	6307	6321	5856	6166	6620	6515	6980	7302	6394
Hoogly	5606	5423	5062	5820	5510	6023	6110	6362	6617	6722	6905
24-Prgs. (N)	4741	4929	5035	5133	5284	5670	5557	6013	6280	6405	5999
24-Prgs. (S)											5248
Kolkata	7732	8021	8016	8188	6365	6397	6674	6926	7391	7701	9864
Nadia	3511	3855	3779	4089	4086	4319	4433	4465	4982	6218	5713
Murshibad	2742	3400	2639	2974	3016	3258	3186	3348	3777	4162	5170
Uttar Dinajpur	2725	2552	2672	2928	2878	3022	4125	2907	3418	3923	6945
Dakshin Dinajpur											
Malda	2953	2842	3087	3232	3036	3621	3313	3525	3797	3995	4993
Jalpaiguri	3419	3407	3393	3824	3544	3821	3921	3938	4396	4791	6056
Darjeeling	3044	3851	2985	3270	3215	3376	4608	3248	3818	4383	6733
Coochbihar	3176	2501	2320	2535	1957	2726	3088	2808	3117	3380	4886
Purulia	3770	3574	2996	3737	3695	4304	4204	4340	4563	4684	4517
West Bengal	4951	4717	4799	5258	5283	5386	5478	5645	5823	5823	5988
RDI (%)	36.84	38.18	42.40	36.47	32.74	29.09	27.49	30.78	28.60	25.81	21.77

TABLE 3 (*Contd.*)

District	*1992-92*	*1991-93*	*1993-94*	*1994-95*	*1995-96*	*1996-97*	*1997-98*	*1998-99*	*1999-00*	*2000-01*	*2001-02*
1	*12*	*13*	*14*	*15*	*16*	*17*	*18*	*19*	*20*	*21*	*22*
Burdwan	8152	8302	8726	9069	9433	10364	10317	11066	11141	11445	12385
Birbhum	4879	5111	5668	6016	6491	6702	7025	7749	7865	7738	8515
Bankura	5888	5910	6130	6676	7220	7467	8029	7983	8947	9361	9649
Medinpur	6572	6410	6989	7235	7601	8069	8177	8225	8810	9263	10253
Howrah	6630	6667	6911	7212	7696	7585	8775	9253	9777	10366	11192
Hooghly	7393	7273	7807	8241	8860	9611	9202	9471	9921	10344	11712
24-Prgs. (N)	5228	6193	6527	6655	7131	7260	8415	9086	9162	9440	8794
24-Prgs. (S)	5756	6028	6231	6745	6640	6917	7390	7769	8159	8395	8619
Kolkata	10065	10139	10465	11028	12179	12308	13674	15624	17660	19896	20560
Nadia	6028	6046	6494	6766	7173	8134	8677	8953	9507	9606	10655
Murshibad	5421	5572	5789	6076	6437	6937	7300	7598	8005	8009	8757
Uttar Dinajpur	4495	4612	4825	5245	5296	5644	5858	6273	6402	6779	6705
Dakshin Dinajpur			5389	5850	6091	6584	6708	7244	8376	8866	8953
Malda	5104	5050	5493	5786	6330	6689	7374	7264	7902	8339	8660
Jalpaiguri	6329	6236	6512	6637	7048	7339	7768	8097	8524	8831	9157
Darjeeling	7546	5208	7715	8152	8270	8294	10601	9724	9785	10416	11156
Coochbihar	5271	5208	5564	5659	6126	6458	6750	7138	7326	7780	7702
Purulia	7881	5093	5263	5855	6171	6478	7628	6900	7753	7905	8810
West Bengal	6330	6406	6756	7094	7492	7880	8407	8814	9330	9779	10376
RDI (%)	21.84	22.19	21.17	20.58	21.65	21.04	21.72	24.40	26.10	29.44	38.05

Note: RDI: Regional disparity Index.
Source: Same as in Table 1.

(b) Districts above the state level: Burdwan, Howrah, Hooghly, 24-Parganas (N), Kolkata, Uttar Dinajpur, Jalpaiguri and Darjeeling—8 districts.

(iii) 2001-02

(a) Districts below the state level: Birbhum, Bankura, Medinpur, 24-Parganas (N), 24-Parganas (S), Murshidabad, Uttar Dinajpur, Dakshin Dinajpur, Malda, Jalpaiguri, Coochbihar and Purulia—12 districts.

(b) Districts above the state level: Burdwan, Howrah, Hooghly, Kolkata, Nadia and Darjeeling—6 districts.

From the above analysis we observe that disparity in per capita DDP exists among the districts of West Bengal during the period under study. Among the districts Nadia and Darjeeling have relatively increased their per capita DDP more so that these two districts have improved their position from below the state level to above the state one.

District-wise per capita DDP reveals that Kolkata has achieved all through the prime position during 1980/81-2001/02. The lowest position is achieved by (i) Uttar Dinajpur in 1980-81 and during 1992/93-2001/02, and (ii) Coochbihar during 1981/82-1990/91. Thus we see that the position of Uttar Dinajpur has improved during 1981/82-1990-91 and remained same during 1991/92-2001/02, while the position of Coochbihar has improved during 1991/92-2001/02 as compared to the 1980s.

Let us now measure the extent of disparity in per capita income among different districts of West Bengal. Conventionally, it is measured by the ratio of minimum per capita DDP to maximum per capita DDP. Alternatively, it is measured by the co-efficient of variation. For the sake of simplicity, we first use the former one.

At the all-India level the inter-state disparity in income reveals that the ratio of minimum GSDP per capita to maximum GSDP per capita after excluding Goa decreased from 30.5% in 1993-94 to 26.1% in 1995-96. Thereafter, it went up and then came down to 26.5% in 2001-02. On the other hand, the Gini co-efficient reflects inter-state income inequality assuming that all persons within a state are located at the mean income of that state. This co-efficient shows a progressive increase in income disparity. It increased from

0.192 in 1993-94 to 0.217 in 1999-00. Thereafter it has shown a decline even though its level at 0.210 in 2001-02 was higher than that in 1993-94 (*Rangarajan*, 2005).

In West Bengal the extent of per capita income disparity is measured at three levels by taking (a) maximum and minimum per capita DDP among all the districts, (b) maximum and minimum per capita DDP among the districts below the State level's SDP, and (c) maximum and minimum per capita DDP among the districts above the State level's SDP.

We have computed the extent of per capita income disparity among the districts of West Bengal in different years: 1980-81, 1990-91 and 2001-02. Estimates reveal that taking all the districts the income disparity has widened significantly from 35.24% in 1980-81 to 49.53% in 1990-91 and then decreased to 32.61% in 2001-02 which is still lower than that in 1980-81. Also, income disparity has widened significantly from 57.48% in 1980-81 to 78.68% in 1990-91 and then reduced to 65.40% in 2001-02 which is still higher than that in 1980-81 in cases of districts 'DDP below the States' SDP. But a decelerating trend has been observed in cases of districts' DDP above the States' SDP: 72.50%, 60.82% and 54.26%. Thus we see that income disparity is very much high in the districts having below the state level income compared to all the districts and the districts having above the state level income in 2001-02. These districts are: Birbhum, Bankura, 24-Parganas (N), 24-Parganas (S), Murshidabad, Uttar Dinajpur, Dakshin Dinajpur, Malda, Jalpaiguri, Coochbihar and Purulia. Also, the disparity is high among the developed districts namely Burdwan, Howrah, Hooghly, Kolkata, Nadia and Darjeeling whose per capita income is above the states' per capita income. This is the analysis of inter-regional per capita income disparity of the districts below the state level income and above the state level one.

We have also computed the measure of income disparity among the districts of West Bengal during 1980/81-2001/02. Estimates reveal that the per capita income disparity has reduced from 36.84% in 1980-81 to 21.77% in 1990-91 and then significantly widened to 38.05% in 2001-02, which is higher than that in 1980-81. Thus there is a tendency of divergent of per capita income disparity among the districts of West Bengal during the period under study.

III. PER CAPITA INCOME GROWTH

To underground regional disparity in West Bengal we need to analyse per capita DDP growth. We have estimated the trend growth rate of per capita DDP during 1980/81-2001/02. Here we have taken two sub-periods: 1980/81-1990/91 and 1991/92-2001/02. The growth rates of per capita DDP for 18 districts along with West Bengal's per capita SDP are presented in Table 4. These growth rates are statistically significant in most of the cases. Estimates reveal that the growth rate of per capita SDP/DDP has varied in West Bengal and across the districts over time. The economy of West Bengal as a whole has grown at the rate of 3.69% during 1980/81-2001/02 while it has increased its per capita SDP growth tremendously from 2.35% in the 1980s to 5.30% in the 1990s. District-wise analysis reveals:

(i) In the 1980s, Kolkata has recorded the lowest per capita DDP growth (0.48%) while Uttar Dinajpur the highest rate of growth (7.04%). That is to say, the income growth disparity range has widened from 0.48% in Kolkata to 7.04% in Uttar Dinajpur.

(ii) In the 1990s, Purulia has recorded the lower growth rate (3.72%) and Kolkata the highest one (8.18%).

(iii) During the entire period the lowest rank is achieved by Howrah (2.65%) while the highest one by Medinpur (6.95%).

(iv) Per capita growth rate of DDP has improved in all the districts excepting Bankura, Medinpur, Uttar Dinajpur and Jalpaiguri in the 1990s as compared to the 1980s. This indicates an improvement of standard of living of the people of these districts. Specially, we may mention that the standard of living has improved faster in the districts of Burdwan, Howrah, Hooghly and Kolkata where developmental activities have been generated significantly in the 1990s.

Regional Income Growth Divergence

So far we have discussed the per capita DDP growth by districts of West Bengal during 1980/81-2001/02. The growth rate has varied across the districts and disparity has been observed by high and low growth values.

TABLE 4

Trend Growth Rates (%) of Per Capita Income of Districts in West Bengal during 1980/81-2001/02 at Constant Prices (1993-94)

Districts	*1980/81-1990/91*	*1991/92-2001/02*	*1980/81-2001/02*
Burdwan	2.08	4.27	3.61
Birbhum	3.94	5.62	4.41
Bankura	5.76	5.52	6.21
Medinpur	6.07	4.38	6.95
Howrah	1.52	5.65	2.65
Hooghly	2.75	4.40	3.71
24-Pgs. (N)	3.00	4.85	3.21
24-Pgs. (S)	-	4.22*	4.43*
Kolkata	0.48*	8.18	5.17
Nadia	5.06	6.18	5.41
Murshidabad	4.98	5.02	6.23
U. Dinajpur	7.04	4.51	5.10
D. Dinajpur	-	6.90*	6.93*
Malda	4.53*	5.93	5.89
Jalpaiguri	4.80*	4.22	5.50*
Darjeeling	5.20*	5.64	7.25
Coochbihar	4.56*	4.54	6.78
Purulia	3.40*	3.72	4.60
West Bengal	2.35	5.30	3.69
IGDI (%)	43.18	21.49	26.36

Notes: * Not significant even at 5% level of significance.
IGDI: Income Growth Disparity Index.

Source: Same as in Table 1.

Balance growth implies that district-wise per capita DDP growth rates coincide with the overall (states') per capita SDP growth rate. Otherwise, the problem of unbalanced growth would appear: districts grow at different rates and the overall rate differs from district-wise growth rates. Such growth divergence may be examined in the present context among the districts of West Bengal. The co-efficient of variation may be used as a system index for per capita income growth disparity. The regional per capita income growth disparity index (IGDI) is defined as:

$$IGDI = \left(\frac{1}{(n-1)} \sum_{i=1}^{n} (g_i - G)^2 \right)^{1/2} / G,$$

where G: overall annual compound growth rate of per capita SDP in West Bengal,

g_i: annual compound growth rate of per capita DDP of district i in West Bengal, and

i: number of districts.

Obviously, IGDI takes the minimum value of zero when all the districts grow at the same constant rate. Any deviation from the minimum value reflects the presence of per capita DDP growth divergence among the districts in West Bengal.

Estimates (Table 4) reveal that IGDI is non-zero indicating that per capita DDP of districts have been divergent. IGDI was 43.18% in the 1980s and 21.49% in the 1990s and 26.36% during the entire period. Thus widening of the per capita DDP growth disparity among the districts has been reduced in the 1990s as compared to the 1980s.

IV. DISPARITY IN HUMAN DEVELOPMENT

Development of any economy has several indicators. These indicators are heterogeneous. The pattern of development varies from country to country, state to state within the country and district to district within the state and so on. In our interest in this paper we are to examine the district-wise disparity in human development in West Bengal by using Human Development Index (HDI) suggested by the UNDP (1990). The HDI is a good indicator of all-round development of the economy by expanding people's capabilities in terms of three indicators: life expectancy, educational attainment and a decent standard of living (i.e., adjusted GDP per capita). Thus the HDI is the simple arithmetic mean of the health index, education index and income index. The HDI value has been constructed on the basis of the values of these variables. Here we have taken into account the HDI data for different time periods: 1991, 2001 and 2004 and the HDI values are different due to using different time period data. For example, in *SIPRD Report* (2001) the HDI calculation has three dimensions:

(i) **Health Index:** Here life expectancy at birth was considered but district level data was not available. Infant mortality rate in 1991 was taken for calculation of survival index.

(ii) **Education Index:** Attendance of children of 6-14 years (1991 data) in school for school enrolment and literacy data (2001) were taken.

(iii) **District Domestic Product (DDP) Index:** Per capita district domestic product for 1995-96 was considered.

But in West Bengal Human Development Report (2004), the HDI calculation is based on:

(a) **Health Index:** Here life expectancy at birth (2001 data) was considered.

(b) **Education Index:** Here literacy rate (2001 data) and school enrolment ratio (NSSO data) were considered.

(c) **Income Index:** Per capita income (2001 data), per capita consumption expenditure (NSSO data) and population living above the poverty line (NSSO data) were considered.

On the other hand, Jana and Roy (2004) have made a paper on "Human Development Index for the Districts of West Bengal." Here the HDI calculation is based on:

(i) **Health Index:** Since district-wise life expectancy data in 1991 was not available, under-five mortality rate (1991 data) was taken as a proxy for life-expectancy at birth.

(ii) **Education Index:** Adult literacy rate of 15 years and above (1991 data) and combined enrolment ratio (percentage of students at primary, secondary and tertiary levels) (1991 data) were considered.

(iii) **Income Index:** Per capita income for the year 1990-91 at 1980-81 prices was taken.

As a result, the HDI values are different in the above two Reports: (SIPRD Report and West Bengal Human Development Report) and Jana and Roy's paper.

Estimates of the HDI of the districts in West Bengal are presented in Table 5. The estimates reveal that the HDI values are different in 1991, 2001 and 2004 across the districts in West Bengal.

TABLE 5

District-wise Human Development Index in West Bengal

Districts	1991					2001					2004				
	Health Index	Edu. Index	Income Index	HDI value	HDI Rank	Health Index	Edu. Index	Income Index	HDI value	HDI Rank	Health Index	Edu. Index	Income Index	HDI value	HDI Rank
Burdwan	0.926	0.544	0.557	0.675	3	0.528	0.665	0.585	0.593	4	0.74	0.71	0.47	0.64	5
Birbhum	0.883	0.430	0.278	0.563	11	0.157	0.361	0.317	0.278	13	0.53	0.61	0.27	0.47	14
Bankura	0.915	0.453	0.385	0.584	9	0.500	0.472	0.463	0.479	7	0.67	0.62	0.26	0.52	11
Medinpur	0.910	0.593	0.321	0.608	8	0.357	0.797	0.439	0.531	6	0.68	0.74	0.45	0.62	7
Howrah	0.929	0.611	0.449	0.663	4	0.757	0.815	0.463	0.678	3	0.77	0.75	0.53	0.68	2
Hooghly	0.936	0.596	0.506	0.679	2	0.728	0.787	0.731	0.749	2	0.77	0.67	0.46	0.63	6
24-Pgs. (N)	0.899	0.614	0.340	0.617	7	0.300	0.824	0.292	0.472	8	0.72	0.76	0.49	0.66	3
24-Pgs. (S)	0.894	0.484	0	0.459	16	0.314	0.562	0.097	0.325	12	0.71	0.68	0.40	0.60	8
Kolkata	0.957	0.734	1	0.897	1	1.000	1.000	1.000	1.000	1	0.82	0.80	0.73	0.78	1
Nadia	0.897	0.463	0.207	0.522	12	0.257	0.508	0.219	0.328	11	0.65	0.66	0.42	0.58	9
Murshidabad	0.878	0.332	0.230	0.480	14	0.300	0.149	0.243	0.231	16	0.57	0.52	0.29	0.46	15
U. Dinajpur }	0.887	0.344	0.632	0.621	6	0.128	0.016	0.000	0.048	18	0.62	0.53	0.39	0.51	13
D. Dinajpur }						0.128	0.339	0.243	0.237	15	-	-	-	-	-
Malda	0.860	0.308	0.125	0.431	17	0.028	0.042	0.097	0.056	17	0.49	0.48	0.36	0.44	17
Jalpaiguri	0.891	0.386	0.365	0.547	10	0.271	0.461	0.341	0.358	9	0.61	0.60	0.38	0.53	10
Darjeeling	0.925	0.511	0.493	0.643	5	0.571	0.696	0.439	0.569	5	0.73	0.72	0.49	0.65	4
Coochbihar	0.872	0.398	0.248	0.506	13	0.000	0.453	0.268	0.240	14	0.50	0.65	0.41	0.52	11
Purulia	0.924	0.366	0.107	0.465	15	0.614	0.248	0.146	0.336	10	0.61	0.55	0.18	0.45	16
West Bengal									0.404		0.70	0.69	0.43	0.61	
DHDI (%)	2.85	25.14	63.88	19.25		64.47	55.61	62.33	59.15		14.90	14.28	30.53	16.68	

Note: DHDI—Disparity in Human Development Index.

Sources: West Bengal Human Development Report, 2004.
In search of A District Development Index, SIPRD, 2001.
Jana & Roy (2004).

The HDI is highest in Kolkata (0.891 in 1991,1 in 2001 and 0.78 in 2004) and lowest in Malda (0.431 in 1991 and 0.44 in 2004) and in Uttar Dinajpur (0.048 in 2001). The HDI in West Bengal has increased from 0.404 in 2001 to 0.61 in 2004. The highly developed districts (based on the HDI value in 2004 above the West Bengal) are: Burdwan, Medinpur, Howrah, Hooghly, 24-Parganas (N), Kolkata and Darjeeling while the less developed districts are: Birbhum, Murshidabad, Malda and Purulia where the HDI values are less than 50. Interestingly, we note that the HDI value is higher in almost all the districts in 1991 compared to the values in 2001 and 2004. This is due to the fact that in 1991 the health index value is significantly higher than education and income indices. However, the HDI rank of the districts are different in the years of 1991, 2001 and 2004 except in Kolkata and Malda. The HDI value has significantly improved in the districts of Birbhum, 24-Parganas (N), 24-Parganas (S), Nadia, Murshidabad, Uttar Dinajpur, Malda and Coochbihar during 2001-04. This indicates an improved well-being of people of these districts.

From the above analysis we observe that there exists disparity in HDI and its components among the districts of West Bengal during 1991-2004. We have computed the value of disparity in HDI (DHDI). Estimates reveal that the DHDI has significantly widened from 19.25% in 1991 to 59.15% in 2001 and then reduced to 16.68% in 2004. Thus a high degree of disparity in HDI among the districts of West Bengal has happened in 2001 as compared to 1991 and 2004. This is due to the fact that in 2001 these exists a high disparity in the components of HDI: health index, education index and income index among the districts of West Bengal. Regional disparity among the districts is very much low in 2004 in all the components of the HDI. This reveals that there is a tendency to get better standard of living of the people of the districts in respects of health, education and per capita income.

V. RELATIONSHIP BETWEEN PER CAPITA INCOME AND HUMAN DEVELOPMENT INDEX

We have already said, per capita income is the indicator of economic development while human development index the human development in respects of education, health and a decent standard of living. It is expected that a high level of per capita income may yield a high level of human development if income is properly used for productive sectors in the economy. But this is not always true. Here we have hypothesed that human development directly affects per capita income of the district: higher (lower) the level of human development, higher (lower) the income of the district. Per capita income (PI) of the districts are regressed on the HDI of the districts:

Log PI = Log a + b Log HDI

The estimated regression equations are the following:

(a) 1991 : Log PI = 9.131 + 0.689* HDI, $R^2 = 0.37$
(67.893) (2.967)

(b) 2001 : Log PI = 9.267 + 0.062 HDI, $R^2 = 0.04$
(86.416) (0.832)

(c) 2004 : Log PI = 9.818 + 1.089* HDI, $R^2 = 0.54$
(63.658) (4.184)

Note: Figs. in ( ) are t-values, * significant at 1% level of significance.

Estimates reveal that the HDI has turned out positive and statistically significant in influencing the per capita income of the district of West Bengal. This shows that there is a strong positive relationship between HDI and per capita income of the districts in West Bengal, which is the indication of the policies undertaken by the Government towards better standard of living of the people in terms of both economic and human developments.

VI. CONCLUDING REMARKS

Regional disparities in per capita income are observed in West Bengal during 1980/81-2001/02. Sectoral distribution of SDP in West Bengal has changed over time: tertiary sector is the prime one during 1980/81-2003/04 excepting 1985/86-1987/88. This is also true in almost all the districts (16) excepting Dakshin Dinajpur and Malda.

Disparity in per capita income exists among the districts of West Bengal during the period under study. Among the districts, Nadia and Darjeeling have relatively improved their position. The extent of per capita income disparity is very much high in the districts whose income below the state income compared to the all districts and the districts whose income above the state level. These districts are Birbhum, Bankura, 24-Parganas (N), 24-Parganas (S), Murshidabad, Uttar Dinajpur, Dakshin Dinajpur, Malda, Jalpaiguri, Coochbihar and Purulia. Also, the income disparity is high among the developed districts namely Burdwan, Howrah, Hooghly, Kolkata, Nadia and Darjeeling.

Per capita SDP in West Bengal has grown at the rate of 3.69% during 1980/81-2001/02. But its growth rate has significantly increased from 2.35% in the 1980s to 5.30% in the 1990s. Per capita DDP growth has varied across the districts over time. It has improved in all the districts of West Bengal excepting Bankura, Medinpur, Uttar Dinajpur and Jalpaiguri in the 1990s as compared to the 1980s. Per capita DDP growths have been divergent. But the divergency among the districts has been reduced in the 1990s as compared to the 1980s.

Development pattern of the districts of West Bengal may be examined in respect of either economic development or human development or both. Human Development Index (HDI) is a good measure of all-round development of the districts by expanding people's capabilities in respects of three indicators: life expectancy, educational attainment and a decent standard of living. The HDI is highest in Kolkata and lowest in Malda in 1991 and 2004. Burdwan, Medinpur, Howrah, Hooghly, 24-Parganas (N), Kolkata and Darjeeling are the developed districts while the less developed districts are: Birbhum, Murshidabad, Malda and Purulia. Thus disparity in HDI is observed among the districts of West Bengal during 1991-2004. Also, there is a strong positive relationship between HDI and per capita income of the districts in West Bengal, which is the indication of the policies undertaken by the Government of West Bengal towards better standard of living of the people in terms of both economic and human developments. The Govt. of West Bengal should take some special measures for the less developed districts so as to improve better quality of life through the spread of primary education, health facilities and creation of job opportunities in the remote areas of these districts. As a result, the regional disparity may be reduced in West Bengal.

References

Bhattacharya, B.B. and Saktivel, S. (2005), "Growing Apart Growth, Employment and Wage Inequality in the 1980s and 1990s", presented at the National Seminar on "Accelerated Economic Growth and Regional Balance", organized by IEA, ISID and IHD held at New Delhi during Sept. 16-18, 2005.

Chatterjee, Biswajit and Ghosh, Dilip Kumar (2001), *"In Search of a District Development Index"*, State Institute of Panchayats & Rural Development, West Bengal, 2001.

Chatterjee, Biswajit (2005), "Growth, Poverty and Human Deprivations in West Bengal—An Analysis of Regional Variations" presented at the National Seminar on "Accelerated Economic Growth and Regional Balance" organized by IEA, ISID and IHD held at New Delhi during Sept. 16-18, 2005.

Das, T.K. (1998), "Conveyance and Catch-up: An Empirical Analysis with Fourteen Major States in India", mimeographed, Deptt. of Economics, Utkal University, Bhubaneswar, Mimeo.

Dholakia, R.H. (2003), "Regional Disparity in Economic and Human Development in India", *EPW*, 37, 39, 4166-72.

Economic Review, Govt. of West Bengal, various issues.

Human Development Report (UNDP): 1990, 1994, 1996, 2001.

Jana, Siali and Roy, Mou (2004), "Human Development Index for the Districts of West Bengal", *Artha Beekshan*, Vol. 13, No. 1, 2004.

Mathur, Ashok (2005), "Spatial Income Inequality and Economic Development presented at the National Seminar on "Accelerated Economic Growth and Regional Balance" held at New Delhi during Sept. 16-18, 2005.

National Human Development Report (2002), Planning Commission, Govt. of India, 2002.

Pal, P.K. (2001), "Development Pattern in India: An Inter-State Analysis", *Occasional Papers*, Department of Economics, Rabindra Bharati University, Vol. IX, March, 2001.

Pal, P.K. (2004), "Development Pattern in West Bengal since 1980's" presented the National Seminar on "25 years of West Bengal Economy" organized by Bengal Economic Association at Xevier's College held on 26th September, 2004.

Rangarajan, C. (2005), "Fiscal Transfers", inaugural address presented at the National Seminar on "Accelerated Economic Growth and Regional Balance", held at New Delhi on Sept. 16, 2005.

Statistical Abstract, Government of West Bengal, Various Issues.

West Bengal Human Development Report (2004), Development & Planning Deptt., Govt. of West Bengal, 2004.

12

Development Paradigm of Health-Education Nexus—An Examination of Regional Disparities

Dhiraj Kumar Bandyopadhyay

This study is an attempt to study of distributive strategies of public health and educational facilities in the districts of West Bengal in terms of physical resources and output in terms of pattern of utilization in relation to curative aspect as well as preventive care in health sector and enrolment and attendance of schools in school education sector. Here we are essentially concerned with school education and not covered higher education, although obviously of great significance of the same. There has been considerable interest the world over on issues pertaining to health and school education. For human welfare, freedom (which derived from entitlement, capabilities and social opportunities) from ignorance, diseases and fear is as important as freedom from want. We know that education, health care, water and sanitation services and environment that promote health and social safety nets which are required to provide such freedom, can not be obtained easily by all through private action and, therefore, there is need for public action. These facilities are collectively termed as 'Social infrastructure' which are critical for planned economic development. In a sense of enhancement off 'Capability', illiteracy is a prison of poverty and education frees one from that prison. Again the broader and more foundational views of poverty has to be kept in mind while concentrating on the deprivation of such basic capabilities as the freedom to lead normal spans of life, say, undiminished by premature mortality; or the freedom to read or write, say, without being constrained by illiteracy. So, education and health can be seen to be valuable to the freedom of person in many ways. The importance of health and educational facilities in particular and promoting social opportunities in general have long been advocated with practical evidence by several eminent economists and social scientists like Amartya Sen, Amiya Kr. Bagchi, Jean Dreze, Pranab Bardhan, Satish B. Agnihotri, R.K. Sen and many others. Amartya Sen and Jean Dreze's (2002) lucid and pragmatic discussion on 'India—Development and Participation' has placed development theory a new height in the necessity of social opportunity like health and education sector facilities.

The structure of our study is as follows:

> Section-II deals with the methodology adopted. Section-III discusses the distribution, pattern of utilization and efficiency thereon in public health facilities. Section-IV examines the nature of distribution of school education facilities in West Bengal. Section-V explores some social indicators on health and school education spheres in order to capture the achievement of facilities. Section-VI concludes with remarks on some policy prescriptions.

I. INTRODUCTION: METHODOLOGY

It is to be noted that the levels of urbanization and industrialization are taken as two major indicators for ranking the districts of West Bengal in terms of development and divided all districts into two groups. The districts have been classified as more urbanized and less-urbanized districts as cutoff point of 28.03% of state level of urbanization. So, more-urbanized districts are: Kolkata, Howrah, North 24-Parganas, Burdwan, Hooghly and Darjeeling. Similarly, the districts have been classified as more industrialized districts as cutoff 17.14% of state level of proportion of workers working registered manufacturing industry. So again, more-industrialized districts are: Howrah, North 24-Parganas, Burdwan and Hooghly with the exception of Kolkata and Darjeeling. Here, we like to include Kolkata as developed group as its share of services sector is highest and if we take into consideration of plantation industry then Darjeeling could be treated as developed district, besides its higher level of urbanization.

Now, common set of districts of developed group are: Kolkata, Howrah, North 24-Parganas, Burdwan, Hooghly and Dajeeling.

Now by comparing the mean values of the groups, 1 and 2, one more developed (Group-1) and the other less developed (Group-2) for a particular variable, the idea of distribution of resources is obtained. The significance of difference in the average values between two groups is found by the 't'-test; the difference is taken as statistically significant when value of t-test is less than the critical value of t (in two tail test) at 95% confidence intervals, as we have assumed unequal varience of two groups of districts. The intra-group disparity in distribution is obtained from the coefficient of variation (CV) for each group and has been indicated as CV_1 and CV_2. Similarly, means and standard deviation for the two groups have been denoted by $mean_1$, $mean_2$, sd_1 and sd_2 respectively. We have avoided large data base and like to present only calculated tables from different data sources.

II. PUBLIC HEALTH FACILITIES (BOTH CURATIVE AND PREVENTIVE CARE)

Distribution

In this section, the focus has been on the trend of distribution of public health in the 19 districts of West Bengal, from 1981 to 2001, with more emphasis on 1990s. The main idea is to examine whether the distribution is biased against the less-developed regions and whether there exist a clear trend in the pattern of distribution over the years. The intra-group differences in the provision of the public health services have also been observed. In West Bengal, the Government of West Bengal has been continuing its efforts to strength and upgrade the curative health services on the one hand and pursuing the expansion of preventive health care measures on the other side. We know that there exist a network of public health care (PHC) system both in the urban and rural areas of the state. At present on an average, in PHC there are 6 beds, in BPHC 15 beds and in a rural hospital 40 beds. Taking stock of the total beds in hospitals of the state government health system, district-wise numbers are taken for the year 1981, 1991 and 2001. Then taking into consideration the total population of the State as in 1991 census and 2001 census, availability of beds per 10,000 population is calculated. The average availability in 2001 at the state level is found to 6.5. The availability of per doctor population has also been calculated only in 2001 as 1991 data were not available.

It is important to be noted that there are as many as 13 districts out of 19 districts in West Bengal (2001; in 1991 it was 18) in the year of 2001, where per 10 thousand availability of bed is lower than the state average, only in Kolkata [where there are 4 Medial Colleges and 23 State General Hospital (S.G.H.)] and in Darjeeling, situation is somewhat better.

So when districts are classified, the following results emerge:

(1) It has been observed that if we include S.G.H. and Medical College and Hospitals the number of doctors increases marginally during 1981 to 1991 and from 1991 to 2001 for Group-1 and Group-2 declines. But if we exclude S.G.H. and Medical College and Hospitals then Group-2 dominates over Group-1 upto 1991, although during 1991-2001 the space was slow. If rural and urban areas are merged together then the desired norm of population served per doctor recommended by Mudaliar Committee is well satisfied by the State (3500 population per doctor). But if rural and urban areas are considered separately then for the rural areas this norm is not satisfied.

(2) Number of Health Centers grow more in Group-2 than in Group-1. The difference between the two statistically significant.

(3) In case of Nurses and Health Associates the same pattern follows as in "(2)".

(4) Number of Clinics and Welfare Centres are statically significant for the two Groups.

(5) Average number of dispensaries per 10,000 population for both the groups fell over the years. Now, taking stock of the total beds in hospitals of State Government Health System, district-wise numbers are compared.

(6) Availability of beds per 10,000 population increase for

both the groups over the years though the increase is more substantial in Group-1, if we include S.G.H. and Medical College and Hospitals and include Kolkata in Group-1.

(7) The pressure on District General Hospitals and State Medical Colleges are higher in both the Groups and even in all urban areas.

On the whole, our observation on the availability of health institutions, number of beds and doctors have shown that variation between two groups are statistically significant in 1981, 1991 and 2001 [($Mean_1 > Mean_2$; t-values are significant as it is less than the critical values of all variables), Calculated t-values and other statistical results are given in Appendix Table 1 to 4].

What is important to note that in all the districts of West Bengal there is a variation of availability of health facilities at the sub-divisional level, i.e. even in a particular districts there is a variation of availability of health facilities, irrespective of whether the district belongs to developed or less developed. So, there is some sort of imbalances in health facilities in itself of all the districts in West Bengal.

Curative Health Care

Now, we like to deal, at first, with the utilization of the curative aspects of the general health care system in West Bengal, from 42nd and 52nd NSS survey, by citing information side by side to India as a whole and other states, if required so. Again, to measure extent of utilization of health services we require the information on prevalence of morbidity.

In rural West Bengal, the number of persons suffering from an acute ailment is 47 per 1000, out of that for male it is 44 and for female it is 49. The share of highest suffering is at the age group of 60 and above and female suffered more for all age group and old age group. In case of chronic suffering the figure is 19 per thousand persons, out of which the share of male is 17 and female is 21 and in this case by age specific group 60 and above male share dominate over female (male-111; female-76). So, in rural West Bengal prevalence of an acute and chronic ailment witnessed a perceptible gender difference. Again, let us take up the case of urban West Bengal, where the morbidity rate for an acute ailment of all persons is 49, out of which for male is 47 per thousand and for female is 50 and for chronic ailment the rate for male 14 per thousand and for female the rate is 18 per thousand and for all it is 16. For any type of ailment rate in urban West Bengal the share of female is 68 per thousand and for male the rate is 61 (for all persons the rate is 65). Here again, the morbidity rate of female is more than male.

In each of the surveys, the percentage of ailing persons treated was found to be higher in urban areas of West Bengal (as well as in India as a whole) than in rural areas. The reported rates of treatment of the sick do not indicate any perceptible gender bias in either of the surveys. Moreover, the results of the two rounds do not reveal any perceptible change over time in the percentage of ailing persons treated in West Bengal (period between 1986-87 to 1995-96). We came to know that across majority of the states in India, over 70 percent of the population is utilizing the services of a private practitioner in case of non-hospitalized services and West Bengal is not exception to that. But, in case of in-patient more than 70 per cent of hospitalized cases in rural areas were in public institutions in West Bengal. Therefore, what we need to interpret utilization patterns in relation to availability, accessibility, quality, cost and nature of ailment. These sort of variables related to health issues are crucial in determining choice and utilization of services.

Again, it is interesting to note that over 50 per cent of hospitalized cases get treated in public hospitals in West Bengal. What is more, if we examine the share of hospitalized cases in the public sector, it is clear that the share of the bottom 20 per cent is greater in West Bengal. Besides this, what is important to note that in West Bengal the share of the top 20 per cent utilizing public hospitals is significant. In West Bengal more than 70 per cent of the upper income groups use public hospitals. So, what emerges utterly from the data of 42nd round of NSS is the dependence of both top and bottom 20 per cent on public hospitals in West Bengal.

From NSS 52nd round what we have observed that in rural and urban areas of all the major states, except for rural Assam and rural Orissa, the private sector is the main provider of non-hospitalized treatment of illness.

We have covered the variables like indoor, outdoor treatment of patients in public hospitals. These figures show the pattern of utilization of public health facilities at the district level of West Bengal, which help us to estimate that about 70% of rural population, a good number of rural middle income group and urban middle and upper income group, are using hospitalized treatment from the same source. So, it is clear that in rural West Bengal 82% of hospitalized treatment provided by Government sources and in urban areas 72% of hospitalized treatment provided by Government sources.

In West Bengal expenditure per treated ailment for non-hospitalized treatment is Rs. 115 (average of rural-urban combine) from public institutions and Rs. 134 from private institutions. (Table 4.19, p. 33, 52nd round of NSS). So, from Government source medical expenditure per treated ailment for non-hospitalization is much lower than private source and are much lower than all India level or comparable to many other states in India. Again in case of hospitalization treatment, coverage total expenditure per hospitalization by Government source is much lower than private sources and could be comparable to other states and India as a whole. So, the state of West Bengal has been catering hospitalized treatment to the majority of the people than the private sectors and cost is lower than the private sectors.

In West Bengal, Health and Family Welfare Department develops Health Management Information System (HMIS) for grading of hospitals in the state sector and measuring their efficiency on the basis of six indicators. The indicators are listed as follows:

(i) Bed turn over rate per month

$$= \frac{\text{Total number of discharges (including deaths) during the month}}{\text{No. of beds}}$$

(ii) Bed occupancy rate

$$= \frac{\text{Total patient days during the month}}{\text{No. of beds} \times \text{No. of days in the month}}$$

Where total patient days is calculated by adding the number of patients remaining at the end of each day of the month.

(iii) Out patient per bed day

$$= \frac{\text{Total No. of outpatients}}{\text{No. of beds} \times \text{No. of days in the month}}$$

(iv) Percentage of major surgeries to total admissions

$$= \frac{\text{No. major surgeries performed}}{\text{No. of admissions}} \times 100$$

(v) Percentage of lab tests to total admissions

$$= \frac{\text{Total No. of laboratory tests done}}{\text{Total No. of IPD (in patient days)}} \times 100$$

(vi) Percentage of imaging to total admissions

$$= \frac{\text{Total No. of X-rays etc. done}}{\text{Total No. of IPD (in patient days) and OPD attendance}} \times 100$$

So, on the basis of these six performance indicators, Department of Health and Family Welfare develops scores for every district hospitals, sub-divisional and stage general hospitals of the districts with reference to the year 2001. To get the district score, we have calculated average of district hospitals score and DD/SG hospitals score (Appendix Table 5). Here, rural hospitals can not be included because the scores of performance indicators for the year 2001 are not available. So, the districts which show lower level of efficiency in relation to utilization of curative health care services are South 24-Parganas, Murshidabad, Uttar Dinajpur, Dakshin Dinajpur, Malda, Jalpaiguri, Darjeeling and Purulia.

Preventive Health Care

Now, we like to examine the pattern of utilization of preventive health care facilities in West Bengal with reference to other major states of India. The proportion of children of 0-4 years of age receiving the vaccine were taken as the indicators. In the case of DPT and OPV, where the dosage consists of 3 doses in the first and a booster dose in the second year, the proportion of children of ages 3 and 4 years who have received all the doses has been taken as the indicator. The place of West Bengal in BCG is 11, measles is 11; in pediatric care is 9 and in supplementary food to the first year is 2. The indicators for maternal health care are: Proportion of women registered for pre-natal care per 1000 pregnant women, proportion of pregnant women who had received at least two doses of tetanus toxic, proportion of pregnant women who had received IFA tablets, proportion of women who had delivered in health institutions and proportion of mothers registered for post-natal care. The place of West Bengal in registered pregnant mother is 8, in recipient of that is 4 (two doses of TT) and IFA tablets is 8, in institutional delivery it is 7, in post-netal core it's rank is 12.

Extent of Utilization of Family Welfare Programme and Maternal Health Care

We have calculated the couple protection rate (CPR) which is simply the ratio of total current contraceptive user and number of eligible couples multiplied by 100. Data on contraception use as provided in "Health on the March" shows that in West Bengal, sterilization is the most commonly used method. District-wise couple protection rate for three years from 1998-99 to 2000-01 are calculated. The marks of the districts are calculated for the sake of organization is on the basis of 2000-01 data. So, the districts which show lower level of CPR are South 24-Parganas, Murshidabad, Uttar Dinajpur, Dakshin Dinajpur, Malda, Jalpaiguri, Darjeeling and Purulia (Appendix Table 5).

Regarding sterilization method adopted, female sterilization is common. The year-wise achievement of the State as a whole corroborates this fact. However, male sterilization was very much common in 10-20 years back.

Here, one important point is to be noted that the spread of literacy, formal and informal particularly among the females, has considerable influence on the progress of family welfare programmes in the State. The ranks of the districts on the basis of CPR (2000-01) and female literacy rate (2001) have been calculated on these two indicators and the rank correlation coefficient is found to be 0.77, which means that, they are highly correlated (Appendix Table 5).

Antenatal care, safe deliveries and post-partum monitoring are the main factors in ensuring safe motherhood. We have observed District-wise data under RCH programme which are available in respect of antenatal check up and institutional deliveries during the years 1999-2000, 2000-01 and 2001-02. With these two data set, safe motherhood index (SMI) is calculated for each district for three respective years mentioned above. Here, SMI is simple average of the proportion of pregnant mothers receiving ante-natal check up (3 check ups) and the proportion of institutional deliveries. These two proportions are highly correlated (Krishnaji, 2002). Districts which show poor SMI are South 24-Parganas, Murshidabad, Uttar Dinajpur, Dakshin Dinajpur, Malda, Jalpaiguri (Appendix Table 5).

Extent of Utilization of Child Health Care

Let us examine the extent of utilization of child immunization programme in West Bengal. Achievement of UIP at the districts level in West Bengal has been computed from Health of March, 2001-02. There is a variation among the districts in relation to utilization of UIP but as a whole performances of the districts are satisfactory.

III. NATURE OF DISTRIBUTION OF SCHOOL EDUCATION FACILITIES IN WEST BENGAL

Distribution

In this section, we like to highlight on the nature and trend of distribution of school education facilities and utilization thereon in the 19 districts of West Bengal, from 1991 to 2001. The intention here is also to examine whether the distribution is biased against the less-developed regions and whether there exist clear trend in the pattern of distribution over the years. The infra-group differences in the provision of the school educational services have also been observed.

Now, the enrolment of children indicates the current spread of education, in our study, gross enrolment ratios for primary, secondary and higher secondary stage are calculated for all districts during the period 1991 and 2001 separately. In order to calculate for 2001 we have to estimate it indirectly as age-wise district level data in 2001 census still yet to be published. So, for the year 2001, the estimates of population at different age groups are calculated on the basis of total population estimates done by Bureau and Share of each schooling age group population as in 1991 census. The percentage of enrolment of eligible age group in primary, secondary, and higher secondary education for the year 1991 and 2001 are given in Tables 24 and 25. From these two tables it has been observed that the enrolment of eligible age group ratio declines in the later stage in comparison to the primary stage for both the years, 1990/1 and 2000/1. This phenomenon is due to lower enrolment in higher classes or high dropout rates. The proposition of the enrolment of eligible age group also falls from that in secondary education. Here, it is to be noted that the lower enrolment and high dropout are obviously stimulated the enrolment ratio but it is also fact due to large number of students of other than age group 6 to 10 years in primary and at the same time there being a greater proportion of students of the specified age group in secondary and higher secondary stage. This view can be substantiated the argument put forwarded by National Human Development Report—2001 and Human Development Report (West Bengal)—2004, Government of West Bengal—as saying that the proportion of students starting early or late schooling as per the prevalent school enrolment norms is considerably large in the developing countries in general and India in particular (in case of West Bengal also).

Our next issue in this section is student-teacher ratio. It is important to note that this ratio has a close bearing on quality of education as well as on retention of enrolled children in schools. In West Bengal, during the period 1995/6 to 2000/1, in all three stages of school education there is an increasing trend of student-teacher ratio which means recruitment of teachers remain stagnant while flow of students increases. In Appendix Tables 7 and 8 we have calculated mean, standard deviation and t-distribution district-wise student-teacher ratio at primary, secondary and higher secondary level during the year 1990/1 and 2000/1 were presented.

From district-wise two tables (1990/1 and 2000/1) it can be seen that except in 3 districts (Kolkata, Bankura and Darjeeling), no districts in West Bengal pupil-teacher ratio is 40:1, although Report on Education Commission (1991) claimed that student-teacher ratio in primary school is 40:1. Now, the government intention is to bring it down further to 30:1. But, if this ratio is to maintain then state government will have to recruit more or less double the existing teachers in 2000/1 (present amount is 1,56,713).

Our next course of discussion is availability and access to primary education in terms of average number of students enrolled (6 to 10 years) per school (student/institution ratio. Availability and access to primary education in the state can also be captured through school density in terms of number of schools per 1000 sq. kms. and per 1 lakh children of eligible age group (6-10 years). Besides this, average catchments area per school (in sq. kms and average number of children enrolled per school are also calculated for the period 1995/6 to 2000/1 for showing the access to schooling. We know that the average area per school gives some idea regarding the efficient coverage in terms of distance. The computational results are as follows:

Availability and Access to Primary Schooling in West Bengal

Year	*School density*		*Catchment area*	
	Per 1000 sq. km.	Per 1 lakh children	Area in sq. km.	No. of children
2000/1	558	445	1.793	170

Source: DSHB, Govt. of West Bengal.

From our above calculated table it has been observed that availability per 1000 sq. km. remaining constant for a period of 4 years from 1995/6 to 1998/9 and after that it increases with a smaller margin. So, it indicates that access to schooling is not improving very much in the state. It is to be noted that due to regular increase in eligible children, availability of primary schools is declining. This sort of issue requires direct government intervention.

Now, as in previous case of health facilities, by comparing the mean values of the two groups, 1 and 2, one more developed and the other less developed for a particular variable (say, either student-teacher ratio or student-institution ratio), the idea of distribution of resources is obtained. The significance of difference in the average values between two groups is found by 't' test; the difference is taken as statistically significant when the value of 't' is greater than the relevant expected value found in t-table for a given number of observations. The intra-group disparity is distribution is obtained from the variance for each group and has been indicated as v_1 and v_2. Similarly, means and standard deviations for the two groups have been denoted by $mean_1$ and

$mean_2$, sd_1 and sd_2 respectively. Now, districts are classified as more-developed and less-developed, the following results emerge:

(i) In 1990/1 (Appendix Tables 7 and 8) (i) $Mean_1$ (i.e. developed districts) of variables like student-institution ratio, student-teacher ratio and enrolment of eligible age group at primary level are 164.62, 45.18 and 86.21 respectively. On the other hand, for the less developed districts $Mean_2$ are 145.07, 44.43 and 75.23 respectively.

(ii) The $variance_1$ of developed districts for the above mentioned three variables are 1570.14, 36.47 and 195.52 respectively at the primary level. On the other hand, for less-developed districts $variance_2$ are 1451.16, 88.94 and 259.24 respectively.

(iii) 't' values for the variables student-institution ratio, student-teacher ratio and enrolment of eligible age group are 0.91, 0.16 and 1.31, which are less than two-tailed respective critical values. So, usually differences of these variables of two groups districts are not significant at primary level.

(iv) At the secondary level, in group-1, the $mean_1$ values of student-institution, student-teacher ratio and eligible age group are 455.62, 38.66 and 44.85, on the other hand for less-developed these are 393.07, 36.75 and 36.16 respectively.

(v) At the secondary level, the values of $variance_1$ of developed districts are 14673.68, 28.33 and 100.05 for the above mentioned three variables and for the less-developed districts $variance_2$ are 7912.13, 61.19 and 122.70 respectively.

(vi) At the secondary level also t-values for the respective variables are less than the two-tailed critical values. So differences of variables for the two groups are not very significant.

(vii) At the higher secondary level, the $mean_1$ values of developed districts of the variables student-institution ratio, student-teacher ratio and enrolment of eligible age group are 0.001, 34.30, 19.41 respectively. On the other hand, for the less-developed districts, the values of respective variables are 0.002, 26.63 and 11.99.

(viii) At the higher secondary level, the $variance_1$ of the above mentioned respective variables for the developed districts are 4.30, 173.34 and 13.36 respectively. On the other hand, for the less-developed districts the $variance_2$ and 3.005, 194.95 and 44.85 respectively.

(ix) The 't' values for the respective variables are –1.30, 1.00 and 2.27 and which are less that two-tailed critical values. So differences for the two groups at the higher secondary level are not very significant.

Now, we like to present the results of 2000/1 (Appendix Tables 7 and 8) and which are as follows:

(i) At the primary level, the $mean_1$, values of variables—student-institution, student-teacher and eligible age group of the developed districts are 169.75, 42.94 and 78.18 respectively. On the other hand, the $mean_2$ values of less-developed districts are 178.29, 59.67 and 81 respectively.

(ii) At the primary level, the value of $variance_1$ of the variables student-institution, student-teacher and enrolment of eligible age group of the developed districts are 622.92, 73.67 and 466.94 respectively. On the other hand, the values of such variables for the less-developed districts and 2896.34, 158.38 and 84.37 respectively.

(iii) At the secondary level, the $mean_1$ values of developed districts of the variables—student-institution, student-teacher and eligible enrolment are 603.61, 43.76 and 50.20 respectively. On the other for the less-developed districts are 574.57, 51.74 and 44.07 respectively.

(iv) At the secondary level, the variance values of developed districts of the variables mentioned above are 6758.68, 43.75 and 320.86 respectively. On the other hand, for less-developed districts the values of the $variance_2$ are 16146.95, 56.77 and 73.71 respectively.

(v) At the higher secondary level, the $mean_1$ values of the developed districts of the variables mentioned above chronologically are 435.50, 85.82 and 46.21 respectively. On the other hand, for the less developed districts these are 368.46, 46.06 and 45.30.

(vi) At higher secondary level, the values of the variance$_1$ for the developed districts of the said variables are 4211.46, 106.96 and 196.62 respectively. On the other hand, for the less-developed districts these are 8134.04, 58.89 and 88.00 respectively.

(vii) The 't' values at primary, secondary and higher secondary levels are less than two-tailed critical values of the three variables—student-institution ratio, student-teacher ratio and enrolment of eligible age group. So, the differences of such variables between the two groups of districts are not very significant. But, here it is important to note that 't' distribution gives us the gross approximation of distribution of variables for a given resources. We will have to examine further intra-group differences in order to verify whether any regional imbalances have been occurred during 1990's.

Now in order to examine intra-group differences, i.e. imbalances within the group as well as within the districts over the period 1990/1 to 2000/01 we will have to consider the values of variables (student/institution, student/teacher and enrolment of eligible age group). What we have observed that except student-teacher ratio and enrolment of eligible age group at the primary level the mean values increases for all variables for developed districts and less-developed districts at primary, secondary level and higher secondary level. It means, on an average, student-teacher ratio of developed distracts have decreased and also in the case of enrolment of eligible age group. The mean values have increased of less-developed districts, for the three variables at the required level of institutions and teachers which are in conformity with the increase of enrolment of students for primary, secondary and higher secondary level. So, there is an imbalances in less-developed districts compared to developed districts, although at the primary level the developed districts have a clear advantage in relation to availability as well as accessible of primary schools. The disparity with the group will regard to student/institution and student/teacher ratio are noticeable and can not be ignored, particularly, in less-developed group. There are wide disparities will regard to availabilities of institutions, availability of teachers (i.e. per teacher catering how much students) and enrolment of eligible age group within the less-developed group as well as within the districts at less-developed group. The districts which are affected due to imbalances-effect are south 24-Parganas, Nadia, Malḍa, Murshidabad, Uttar Dinajpur, Dakshin Dinajpur, Coochbihar, Jalpaiguri. The imbalance in a district means there is a variation of availability and accessibility of educational facilities between the sub-divisions of the district (Appendix Tables 7 and 8). These can also be seen in developed districts also where values of standard deviation of educational facilities are noticeable.

It is evident from our foregoing analysis that a significant proportion of children in the age group 6-14 year were not effectively enrolled in schools in the rural West Bengal even in 1998-99. From 2001 census data we can say that about 22% of rural boys and about 28% of rural girls are in group of never-enrolled children, which are as proxy indicator of enrolment, as these are figures of percentage of non-literate children. There are a number of reasons for the relatively low ratio of attendance at schools in West Bengal, compared to say, Kerala. Here, the most important reason relates to the sheer physical lack of schools in the vicinity. What we have been observed from our study is that lack of basic infrastructural facilities continues to be serious concern for the proper growth of primary education in West Bengal. It is not in case that there are not enough schools, even those that exists often do not have buildings to speak of, not to mention other facilities and equipment. Despite the rapid increase in the number of schools and school teachers during 1980's than 1990's, there are gaps in physical availability of schools. The number of schools with no room is depressingly high, and amounts to nearly one-fifth of all schools. It is argued that when a school does not have a building, it does not only affect the quality of the learning experience, but also affect the quantity of instruction since such schools can not function well in rainy seasons. Again, school with only one room amounted to nearly another one-fifth. This means that all the primary classes are therefore taught together in one room which is not desirable for achieving competencies in learning. What is more, in West Bengal the average number of teachers per school is 3, this is still below the number of classes. This also means that at least two classes would be taught together on average. It was estimated in 1997 (*Nagi Reddy*, 2003) that more than half of the schools had only one or two teachers, so that multi-grade simultaneous classes were the norm in these schools. In addition, there are major inadequacies with respect to the physical condition of schools and the absence of necessary toilets and drinking water facilities, basic equipments and teaching materials. NSS 52 round of attendance of School Education (July, 1995 - June 1996) confirms that state government (government and government-aided schools) is the major provider for enrolling the eligible age group in school education.

The state of West Bengal was launched a new system of alternative schooling in 1997, the Sishu Siksha Kannasuchi. The essential purpose was to provide access to basic education to the large number of children in the age group 5-9 years who are unable to get enrolled in the formal primary school because of lack of easy access, unsuitable school timings, lack of accommodation or similar problems. This programme ensured more than 11,000 Sishu Shikha Kendras, catering to 7.5 lakh students, were set-up between 1997 and 2001. What is more, the programme is under the supervision and control of the Department of Panchayats and Rural Development, this in turn means that the local panchayats have authority over the SSKs in their own villages and monitoring is done by the Village Education Committees. The SSKs do not receive any infrastructural facilities from the state government. All such facilities, even buildings, etc. are to be provided by the panchayats from own resources. The government provides the salaries of Sahayakas (must be women and normal monthly honorarium of only Rs. 1,000) and the free text books.

Public Expenditure on Education in West Bengal

We know that the state of West Bengal is directly responsible for much more of the overall educational system than in many other "advanced" states. As a consequence, education expenditure as a proportion of SDP increased from about 3% in the early 1980s to 4.8% in early 1990s, and was around 3.5% in the 1998/9. In West Bengal, more than 90% of the total public expenditure on education is spent through the Education Department. Again, per student expenditure at 1997/8 prices was about Rs. 590 in 1980/1 and increased to about Rs. 1302 by 1997/8. But, a system where large amount of money expenditure is being incurred by state government, an outcome in respect of literacy, enhancement of enrolment and achievement in public examination to be evaluated, so far as effectiveness of educational system is concerned. So, we can look upon the achievement of these variables.

IV. SOME SOCIAL INDICATORS ON HEALTH AND EDUCATION SPHERES

Infant Mortality Rate

There is an Universal concerns as that infant mortality rate (IMR) is an accepted indicator for social development. The decline in the level of infant and child mortality depends upon the performance of Safe Motherhood Index (SMI) and child immunization which also in turn depends the extent of utilization preventive maternal and child health care. Although curative aspect sets itself as a saver of last resort. It is fact that India has made considerable progress in reduction of infant mortality rate since 1950-51, but this progress has slowed down in last few years with IMR 70 per thousand live births. We have analyzed the data for West Bengal—a state that has done quite well in reducing mortality among children (both infant and under-five). It is to be noted here that the SRS estimates for rural IMR for 1999 (*SRS Bulletin*, April 2001, S.B. Agnihotri, *EPW*, September 8, 2001) put West Bengal in the second place among the 16 major states—just below Kerala. But in West Bengal there are seven districts viz., Coochbihar, Malda, Birbhum, South 24-Parganas, Uttar and Dakshin Dinajpur (jointly West Dinajpur upto 1991), Jalpaiguri and Murshidabad where IMR rates are high and these districts exhibit higher IMR in rural areas than urban areas (except Birbhum). These district have lack on many factors which we like to come one by one (Appendix Table 6):

(i) In these district there are lower level of urbanization and higher level of female illiteracy;

(ii) These district also exhibit lower value of SMI, in turn explain lower level of utilization of maternal and child health care;

(iii) Again, in majority of these districts life expectancies are also lower (except South 24-Parganas);

(iv) What is more, in these districts population growth from 1991 to 2001 were also at higher level and lower levels of public health facilities particularly in terms of number of beds per 10,000 population as well as number of public health institutions;

(v) At last, in these districts also the rate of using adequate sanitation facilities are very poor.

So, reduction of IMR in West Bengal as a whole is no doubt a gain of good score at country level but many regions and groups have been existing with unacceptably high IMR exist and the state must direct its efforts to reduce these. The bottlenecks by which seven districts have been suffering to be removed by identify pockets with high mortality levels and intensify efforts in relation to the problems identified above. The quote S.B. Agnihotri: "such an approach has considerable utility for two reasons: not only do these high IMR groups 'spoil' the average IMR figures, it is also easier to reduce IMR among these to a lower level compounded with reducing IMR in pockets where its levels are already low."

Intensity of Formal School Education

We have developed an indicator as 'Intensity of formal education' (IFE) for each district for the 2001 which is on the basis of National Human Development Report -2001. Our indicator is based on class-wise enrolment rates. What is important is that, this indicator not only values education in early years of an individual's life, but it lays importance on a structural formal system of education and, more precisely, weighs progressively the capacity of the education system to retain enrolled students over successive classes from I to XII. Here, IFE has been estimated as the weighted average of the enrolled students from classes I to XII. The result is shown below:

Measures of Intensity of Formal Education

District	*Intensity of formal education*	*Rank*
Burdwan	6.3	5
Birbhum	5.70	9
Bankura	6.03	7
Medinpur	6.24	6
Howrah	6.4	3
Hooghly	6.44	2
North 24-Parganas	6.7	1
South 24-Parganas	5.40	13
Kolkata	5.03	11

(Contd.)

District	*Intensity of formal education*	*Rank*
Nadia	6.30	4
Murshidabad	5.33	14
Uttar Dinajpur	5.03	17
Dakshin Dinajpur	5.31	15
Malda	5.6	10
Jalpaiguri	5.40	13
Darjeeling	5.8	8
Coochbihar	5.19	16
Purulia	5.51	12
West Bengal	5.90	

Source: Calculation based on educational tables of 1991 and 2001.

From the above table we see that the intensity of formal education in West Bengal is 5.90. The more urbanized and industrialized districts (Group-I) have higher ranks than the less-urbanized and industrialized district (Group-II).

Literacy

The literacy rate in West Bengal has always been higher than the all-India average. Now, what is important to note is that performance of developed districts (in terms of more urbanized and industrialized districts) in literacy rate achievement is better than less-developed districts (lower level of urbanization and industrialization). But, it is also encouraging that the largest improvements in literacy in the past decade have been in some of what were the most 'backward' districts in less-developed group, and which is especially among females.

The proportion of households without any female adult literate was substantially higher, at 51% and 31% in the rural and urban areas of West Bengal respectively. Besides this, there is a substantial rural-urban gap of literacy rate in South 24-Parganas, Nadia, Malda, Murshidabad and Jalpaiguri and Uttar Dinajpur. What is more, in these districts there is a literacy gap between male and female in urban and is more pronounced in rural areas..

Therefore, our foregoing analysis of this section suggests as well as identifies the less-urbanized and industrialized districts which have problem of social indicators like infant mortality rate, lower intensity of formal education and higher level illiteracy, particularly in rural areas and among females. The districts which have higher level of infant mortality ratios in rural areas as well as in district level and in rural females are Coochbihar, Malda, Murshidabad, Dinajpur (Uttar and Dakshin), Birbhum, South 24-Parganas and Jalpaiguri. Similarly, the districts which have lower level of intensity of formal education and lower level of literacies, particularly in rural female are—South 24-Parganas, Nadia, Malda, Murshidabad, Uttar Dinajpur and Jalpaiguri. The districts which both have serious problem in health and educational achievement are South 24-Parganas, Malda, Murshidabad, Uttar Dinajpur and Jalpaiguri. Therefore, these districts require more attention to state government for curing lack of social indicators in order to achieve balance developmental efforts.

V. CONCLUDING REMARKS

Our study highlights the fact despite being ahead of many other states on many development initiatives such as land reforms and role of panchayats in local governance, and also better performances in terms of decline in rate of population growth and positive change in sex-ratio. It is evident that behavioural response to illness is shaped by a number of factors like availability, accessibility, quality and cost of services. So, merely interpreting data on utilization patterns without relating it to the availability of services could lead to erroneous conclusions. We have observed from our study that the issues like distribution, utilization, efficiency and performance of seven districts of West Bengal mentioned above have been biased against less developed regions. There is a variation at sub-division level of more or less each districts in health facilities provided by public health system, it is also true in case of utilization of preventive care also. The rural-urban divide in healthcare infrastructure for public health system was substantial before eighties but reduced substantially due to the growth of primary health centers and sub-centres (particularly during 1981 to 1991). An urban doctor serves less people that a rural doctor serves. Similarly, an urban bed serves more people while a rural bed serves less. Urban-rural disparity in government health spending leads to rural people spend more of their income on health compared to urban people. This phenomenon is also true for India as a whole. The implication of social cost of rural areas in West Bengal as well as in India is to be taken as a serious issue in near future.

In our study, we have observed that the public sector is the major provider of curative services, particularly in hospitalized treatment. In preventive health care facilities in West Bengal the public sector is not only a major player but also proved us the fact that private sector is largely comprised of small establishments and which are mostly urban-based. So, any attempt to cut-back of public services, the private and voluntary sectors will not be able to fill the gap by keeping in mind in social costs. The preventive health care in West Bengal is heavily depended on public sector, it is in right track. The utilization and performance could be enhanced more and less-developed districts should get priority in the issues mentioned earlier.

There is the need to disaggregate the mortality rates at the district level (particularly in seven districts mentioned earlier) of West Bengal by the factors like region, location (urban/rural, block level as well as panchayat level), social groups and gender to identify pockets of higher mortality rate and less availability of curative and preventive health care services. It is important to be noted that the performance of the public health systems in rural areas is of great significance as they are available, accessible and affordable to people in areas where the private health sector is virtually non-existent (there are evident in several blocks at the district level in West Bengal and except for a few quacks). In West Bengal the Homeopath Doctors acted as a safety valve for the poor masses in both urban and rural areas.

REFERENCES

Census of India, various issues of 1981, 1991, 2001, Govt. of India, National Sample Survey (42nd round, 52nd round and 54th round) Reports.

Bureau of Health Intelligence, *Health on March*, various issues, Govt. of West Bengal.

Bureau of Applied Economics and Statistics, Govt. of West Bengal, (i) *Statistical Abstract*, 2001. (ii) *District Statistical Handbooks* (DSH), 2001.

Chatterjee, Biswajit and Ghosh, Dilip Kumar (2001), In search of District Development Index, State Institute of Panchayats & Rural Development, West Bengal.

Dreze, Jean and Sen, Amartya (1995), *India: Economic Development and Social Opportunity*, Oxford University Press.

Sen, Raj Kumar (ed.) (2004), *Social Sector Development in India*, Deep & Deep Publication Pvt Ltd., New Delhi.

Burgess, R. and Stem, N. (1991), 'Social Security in Developing Countries: What, When, Why, Who and How?' in Ahmad, E., Dreze, Jean, Hills, John and Sen, Amartya (eds), *Social Security in Developing Countries*, Clarendon Press, Oxford.

Creese, A. (1990), *User Charges for Health Care: A Review of Recent Experiences*, WHO, SHS, Paper No. 1, Geneva.

Ferranti, David (1985), 'Paying for Health Services in Developing Countries', *World Health Forum*, Vol. 6.

Government of India (1961), *Report of the Health Survey and Planning Committee*, Ministry of Health, New Delhi.

Kannan, K.P., Thankappan, K.R., Raman Kutty, V. and Arvmdan, K.P. (1992), *Health and Development in Rural Kerala*, KSSP, Thiruvananthapuram.

Nandraj, S. (1994), 'Quality of Private Health Care', *Economic and Political Weekly*, Vol. XXIX, No. 27.

Rao, Mohan (1995), 'An Investigation into the Differential Behaviour of Economic Classes in Relation to the Family Planning Programme in Mandya District, Karnataka', Ph.D. thesis, Centre of Social Medicine and Community Health, Jawaharlal Nehru University, New Delhi.

Bagchi, A.K., 'Political Economy of Under Development', Cambridge.

Basu, Ram, V., 'The Structure and Utilization of Health Services, Mohon Rao, edited, *Disinvesting in Health*.

Banerji, Debabar, *Political Economy of Public Health in India*.

Agnihotri, S.B. (1999): 'Inferring Gender Bias from Mortality Data—A Discussion Note', *Journal of Development Studies*, 35 (4), pp. 175-200.

—— (2000): *Sex Ratio Patterns in the Indian Population—A Fresh Exploration*, Sage, New Delhi.

—— (2001): Declining Infant and Child Mortality in India: How Do Girl Children Fare?' *Economic and Political Weekly*, 36(3), January 20-26, pp. 228-33.

—— Infant Mortality variations in Space and Time: An analysis of West Bengal data, *EPW*, Sept. 2001.

Kanch, J. and A.K. Sen (1983): 'Indian Women: Well Being and Survival', *Cambridge Journal of Economics*, 83(7), pp. 363-80.

Rajan, S. Irudaya and Mohanachandran (1998): 'Infant and Child Mortality Estimates: Part 1', *Economic and Political Weekly*, 35(51), December 16.

Krishnan, T.N. (1999): 'Access to Health and the Burden of Treatment in India: An Inter-State Comparison' in M. Rao (ed), *Disinvesting in Health: The World Bank's Prescriptions for Health*, Sage Publications, New Delhi, 208-32.

World Bank (2004): *Attaining the Millennium Development Goals in India: Role of Public Policy and Service Delivery*, Human Development Unit, New Delhi, World Development Report (2004).

World Bank (1993): *World Development Report, 1993: Investing in Health*, Oxford University Press, Washington, DC.

Dreze J., A. Sen (2002): *India: Development and Participation*, Oxford University Press, New Delhi.

Pratichi (India) Trust (2002): *The Delivery of Primary Education: A Study in West Bengal (The Pratichi Education Report)*, New Delhi.

Parikh, K. (2002): *Social Infrastructure—As Important As Physical Infrastructure.*

HDR (2004): Govt. of West Bengal.

APPENDIX
TABLE 1

Mean and Standard Deviation of Table 2 (in relation to Availability of Bed)

1991

District	*Availability of Bed*		*District*	*Availability of Bed*	
	X	*S.P.*		*X*	*S.D.*
Burdwan	7.11	3.41	Maldev Town	4.36	1.92
Hooghly	8.12	3.44	Murshidabad	5.67	2.39
Howrah	9.17	6.42	Jalpaiguri	5.06	0.46
North 24-Parganas	3.52	0.63	Coochbihar	4.97	3.55
Darjeeling	34.54	36.02			
Bankura	8.41	4.81			
Medinpur	4.3	2.24			
South 24-Parganas	3.63	1.77			
Birbhum	6.81	4.54			
Nodia	16.75	14.78			

X = Mean

SD = Standard Deviation.

Source: District Statistical Handbooks, Bureau of Applied Economics and Statistics, Government of West Bengal.

TABLE 2

Mean and Standard Deviation of Availability of Bed and Doctors of Table 3

2001			Avaiiablity of Doctors		Avaiiablity of Doctors		Availability Beds	
	7(X)	7(SD)	(X)	SD	(X)	SD	(X)	(SD)
Birbhum	44.33	13.31			12007.48	2164.50	7.94	4.92
Nadia	128.25	60.70			20430.81	15528.00	12.21	14.09
Malda	243.00	118.79			29280.07	7770.02	3.24	0.97
Murshidabad	48.20	12.47			27324.76	12021.71	4.61	3.04
Jalpaiguri	89.00	29.69			9942.48	1961.25	16.62	3.71
Coochbihar	15.60	3.04			14499.41	3618.72	5.97	2.86
Uttar Dinajpur	165.50	13.43			22317.43	8661.96	3.05	1.97
Dakshin Dinajpur	129.00	49.49			17661.58	4256.99	23.17	24.16
Burdwan	163.66	28.01			11714.95	7278.27	8.99	6.55
Hooghly	203.25	52.27			13262.13	3254.11	5.55	3.97
Howrah	109.50	50.20			3865.48	2509.24	31.16	25.90
North 24-Parganas	158.50	127.87			16362.32	5896.39	3.46	1.46
Darjeeling	22.00	6.48			5103.71	664.73	18.64	7.08
Purulia	65.50	50.20			11041.90	2584.96	9.09	0.56
Bankura	216.00	36.00			15348.13	7074.15	8.30	5.49
Paschim Medinpur	237.00	68.58			11707.64	2195.73	6.42	3.19
Purba Medinpur	177.50	59.07			24052.86	8504.92	3.01	0.625
South 24-Parganas	91.5	44.54			32464.64	7582.15	2.35	0.26

TABLE 3

Mean, Standard and T-Distribution of Availability of Health Facilities: 2000-01

More developed	*More developed health hospitals/ centres etc.*	*Less developed health hospitals/ centres etc.*	*More developed availability of doctors*	*Less developed availability of doctors*	*More developed availability of beds*	*Less developed availability of beds*
Mean	494.8333333	379.3846154	9972.93391	35766.70974	14.25467345	6.275943774
Standard Error	168.0875599	73.19061332	2073.752612	19214.14461	5.450521105	1.024392601
Median	506.5	270	8140.971429	14081.13636	9.754501011	5.963813613
Mode	#N/A	#N/A	#N/A	#N/A	#N/A	#N/A
Standard Deviation	411.7287538	263.8925092	4637.051809	69277.58362	13.35099554	3.69350005
Sample Variance	169520.5667	69639.25641	21502249.48	4799383592	178.2490819	13.64194262
Kurtosis	-2.85364005	0.079119931	-0.42524266	12.71220873	4.250070123	-0.53858033
Skewness	0.048218477	0.927448723	0.846345538	3.55125433	1.974245112	0.264053515
Range	909	871	11586.93673	255084.9801	37.28632773	12.67123493
Minimum	73	78	5230.944625	10246.95541	2.975265655	0.348012046
Maximum	982	949	16817.88136	265331.9355	40.26159338	13.01924698
Sum	2969	4932	49864.66955	464967.2267	85.52804072	81.58726906
Count	6	13	5	13	6	13

Note: Calculated table based on data-base of district statistical handbooks, (Bureau of Applied Economics & Statistics, W.B.), census various issues.

TABLE 4

t-Test: Two Samples Assuming Unequal Variances for Developed and Less Developed Districts

	Hospitals and centres		*Availability of doctors*		*Availability of beds*	
	Variable 1	*Variable 2*	*Variable 1*	*Variable 2*	*Variable 1*	*Variable 2*
Mean	494.8333333	379.3846154	9972.93391	35766.70974	14.25467345	6.275943774
Variance	169520.5667	69639.25641	21502249.48	4799383592	178.2490819	13.64194262
Observations	6	13	5	13	6	13
Hypothesized Mean Difference	1		1		1	
df	7		12		5	
t-Stat	0.624273326		-1.33473753		1.258347043	
P (T<=t) one-tail	0.276121204		0.103367181		0.131913362	
t Critical one-tail	1.894577508		1.782286745		2.015049176	
P (T<=t) two-tail	0.552242408		0.206734363		0.263826723	
t Critical two-tail	2.36462256		2.178812792		2.570577635	

Source: Same as Table 3.

TABLE 5

CPR and its Relation with Literacy, Efficience of Hospitals, SMI

CPR (figures in percentage)

Districts	*2001*	*Rank*	*Female literacy rate (Rank)*	*Efficiency (Hospitals) Average Score*	*SMI*
Burdwan	54.26	1	7	53.5	55.61
Birbhum	42.77	4	9	49.0	47.87
Bankura	43.75	3	14	49.5	60.49
Medinpur	37.40	9	5	52.5	38.60
Howrah	29.15	13	3	51.5	51.46
Hooghly	34.49	12	4	51.5	54.59
North 24-Parganas	24.29	15	2	51.0	40.54
South 24-Parganas	20.53	17	9	52.5	27.61
Kolkata	38.11	8	1	50.5	74.22
Nadia	36.69	11	8	52.5	57.42
Murshidabad	36.85	10	15	49.0	33.85
Uttar Dinajpur	19.30	18	17	49.5	32.05
Dakshin Dinajpur	28.50	14	11	29.0	41.90
Malda	21.24	16	16	24.0	33.83
Jalpaiguri	38.52	7	12	49.0	39.93
Darjeeling	41.59	5	6	45.5	82.99
Coochbihar	41.10	6	10	47.0	43.00
Purulia	45.12	2	18	49.0	46.71
West Bengal	35.34	—	—	51.0	46.50

Source: Health on March, 2000-01.

TABLE 6

Life Expectancy and Infant Morality Rate of the Districts in West Bengal

Districts	*Life Expectancy*	
	Male	*Female*
Darjeeling	67	71
Jalpaiguri	61	63
Coochbihar	53	57
Uttar Dinajpur	61	63
Dakshin Dinajpur		
Malda	54	55
Murshidabad	58	60
Birbhum	56	58
Bardhaman	68	71
Nadia	63	65
North 24-Pgs.	66	71
Hooghly	69	73
Bankura	62	68
Purulia	60	63
Medinpur	65	67
Howrah	70	73
Kolkata	74	75
South 24-Pgs.	65	70

District-wise Infant Mortality Rate (1991, 2001 in West Bengal)

Sl. No.	*Districts*	*1991 Infant Mortality*	*Infant Mortality Rate 2001*		*2001*
			Male	*Female*	
1.	Burdwan	61	38	40	39
2.	Birbhum	87	60	65	63
3.	Bankura	63	41	45	43
4.	Medinpur	73	47	51	49
5.	Howrah	45	22	33	28
6.	Hooghly	47	25	25	25
7.	North 24-Parganas	77	46	54	50
8.	South 24-Parganas	76	54	66	60
9.	Calcutta	28	15	18	17
10.	Nadia	80	56	57	57
11.	Murshidabad	88	61	59	60
12.	Uttar Dinajpur	89	68	59	64
13.	Dakshin Dinajpur	89			
14.	Malda	96	57	89	73
15.	Jalpaiguri	79	62	58	60
16.	Darjeeling	58	39	43	41
17.	Coochbihar	98	76	76	76
18.	Purulia	55	46	46	46

Source : Census of India, 1991, 2001, Series-20, West Bengal.
Human Development Index, 2004, Dept. of Planning & Implementation, Govt. of West Bengal.

TABLE 7

Primary

Districts	*Student/ Inst.*		*No. of teachers*	*Student/ teacher Mean*	*Student/ teacher SD*
	Mean	*S.D.*			
Kolkata			6526		
Burdwan	168.18	26.63	15027	43.71	2.27
Hooghly	154.09	20.08	10475	41.38	3.63
Howrah	159.45	9.20	6933	49.12	6.25
North 24-Parganas	199.95	41.97	12943	65.31	16.75
Darjeeling	130.40	11.32	7392	32.13	5.72
Bankura	95.02	7.76	8156	40.23	1.80
Purba Medinpur	143.64	13.73	8739	50.82	4.43
Paschim Medinpur	103.76	18.69	11527	38.27	5.06
South 24-Parganas	230.42	30.77	11398	73.49	8.70
Birbhum	149.85	28.30	7625	46.02	6.41
Nadia	213.95	30.50	7282	78.02	14.82
Malda	205.05	46.86	6294	63.46	18.52
Murshidabad	244.37	49.88	10072	72.80	17.95
Jalpaiguri	245.07	30.91	6524	79.64	10.77
Coochbihar	199.52	42.14	5651	68.07	3.10
Uttar Dinajpur	223.56	26.93	3964	90.12	36.99
Dakshin Dinajpur	166.83	26.84	4066	47.02	5.50
Parulia	105.80	0.23	6119	53.72	3.46

TABLE 7 (*Contd.*)

Secondary

Districts	*Student/ Inst.*		*No. of teachers*	*Student/ teacher Mean*	*Student/ teacher SD*
	Mean	*S.D.*			
1	*2*	*3*	*4*	*5*	*6*
Kolkata			9380		
Burdwan	657.40	71.60	6471	55.64	6.23
Hooghly	496.64	57.82	7619	47.00	2.45
Howrah	634.30	15.09	4263	55.55	7.74
North 24-Parganas	607.69	152.72	8481	54.86	19.09
Darjeeling	404.26	97.03	2478	31.64	3.20
Bankura	488.64	14.41	3892	44.68	1.02
Purba Medinpur	435.92	210.76	5619	53.68	13.00

(*Contd.*)

1	2	3	4	5	6
Pachim Medinpur	389.47	179.52	6368	40.09	18.13
South 24-Parganas	439.02	71.23	6682	38.96	2.30
Birbhum	420.90	33.82	3746	38.62	2.48
Nadia	777.12	228.88	4772	75.77	12.37
Malda	586.14	35.48	2846	58.99	2.35
Murshidabad	711.33	194.58	4165	67.41	16.62
Jalpaiguri	814.38	154.76	2658	66.44	10.97
Coochbihar	739.39	65.59	2722	81.72	11.70
Uttar Dinajpur	444.40	60.64	1267	52.67	0.17
Dakshin Dinajpur	566.41	150.81	1259	41.76	4.50
Parulia	440.53	40.45	2156	52.40	4.08

TABLE 7 (*Contd.*)

Higher Secondary

Districts	*Student/ Inst.*		*No. of teachers*	*Student/ teacher*	*Student/ teacher*
	Mean	*S.D.*		*Mean*	*SD*
Kolkata			7778		
Burdwan	1054.18	107.68	4461	46.93	7.11
Hooghly	1095.13	128.09	3179	42.48	4.05
Howrah	1016.13	127.59	2842	45.55	14.23
North 24-Parganas	1195.44	201.19	8742	50.55	12.04
Darjeeling	858.71	275.27	1148	58.29	24.28
Bankura	859.78	6.16	2083	41.66	0.30
Purba Medinpur	1068.41	133.81	3155	52.19	4.60
Pachim Medinpur	941.63	226.17	3703	43.19	4.73
South 24-Parganas	926.09	81.11	4239	40.80	1.82
Birbhum	849.70	75.63	1942	40.65	5.20
Nadia	1473.87	163.96	3421	52.16	10.74
Malda	1042.64	248.35	1478	48.84	5.34
Murshidabad	1254.34	225.51	2292	61.09	7.93
Jalpaiguri	1452.78	149.90	1605	198.15	250.30
Coochbihar	1481.10	362.94	1522	74.46	25.25
Uttar Dinajpur	1079.18	172.15	956	57.01	7.21
Dakshin Dinajpur	1094.96	162.90	828	49.36	9.73
Parulia	2253.86	1888.47	1979	44.90	9.02

Source: Same as Table 3.

TABLE 7 (*Contd.*)

	Primary: 1990/91 Developed Districts		
	Student-Inst. Ratio	*Student-Teacher Ratio*	*Enrolment Eligibility age*
Mean	164.62	45.18	86.21
Variance	1570.14	36.47	195.52
T-Stat.	0.91	0.16	1.31
t-critical one tail	1.78	1.78	1.77
t-critical two tail	2.18	2.18	2.14
P (T<=t) one tail	0.19	0.44	1.76+
P (T<=t) two tail	0.38	0.88	0.21
Mean	145.07	44.43	75.23
Variance	1451.16	88.94	259.24
	Secondary: 1990/91 Developed Districts		
Mean	455.62	38.66	44.85
Variance	14673.68	28.33	100.05
T-Stat.	1.14	0.48	1.49
t-critical one tail	1.77	1.78	1.77
t-critical two tail	2.16	2.18	2.14
P (T<=t) one tail	0.14	0.32	0.07
P (T<=t) two tail	0.27	0.64	0.157
Mean	393.07	36.75	36.16
Variance	7912.13	61.19	122.7
	Higher Secondary: 1990/91 Developed Districts		
Mean	0.001	34.3	19.41
Variance	4.297	173.34	13.36
T-Stat.	-1.3	1	2.27
t-critical one tail	1.78	1.78	1.78
t-critical two tail	2.18	2.18	2.18
P (T<=t) one tail	0.11	0.16	0.02
P (T<=t) two tail	0.22	0.33	0.04
Mean	0.002	26.63	11.9
Variance	3.005	194.95	44.85

APPENDIX TABLE 8

	Primary			*Secondary*		
	Student-Inst. Ratio Sample-19 D.f.: 17	*Student-Teacher Ratio Sample-19 D.f.: 17*	*Enrolment eligible age group Sample-19 D.f.: 17*	*Student-Inst. Ratio Sample-19 D.f.: 17*	*Student-Teacher Ratio Sample-19 D.f.: 17*	*Enrolment eligible age group Sample-19 D.f.: 17*
Developed Districts						
Mean	169.75	42.84	78.18	603.61	43.76	50.20
Variance	622.92	73.67	466.94	6758.68	43.75	320.86
T-Stat.	-0.37	-2.95	-0.42	0.51	-2.22	1.03
t-critical one-tail	1.74	1.74	1.74	1.74	1.74	1.74
t-critical two tail	2.11	2.11	2.11	2.11	2.11	2.11
P (T<=t) one-tail	0.36	0.00	0.34	0.30	0.02	0.16
P (T<=t) two tail	0.72	0.00	0.68	0.62	0.04	0.32
U-Developed Districts						
Mean	178.29	59.67	81.11	574.57	51.74	44.07
Variance	2896.34	158.38	84.37	16164.95	56.77	73.71

TABLE 8 (*Contd.*)

	Higher Secondary		
	Student-Inst. Ratio Sample-19 D.f.: 17	*Student-teacher Ratio Sample-19 D.f.: 17*	*Enrolment eligible age group Sample-19 D.f.: 17*
Developed Districts			
Mean	435.50	85.82	46.21
Variance	4211.46	10681.96	196.62
T-Stat.	1.63	1.43	0.17
t-critical one-tail	1.74	1.74	1.174
t-critical two tail	2.11	2.11	2.11
P (T<=t) one-tail	0.06	0.08	0.43
P (T<=t) two tail	0.12	0.17	0.86
U-Developed Districts			
Mean	368.46	46.06	45.30
Variance	8134.04	58.89	88.00

Source: Same as Table 3.

PART IV

INFRASTRUCTURE, URBANIZATION AND SMALL SCALE INDUSTRIES

13

Inter-district Disparity in the Growth of Urbanization

DHIRENDRA NATH KONAR

This paper has concentrated on the feature of Urbanization and inter district disparity observed in West Bengal. It is distributed over the following sections. The concept of urbanisation, trend of Urbanization in West Bengal, trend of Urbanisation in West Bengal at the district level, growth of towns in West Bengal and provisions of Urbanization in West Bengal. It has been concluded on the basis of analysis that the rate of urbanization in West Bengal has been slightly higher than that of India but there has not been proper dispersion of urbanisation in the state as it has been centered basically around Kolkata and on the districts in the neighbourhood of it. A proper dispersion of urban centres is urgently needed, otherwise Kolkata and some 20 towns of the state will have to bear the trimendous burden of growing population leading to huge damage to environment and related problems.

INTRODUCTION

One of the most significant of all post-war demographic phenomena is the rapid growth of cities in the developing countries. In 1950, 275 million people had been living in the cities of the Third World countries, which was a mere 38 percent of the 724 million total urban population. According to the estimates of the United Nations, the world's urban population has reached 1.56 billion by 1975 and more than 50 percent of these people lived in metropolitan areas of the developing countries. Another estimate made by the United Nations reveals that in 2000 over 2.12 billion or 66 percent of the urban dwellers of the world will reside in less developed regions. This is the general trend of urbanization across the world. Needless to say, India and for that matter West Bengal is no exception to this trend. In fact, West Bengal has been following the same track.

THE CONCEPT OF URBANIZATION

The term "urbanization" as used in India is quite old. It started with the setting up of Municipal Corporation of Madras in 1688. Demographically, urbanization means an increase in the proportion of urban population in the total population of a country over a period of time. However, this definition does not express the whole truth of the process of urbanization either in India or in any of the States in India.

In the census of India 2001, the definition of urban area adopted is as follows:

(a) All places with a municipality, corporation, cantonment board or notified town area committee, etc.

(b) A place satisfying the following three criteria simultaneously:

  (i) A minimum population of 5000;

  (ii) At least 75 percent of male working population engaged in non-agricultural pursuits; and

  (iii) A density of population of at least 400 per sq. km. (100 per sq. mile).

Urbanization in India has been brought into three categories, namely: (a) Towns, (b) Cities and "Urban Agglomeration" or Megacities.

Towns with population of 1,00,000 and above are called Cities.

Again, Towns with minimum population of one million have

been called Urban Agglomerations. [Series-20, West Bengal. Census of India. 2001, Final Population Totals.]

TREND OF URBANIZATION IN EAST BENGAL

Economic development is generally associated with the growth of urbanization.

Some Economists observe that the acid test of development of a country lies in the shift of population from the rural areas to the urban areas. In the following paragraph we shall demonstrate the trend of urbanization in West Bengal during the last one hundred years between 1901 and 2001. According to the census of 2001, there lived in West Bengal all population of 80176197 of which 57748946 lived in rural areas while the remaining 2242725 lived in the urban areas. It is a matter of great surprise to see that nearly 72 percent of the population of the State of West Bengal lived in the city of Kolkata and towns like Asansol, Kharagpur, Andal, Durgapur, Habra, Englishbazar, Raiganj, Nabadwip, Raniganj, Ranaghat, Krishnagar, Berhampore, Balurghat, Shiliguri, Alipurduar and some other towns. Again, according to the latest census of 2001, in West Bengal there were fifty-eight towns each having a population of at least one lakh. In 1991, the number of such town was forty-four. Besides, as per the 2001 census, in India there are thirty-five urban agglomerations having a minimum population of one million. These include our capital, Kolkata and Asansol having a population 1090171. Let us now concentrate on the trend of urbanization in West Bengal between 1901 and 2001 as revealed through Table 1.

We see from Table 1 that till 1931 the extent of urbanization was very much limited in West Bengal. Between 1901 and 1931 the percentage of people living in urban areas increased only by three, from 12.20 to 15.32. However, between 1931 and 1941 there was a quick improvement in urbanization in this state as during this inter-censual period there was more than live percentage increase in the rate of urbanization. The first post-independent census taking place in 1951 reveals that about 24 percent of total population of West Bengal lived in urban areas. This percentage improved nominally in the subsequent two censuses and became 26.47 and 27.48 respectively in the censuses of 1981 and 1991. In

TABLE 1

Percentage Distribution of Urban and Rural Population of India and West Bengal between 1901 and 2001

Census Years	*Percentage of Population in*			
	Urban India	*Urban West Bengal*	*Rural India*	*Rural West Bengal*
1901	10.73	12.20	89.27	87.80
1911	10.18	13.05	89.82	86.95
1921	11.03	14.41	88.97	85.59
1931	11.83	15.32	88.17	84.68
1941	13.65	20.41	86.35	79.59
1951	17.03	23.88	82.97	76.12
1961	17.73	24.45	82.27	75.55
1971	19.64	24.75	80.36	75.25
1981	23.04	26.47	76.97	73.53
1991	25.73	27.48	74.27	72.52
2001	27.79	28.03	72.21	71.97

Source: Census of India, 1991 and 2001.

fine, according to the census of 2001, more than 28 percentage of total population of West Bengal lived in the urban areas. It may be mentioned that the level of urban expansion in the state of West Bengal had kept well ahead of India during the first ninety years of the last century. However, the latest census data show that the two rates have almost converged.

The trend of the percentage of urban population of India and that of West Bengal will be more prominent if we minutely look at the graph of this as shown in diagram 1.

TREND OF URBANIZATOIN IN WEST BENGAL AT THE DISTRICT-LEVEL

We have seen that in West Bengal about 28 percent of total population live in the urban areas. However, the trend of urbanization in West Bengal across the districts is not at all encouraging. This phenomenon will appear in Table 2.

TABLE 2

Percentage of Urban People Living in Districts of West Bengal in 1991 and 2001 and Ranks attained by the Districts

District	*1991*		*2001*	
	% of Urban people	*Rank*	*% of Urban people*	*Rank*
Darjeeling	30.47	6	32.44	6
Jalpaiguri	16.36	8	17.74	8
Coochbihar	7.81	17	9.10	15
North Dinajpur	13.34	10	12.06	12
South Dinajpur	1335	9	13.09	10
Malda	7.07	18	7.32	18
Murshidabad	10.43	12	12.79	11
Nadia	22.63	7	21.27	7
North 24-Parganas	51.23	2	54.30	2
South 24-Parganas	13.03	11	15.77	9
Kolkata	100.00	1	100.00	1
Howrah	49.58	5	50.39	3
Hooghly	31.19	5	33.48	5
Burdwan	35.09	4	37.18	4
Birbhum	8.98	15	8.58	16
Bankura	8.29	16	7.37	17
Medinpur	9.85	13	10.49	13
Purulia	9.44	14	10.07	14
West Bengal	27.48	—	28.03	1

(Rank Correlation Coefficient: +0.98)

Source: Calculated from *Censuses of India*, 1991 and 2001.

Table 2 displays that the urban expansion in the State of West Bengal centered, as it was, on the single metropolis of Kolkata. In reality, the districts in the neighbourhood of Kolkata, namely North 24-Parganas, Howrah, Burdwan and Hooghly had seen rapid urbanization in both 1991 and 2001. In this race, the solitary exception is Darjeeling very highly attractive to the tourists all over the world. The present Table just reveals that these districts have occupied the supreme ranks in both 1991 and 2001. Besides, the Spearman's rank correlation coefficient between ranks attained by eighteen districts of the State in 1991 and 2001 has been found to be +0.98. This signifies the fact that the relative position of the

Diagram 1: Percentage of Total Population in Urban India and West Bengal

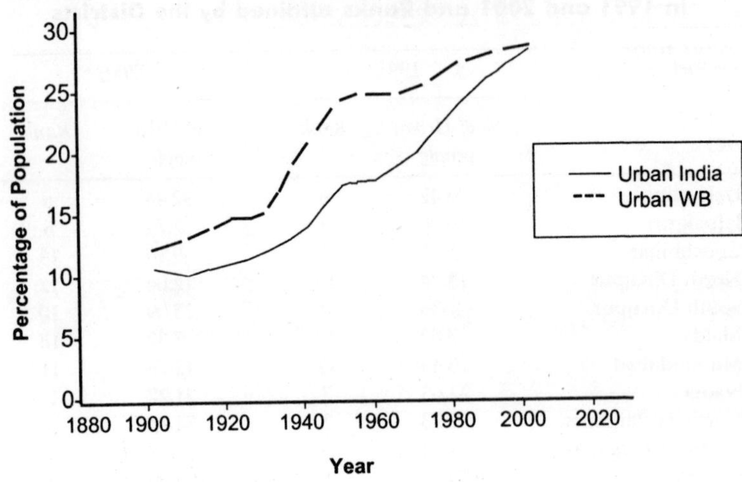

districts of the State in the field of urbanization between 1991 and 2001 has remained almost unaltered. A very surprising aspect of the district-wise spread of urbanization in West Bengal is that though the rate of urbanization in the State in 2001 was slightly higher than that in 1991, some districts, namely North and South Dinajpur, Nadia, Birbhum and Bankura had shown a relatively lower rate of urbanization in 2001 than in 1991. On the other hand, some other districts, viz. North 24-Parganas, Howrah, Burdwan and Hooghly had seen a higher rate of urbanization in 2001 than in 1991. The hilly district of the State, that is, Darjeeling, had also seen an improvement in urbanization in 2001.

The Table also discloses that in both 1991 and 2001 the rate of urbanization in as many as twelve districts has been less than the State figure, signifying that there is a disparity in the growth of urbanization in West Bengal. We now wish to discuss the growth of towns in West Bengal.

GROWTH OF TOWNS IN WEST BENGAL

The total number of towns in West Bengal has been growing at a rapid speed. Table 3 will vindicate this feature.

TABLE 3

Number of Towns in West Bengal Between 1901 and 2001

Census Years	*Number of Towns*
1901	78
1911	81
1921	89
1931	94
1941	105
1951	120
1961	184
1971	223
1981	291
1991	382
2001	375

Source: *Censuses of India,* Various Issues.

Diagram 2: No. of Towns in WB during last 100 Years

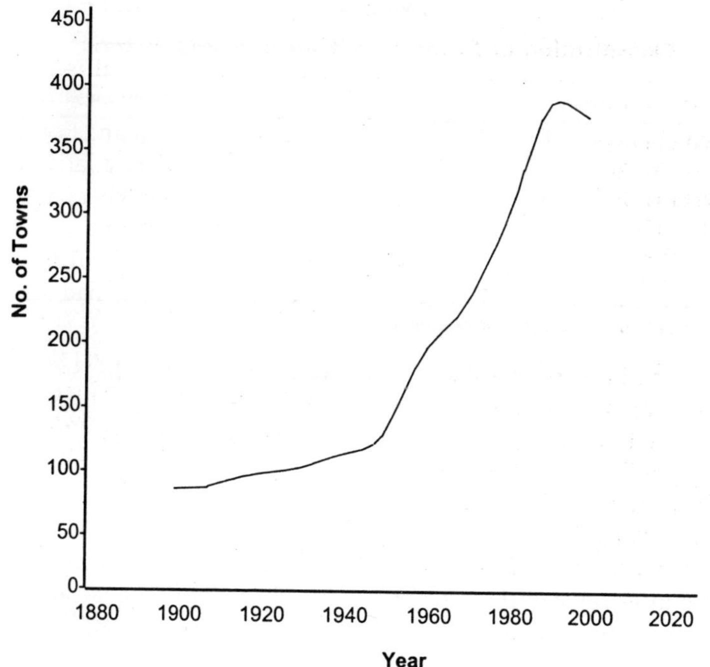

It is seen from Table 3 that between 1901 and 1951 there was a relatively slow growth in the number of towns in this State. However, this slow trend was subsequently broken and in the inter-censual decade 1951-61, there was more than fifty-three percent increase in the number of towns here. Between 1961 and 1971, 39 new towns and between 1971 and 1981, 68 such towns had been added in the map of towns in the State. The total number of towns in the State in 1991 increased to 382 and in 2001 it became 372. According to the latest available information, there are in West Bengal, 126 Municipalities.

The trend of growth of towns in West Bengal over the last one hundred years or so will be clearly visualized if we closely observe the graph of this as shown in diagram 2.

We now wish to discuss the number of different types of towns in West Bengal at the district-level.

In our censuses towns have been grouped into six classes on the basis of the number of population living in a particular town. Such classification has been shown in Table 4.

TABLE 4

Classification of Towns on the Basis of Population

Number of Population	*Nature of Towns*
100000 and more	Class-1
50000 to 99999	Class-2
20000 to 49999	Class-3
10000 to 19999	Class-4
5000 to 9999	Class-5
Below 5000	Class-6

Source: Census of India, Various Issues.

On the basis of this classification of towns in our censuses let us now present the district-wise number of six classes of towns in the State of West Bengal in the census years 1991 and 2001. Table 5 reflects this feature.

A scrutiny of Table 5 reveals that the number of Class-I Towns in West Bengal had increased from 44 in 1991 to 58 in 2001, an increment of about 32 percent. Of these additional towns increased in the inter-censual decade, 1991-2001, North 24-Parganas alone shared as many as six, Hooghly has done three, such towns, though non-existent in South 24-Parganas in 1991, sprang in 2001

TABLE 5

District-wise Classification of Towns in West Bengal

Districts	*Class I*		*Class II*		*Class III*		*Class IV*		*Class V*		*Class VI*	
	1991	*2001*	*1991*	*2001*	*1991*	*2001*	*1991*	*2001*	*1991*	*2001*	*1991*	*2001*
Darjeeling	1	2	1	—	2	2	2	2	1	2	2	1
Jalpaiguri	1	1	2	1	3	4	5	7	4	2	—	1
Coochbihar	—	—	1	1	—	2	5	5	3	1	—	1
North Dinajpur	1	1	—	1	2	1	1	1	1	2	—	—
South Dinajpur	1	1	—	1	1	—	—	—	1	—	—	—
Malda	1	1	—	1	1	—	1	—	1	3	—	—
Murshidabad	1	1	1	3	9	7	1	5	6	13	—	—
Nadia	3	3	4	5	4	3	4	4	11	10	1	—
North 24-Parganas	16	22	7	2	10	4	13	7	11	12	2	1
South 24-Parganas	—	2	4	1	6	6	11	4	19	6	2	2
Kolkata	1	1	—	—	—	—		—	—	—	—	—
Howrah	3	3	1	1	3	7	17	14	22	23	1	5
Hooghly	6	9	4	i	5	4	7	6	12	16	2	3
Burdwan	5	6	4	2	8	6	15	14	23	27	6	11
Birbhum	—	—	2	3	4	2	—		—	1	1	—
Bankura	1	1	1	1	1	1	1	1	2	1	1	—
Medinpur	3	3	2	4	4	4	9	4	1	4	3	2
Purulia	—	1	1	—	1	3	4		3	5	1	1
West Bengal	44	58	35	29	64	56	96	76	121	128	22	28

Source: Census of India, Various Issues.

and numbered two, there sprang an additional town of this type in Darjeeling and in Purulia there was a new development of this town. It is also noted from Table 5 that the total number of Class 2, Class 3 and Class 4 Towns in the State as a whole declined in 2001, while the number of Class 5 and 6 Towns had slightly increased. The rate of decline in Class 2 Towns in two 24-Parganas is really noticeable. In North 24-Parganas the number of Class 3 towns in 2001 declined to 4 from 10 in 1991 and the number of Class 4 towns declined to 7 in 2001 from 13 in 1991. In case of South 24-Parganas the number of Class 4 and Class 5 Towns in 2001 had reduced almost to one-third of their number in 1991. All these information suggest that due to high pressure of population many towns, specially in 24-Parganas, have upgraded their Class, that is, Class 2 towns have been tipped to the status of Class 1 towns Class 3 towns have been tipped to the status of Class 2 towns and so on. However, there can be no denying the fact that the main attraction of the people is to throng in to Class 1 towns.

PROBLEMS OF URBANIZATION IN WEST BENGAL

Basically, there are two major problems of urbanization in West Bengal. The first one is the high degree of urban concentration in and around Kolkata. The second problem is the absence of a strong base of small and medium urban centers. Kolkata is, in fact, a three-in one city: an administrative head quarter, a business center and a center of higher education. Kolkata being the best center of trade and administration and the peculiar nature of employment that job seekers like bureaucrats, military men, office employees, transport workers, mechanics, plumbers, porters, domestic servants, middlemen, etc. usually take up, has attracted many people not only from various parts of India but also from different parts of the globe. Besides, Kolkata has become the cheapest metropolis of India. Naturally, after Greater Mumbai, Kolkata has become the largest Urban Agglomeration in India. It may be mentioned here that between 1991 and 2001 the annual growth rate of population in Kolkata Agglomeration has been 1.93%.

The basic reason behind the high degree of concentration in and around Kolkata is that living in the countryside has become more difficult for thousands of people who constitute the rural labour force.

The small and medium-sized towns of Kolkata's hinterland are hardly in a better position to offer employment to millions of our rural people. The growth of Kolkata's population is thus only partially due to the natural increase in the city's population but mainly due to the influx from outside. It is surprising to note that in this core city with an area of 104 sq. km. had lived a population of 1.02 million in 1911 and in this very city with the same area lived a population of 4.6 million in 2001. In this context it will be worthwhile to mention that since our villages are very underdeveloped, people are forced to come to Kolkata during the day time to earn their livelihood, making the city's day time population about 10% of the State's total population. Many of these people swarm the pavements and kerbs through the day. It is worth mentioning thai 32.55% of total population of Kolkata live in the bustees (*Census*, 2001).

Besides, the infrastructural facilities are extremely concentrated in Kolkata and there is a vast gap between Kolkata and other cities and towns with respect to the quality and level of such facilities. Obviously, in the absence of a few intermediate size cities, it is difficult to reduce the burden of Kolkata without sustained government effort to develop the smaller cities.

CONCLUSION

It is a fact that the rate of urbanization in West Bengal has been slightly higher than that of India. But there has not been proper dispersal of urbanization in this State. Urbanization has been centered basically on Kolkata and on the districts in the neighbourhood of this great city. Unless there is adequate dispersal of the urban centers, Kolkata and some twenty towns of the State will have to bear the tremendous burden of population and this will lead huge damage to environment and related issues.

REFERENCES

Bhattacharya, Basabi (1991): "Urbanization and Human Development", *Economic and Political Weekly*, Vol. XXXIII, Nos. 47 and 48.

Bose, A. (1947): *Studies on Indian Urbanization*, 1901-81, McGraw Hill, New Delhi.

Census of India. Various Issues.

Chatterjee, Mahalaya (1996): "Urbanization and Demographic Changes in India (1961-91), *Business Studies*, Vol. XIX, Nos. 1 and 2.

Economic Review; Govt. of West Bengal, Various Issues.

Giri, Pabitra (1998): "Urbanization in West Bengal, 1951-1991", *Economic and Political Weekly*, Vol. XXXIII, Nos. 47 and 48.

Giri, P. (1999): "Urbanization in West Bengal: Trends and Problems", *Artha Beekshan*, Vol. 8, No. 1, June.

Goon, A.M. and Haider, D. (1990): Calcutta's Population: Changing Size and Age Sex Composition," *Artha Shastra*. Vol. 9, No. 2.

Human Development in South Asia, 1997.

Konar, D.N. (1996): Degree of Urbanization in Orissa and Bihar - An Econometric Analysis", *Artha Shastra*. Vol. 10, Nos. 1 & 2.

Konar, D.N. (1996): "Urbanization in West Bengal and the Problem of Environment," *Economic Affairs*, Vol. 41, No. 1, Jan.-March.

Konar, D.N. (1998): "Population Pressure and the Problem of Environment in Calcutta", *Journal of Commerce*, Vidyasagar University, Vol. 3, March.

Konar, D.N. 1999): "Trend of Urbanization in West Bengal Since Independence", *Artha Shastra*, Vol. 8, No. 1, June.

Konar, D.N. (2004): *The Scenario of Population Growth in India*, Akansha Publishing House, New Delhi.

Munshi, S.K. (1975): *Calcutta Metropolitan Expansion*, People's Publishing House.

Todaro, M. (1987): Economic Development in the Third World, Orient Longman.

World Development Report, Various Issues.

West Bengal: Census of India, 2001, Series 20, Final Population Totals.

Road Transport System and Regional Disparities

DEBASISH BERA, DHIRENDRA NATH KONAR AND DILIP HALDER

Regional disparity is a common characteristic of all developing economies. The nature gives an economy a diversified character associated with the crux of man-nature interaction. As a consequence there emerges a regional disparity in the natural and economic activities. The regional disparities have got different dimensions and in this paper the aspect of economic disparity is more concerned dimension.

Since much discussed reason for underdevelopment is lack of infrastructure or inadequacy in infrastructure, we are trying to focus on the feet that the lack of transport linkages may be considered as one of the factors among others responsible for the existence of regional disparities in an economy. To overcome this problem of regional disparities, road transport system—a safe, flexible and door-to-door service rendering link—is indispensable along with the network of infrastructure.

The objective of the present study is to highlight the fact that the West Bengal economy is suffering from regional disparities reflected in terms of index of agricultural productivity due to non-uniform expansion of transport facilities measured in terms of road length which is quite palpably manifested in the disparities even at the district level. In this paper we work out empirically the relationship between the transport infrastructure and the economic growth by the productivity of agricultural produce (index of productivity of combined commodities). On the basis of the empirical observation, analyzing case by case for all districts of West Bengal, it may be hypothesized that the regional disparities in productivity is mainly due to the disparity of transport infrastructure.

To find the empirical evidences in support of the hypothesis the positive correlation coefficient between the transport infrastructure (road transport network) and the productivity should be worked out at the overall state level of West Bengal and thereafter at the district level separately with respect to time for West Bengal. Therefore, the first task is to judge whether the production, cropping pattern and the cropping intensity at the state level has been positively associated with the transport infrastructure and then to find out the impact of road on productivity. The impact of road development on the productivity will not be the same for all districts as there are so many influencing factors—soil pattern, land use, climate, etc. A few more interesting facts come out of the empirical results that the additional investments on road infrastructure which is highly productive reflected by the high value of correlation coefficient is accompanied by low road density which again justifies the priority of investments on road.

The suggestion for development which has got implications in terms of higher productivity and increase in Gross Domestic Product is to increase road infrastructure of high quality reducing the existing inequality as reflected in the results of the empirical exercise while reducing the inequality of distribution of road infrastructure in different districts. Obviously the greater share of the investment should go in favour of those districts which suffer from the shortage of infrastructure but this does not mean that those who have higher productivity index with high density be denied their share of investment.

Regional disparity is a common characteristic of all developing economies. The nature gives an economy a diversified character—diversity in climate, soil pattern, natural resources and diversity in the crux of man-nature interaction. As a consequence, there emerges a regional disparity in the natural and economic activities. The regional disparities have got different dimensions—economic disparity, cultural disparity and health and educational disparities. In this paper the aspect of economic disparity is more concerned dimension for our analysis and the regional disparities exist due to a number of factors—geographical, topological, historical and demographic, etc. The availability of labour as an input for production, the land-use pattern, the fertility of soil and capital are not uniformly available in all regions and the produced goods are not uniformly demanded in all areas. Automatically, a geographical gap between the production centres and the available input resources or the gap between the production centres and the distribution centres creates a gap between the prices of the inputs and the commodities—finished products, in different places thereby creating regional disparities in economic dimension. Due to this regional gap in mobility, the factors of production are available at a very low price at the place of their availability where there is either no production centres or any access of mobility whereas those are available at a very high price in the areas of production centres and thereby increasing the cost of production and the prices of the products as well.[1] On the other hand, due to the non-existence of sufficient link between the production centres and the markets, the products are sold at a very high price due to huge transport cost. As a result, the demand for the finished goods and the supply of the factors of production are not sufficiently matched by the respective supply of or the demand for and thus arresting the economic activities and the growth of the economy. The price difference of the same commodity in different places due to lack of sufficient link for transportation results in regional disparities thereby breaking the economic and social ties between rural and urban economies.

Since much discussed reason for underdevelopment is lack of infrastructure or inadequacy in infrastructure, in this present paper, we are trying to focus on that. The lack of transport linkages may be considered as one of the factors, among others, responsible for the existence of regional disparities in an economy. To overcome this problem of regional disparities road transport system, a safe, flexible and door-to-door service rendering link, is indispensable along with the network of infrastructure—railways, waterways and airways 'through which factors of production should be brought from various locations of their availability to the production centers and for the finished products to reach the distribution centers wherefrom the customers will take them to their respective places for final consumption'[2] in a very short time and at a very low cost. The factors of production are always changing their places and forms from one sector where they are surplus to other where they are shortage. The improvement of the accessibility by way of constructing road linkages has been followed by the increase in the quantity of production and this positive relationship is an accepted fact supported by the empirical studies.[3]

The objective of the present study is to highlight the fact that the West Bengal economy is suffering from regional disparities reflected in terms of index of agricultural productivity due to non-uniform expansion of transport facilities measured in terms of road length which is quite palpably manifested in the disparities even at the district level. In this paper we work out empirically the relationship between the transport infrastructure and the economic growth by the productivity of agricultural produce (index of productivity of combined commodities). On the basis of the empirical observation, analyzing case by case for all districts of West Bengal, it may be hypothesized that the regional disparities in productivity is mainly due to the disparity of transport infrastructure.

Thus for achieving the scenario of disparities in the West Bengal economy and to analyse the basic reasons behind the disparities the assessment of the existing road network at the regional level along with the respective road densities is indispensable. It is equally important to note that the transport development is one of the factors among other factors which are more or less directly or indirectly responsible for the regional disparities. Towards this purpose the case of all districts of West Bengal have been chosen for investigation and to research out the fact that the regional disparities in terms of index of agricultural productivity is mainly due to the disparities in road transport.

While examining the impact of road network on the index of agricultural productivity the calculation of the correlation coefficient between the road length and the index of the productivity of the combined agriculture commodity group at the district level is important. The differences in the road density per square km in different districts of West Bengal may add another dimension in the analysis of regional disparities.

The study uses the data on the road length of West Bengal and separately for each district for the time period 1990-91 to 1999-00 maintained only by the Public Works (Road) Department, Govt. of West Bengal and that of the changes of productivity, cropping pattern and the cropping intensity of West Bengal and index of productivity of agricultural produce in each district for the same period of ten years. The data are collected mainly from the secondary sources—Publications of the Bureau of Applied Economics and Statistics, Government of West Bengal; *Statistical Abstract*, West Bengal, 2002; Draft of The Five Year Plans, Zilla Parishad (1999), and Annual Plans for different years.

Road Inventory with the NHDP and Disparities in Development

The road transport system in West Bengal is significant in Indian perspective but with respect to population density and land area the system is not adequate. West Bengal has only 2.7 percent of the total land area of India but in terms of population, West Bengal shares over 8 percent as per the Census report of 2001. So in terms of density of the population per sq. km, West Bengal is alarmingly excess over the population density of India in general. In 2001, the population density of India is 324 whereas in West Bengal it is 904. In fact, West Bengal is the most densely populated state in India. This fact should be taken into account as another dimension in analyzing the regional disparities in per capita income, average production and the respective road length in West Bengal.

The lengths of roads of different types in West Bengal are presented in Table 1 and the major roads are presented in Map 1. The inventories of road transport network are not obviously distributed uniformly throughout the region and, thus the impact of road transport on different economic activities—income generation, increase in per capita income, marketability of potential, full utilization of resources is different in different region of the economy thereby creating regional disparities.

West Bengal is a major beneficiary of National Highways Development Project (NHDP) as major lengths of Golden Quadrilateral and East-West Corridor Pass through the State. The progress of National Highways Development Project in West Bengal in case of Golden Quadrilateral is only 115 Kms. against the total project of 398 Kms. Apart from this, the proposed new road transport system, East-West Corridor and the 4-lane

Map 1

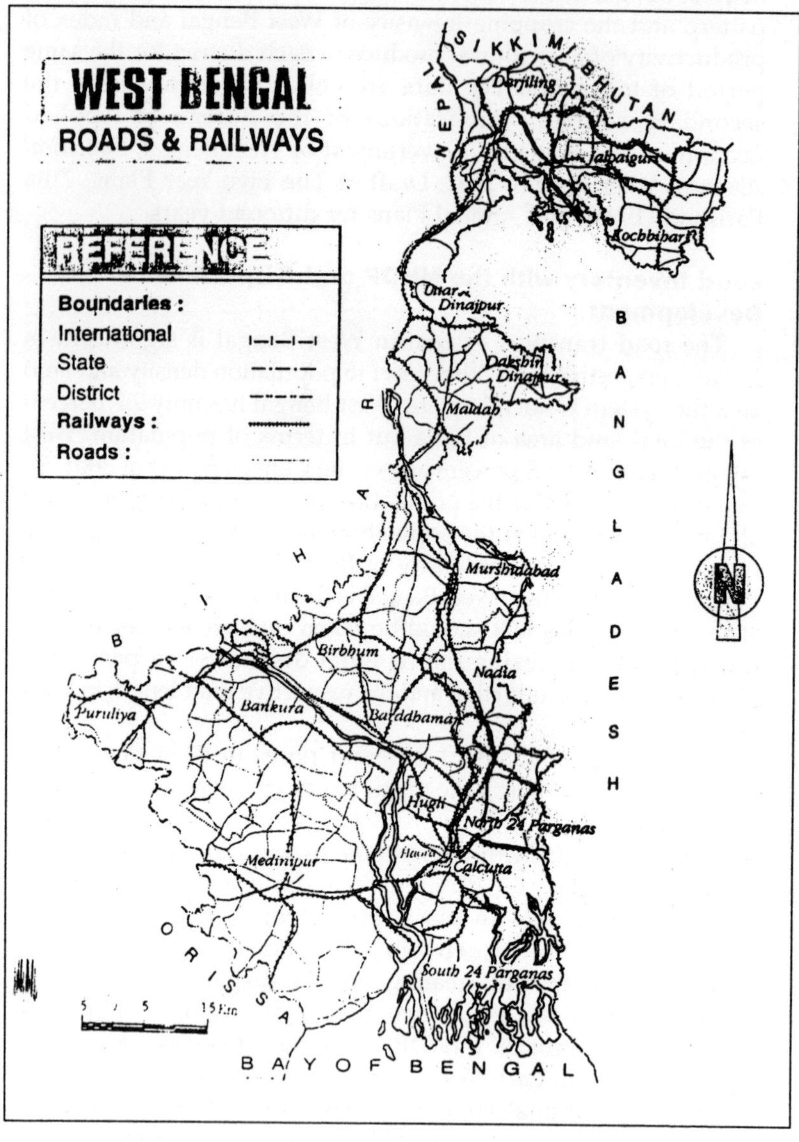
WEST BENGAL
ROADS & RAILWAYS
REFERENCE
Boundaries :
International
State
District
Railways :
Roads :
NEPAL
SIKKIM
BHUTAN
Darjiling
Jalpaiguri
Kochbihar
Uttar Dinajpur
Dakshin Dinajpur
Maldah
BANGLADESH
BIHAR
Murshidabad
Birbhum
Nadia
Puruliya
Bankura
Barddhaman
Hugli
North 24 Parganas
Haora
Calcutta
Medinipur
ORISSA
South 24 Parganas
BAY OF BENGAL
N

TABLE 1

The Length of Roads of Different Types in West Bengal in March, 2001

1.	National Highways	1956 Km.
2.	State Highways	3207 Km.
3.	Major District Roads	6833 Km.
4.	Minor District Roads	10767 Km.
5.	Village Roads	33655 Km.

Source: Institutional Development Study; PWD (Roads), Government of West Bengal.

connectivity to Haldia Port are 330.85 Kms and 53 Kms respectively (Map 2). The development of Highways will create immense benefits to West Bengal in future in terms of the reduction in travel time, lesser fuel consumption, quicker access to big cities of other States and important markets giving a big boost to the agriculture and industry in West Bengal with direct and indirect creation of employment opportunities.[4] Obviously, the existence of the superior types of roads may influence the assessment of the relationship in the empirical study in the respective region.[5]

Relationship between Road Length and the Index of Productivity—District-wise Analysis

To find the empirical evidences in support of the hypothesis the positive correlation coefficient between the transport infrastructure (road transport network) and the productivity should be worked out at the overall state level of West Bengal and thereafter at the district level separately with respect to time for West Bengal. Therefore, our first task is to judge whether the production, cropping pattern and the cropping intensity at the state level has been positively associated with the transport infrastructure. We consider the Table 2 to consider the changes of productivity, cropping pattern and the cropping intensity for the period of ten years from 1990-91 to 1999-2000.

The Index of Cropping Pattern and the Index of Cropping Intensity may be categorically defined as follows:

Index of Cropping Pattern in the jth year = $[\Sigma.\ Cij\ Yio\ Pio\ /\Sigma.\ Cio\ Yio\ Pio\ ] \times 100$

Map 2: West Bengal—Golden Quadrilateral and East-West Corridor

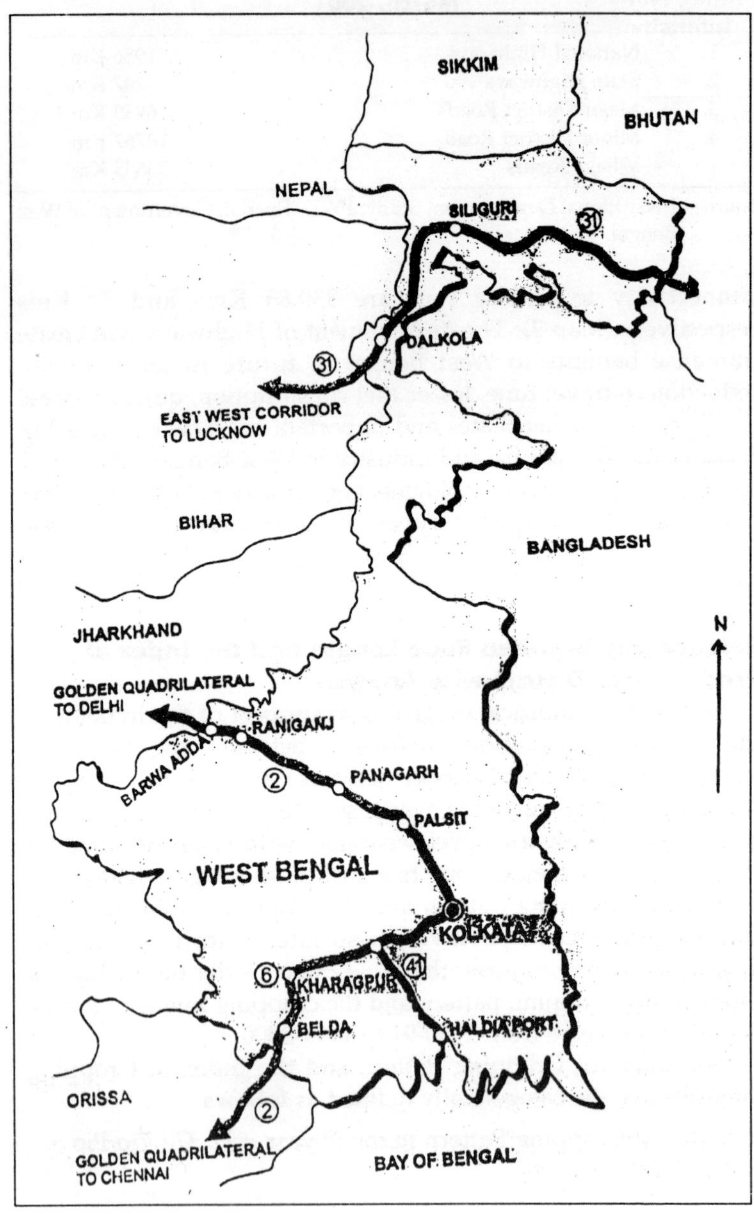

TABLE 2

Index Number of Productivity, Cropping Pattern and Cropping Intensity in West Bengal (Base: Triennium Ending Crop Year 1981-82 = 100)

Year	*Index of Productivity*	*Index of Cropping pattern*	*Index of Cropping intensity*
1990-91	148.2	114.2	111.8
1991-92	167.1	117.5	111.5
1992-93	162.0	116.5	109.3
1993-94	166.3	118.8	112.9
1994-95	172.2	119.6	111.3
1995-96	167.4	121.8	114.0
1996-97	186.6	124.2	114.8
1997-98	179.4	124.3	116.4
1998-99	184.3	130.1	116.6
1999-2000	185.7	129.0	119.4

Source: Statistical Abstract, West Bengal, 2002; Bureau of Applied Economics and Statistics, Government of West Bengal.

where Cio =aio / Σ aio = Proportion of area under i^{th} crop in the base period

Cij = aij / Z aij = Proportion of area under i^{th} crop in the jth period.

Yio = Yield per hectare of the ith crop in the base period

Pio = Price per unit of the ith crop in the base period

Index of Cropping Intensity = [Index of area under crops/ Index of net area sown] × 100

On the other hand, the total road length for the time period 1990-91 to 1999-00 maintained only by the Public Works (Road) Department, Government of West Bengal has been presented in Table 3. It is to be noted here that the changes in the length of roads is due to the transfer of authority of maintenance to other agencies, like Zilla Parishads and municipalities have been carefully adjusted.[6]

The degree of association between the road length and the index of productivity is very positive and is reflected by the value of the correlation coefficient between the road length and the

TABLE 3

Inventory of Total Road Length in West Bengal

Year	*Total Road Length in Km*
1990-91	17271
1991-92	17298
1992-93	17305
1993-94	17367
1994-95	17370
1995-96	17386
1996-97	17357
1997-98	17357
1998-99	17357
1999-2000	17421

Source: Public Works (Roads) Department, Govt. of West Bengal.

index of productivity for the period 1990-91 to 1999-00 which is significantly as high as 0.71495. It may be asserted with confidence that there will be a substantially positive contribution of road infrastructure to agricultural productivity which will ultimately get reflected in increase in Gross Domestic Product. Now we may turn to detailed empirical exercise at the district level. The Map 3 showing the Administrative Map of West Bengal, 1991 with district-wise break up may be used as ready reference. It would be very interesting if we could study the relationship between the transport infrastructure and the different agricultural produce in all the districts of West Bengal separately and in details for the period of ten years. The impact of road development on the productivity will not be the same for all districts as there are so many influencing factors—soil pattern, land use, climate, etc. The district-wise road length and the corresponding index of productivity of the agricultural produce in different years covering the period of ten years are presented in the following Table 4. The Road Length in the Table 4 indicates the total length of the roads constructed and maintained by the Public Works Department and Public Works (Roads) Department in West Bengal and the roads maintained by Zilla Parishads and Municipalities. The table gives an idea at a glance about the association between transport infrastructure (road length in Km) and the index of productivity of the combined agricultural produce in all districts of West Bengal

Map 3

WEST BENGAL
ADMINISTRATIVE MAP
1991
REFERENCES
International
State
District
DISTRICT HEADQUARTER
DARJILING
Siliguri
JALPAIGURI
Jalpaiguri
Kochbihar
KOCHBIHAR
UTTAR DINAJPUR
Raiganj
DAKSHIN DINAJPUR
Balurghat
MALDAH
English Bazar
B A N G L A D E S H
N
Baharampur
MURSHIDABAD
Siuri
BIRBHUM
NADIA
Krishnanagar
BARDDHAMAN
Barddhaman
B I H A R
Bankura
BANKURA
PURULIYA
Chuchura
HUGLI
Basirhat
NORTH 24 PARGANAS
CALCUTTA
Haora
HAORA
Alipur
Medinipur
MEDINIPUR
SOUTH 24 PARGANAS
87°E
88°E
89°E
27°N
26°N
25°N
24°N
23°N
22°N
20
km

TABLE 4

Relationship between the Road Length and the Agricultural Productivity in Different Districts and in Different Periods

Years		1990-91		1995-96		1998-99		1999-00		2000-01	
Name of the Districts of West Bengal		Road length in km	Index of Productivity	Road length in km	Index of Productivity	Road length in km	Index of Productivity	Road length in km	Index of Productivity	Road length in km	Index of Productivity
1.	Burdwan	4274	156.1	4773	160.5	5001	170.3	5338	164.1	5379	161.5
2.	Birbhum	2312	206.4	2446	143.4	2884	189.8	3120	175.5	3224	163.6
3.	Bankura	2404	171.6	2275	206.0	2275	210.7	2326	217.7	2437	223.9
4.	Medinpur	7161	150.0	7763	217.9	7851	226.7	8009	250.5	8045	245.8
5.	Howrah	2466	145.8	2519	143.5	2697	160.0	2712	196.7	2712	193.3
6.	Hooghly	3660	142.0	5927	157.5	9346	151.5	9362	152.5	9399	194.1
7.	24-Pgs. N&S	6765	139.8	10260	139.85	12735	162.7	21250	189	21285	183.3
8.	Nadia	2766	168.9	2811	166.4	3615	188.6	3691	179.2	3691	180.3
9.	Mursidabad	3794	157.2	4259	167.6	4407	192.0	4489	171.1	4489	178.3
10.	Dinajpur N&S	2351	176.3	2627	178.9	2950	225.6	3084	219.1	3198	241.8
11.	Malda	1703	149.6	1676	155.4	1779	183.2	1931	191.3	1931	196.5
12.	Jalpaiguri	2012	113.9	2082	114.8	2203	171.4	2292	179.4	2399	174.2
13.	Darjeeling	3118	107.1	3186	152.2	3193	183.2	3430	189.0	3475	201.6
14.	Coochbihar	1251	141.4	2375	153.8	2408	216.4	2461	197.0	2462	205.9
15.	Purulia	1455	129.2	1594	154.0	3979	142.0	4754	177.7	4849	174.7

Notes: 'Index of Productivity' stands for all combined Index Number of Productivity of all commodity groups—Foodgrains and Non-Foodgrains in West Bengal. (Base: Triennium ending crop year 1981-82 = 100)

Source: *Statistical Abstract*, West Bengal, 2002; Bureau of Applied Economics and Statistics, Government of West Bengal.

having different geographical, climatological, geomorphological (shown in Map 4), economic and social dimensions for the period 1990-91 to 2000-01. This information will help us to analyse the degree of association between the road length and the index of productivity of the combined agricultural production of West Bengal for each district separately.[7]

We can now extend our analysis to test the degree of association between the transport infrastructure and the Index of productivity of agricultural produce keeping other factors constant, which are more or less responsible for the change in production to assess the disparities in the productivity due to inadequate road length.

The district-wise Correlation Coefficient between Road length and Index of Productivity are calculated and presented in the following Table 5.

TABLE 5

District-wise Area, Road Length, Road Density and Correlation Coefficient between Road Length and Index of Productivity

Name of the Districts of West Bengal	*Area in Sq. km*	*Road length (2000-01)*	*Road density per sq. km (2000-01)*	*Correlation coefficient between Road length and Index of Productivity*
1. Burdwan	7024	5379	0.705	0.5547
2. Birbhum	4345	3224	0.742	0.3378
3. Bankura	6882	2437	0.354	-0.1541
4. Medinpur	14081	8045	0.571	0.9969
5. Howrah	1467	2712	1.848	0.8400
6. Hooghly	3149	9399	2.984	0.5109
7. 24-Pgs. N&S	14054	21285	1.514	0.9682
8. Nadia	3927	3691	0.939	0.8793
9. Mursidabad	5324	4489	0.843	0.7221
10. Dinajpur N&S	5359	3198	0.596	0.9436
11. Malda	3733	1931	0.577	0.9283
12. Jalpaiguri	6227	2399	0.385	0.8908
13. Darjeeling	3149	3475	1.103	0.8101
14. Coochbihar	3387	2462	0.726	0.7273
15. Purulia	6259	4849	0.774	0.7421

Source: Statistical Abstract, West Bengal, 2002; Bureau of Applied Economics and Statistics, Government of West Bengal.

Map 4

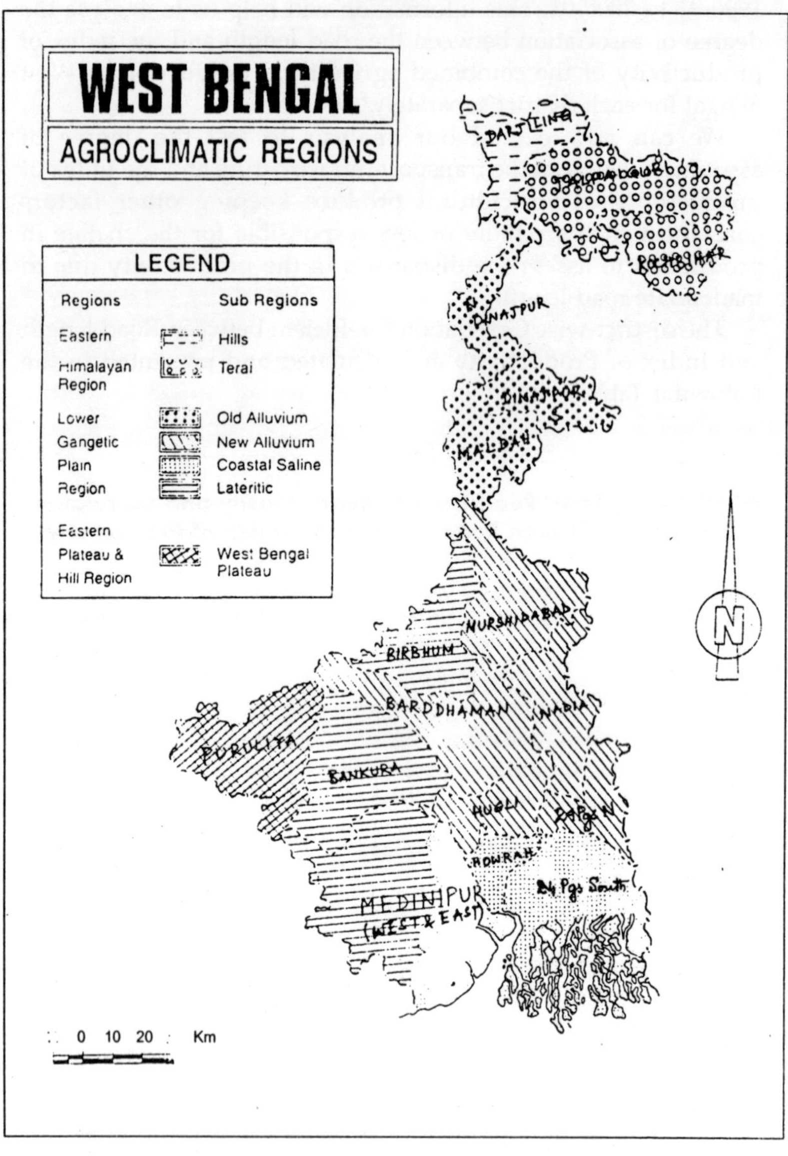
WEST BENGAL
AGROCLIMATIC REGIONS
LEGEND
Regions
Sub Regions
Eastern Himalayan Region
Hills
Terai
Lower Gangetic Plain Region
Old Alluvium
New Alluvium
Coastal Saline
Lateritic
Eastern Plateau & Hill Region
West Bengal Plateau
DARJILING
DINAJPUR
DINAJPUR
MALDAH
MURSHIDABAD
BIRBHUM
BARDDHAMAN
NADIA
PURULIYA
BANKURA
HUGLI
HOWRAH
24 Pgs South
MEDINIPUR
(WEST & EAST)
N
0 10 20 Km

It is interesting to note that (vide Table 5) among all the districts of West Bengal Medinpur has gained the significance by the fact that the 'Correlation Coefficient' between the Road length and the Index of Productivity of the combined commodity group—Foodgrains and Non-Foodgrains (Base: Triennium ending crop year 1981-82 = 100), scores the highest value '0.9969' among other districts of West Bengal. From the value of correlation coefficient between road length and Index of Productivity of the combined agricultural produce it can be straightway said that the marginal productivity of the road development is the highest in Medinpur (Purba and Paschim Medinipur) justifying additional investment on road development. This argument finds further strength in the fact that there is scope for developing road infrastructure, as the road density in the district is very low. This high value of correlation coefficient may also be explained by the lack of adequate substitution for road.[8]

A few more interesting facts come out of the results presented in the Table 5. If we apply the same argument which justifies additional investments on road infrastructure which is highly productive reflected by the high value of correlation coefficient accompanied by low road density, the priority of investments on road is claimed by Jalpaiguri district where the value of correlation coefficient between the road length and index of productivity is 0.89 and the road density 0 38. The another interesting point which emerges out from this exercise is high index of productivity accompanied by high road density per square km. In that category three districts—Darjeeling, Howrah and 24-Pgs. N&S combined stand distinct. In their cases correlation coefficients between the productivity and transport infrastructure are 0.81, 0.84 and 0.96 and road densities 1.10, 1.84 and 1.51 for Darjeeling, Howrah and 24-Pgs. N&S respectively.

In case of Hooghly district a departure is noticed in the sense that the correlation coefficient between the road length and index of productivity is 0.51 but the road density is the highest, to the extent of 2.98 (approximately 3.0). This may perhaps be explained by the fact that the area of this district is very small measuring 3149 sq. km, equal to that of Darjeeling district and second from the lowest order, the lowest being Howrah district. Besides, a considerably large area of Hooghly district is occupied by the river Hooghly, the banks of which constituted the Industrial Estate of

West Bengal. As a result, there is relatively less space for road construction, even then if additional road is constructed that might increase the industrial productivity more than agricultural productivity and the present index of productivity has been constructed by the agricultural products only.

The peculiarity noticed in case of Darjeeling having road density greater than one (1) is explained by the spiral and vertical movement of roads and the existence of space locating other activities are along that road and hence the space devoted to road construction is greater than the space devoted to other activities including housing. In case of Howrah where also the road density is much greater than one the same logic of Hooghly district applies to a great extent.

However, considering all these norms of road density and index of productivity hold good as the instrument of developing the hypothesis mentioned earlier.

If the hypothesis—that the disparities of productivity index is explained by the disparities in the availability of road infrastructure—is accepted as valid on the basis of the above empirical exercise, the suggestions and recommendations are quite evident.

Though as per the title of the paper the road infrastructure has been focused from the standpoint of overall development and investments in transport infrastructure in general, the role of other components of transport infrastructure like railways, river ways, seaport and airport, etc. should not be lost sight. May be, they play an important role for efficient utilization of road infrastructure. If there are possibilities of development of substitute like Inland Water Transport, Coastal Shipping and Railways the principle of Comparative Cost Advantage will decide the investment policy on road transport. A close look at the geographical layout of the District will make it clear that the possibilities of development of substitute are not always feasible. In addition to that the inherent advantage of the road transport that makes the transport services available from door-to-door cannot be substituted fully by other modes just referred. In calculating the Comparative Cost Advantage we should consider not only the cost of haulage but also the cost of travel time, damage of the cargo, cost of accident, cost of interchange and various other components of cost. However, it appears from the choice of mode exercised by the users of the road that the road transport system scores above all and in Medinpur (Purba and Paschim Medinipur) district there is ample scope for development of road transport system as reflected in the road density to give a boost to agriculture, industry and service sector of the district thereby increasing the per capita income of the region.

The suggestion for development which has got implications in terms of higher productivity and increase Gross Domestic Product is to increase road infrastructure of high quality reducing the existing inequality as reflected in the results of the empirical exercise while reducing the inequality of distribution of road infrastructure in different districts. Obviously the greater share of the investment should go in favour of those districts which suffer from the shortage of infrastructure but this does not mean that those who have higher productivity index with high density be denied their share of investment.

NOTES AND REFERENCES

Bera, Debasish, Konar, Dhirendranath and Halder, Dilip (2003): 'Regional Imbalance and the Role of Freight: A Case Study of The Marine Fish In The Coastal Region of Purba Medinipur District, West Bengal', *Artha Beekshan*, Vol. 12, No. 3, December.

Bera, Debasish (2005), 'Road Infrastructure And Its Impact on Regional Development with Special Reference to Medinpur District'—A Thesis for the Degree of Doctor of Philosophy in Economics, Department of Economics, University of Kalyani, West Bengal.

District Planning Committee, Annual Plans, Government of West Bengal.

District Statistical Handbooks: 1990-2000, Bureau of Applied Economics and Statistics, Government of West Bengal.

Government of India: Reports of the National Highways Authority of India (NHAI), 2002, Ministry of Road Transport and Highways.

Halder, Dilip (1996): The Transport Infrastructure: Role in Social and Economic Development, *Artha Beekshan*, Vol. 4, No. 1, June.

The Statesman (11th November, 2003): 'Destination West Bengal'.

Zilla Parishad (1999), Draft of the Five Year Plan, for different Districts, Government of West Bengal.

Disparity in the Development of Small Scale Industries

MOHASIN MALLICK

The objective of the present study is to find out and highlight the extent of uneven development of Small Scale Industries (SSI) in North and South Bengal, particularly emphasising on the growth of employment and number of factories in this sector.

The study will cover the period 1980-81 to 2000-01 to locate the pattern of development of this sector after thirty years of planning. It is also the objective of the study to measure the unevenness in SSI sector in the districts of West Bengal (W.B.) during the period of economic reform commenced in 1991

Our hypotheses of the study are: (i) During the period of the study disparity in employment in the SSI between the N.B. and S.B. districts is increasing over the years. (ii) Disparity in the number of registered units of SSI between the N.B. and S.B. districts is also increasing during the same period.

From the study it is observed that N.B. districts are comparatively backward than the S.B. districts in respect of both employment generation in SSI sector and also in the growth of SSI units during the period under study. Secondly, the extent of unevenness in both the cases was high in S.B. districts. Thirdly, disparity in both the cases among the N.B. districts was comparatively low. Fourthly, the disparity between the N.B. and S.B. districts in both the cases were quite high during the period. Fifthly, during the period of economic reform the employment generation and number of SSI units have declined for W.B., for S.B. and also for N.B. districts. This implies that Government is indifferent to the growth of SSI units and also for the employment generation aspect. The market forces have pushed the SSI units to a backward stage.

Lastly, it is also observed that during the period of economic reform disparity in employment generation and number of units for the S.B. and N.B. districts in the SSI sector are declining. Also the disparity between the North and South Bengal districts are declining since 1995-96.

INTRODUCTION

The objective of the present study is to find out and highlight the extent of uneven development of Small Scale Industries (SSI) in North and South Bengal, particularly emphasising on the growth of employment and number of factories in this sector. It is generally found that the North Bengal (N.B.) districts are neglected during the plan period and hence the standard of living of the people of this region is comparatively lower than the South Bengal (S.B.) districts.

For the development of N.B. districts SSI may play a major role in solving the unemployment problem and poverty by setting up SSI units according to the resources available in the different districts. The study will cover the period 1980-81 to 2000-01 to locate the pattern of development of this sector after thirty years of planning. It is also the objective of the study to measure the unevenness in SSI sector in the districts of West Bengal (W.B.) during the period of economic reform commenced in 1991.

Regarding the overall backwardness of the N.B. districts, Pal (2005) in a study concluded "According to an estimate made by the State Statistical Bureau, Government of W.B., during the plan period 1955-56 to 1960-61, about 50 per cent of the State income was generated in Kolkata and three other districts (Howrah, Hooghly, and 24-Parganas) which were roughly identified with Kolkata industrial areas. Adding Medinpur and Burdwan, the contribution to State's income of these six districts was of the order of 70 per cent. The remaining ten districts, viz., West Dinajpur, Jalpaiguri, Malda, Darjeeling, Purulia, Nadia, Bankura, Birbhum, Murshidabad, and Coochbihar were considered as the most backward districts in the State. The disparity in the development among the districts of W.B. remained almost unchanged till recently. Kolkata, Howrah, Hooghly, 24-Parganas, Burdwan and Medinpur, the six S.B. districts with varying rates of industrial and agricultural development accounted 69.49 per cent of State income in 1980-81, estimated at current prices, was generated in these six districts. "In recent years also wide disparities in district per capita incomes are found and it is seen that most of the N.B. districts are lagging behind the S.B. districts in per capita income. For exemple, the State per capita income in 1999-2000 (P), at constant prices (1993-94), was Rs. 9330 while the districts Malda, Dinajpur, Jalpaiguri and Cooch-Bihar had lower per capita income than state average (Table 1).

On the basis of the above reality our hypotheses of the study are:

(I) During the period of the study disparity in employment in the SSI between the N.B. and S.B. districts is increasing over the years.

(II) Disparity in the number of registered units of SSI between the N.B. and S.B. districts is also increasing during the same period.

In section-I, employment pattern in the SSI sector in the districts of W.B. will be examined for the period 1980-81 to 2000-01 and also a comparison of the unevenness of employment generation in the districts of North and South Bengal will be made. In section-II, the growth of SSI units during the same period in the districts of W.B. will be studied. A comparison of unevenness of the same in the North and South Bengal districts will be made for the same period. The extent of disparity between the N.B. and S.B. districts in regard to employment generation and number of SSI units is also proposed to be made in this section. In section-III, the causes of unevenness in employment and SSI units in the districts of W.B. will be highlighted and also the general policy prescriptions and conclusions will be made. The disparity is measured in this study, by the co-efficient of variation defined as C.V. = (S.D. / Mean) × 100.

TABLE 1

Estimates of per capita Income by Districts of West Bengal at Constant Prices (1993-94)

(*in Rs.*)

Sl. No.	*District*	*Year*			
		1993-94	*1995-96*	*1997-98*	*1999-00(P)*
1.	Burdwan	8726	9433	10317	11141
2.	Birbhum	5668	6492	7025	7865
3.	Bankura	6131	7220	5029	8948
4.	Medinpur	6789	7601	8177	8810
5.	Howrah	6911	7696	8775	9777
6.	Hooghly	7807	8860	9202	9921
7.	24-Parganas (N)	6527	7131	8415	9162
8.	24-Parganas (S)	6231	6640	7390	8159
9.	Kolkata	10465	12179	13674	17660
10.	Nadia	6494	7173	8677	9507
11.	Murshidabad	5789	6437	7300	8005
12.	Purulia	5263	6171	7628	7753
13.	Malda	5493	6330	7374	7902
14.	Uttar Dinajpur	4825	5296	5858	6403
15.	Dakshin Dinajpur	5389	6091	6708	8376
16.	Jalpaiguri	6512	7048	7768	8524
17.	Darjeeling	7715	8270	10601	9785
18.	Coochbihar	5564	6127	6750	7326
	West Bengal	6756	7492	8408	9330

Note: P = Provisional.

Source: Estimates of State Domestic Product and District Domestic Product of W.B., Bureau of Applied Economics & Statistics, W.B., 2002, Table number 20, p. 78.

I

During the period under study it is found that the S.B. districts as a whole (e.g. Burdwan, Birbhum, Bankura, Medinpur, Howrah, Hooghly, 24-Parganas, Kolkata, Nadia, Murshidabad, Purulia) recorded about 93 per cent of the total registered factories and about 95 per cent of the daily workers were in these factories. The corresponding figures for the N.B. (Malda, Dinajpur, Jalpaiguri, Darjeeiing, and Çoach Behar) districts were about 7 per cent and 5 per cent during the same period (Table 2).

TABLE 2

District-wise Number of Registered Factories in W.B. and Number of Workers Employed therein

Sl. No.	*Districts (Name)*	*1980*		*1991*		*2000*	
		Units	*Employ.*	*Units*	*Employ.*	*Units*	*Employ.*
1.	Burdwan	367	N.A.	562	12442	752	83338
2.	Birbhum	82	N.A.	115	4289	143	4815
3.	Bankura	66	N.A.	99	2176	136	3519
4.	Medinpur	92	N.A.	186	24025	217	29788
5.	Howrah	1394	N.A.	2052	152204	2512	168477
6.	Hooghly	221	N.A.	415	100271	536	100315
7.	24-Parganas (N&S)	2979	N.A.	4525	409257	5596	395168
8.	Kolkata	594	N.A.	879	18698	955	19260
9.	Nadia	91	N.A.	155	12341	166	13327
10	Murshidabad	14	N.A.	21	3575	25	4157
11	Purulia	50	N.A.	59	4288	68	4927
12.	Malda	8	N.A.	21	623	34	1222
13.	Dinajpur (U&D)	30	N.A.	42	2423	67	3995
14.	Jalpaiguri	254	N.A.	361	20374	434	26571
15.	Darjeeling	166	N.A.	223	10428	255	12602
16.	Coochbihar	13	N.A.	22	880	28	1015
	S.B. Total	5950	—	9068	743566	11106	827091
	N.B. Total	471	—	669	34728	818	45405
	W.B. Total	6421	—	9737	778294	11924	872496
	S.B. (%)	93%	—	93%	95%	93%	95%
	N.B. (%)	07%	—	07%	05%	07%	05%

Notes: Figures exclude defence factories, Employ. = Average daily employment.

Source: *Economic Review* (Statistical Appendix), Govt. of W. B., 1997-98, p. 88, 1997-98, p. 114, and 2002-03, p. 103.

So in respect of number of industries and employment S.B. districts are much ahead than the N.B. districts. N.B. districts are backward both in respect of overall development and industrial progress.

Let us examine the district-wise employment situation in both the group of districts. Among the districts, Kolkata occupied the highest position in respect of generation of employment in the SSI sector followed by Burdwan, North 24-Parganas, Howrah, and Hooghly (Table 3). The N.B. districts have comparatively smaller figures except Darjeeling.

TABLE 3

District-wise Employment in SSI in West Bengal (in number)

Sl. No.	*District*	*1980-81*	*1985-86*	*1990-91*	*1995-96*	*2000-01*
1.	Burdwan	13484	13108	13852	13612	4727
2.	Birbhum	5061	6060	3946	3407	1592
3.	Bankura	3110	2885	4899	2504	1954
4.	Medinpur	10451	17850	17915	8007	4811
5.	Howrah	10163	10371	10097	9010	3243
6.	Hooghly	8638	14066	11789	6019	4979
7.	24-Parganas (N)	9306	48305	25527	14878	7504
8.	24-Parganas (S)	—	—	11356	8678	2099
9.	Kolkata	13532	13961	20563	10449	9152
10.	Nadia	3290	4884	6473	3108	1283
11.	Murshidabad	2763	5939	6275	6499	3360
12.	Purulia	3808	5807	5147	5223	1296
13.	Malda	3488	2659	5056	2133	1222
14.	Dinajpur (U)	1674	3695	3962	1705	876
15.	Dinajpur (S)	—	—	—	918	873
16.	Jalpaiguri	1712	6918	8092	4352	1923
17.	Darjeeling	8999	3945	6180	1202	910
18.	Coochbihar	1562	1922	2003	628	1448
	Total W.B.	101041	162375	163132	102332	53252

Source: *Economic Review* (Statistical Appendix), Govt. of W.B., 1981-82, p. 122; 1997-98, p. 132; 2003-04, p. 126.

Of the total employment generated in the SSI sector in 1980-81 in W.B., 82.74% was for S.B. districts and only 17.26% was for N.B. districts. This figures increased for S.B. in 2000-01 while decreased for the N.B. districts (Table 4).

The trends of employment pattern in SSI during the period 1980-81 to 2000-01 for W.B., S.B. and N.B. are shown in Figure 1. It is found that upto 1990-91 the employment for W. B. in this

TABLE 4

Regional Employment of SSI in W.B. (in number)

Region	*Year*				
	1980-81	*1985-86*	*1990-91*	*1995-96*	*2000-01*
S.B.	83606	143236	137839	91394	46000
S.B.(%)	82.74	88.21	84.49	89.31	86.38
N.B.	17435	19139	25293	10938	7252
N.B. (%)	17.26	11.79	15.51	10.69	13.62
W.B.	101041	162375	163132	102332	53252
W.B.(%)	100.00	100.00	100.00	100.00	100.00

Source: Calculated from the Table 3.

sector gradually increased and after that it showed a steep decline. Approximately, the same trend is found for the S.B. districts and for the N.B. districts also. It indicates that before the economic reform in 1991 employment in this sector increased in W.B. and also for the groups of the S.B. and N.B. districts while during the period of economic reform employment generation in this sector severely declined and this was more for the N.B. districts.

To find out the extent of disparities in employment of SSI in W.B., Co-efficient of variations (C.V.) of employment for W.B., S.B. and N.B. have been estimated and the result is shown in Table 5.

TABLE 5

C.V. of Regional Employment of SSI

Region	*Year*				
	1980-81	*1985-86*	*1990-91*	*1995-96*	*2000-01*
W. Bengal	80.65	107.43	83.87	87..90	79.38
S. Bengal	51.94	95.53	74.44	69.67	66.62
N. Bengal	81.64	44.61	40.51	58.83	24.99

Source: Calculated from Table 3.

It is observed that overtime the disparities were declining for

Fig. 1: Line Diagram of Regional Employment of SSI

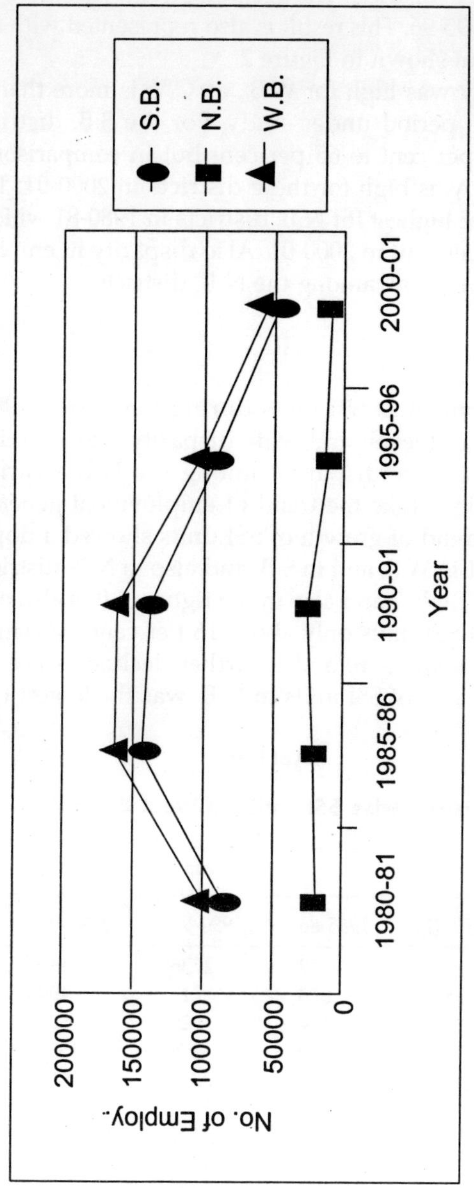

W.B., S.B. and N.B. districts. The declining trend was more for N.B. districts since 1995-96. This result is also represented with the help of a line diagram shown in Figure 2.

The disparity was high for W.B., as C.V. is more than 80 per cent during the period under study. For the S.B. districts C.V. varies from 95 per cent to 65 per cent but in comparison to the year 1980-81, C.V. is high for these districts in 2000-01. The C.V. (81.64%) was the highest for N.B. districts in 1980-81 which came down to 24.99 per cent to 2000-01. Also disparity in employment was comparatively low among the N.B. districts.

II

The development of SSI units during the period 1980-81 to 2000-01 was also uneven and wide disparity was found among the S.B. districts. The disparity among the N.B. districts was comparatively low. Like the trend of employment generation in SSI sector, the trend of growth of SSI units showed a downward trend since 1991 in W.B. and in S.B. and also in N.B. districts. This is shown in the Table 7 and also in the figure 3. It is also observed that of the total SSI units only about 16 per cent was situated in the N.B. districts (Table 6) and it further declined since 1991. In 1995 the percentage of SSI units in N.B. was the lowest (11.10%).

TABLE 6

Dristrict-wise SSI Units in West Bengal

District	*Year*				
	1980-81	*1985-86*	*1990-91*	*1995-96*	*2000-01*
Burdwan	1646	2229	2736	2180	625
Birbhum	553	820	713	404	175
Bankura	450	464	929	624	358
Medinpur	1231	2859	3658	1512	1058
Howrah	1198	2665	2338	1669	539
Hooghly	692	1504	1719	801	425
24-Parg. (N)	1503	4570	4621	2558	997
24-Parg. (S)	—	—	1286	1207	280
Kolkata	1881	1566	2825	1465	1440

(Contd.)

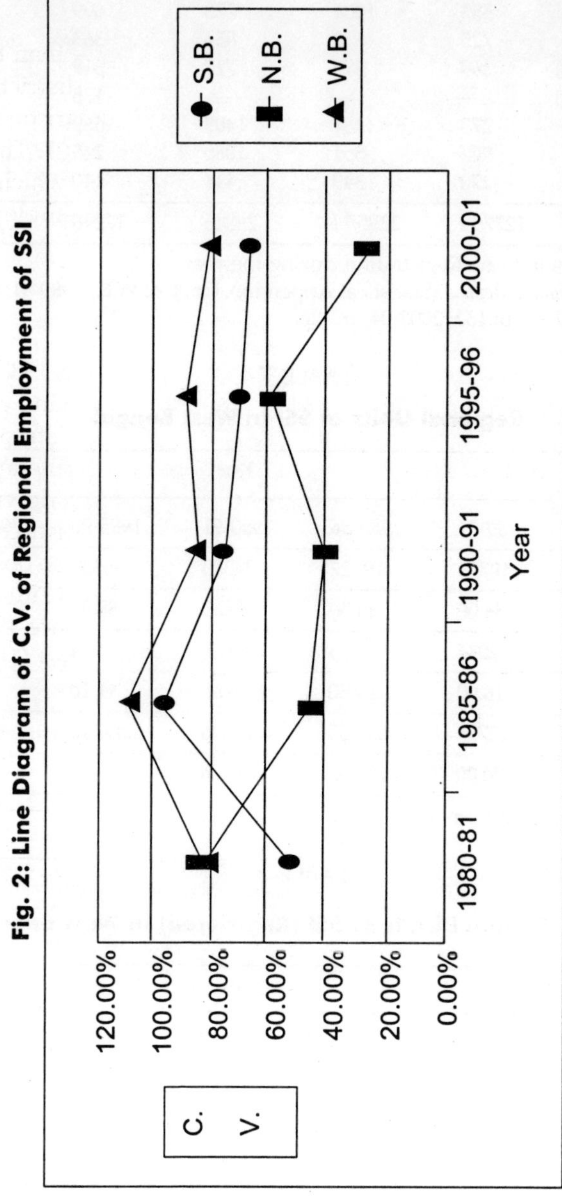

Fig. 2: Line Diagram of C.V. of Regional Employment of SSI

Nadia	387	954	1365	550	345
Murshidabad	637	962	1370	1663	836
Purulia	553	1034	773	699	212
Malda	725	672	854	363	351
Dinajpur (U)	269	575	727	319	179
Dinajpur (D)	—	—	—	178	137
Jalpaiguri	273	1181	1408	669	272
Darjeeiing	507	551	1080	245	176
Coochbihar	270	349	444	140	199
W.B. (Total)	12775 !	22955 I	28846	17246	8604

Note: Figures indicate Registration during the year.
Source: *Economic Review* (Statistical Appendix), Govt. of W.B., 1980-81, p. 122; 1997-98, p. 132; 2003-04, p. 126.

TABLE 7

Regional Units of SSi in West Bengal

Region	*Year*				
	1980-81	*1985-86*	*1990-91*	*1995-96*	*2000-01*
S.B.	10731	19627	24333	15332	7290
S.B. (%)	84.00	85.50	84.35	88.90	84.73
N.B.	2044	3328	4513,	1914	1314j
N.B. (%)	16.00	14.50	15.65	11.10	15.27
W.B.	12775	22955	28846	17246	8604 I
W.B. (%)	100.00	100.00	100.00	100.00	100.00

Source: Calculated from Table 6.

TABLE 8

C.V. of Regional Units of SSI (Registered) in West Bengal

Region	*Year*				
	1980-81	*1985-86*	*1990-91*	*1995-96*	*2000-01*
S.B.	52.06	64.60	66.83	66.77	62.31
N.B.	44.69	41.81	36.08	48.63	25.41
W.B.	63.46	76.56	76.54	84.31	72.74

Source: Calculated from Table 6.

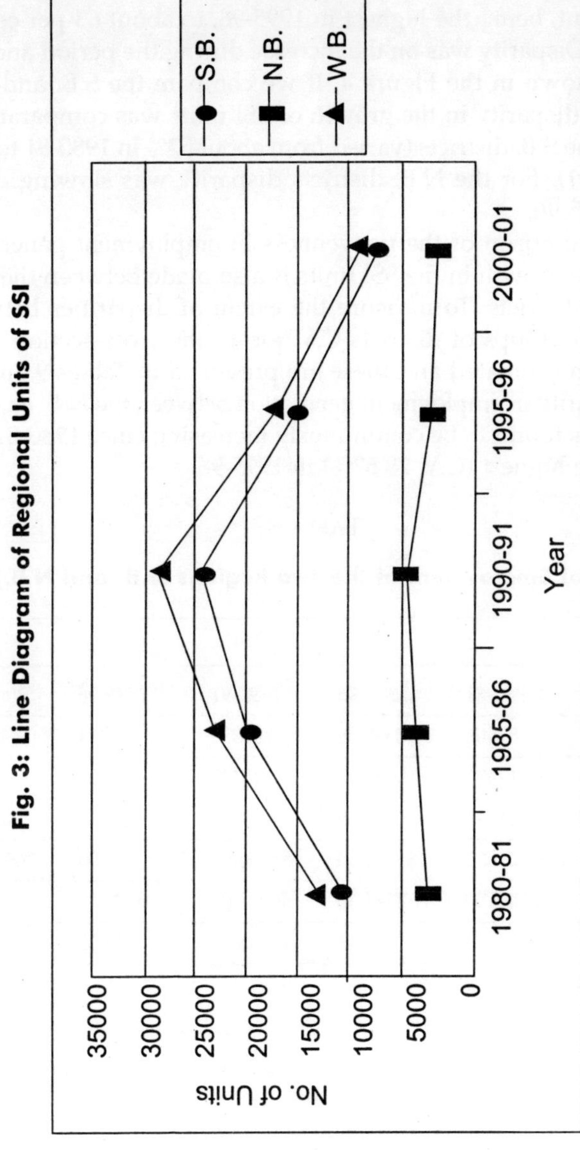

Fig. 3: Line Diagram of Regional Units of SSI

Regarding the disparity in the growth of SSI units, it is found that the disparity was quite high for W.B.; it varied from about 84 per cent, being the highest in 1995-96, to about 63 per cent in 1980-81. Disparity was on the increase during the period and this is also shown in the Figure 4. If we compare the S.B. and N.B. districts, disparity in the growth of SSI units was comparatively high in the S.B. districts (varied from about 52% in 1980-81 to 62% in 2000-01). For the N.B. districts disparity was slowing down since 1995-96.

A comparison of the unevenness in employment generation and in the growth in the SSI units is also made between the N.B. and S.B. districts. To measure the extent of disparities between these two groups of districts C.V. for all the cross-section years have been estimated and these are presented in Tables 9 and 10. The disparity in employment generation between the N.B. and S.B. districts is found to be continuously increasing since 1980-81 and it was the highest (C.V. 78.52%) in 1995-96.

TABLE 9

C.V. of Employment of the Two Regions (S.B. and N.B.)

Region	*Year*				
	1980-81	*1985-86*	*1990-91*	*1995-96*	*2000-01*
S.B. (total)	83606	143236	137839	91394	46000
N.B. (total)	17435	19139	25293	10938	7252
W.B. (total)	101041	162375	163132	102332	53252 I
A.M.	50520.50	81187.50	81566.00	51166.00	26626.00
S.D.	33085.50	62048.50	56273.00	40177.27	19374.00
C.V. (%)	65.84	76.43	68.99	78.52	72.76

Source: Calculated from Table 4.

In regard to the disparity in the growth of SSI units approximately the same trend is found during the period under study. For example, the C.V. in number of SSI units between the N.B. and S.B. districts was 68.00 per cent in 1980-81; it increased to 77.80 per cent in 1995-96 and again came down to 69.46 per cent in 2000-01 (Fig. 5).

Fig. 4: Line Diagram of C.V. of Regional Units

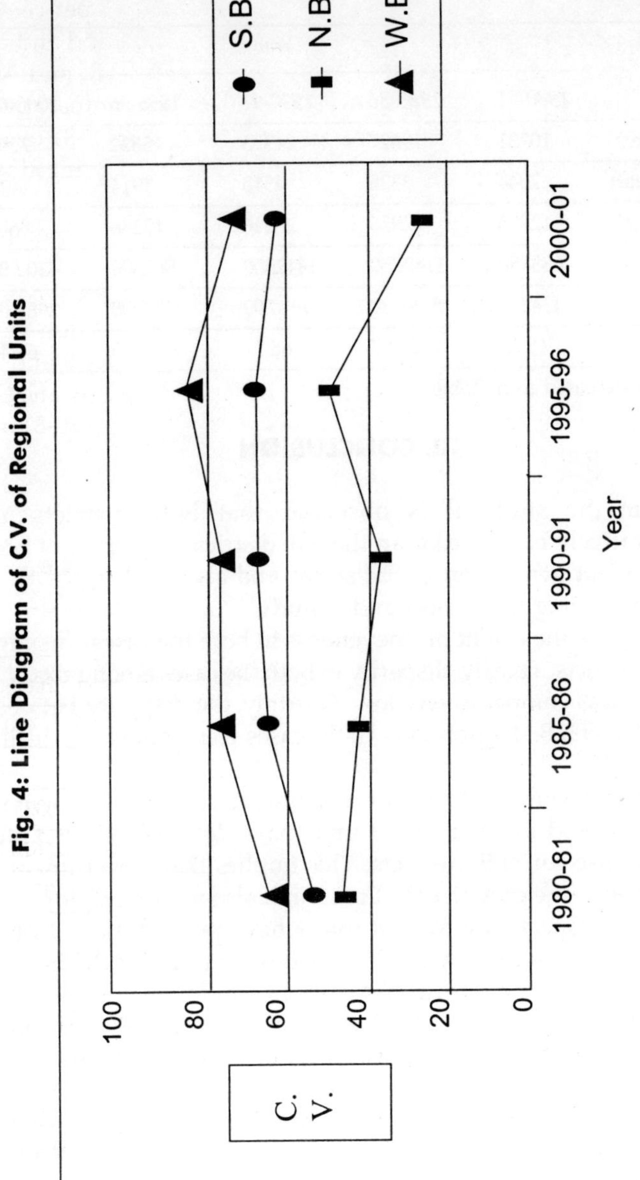

TABLE 10

C.V. of SSI Units of the Two Regions (S.B. and N.B.)

Region	*Year*				
	1980-81	*1985-86*	*1990-91*	*1995-96*	*2000-01*
S.B. (total)	10731	19627	24333	15332	7290
N.B. (total)	2044	3328	4513	1914	1314
W.B. (total)	12775	22955	28846	17246	8604
A.M.	638750	1147750	1442300	862300	4302.00
S.D.	434350	8145.39	9910.00	6709.00	2988.00
C.V. (%)	68.00	70.97	68.71	77.80	69.46

Source: Calculated from Table 6.

III. CONCLUSION

From the study it is observed that N.B. districts are comparatively backward than the S.B. districts in respect of both employment generation in SSI sector and also in the growth of SSI units during the period under study.

Secondly, the extent of unevenness in both the cases was high in S.B. districts. Thirdly, disparity in both the cases among the N.B. districts was comparatively low. Fourthly, the disparity between the N.B. and S.B. districts in both the cases were quite high during the period.

Fifthly, during the period of economic reform the employment generation and number of SSI units have declined for W.B., for S.B. and also for N.B. districts. This implies that Government is indifferent to the growth of SSI units and also for the employment generation aspect. The market forces have pushed the SSI units to a backward stage. Lastly, it is also observed that during the period of economic reform disparity in employment generation and number of units for the S.B. and N.B. districts in the SSI sector are declining. Also the disparity between the North and South Bengal districts are daclining since 1995-96.

One of causes of the wide unevenness in SSI sector development is that most of the units are situated in Kolkata and its surrounding few districts like Howrah, Hooghly, North 24-

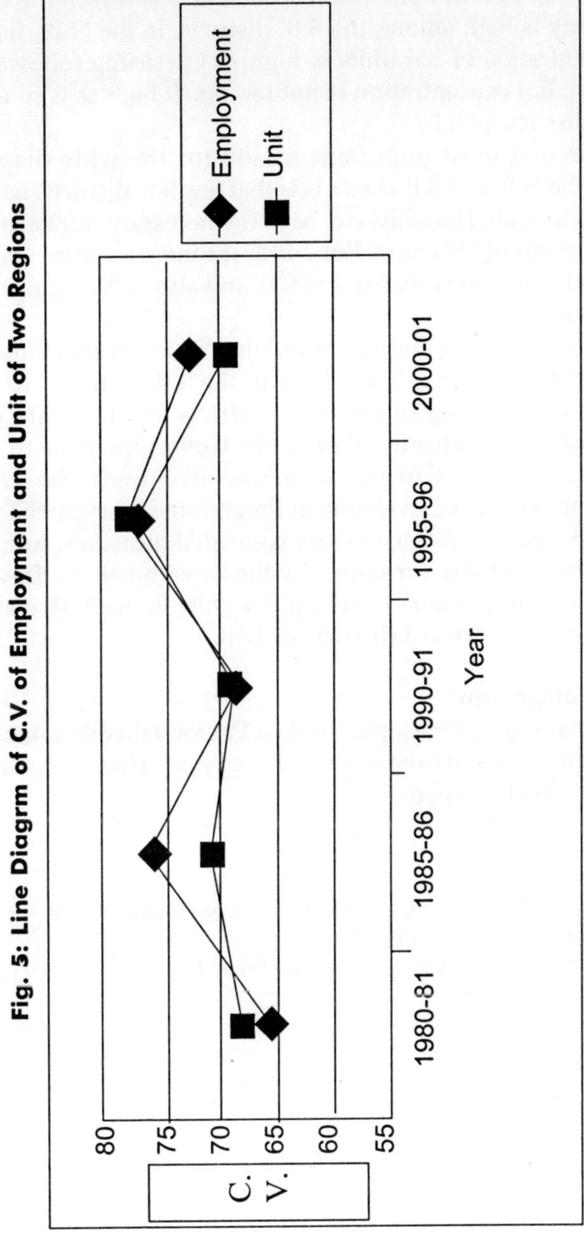

Fig. 5: Line Diagrm of C.V. of Employment and Unit of Two Regions

Parganas and also in Burdwan district. For this reason the extent of disparity is high among the S.B. districts. In the N.B. districts the concentration of SSI units is high in Darjeeiing followed by Jalpaiguri. But concentration is not too much high as is found in the few districts of S.B.

The second most important reason for the wide disparity between the N.B. and S.B. districts is that few S.B. districts, namely, Kolkata, Howrah, Hooghly, etc. have the necessary infrastructure for the growth of SSI units. But sufficient infrastructure was not developed in the other districts of S.B. and also of N.B. during the plan period.

W.B. Is one of the densely populated States in India and the density of population is quite high in the S.B. districts. To raise the standard of living of the N.B. districts and to create more employment opportunity there, the Government is to take sufficient measure and to give some incentives under the scheme of Backward Districts Development Programme to set-up SSI units in the N.B. districts. As a necessary co-related measures, sufficient infrastructure is to be developed by the Government to draw the attention of the investors to set-up SSI units in the N.B. districts and also other backward districts of W.B.

Acknowledgement

I am thankful to Dr. Gopal Krishna Pal for valuable comments in different phases in preparation of the paper. However, for any error, I am solely responsible.

References

Government of India (1956), Planning Commission; *Second Five Year Plan* New Delhi, Chapter-xx, pp. 450-51.

Government of West Bengal (1989-90): *Economic Review*, Chapter 5, pp. 47-52.

Government of West Bengal (2002): *West Bengal: 25 Years of Stability and Process*; Information and Cultural Department, Kolkata, p. 51.

International Bank for Reconstruction and Development (Feb. 1978): *Employment and Development of Small Enterprise—Sector Policy Paper*, Washington, Chapter-II, p. 6.

Kuchhal, S.C. (1985): *The Industrial Economy of India*, Chaitanya Publishing House, Allahabad, pp. 155-86.

Kuznets, Simon (1959): *Six Lectures on Economic Growth*; The Free Press (Corporation), New York, Lecture-III, p. 54.

Mukherjee, Nilmony (1997): *Small Scale Industries: Problems with Special Reference to Darjeeling District (1951-85)*, 1st edition, Progressive Publisher's, Kolkata.

Nair, K.R.G. (1981), *Regional Experience in a Developing Economy*, Wiley Eastern Ltd., New Delhi.

Pal, Gopal Krishna (2005): *Regional Disparities in Developing Economy*, Deep & Deep Publications Pvt. Ltd., New Delhi, pp. 2-40.

16

Regional Disparities in Development

KALIPADA BASU

There are regional economic disparities in the country and also within the state. West Bengal is not an exception. Here in this article the state of West Bengal has been divided into four regions: Regions A, B, C and D.

Region A (Kolkata Region) consists of Kolkata, Howrah, Hooghly, 24-Parganas (N & S).

Region B (Burdwan Region) consists of Burdwan, Birbhum, Bankura, Medinipur (E & W) and Purulia.

Region C (Malda Region) covers Malda, Murshidabad, Dinajpur (E & W) and Nadia.

Region D (North Bengal Region) encircles Darjeeling, Jalpaiguri, Coochbihar.

An analysis shows that there are regional disparities in industrial development. In Banking services there is also unbalanced development. Regional disparities are conspicuous also in the field of literacy. In Health Care discrepancies have also been noticed.

Urbanisation is an indicator of economic development. Here also, we find regional disparities.

Infrastructural developments outside Kolkata Region, especially in Region C and D are dismal.

There are also wide discrepancies in Human Development Index (HDI) among the districts.

If things go on in this fashion resentments among the masses of backward areas will cross the limit and the state will be disintegrated.

West Bengal has 19 districts including Kolkata. West Bengal based political parties, especially the Left, and the Congress during the regime of Sidhartha Sankar Ray alleged that the State was discriminated against others, especially Maharashtra, Gujarat, Tamil Nadu, Karnataka, etc. on the question of granting of industrial licenses, setting up public sector units, infrastructural development and the like. These were also political issues. The people of West Bengal were made to think that the State got step-motherly treatment from the Centre. The anti-Delhi propaganda by the Left was swallowed by the people of the State. The Left parties came to power in 1967, 1969 and 1977 mainly on this issue or slogan against the Union Government.

But during 30 years of Left Front rule in the State at a stretch the same thing had happened within the State itself. Development in the State has been lop-sided during last three decades, in other words development in the State had been unbalanced. Some districts, namely Bankura, Birbhum, Purulia, West Dinajpur and East Dinajpur have remained backward and the people of those areas have not felt any touch of development and they complained that they were discriminated against other districts. The three North Bengal districts, namely, Darjeeling, Jalpaiguri and Coochbihar are also the victims of neglect for which centrifugal forces have raised their ugly heads against the State Government. Kamtapuri, Naxalite Gorkhaland movements are the outcome of regional imbalance in development. The ministers, bureaucrats are more concerned with development in Kolkata and around it. The investors or entrepreneurs are unwilling to invest in those backward districts because of lack of infrastructural facilities like roads, rails, power, banking services, tele-communication, hotels, etc. Social sectors like education and health were also neglected.

UNBALANCED POPULATION BURDEN

Population-wise the districts can be divided into high, medium and low populated regions. North 24-Parganas with 89.34 lakh people has the highest population, followed by South 24-Parganas and Burdwan (69 lakh each), Murshidabad (59 lakh), Hooghly (50 lakh). These districts are in the first category. In the second category, range of population is between 30 lakh to less than 50 lakh and Nadia, Kolkata, Howrah, Bankura, Malda, Birbhum belong to this category. In the third category of districts, population is below 30 lakh. Dakshin Dinajpur (15 lakh) and Darjeeling (15 lakh) have the lowest population.

URBANIZATION: INDICATOR OF DEVELOPMENT

Urbanization is an indicator of development. On this count Kolkata is the most developed district with 100 per cent of people living in urban areas. Only in two districts—North 24-Parganas and Howrah more than 50 per cent of people live in urban areas. Burdwan, Hooghly, Darjeeling are in the third group having urban population between 32 and 37 per cent. Medinpur, Nadia, Murshidabad, Uttar Dinajpur, Dakshin Dinajpor, South 24-Parganas, Jalpaiguri, Nadia are in the fourth group having urban population from 12 per cent to 21 per cent. Malda (7.32%), Bankura (7.37%), Birbhum (8.57%) Coochbihar (9.10%), Purulia (10%) are in the fifth group. Districts having urban population less than 20% can be termed as backward.

Four Regions

On the count of development we can divide the whole of the State into four regions: Region A (Kolkata, Howrah, Hooghly, 24-Parganas (N & S)); Region B (Burdwan, Birbhun, Bankura, Medinpur (E & W), Purulia); Region C (Malda, Nadia, Murshidabad, Dinajpur (E & W)); and Region D (Darjeeling, Jalpaiguri & Coochbihar). Alternatively Region A can be called Kolkata Region, Region B as Burdwan Region, Region C as Malda Region and Region D as North Bengal Region.

Industry: Unbalanced Regional Development

An analysis of industrial development shows that industrial development has been concentrated in Region A, out of 13,204 registered factories in the State 10,463 factories, i.e., 79 per cent are concentrated in Kolkata and around it. Kolkata has 959 factories, Howrah 2,721, Hooghly 6,582, 24-Parganas (N & S) 6,191. Region B has 1,507 units or 11 per cent of the total. Here also there are disparities within this region. Burdwan alone has

863 units, i.e., 55 per cent of the total factories of this region (Region B). Region C consisting of Malda, Nadia, Murshidabad, Dinajpur (N & S). Malda has only 367 units (2 per cent), Region D or North Bengal region, namely Jalpaiguri, Darjeeling and Coochbihar has 817 units, i.e., 6 per cent of the total. From these analysis it is found that Kolkata and Burdwan regions or Region A and B have the maximum number of registered factories (11,941) or in other word, these two regions have the lion's share of the total factories of the State (90 per cent).

Banking Service

In banking services there are also regional disparities among 4 regions of West Bengal—Kolkata, Burdwan, Malda and North Bengal. As per Economic Review, Govt. of West Bengal (2004-05) of the total bank offices (4,475) in the State, 47 per cent are in the Kolkata region, 26 per cent in Burdwan region, 15 per cent in Malda region and 10 per cent in North Bengal region. Kolkata and Burdwan regions have 73 per cent of bank offices. Kolkata alone has 1,010 branches (22 per cent).

Education

Kolkata region is comparatively more developed in education than other regions. As per census report (2001) Kolkata itself has the highest literacy rate (80.86 per cent). Kolkata region's literacy rate is 76 per cent. Burdwan region 65.11 per cent, Malda region 56.45 per cent and North Bengal region 67 per cent. Low literate districts are Uttar Dinajpur (47.89%), Malda (50.28%) Murshidabad (54.35%). The average literacy rate in West Bengal is 69.2 as per census report 2001 (All India 65.4%). This shows that there are disparities in the spread of elementary education in the districts or regions (A, B, C and D).

Health Care

In health care also discrepancies have been noticed. Government health centers including those of local bodies are not evenly distributed. The State runs 12,058 health centers including hospitals and of these 37 per cent is in Burdwan region, 28 per cent in Kolkata region, 22 per cent in Malda region and only 11 per cent in North Bengal region. Here also Kolkata and Burdwan regions have the highest percentage (65%) of health care centers.

Lowest number of healthcare center has in the city of Kolkata (71). This is because Kolkata has large number of private doctors and nursing homes. Serious patients are sent to Kolkata from districts, because district hospitals and health centers are not well equipped and cannot meet up demand of patients.

Infrastructure

Infrastructure are the main boosters for economic development. Infrastructure include roads, rails, power, banking services, tele-communication system, air and sea ports, post offices, etc. But districts of West Bengal lacks infrastructure. PWD, Municipal and Panchayat roads are in shambles in most of the districts. Roads are not repaired regularly although conditions of 60 per cent roads are in bad shapes for years together. Industrialists do not like to go to the districts where infrastructures are insufficient.

Per Capita Income

There are differences in per capita income among the four regions: A, B, C, and D.

Kolkata region had the highest per capita income for the year 2001-02 (1993-94=100). This region had annual average per capita income to the tune of Rs. 13,043—Kalkata Rs. 20,560, Howrah Rs. 11,192, Hooghly Rs. 11,712 and 24-Parganas (N & S) Rs. 8,007.

Burdwan region had the second highest per capita average annual income, Rs 9,922. Separately Burdwan had a record of Rs. 12,385, Bankura Rs. 9,649, Birbhum Rs. 8,515, Purulia Rs. 8,810, Medinpur Rs. 10,253. Malda region's average per capita income was Rs. 8,975. The break-up is: Nadia Rs. 10,655, Murshidabad Rs. 8,757, Malda Rs. 8,660, Dinajpur (combined) Rs. 7,829.

North Bengal region was endowed with average per head income of Rs. 9,339. Darjeeling had the highest income of Rs. 11,156, followed by Jalpaiguri Rs. 9,157, and Coochbihar Rs. 7,702.

Average per capita income of West Bengal was Rs. 16,072 (current price 2000-01). India's average per capita income was Rs. 16,707 at that period.

Nature of Poverty

Discrepancies in poverty are also noticed among the districts. In Purulia 78.72% of the people live below the poverty line. Other high poverty level districts are: Bankura 59.62%, Birbhum 49.37%, Murshidabad 46.12%. The lowest poverty level districts are: Kolkata 5%, Howrah 7.63%, North 24-Parganas 14.41%. Percentage of poverty in West Bengal, as a whole, is 27% and India 26%.

Disparities in Human Development

There are wide discrepancies in Human Development Index (HDI) among the districts. In HDI determination full mark is supposed to be one. Kolkata's score is the highest (0.78), followed by Howrah (0.68), North 24-Parganas (0.66), Darjeeling (0.65), Burdwan (0.64), Hooghly (0.64), Medinpur (0.62), South 24-Parganas (0.60).

District's whose scores are above half or 0.5 and below 0.6 are Nadia, Jalpaiguri, Coochbihar, Bankura and Dinajpur.

In the lowest category are Birbhum, Murshidabad, Purulia and Malda. Malda's score is 0.44.

Rank-wise Kolkata is at the top and Malda is at the bottom (Rank-17). In the second position is Howrah; North 24-Pargana's position is the third.

Here it can be mentioned that West Bengal's position is the eighth in India. West Bengal's position is 0.472. Kerala with 0.638 is in the top position.

India's position in the world is 127 having HDI 0.595. Norway with 0.956 is at the highest position (Rank 1). HDI is prepared on the basis of per capita income, education and health life expectancy, etc.

Development Authorities

The State Government has set-up development authorities like KMDA, Durgapur Development Authority, Haldia Development Authority, Digha Development Authority, Sunderban Unnyan Parishad, Uttar Banga Unnayan Parishad, Darjeeling Hill Council, etc. But these development authorities depend fully on the State Government for the implementation of development projects. For instance, Uttar Banga Unnayan Parishad was set-up in 2000-01. In 2001-02 Rs. 42 crore was sanctioned to the Parishad; but in 2003-04 the allotment was reduced to Rs. 5 crore. In 2004-05, the allocation was Rs. 10 crore. These amounts are meager in consideration of their needs. If a development authority demands, say, Rs. 100, it gets only Rs. 10. These development agencies do not get money as per requirements. Hence, people have lost faith on these agencies. These authorities are nothing but cosmetics in the development scenario of the State.

State Finance Commission

District municipalities have meager income. They also depend on grants from the State Government. Bhabatosh Datta Committee suggested constitution of a State Finance Commission in the light of Central Finance Commission for the distribution of resources from the exchequer of the State Government; and that recommendation was accepted. A Finance Commission Act was passed in the Assembly in 1994, but the fact is that the commission has been a non-functioning body. Money is not distributed to local bodies as per principles recommended by Datta Committee. Municipalities and Panchayats can demand shares of Sales Tax (VAT), Motor Vehicle Tax, Land Tax, Amusement Tax, etc. as these taxes are collected from the municipal and panchayat areas. Development authorities should also get a portion of revenues collected from the areas of the development authorities, otherwise, the financial problems of the municipalities, local bodies and development authorities will not be solved.

Level of Development

If we consider the level of development of the districts on the basis of total score, the most developed districts are: (in descending order): Kolkata, Hooghly, Howrah, Burdwan and 24-Parganas (N). Less developed districts are (in the ascending order): Malda, Uttar Dinajpur, Murshidabad, Jalpaiguri, Coochbihar. Other districts are in the middle position of developed and less developed areas.

The Gorkhaland, Kamtapuri, Naxal and other anti-state movements in the backward regions are the impacts of the disparities in development. Centrifugal forces have been raising their ugly heads in the backward regions. The State and the Central Governments are not serious about the uplift of the backward areas. Development (if any) has been concentrated in few pockets like Greater Kolkata, Durgapur, Asansol, Haldia regions. No serious attempt has been made yet for the all-round development of the Malda and North Bengal regions, i.e. Regions C & D.

Kolkata centric attitudes of ministers, bureaucrats, even

people's representatives are responsible for this unbalanced development. MLAs of the districts also arrange for permanent shelters in Kolkata. They do not look back towards their places after elections. They are not also vocal for the development of their areas. If these things go on resentment among the masses of backward areas will have no limit and it will be very difficult to suppress them. That sign is already there.

TABLE 1

West Bengal: Regional Disparities in Industrial Development

Regions	*No. of registered factories (2004)*	*% of the state's total**
Region-A		
Kolkata	959	
Howrah	2,721	
Hooghly	592	
24-Parganas (N & S)	6,191	79
Total	10,463	
Region-B		
Burdwan	863	
Birbhum	155	
Bankura	162	
Medinpur (E & W)	298	
Purulia	79	11
Total	1,557	
Region-C		
Malda	50	
Murshidabad	50	
Dinajpur (E & W)	87	
Nadia	180	2
Total	367	
Region-D		
Darjeeling	286	
Jalpaiguri	493	
Cooch Bihar	38	6
Total	817	
Grand Total	13,204	

Data are re-arranged and percentage calculated.

*Percentages are approximate.

Source: *Economic Review*, Government of West Bengal, 2004-05.

TABLE 2

West Bengal: Regional Disparities in Education as on 31.03.2004

Regions	*Percentage of literacy as per census 2001*	*Average percentage in the region**
Region-A		
Kolkata	80.86	
Howrah	77.01	
Hooghly	75.11	
24-Parganas (N & S)	73.76	76
Region-B		
Burdwan	70.18	
Birbhum	61.48	
Bankura	63.44	
Medinpur (E & W)	74.90	
Purulia	55.57	65.11
Region-C		
Malda	50.28	
Murshidabad	54.35	
Dinajpur (E & W)	55.74	
Nadia	66.14	56.45
Region-D		
Darjeeling	71.79	
Jalpaiguri	62.85	
Cooch Bihar	66.30	67

Data and percentage are calculated.

* Percentages are approximate.

Source: *Economic Review*, Government of West Bengal, 2004-05.

TABLE 3

West Bengal: Regional Disparities in Health as on 31.03.2004

Regions	*Number of health centre*	*Average percentage of the grand total**
Region-A		
Kolkata	71	
Howrah	529	
Hooghly	782	
24-Parganas (N & S)	2,047	28
Total	3,429	
Region-B		
Burdwan	938	
Birbhum	571	
Bankura	667	
Medinpur (E & W)	1,777	
Purulia	572	37
Total	4,525	
Region-C		
Malda	567	
Murshidabad	944	
Dinajpur (E & W)	565	
Nadia	560	22
Total	2,636	
Region-D		
Darjeeling	300	
Jalpaiguri	640	
Cooch Bihar	457	11
Total	1,397	
Grand Total	12,058	

Data and percentage are calculated.
*Percentages are approximate.
Source: *Economic Review*, Government of West Bengal, 2004-05.

Regional Disparities in Industrial Development in per cent in West Bengal

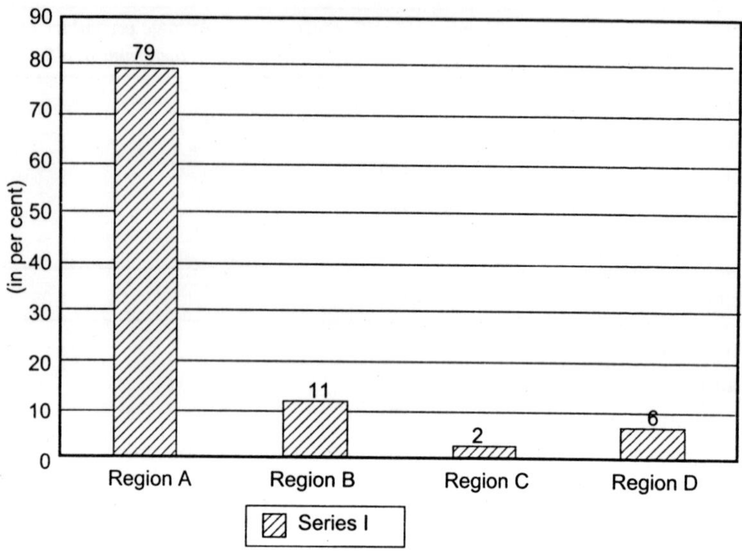

Regional Disparities in Education in West Bengal (%)

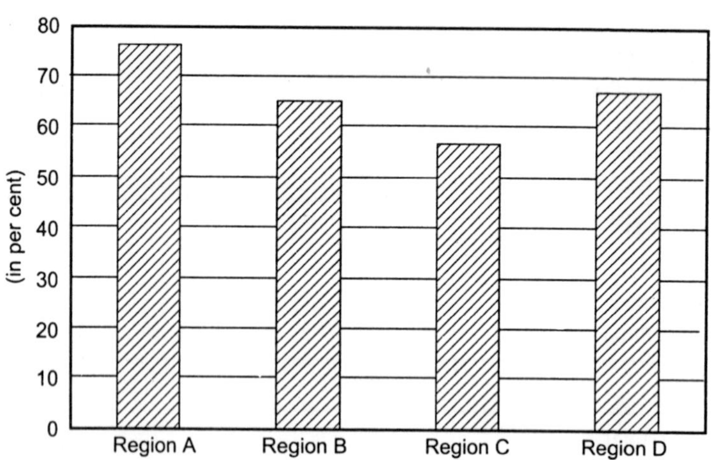

Regional Disparities in Health (%) in West Bengal

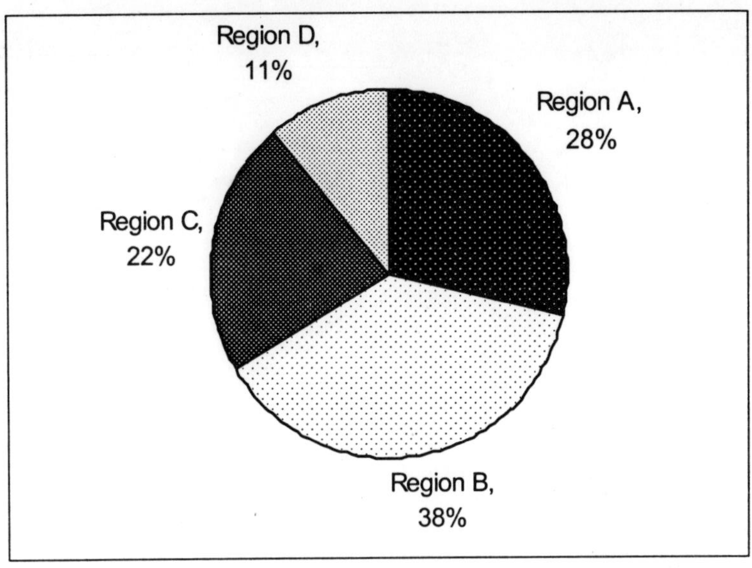

References

Artha Beekshan (Bengal Economic Association), 26th Conference Number (Dec. 2005 and March 2006), Articles by several authors.

Census Report, 2001, Series 1, RGCC, India (District Totals)

Economic Review (Statistical Appendix), 2004-05, Government of West Bengal.

National Human Development Report, 2001.

Statistical Abstract, Government of West Bengal, several issues.

West Bengal Human Development Report, 2004.

PART V

BACKWARDNESS IN NORTH BENGAL

Comparative Backwardness of North Bengal: Strategies for its Development

Kanak Bagchi and Satyen Sarkar

West Bengal economy is characterized by dualistic development. There is the coexistence of most and least developed regions. Data on various aspects of socio-economic development reveal that North Bengal region is comparatively backward in West Bengal in terms of certain important socio-economic indicators of development. Of late both the State and the Central Government have recognized this fact. A special development strategy for North Bengal has been adopted by the State Government for North Bengal by constituting the North Bengal Development Council (NBDC). This Council is yet to deliver services to the people of the region.

This paper is broadly divided into two parts. In the first part an attempt has been made to show the comparative backwardness of North Bengal in terms of secondary data collected from various official publications. In the second part we have outlined some strategies for development of North Bengal considered as a backward region and so also for other backward districts of the State. This paper recognizes the fact that special strategy for development of all backward areas of West Bengal including North Bengal is to be adopted simultaneously. The paper ends with the note that ultimately the Governments both at the State and the Centre have been found to intervene to address the problems of underdevelopment of North Bengal. It is hoped that overcoming the initial difficulties the NBDC will be able to perform its role properly and fulfil its objective of ameliorating the plight of the depressed people of North Bengal.

I. INTRODUCTION

The West Bengal economy is characterised by a sharp dualism in respect of state of development. There is the coexistence of areas with both the highest and the lowest levels of development. The development of the State, as in most other states, has been mostly State capital-centric while its far-flung areas have been neglected for a long time. Regional disparity in socio-economic development in West Bengal is a chronic problem. But, adequate studies have not been done on this issue. This paper is a modest attempt in fulfilling the research gap in this direction.

The existence of sharp inter-district disparity in development had been recognised and brought to focus in 1971 by the Bengal Chamber of Commerce and Industry, Calcutta (*BCCI*, 1971) when it stated: "While the Calcutta Metropolitan District or the district of Burdwan in the coal-iron ore belt represents a relatively high level of development, the outlying regions like Darjeeling-Coochbihar-Jalpaiguri in the north or Purulia-Bankura-Murshidabad in the west reflect a sorry plight of stagnation and decay. Indeed, a greater degree of intra-State regional imbalance is not witnessed in any other state of the Indian Union, as ... the data provided by the Census of India, reveals." Later studies have also found that inter-district disparities in development are persisting in West Bengal (e.g. *Pal*, 1995).

Since 1971 the position of West Bengal has slipped to a lower position *vis-a-vis* other States as far as various development indices are concerned (*Konar*, 1999). At the same time regional disparity in development is persisting. Although, as it would be evident that disparities in certain areas have been reduced, in some other areas it has probably increased. It requires a thorough investigation to find out the nature of disparities and to examine whether they are increasing or decreasing over time.

However, it is only recently that debates and discussions are going on regarding the relative backwardness of outlying regions of West Bengal specially the North Bengal region *(Lok Sabha Debate,* 2002) but they are mainly concentrated in political circles rather than in academic circles. In recent years a political movement known as *Kamatapuri* movement for a separate State comprising the six districts of North Bengal is going on in North Bengal. One of the causes of this movement is said to be the socio-economic backwardness of this region (*Government of West Bengal,* 1997, 2000, 2001). In response to these debates discussions and movements, the Government of West Bengal has taken several steps to redress the problem. For example, the State Government has constituted a body named *Uttar Banga Unnayan Parishad* in September 1999 with the objective of formulating schemes for the development of North Bengal region. It may also be noted that, recently a research-based study report entitled: 'Comparative Backwardness of North Bengal' has been brought out by the Planning Commission (*Govt. of India,* 2002) in order to understand and address the issues involved in it.

The objective of this paper is first to show through analysis of data that North Bengal is a comparatively backward region with respect to different aspects of socio-economic development and then to suggest strategies for faster development of North Bengal so that the districts comprising the region may possibly catch up with the other relatively developed districts of West Bengal.

In order to study the relative backwardness of North Bengal we shall divide the state of West Bengal into three regions, viz., North Bengal, South Delta and West Plain. The rationale for this type of regionalization is discussed in the next section. By using data obtained from various authentic sources like Census Reports, Statistical Abstracts, Economic Reviews, etc., we shall try to understand how backward the North Bengal region is compared to the other two regions of West Bengal. Simple statistical tools like averages, ratios and coefficient of variation will be used for this purpose.

The paper is divided in five sections. In the next, i.e., second section we shall delineate the regions of West Bengal for the purpose of our analysis and shall provide a brief profile of North Bengal region. In the next section we shall attempt to show the comparative backwardness of North Bengal. Section four will deal with the strategy of development for North Bengal as a backward region. Finally in the last section we shall conclude our discussion.

II. REGIONALIZATION OF WEST BENGAL AND NORTH BENGAL REGION IN PROFILE

Since in this paper we are dealing with the problems of backwardness of North Bengal region, therefore, we selected this region. The rest of Bengal has been divided into two regions: South Delta and the West Plain regions. The North Bengal region includes the districts of Coochbihar, Jalpaiguri, Darjeeling, Uttar Dinajpur, Dakshin Dinajpur and Malda; the South Delta region consists of the districts of Murshidabad, Nadia, Burdwan, 24-Parganas (North), 24-Parganas (South), Hooghly, Howrah and Kolkata; while the West Plain region comprises of Birbhum, Bankura, Medinpur and Purulia districts.

It may be noted that according to the norms of regional taxonomy at least three fairly distinct schema are available, namely, natural regions based on geographical factors, agro-climatic and planning regions and socio-cultural and linguistic regions (*Bhat and Zaviex*, 1999). In the first approach a country is divided into natural regions. This approach has evolved from the works of L. Dudley Stamp, J.N.L. Baker, D.H.K. Spate and others during the first half of the 20th century. In these attempts there was emphasis on the physiography, geological structure, climate and soils (*Spate and Learmonth*, 1967). In the second approach, there has been an attempt to identify agricultural and economic regions for planning purposes. Here the emphasis is on production specialisation and economic dependency as the basis for regional classification. The Planning Commission has from time to time made attempts to delineate resource development divisions, backward areas and agro-climatic region (*Thorner and Thorner*, 1962). In the third approach of regionalization schema, the purpose has been to identify regions of socio-cultural and linguistic similarities that had historically evolved out of socio-political interactions (*Khan*, 1973, *Mitra*, 1965, *Bose*, 1994).

For the purpose of delineation of the regions in West Bengal we have adopted the first approach, that is, natural regions based more or less on geographical factors. Thus, North Bengal commonly known as *'Uttar Banga'* is largely comprised of the sub-

Himalayan West Bengal and South Delta usually known as *'Dakshin Banga'* or *'Gangeya Samabhumi'* region mostly consists of the Gangetic or deltaic West Bengal, and West Plain region is normally known as *'Rarh Anchal'*.

The delineated regions are not too small or too large as can be seen from Table A-1. In terms of area, North Bengal, West Plain and South Delta occupy about 25 percent, 36 percent and 40 percent of geographical areas respectively while they comprise about 18 percent, 23 percent and 59 percent of the population respectively of West Bengal as per 2001 Census (*Census of India*, 2001).

The northern part of West Bengal, specifically, the area lying to the north of the river Gangaes is called North Bengal. It consists of six districts as noted above. Physiographically, the Sub-Himalayan districts of Darjeeling, Jalpaiguri and Coochbihar are much similar, while the other three districts, namely, North Dinajpur, South Dinajpur and Malda together are much similar from physiographic and climatic point of view. Thus, as per agro-climatic regional classification, the districts of North Bengal fall under two classes: (i) the Eastern Himalayan Region, which is again divided into two sub-regions, namely, Darjeeling Hills sub-division and Jalpaiguri and Coochbihar Terai sub-division; (ii) the lower Gangetic Plain comprising of older alluvium sub-region of Malda, Uttar Dinajpur and Dakshin Dinajpur districts (*GoI*, 2002, p. 2). In Eastern Himalayan region annual average rainfall varies between 2500 to 3500 mm. It has low temperature and high humidity. Poor sunshine coupled with low soil nutrients affects agricultural productivity. The lower Gangetic Plain has an annual rainfall between 1500-2000 mm.

As per the 2001 Census, the total population of the districts under North Bengal was 1,47,22,015 persons, which was 18.35 percent of the State of West Bengal (Table 1). The decennial population growth of the region (1991-2001) was 22.31 percent as against 17.84 percent in the case of the State as a whole. The region is predominantly rural where only 14.14% of population lives in urban areas compared to 31.15% of the same in the rest of Bengal. The districts of Coochbihar, Jalpaiguri, Uttar Dinajpur and Dakshin Dinajpur are characterised by incidence of higher proportion of Scheduled Caste population, which is well above the State average. In Jalpaiguri and Darjeeling districts, the

TABLE 1

Socio-Demographic Profiles of the Three Regions of West Bengal

Dist./Region/ State	*Constituent Districts*	*Area (in sq. km.)*	*Population*	*Density of Population/ sq.km.*	*Land-Man Ratio*	*Proportion of SC&ST Population to Total Population*	*Proportion of Urban to total population*	*Population growth (1991-2001)*
North Bengal (Uttar Banga)	Coochbihar, Jalpaiguri, Darjeeling, North Dinajpur, South Dinajpur, Malda	21855 (24.62)	1,47,22,015 (18.35)	674	0.15	34.07	14.17	22.46
West Plain (Rarh Anchal)	Birbhum, Bankura, Medinpur, Purulia	31767 (35.79)	1,83,78,074 (22.91)	578	0.17	27.43	9.58	15.37
South Delta (Dakshin Banga)	Murshidabad, Nadia, Burdwan, 24-Parganas (N), 24-Parganas (S), Hooghly, Howrah, Kolkata.	351309 (39.58)	4,71,21,082 (58.74)	1341	0.07	20.87	39.57	16.94
West Bengal		88752	80221171	904	0.11	24.79	31.15	17.84

Note: Figures in parentheses indicate percentages of total.
Sources: (i) *Economic Review*, 2001-02. (ii) *Census Report*, 1991.

Scheduled Tribe population accounts for a sizable proportion, i.e., 21.0 percent and 13.8 percent respectively as compared to the State average of 5.6 percent (*Government of West Bengal*, 2002a).

North Bengal region covers an area of 21,000 square kilometres, which is about 24 percent of total area of the State. Teesta, Torsa, Jaldhaka and Mahananda are the four major rivers of the region. These rivers are characterised by erratic changes in their courses and flooding. The other rivers of the region are Sankosh, Raidak, Kaljani, Mujnai, Atrai, Punarbhaba and Tangan. The river Ganges flows through the Western and Southern boundary of Malda district, which also forms a natural boundary between North and South Bengal. The hills and adjacent areas are covered with temperate and tropical forest composed *of Pine, Fir* and other evergreen types like *Gurjan. Sal* is also quite abundant in the forest. About 18 percent of the region is classified as forest land, much of which is concentrated in the districts of Darjeeling and Jalpaiguri (*GoI*, 2002).

III. COMPARATIVE BACKWARDNESS OF NORTH BENGAL

Ample evidences are there to illustrate that, there are regional disparities in socio-economic development in West Bengal and North Bengal is a backward region compared to South Delta and West Plain regions in many respects. In what follows we have shown these disparities in terms of per capita income, human development and social development in West Bengal.

III.1 Disparities in Per Capita Income

In order to measure the disparities in development we have first used District Per Capita Income (DPCI) as a measure of development. Table 2 presents DPCI in West Bengal from 1980-81 to 2000-01. To realise the pace of development of different regions, DPCI relatives have been worked out. By expressing each of the DPCI as a percentage of the State per capita income for the same year, DPCI relatives are calculated at constant prices and are presented in Table 3.

Table 2 shows that per capita income of North Bengal region was lower both in 1980-81 and 2000-01 than that of the West Plain and South Delta regions. However, it can also be seen that though per capita income of West Plain region was higher than that of

TABLE 2

District Per Capita Income in West Bengal: 1980-81 to 2000-01 (at Constant Prices)

Dist./Region/State	*1980-81*	*1990-91*	*2000-2001*	
Coochbihar	1000.00	1886.62	7779.86	
Jalpaiguri	1197.00	2120.39	8830.71	
Darjeeling	2235.00	2410.69	10415.88	
Uttar Dinajpur & Dakshin Dinajpur (Combined)	1090.00	2777.97	6778.81	(U. Dinajpur)
			8866.40	(D. Dinajpur)
Malda	986.00	1667.13	8339.28	
North Bengal	1301.6	2172.56	8501.82	
Birbhum	1456.00	1944.43	7738.07	
Bankura	1322.00	2164.38	9361.52	
Medinpur	1093.00	2028.71.	9263.49	
Purulia	1363.00	1633.17	7905.00	
West Plain	1308.5	1942.67	8567.02	
Murshidabad	983.00	1853.07	8009.30	
Nadia	1111.00	1808.04	9606.47	
Bardwan	2114.00	2571.89	11445.13	
24-Parganas (N)	1789.00	2968.55	9440.25	
24-Parganas (S)	(Combined)	1465.82	8394.74	
Hooghly	1988.00	2448.81	10344.55	
Howrah	2219.00	2308.55	10365.59	
Kolkata	3156.00	4026.47	19895.96	
South Delta	1908.57	2317.77	10937.75	
West Bengal	1612.00	2144.69	9778.09	

Source: Bureau of Applied Economics and Statistics, Govt. of West Bengal (1978-89, p. 662; 1997-98, p. 560; 2001-02, p. 449).

the North Bengal region, the difference is too small to merit attention. This indicates that, as far as per capita income is concerned, both the North Bengal and West Plain regions are comparatively poorer than the South Delta region.

Per capita income relative for North Bengal, which was 80.74 in 1980-81, has increased to 86.95 in 2000-01 (Table 3). But DPCI relatives of all North Bengal districts except Darjeeling were lower than West Bengal average both in 1980-81 and 2000-01. However, from Table 2 it can be seen that per capita income of North Bengal was 19.26 percent lower than State per capita income in 1980-81 and 14.06 percent in 2000-01. This indicates that the position of North Bengal region has improved by about 5 percentage points over the ten-year period. However, though the per capita income of Darjeeling district in both the years were higher than the State average income, its position deteriorated by 32 percentage points over the ten-year period. But the position of other districts improved moderately over the period.

TABLE 3

District Per Capita Income Relatives of West Bengal: 1980-81 to 2000-01

Dist./Region/State	*1980-81*	*1990-91*	*2000-2001*
Coochbihar	62.03	87.96	79.56
Jalpaiguri	74.25	98.87	90.31
Darjeeling	138.65	112.40	106.52
Uttar Dinajpur & Dakshin Dinajpur (Combined)	67.62	129.53	69.33
Malda	61.17	77.73	85.28
North Bengal	80.74	101.29	86.95
Birbhum	90.32	90.66	79.14
Bankura	80.00	100.92	95.74
Medinpur	67.80	94.59	94.74
Purulia	84.55	76.15	80.84
West Plain	81.17	90.58	87.61
Murshidabad	60.98	86.40	81.91
Nadia	68.92	84.30	98.24
Bardwan	131.14	119.92	117.05
24-Parganas (N)	110.98	96.45	96.54
24-Parganas (S)	(Combined)	67.93	85.85
Hooghly	123.32	114.18	105.79
Howrah	137.65	107.64	106.00
Kolkata	195.78	187.74	203.47
South Delta	118.39	108.07	111.86
West Bengal	100	100	100

Source: Calculated from Table 2.

To understand the magnitude of regional income variation for different years, coefficients of variation (CVs) for DPCI are worked out and presented in Table 4. It is revealed from this table that the regional disparity tended to reduce over the years.

TABLE 4

Coefficients of Variation of District Per Capita Income (DPCI) for Different Regions of West Bengal: 1980-81 to 2000-01

(*in percent*)

Region/State	*1980-81*	*1990-91*	*2000-01*
North Bengal	59.83	48.87	13.08
West Plain	301.73	10.05	8.74
South Delta	53.54	31.44	32.36
West Bengal	54.00	36.19	28.61

Source: Computed from Table 2.

III.2 Disparities in Human Development Index (HDI)

Since the publication of Human Development Report in 1991, various countries of the world including India have started publishing Human Development Reports which contain Human Development Index that is believed to express the level of development in a better way than per capita income. Recently State Governments in India are also publishing State Human Development Reports that contain HDI at district level. In addition, individual scholars have also made attempts to construct HDI at district level (*Banerjee and Roy*, 1998; *Rani*, 1999; *Roy and Bhattacharya*, 1999) The advantage of such an exercise is that it enables us to make an inter-district comparison in development, which helps to adopt appropriate policies at state level to address the problems of backward districts. One attempt at constructing HDI for West Bengal districts has been made by Bhattacharya (*Bhattacharya*, 1998) for the years 1981 and 1991. In this study we are using the HDI for West Bengal districts estimated by Bhattacharya for our purposes of inter-district comparison. This has been shown in Table 5.

Table 5 represents the HDI of West Bengal districts for 1981 and 1991. It reveals such a pattern of values and ranks of HDI that it mostly conforms our regional classification of the districts of West Bengal for both the years. The average values of HDI in 1981 for the South Delta, West Plain and the North Bengal regions were 0.5739, 0.3473 and 0.1996 respectively. This indicates that South Delta is the most developed, West Plain is the moderately developed and North Bengal is the least developed region in terms of Human Development. In the most developed South Delta

TABLE 5

Human Development Index (HDI) in West Bengal Districts, 1981 and 1991

Dist./Region/State	*Value 1981*	*Rank 1981*	*Value 1991*	*Rank 1991*
Coochbihar	0.0766	15	0.1034	15
Jalpaiguri	0.2528	12	0.3026	12
Darjeeling	0.5581	5	0.3979	9
U&D/Dinajpur (Combined)	0.1107	14	0.0524	16
Malda	0.0000	16	0.1980	13
North Bengal	0.1996		0.2109	
Birbhum	0.3057	9	0.4866	7
Bankura	0.4373	7	0.4344	8
Medinpur	0.2832	11	0.5398	6
Purulia	0.3631	8	0.3351	11
West Plain	0.3473		0.4490	
Murshidabad	0.1707	13	0.1852	14
Nadia	0.2966	10	0.3891	10
Bardwan	0.5990	4	0.6521	4
24-Parganas (N) & (S) (Combined)	0.5367	6	0.6409	5
Hooghly	0.6767	3	0.6956	3
Howrah	0.7374	2	0.7671	2
Kolkata	1.0000	1	1.0000	1
South Delta	0.5739		0.6186	
West Bengal	0.4003		0.4488	

Source: Bhattacharya (1998), pp. 3027-28.

region except Murshidabad (0.1707) and Nadia (0.2966) in five other districts, HDI values are higher than the State average value (0.4003) in 1981. In the moderately developed West Plain region, HDI values of all the districts except Bankura fall short of the State average value. In the least developed North Bengal region, HDI values of all the districts except Darjeeling fall much short of the State average value.

In 1991, the HDI values followed the similar pattern as that of 1981. The high degree of disparity among the districts persisted in 1991 also. In the developed South Delta region of the 7 districts, the HDI of 2 districts (Murshidabad and Nadia) fell short of the State average. In the West Plain region out of 4 districts, HDI values of 2 districts (Bankura and Purulia) fell short of the State average and in the North Bengal region consisting of 5 districts, HDI value was lower than the State average in all the districts.

The HDI also reveals indirectly the relative deprivation of the people living in a spatial unit—the highest level of human development implies the lowest level of deprivation and *vice versa.* Therefore, the lower the value of HDI and lower the rank of a district, the more deprived is the district. Since the districts in North Bengal except Darjeeling occupies lower ranks in HDI compared to most other districts of the other two regions and since the average HDI value of North Bengal region is the lowest among the regions both in 1981 and 1991 it implies that this region and the districts comprising it are the most deprived and therefore backward in West Bengal. Comparatively speaking in terms of HDI, West Plain region is moderately deprived and South Delta region is the least deprived region.

In 1981, the coefficient of variation (CVs) of HDI values for all the districts of West Bengal was 0.67 while at the all India level it was 0.53 (*Bhattacharya,* 1998). This indicates a very high degree of relative deprivation in West Bengal. The rank correlation coefficient between HDI and per capita district domestic product is 0.94. This implies that those districts of West Bengal that are deprived in terms of income are also deprived by and large in terms of human development.

In 1991, the degree of relative deprivation has decreased a little. The CV in HDI was 0.58 in 1991 as against 0.67 in 1981 for all the districts of the State. For the States of India the CV was 0.47 in 1991. This shows that though the value of CV had decreased in West Bengal in 1991, it was still higher than that of India. This indicates that the degree of relative deprivation is still higher in West Bengal than in India. The rank correlation coefficient between HDI and per capita domestic product at district level was 0.90 in 1991 as compared to 0.94 in 1981. This implies that the degree of association between HDI and per capita domestic product has not decreased. It also means that development in West Bengal during 1980 and 1990 have primarily followed the gradient of income growth (*Bhattacharya,* 1998). Considering all these aspects it can be stated that the extent of relative deprivation in West Bengal has not changed between 1981 and 1991. This also signifies that the backward regions have remained backward over this period.

III.3 Disparities in Social Development

In a recent paper (*Bagchi and Sarkar*, 2003) we have shown inter-district and interregional disparities in social development in West Bengal by taking 6 indicators each from health and education sectors. The indicators that we have taken from health dimension are—access to toilets, rural water supply, availability of doctors, availability of beds in State Government health system, infant mortality and percentage of safe delivery. The six indicators from education dimension are—total literacy rate, number of primary schools per ten thousand population, teacher-student ratio at primary level, Scheduled Caste and Scheduled Tribe literacy rate and percentage of schools having drinking water facilities.

In this paper following V. Nath's study (*Nath*, 1970) we have attempted to highlight disparities in social development in respect of selected indicators among different regions and different districts of West Bengal. As a requirement for Nath's method we have assigned ranks (better the situation higher the rank and *vice versa*) to different districts in the case of all the twelve selected indicators. Ranks have then been added up to obtain the total rank score of that district (Table 6). Districts are then arranged in an ascending order of total rank score (Table 7). The districts having the lowest total rank score are designated as the most developed and the districts having the highest rank score are considered as least developed.

It can be seen from Table 7 that the metropolitan district of Kolkata is the most developed and Malda is the least developed district in terms of social development. We have divided the districts into two categories—developed and less developed on the basis of the State average rank score value (=109.89). Districts having score below this average value has been categorized as developed and districts having score above this average score have been categorized as less developed districts. Of the 18 districts, 10 districts belonged to the 'developed' category and the other 8 districts belonged to the 'less developed' category. The table reveals that all the six districts of North Bengal except Darjeeling belonged to less developed category. While of the 4 districts of West Plain region, three belonged to developed

TABLE 6

Rank Score of the Districts of West Bengal on the Basis of 12 Social Indicators

Districts & Regions/Indicators	*1*	*2*	*3*	*4*	*5*	*6*	*7*	*8*	*9*	*10*	*11*	*12*	*Total Rank Score*
Coochbihar	10	8	9	6	16	16	13	14	14	14	8	8	136
Jalpaiguri	8	15	11	9	11	14	14	13	15	6	11	9	136
Darjeeling	5	17	1	2	5	8	7	18	10	3	7	18	101
Uttar Dinajpur	11	3	12	17	14	18	18	17	16	8	15	17	166
Dakshin Dinajpur	11	2	13	13	14	12	12	16	9	10	14	7	133
Malda	13	13	16	14	15	17	17	12	13	9	16	15	170
North Bengal	9.67	9.67	10.33	10.17	12.5	14.17	13.5	15.0	12.83	8.33	11.83	12.33	140.33
Birbhum	14	5	3	5	13	4	11	10	3	11	18	16	113
Bankura	17	4	6	4	7	6	10	5	5	2	17	11	94
Medinpur	15	14	7	12	8	10	2	1	7	12	3	5	96
Purulia	16	1	2	7	4	15	15	7	12	1	13	13	106
West Plain	15.5	6	4.5	7.0	8.0	8.75	9.5	5.75	6.75	6.5	12.75	11.25	102.25
Murshidabad	12	9	17	8	10	13	16	6	15	18	12	10	146
Nadia	6	7	10	3	12	2	9	9	12	15	6	2	93
Burdwan	7	11	8	10	6	9	6	3	8	5	10	3	86

24-Parganas (N)	2	12	14	15	10	7	4	2	2	16	2	4	90
24-Parganas (S)	9	16	15	16	9	11	8	4	11	17	4	12	132
Hooghly	4	6	5	7	3	5	5	8	4	13	9	6	75
Howrah	3	10	4	11	2	3	3	11	6	4	5	14	76
Kolkata	1	–	–	1	1	1	1	15	1	7	1	1	29
South Delta	5.5	8.87	9.12	8.87	6.62	6.37	6.5	7.25	7.37	11.87	6.12	6.5	90.96

Indicators: 1. Access to toilets; 2. Rural water supply; 3. Availability of doctors; 4. Availability of beds; 5. Infant mortality rates; 6. Percentage of safe delivery; 7. Percentage of total literacy; 8. Primary schools per ten thousand population; 9. High and higher secondary schools per ten thousand population; 10. Teacher-student ratio in primary schools; 11. SC/ST literacy rate; 12. Percentage of schools having drinking water facility.

Source: Bagchi and Sarkar (2003).

category and one belonged to the less developed category. Again, of the 8 districts of South-Delta region 6 belonged to developed category and 2 belonged to less developed category.

TABLE 7

Levels of Development of the Districts on the Basis of Total Rank Score

District/Level of Development	*Total Rank Score*	*Rank*
Developed		
Kolkata	29	1
Hooghly	75	2
Howrah	76	3
Burdwan	86	4
24-Parganas (N)	90	5
Nadia	93	6
Bankura	94	7
Medinpur	96	8
Darjeeling	101	9
Purulia	106	10
Less Developed		
Birbhum	113	11
24-Parganas (S)	132	12
Dakshin Dinajpur	133	13
Coochbihar	136	14
Jalpaiguri	136	15
Murshidabad	146	16
Uttar Dinajpur	166	17
Malda	170	18

Source: As in Table 6.

In this study we have made an addition to Nath's study. After adding up the rank score of all the districts, we have again added the rank score of the districts falling within a region and then obtained the average score for the region (Table 6). In this way we have worked out the relative level of development of the three regions. From this exercise, on the basis of average rank score, it can be seen that South Delta is the most developed, West Plain is the moderately developed and North Bengal is the least developed region.

There are some other studies also which provide evidence to the fact that North Bengal is a relatively more backward region. We may mention here results of one such study, which support this. The National Institute of Population Sciences, Mumbai conducted 'National Family Health Survey', in 1992-93. Using these data Bhat and Zavier (1999) made a regional analysis of the findings of National Family Health Survey. They have delineated the most backward regions in each major state with respect to eight indicators of development. These indicators are—asset poverty, underweight children, under-5 mortality rates, trained birth attendance, child immunisation, total fertility rate, contraceptive practice, and female literacy. According to this study, in West Bengal, the West Plain region is the most backward region with respect to only one indicator, that is, in the case of underweight children. While with respect to all other seven indicators North Bengal is the most backward region.

TABLE 8

Classification of NSS Regions by Rural Poverty Ratio (1993-94) in West Bengal

Medium Poverty Region (21-40 percent)	*Poverty Ratio*	*High Poverty Region (41-60 percent)*	*Poverty Ratio*
WB-Central Plains	31.0	WB-Himalayan	58.7
WB-Western Plains	40.3	WB-Eastern	47.1

Note: *Himalayan Region* consists of Coochbihar, Jalpaiguri and Darjeeling districts.
Eastern Plains region constitutes Uttar Dinajpur, Dakshin Dinajpur, Malda, Murshidabad, Birbhum and Nadia districts.
Central Plain region includes Burdwan, Howrah, Hooghly, North 24-Parganas, South 24-Parganas and Kolkata districts.
Western Plain region comprises of the districts of Bankura, Purulia and Medinpur.

Source: Calculation made by NIRD and Haque as reported in India Rural Development Report, 1999, cited in IDBR, Bhubaneswar (2000)

Finally we may mention data relating to poverty variations in West Bengal (Table 8). Classification of National Sample Survey (NSS) regions by rural poverty ratio (1993-94) shows that of the 4 NSS regions in West Bengal, Himalayan region is a high-poverty region (41-60 per cent) having poverty ratio of 58.7 in 1993-94 (*Institute for Development of Backward Regions (IDBR)*, Bhubaneswar, 2000). This also shows that North Bengal is the most deprived region of West Bengal.

IV. STRATEGY FOR DEVELOPMENT OF NORTH BENGAL

Our discussions above perhaps have made it clear that there are regional disparities in development in West Bengal, and North Bengal is a comparatively backward region. It has also appeared to us that the position of the West Plain region is also not much advanced as far as selected socio-economic indicators of development are concerned. We have also noticed that in the so-called developed South Delta region there are districts like South 24-Parganas and Murshidabad, which are more or less at the same level of development as the backward districts of West Plain and North Bengal regions. Therefore, there are both inter-regional as well as intra-regional disparities. Now the question is what strategies can be adopted for the rapid development of the most backward region and most backward districts of the comparatively advanced regions. This is of utmost importance because it is only through the accelerated development of the backward areas of West Bengal along with other parts that its relative position among the Indian States can be improved. This is not possible only through the state capital-centric or certain other urban area-centric development in the state.

However, all disparities cannot perhaps be removed. With free-market economic policies as today's prevailing trend, the scope for government intervention is also limited. The primary challenge for any government is to ensure that all (rich and poor, urban and rural alike) can participate in the economic growth. Here participation means (a) taking part in the decision-making regarding policies and programmes that aim at bringing about development, (b) contributing to economic growth with labour, skills, knowledge and entrepreneurship according to the full capabilities of the people concerned, and (c) benefiting from economic growth through income and asset accumulation resulting in a good quality of life (*ESCAP*, 2001).

For a people-centric development strategy let us first see what measures have so far been adopted by the Government of West Bengal to accelerate the pace of development of North Bengal for improving the standard of living of the people. The State Government has constituted a body named *Uttar Banga Unnayan Parishad* (North Bengal Development Council) in September 1999, with the objective of formulating schemes for the development of the North Bengal region. The University of North Bengal had prepared a socio-economic perspective plan for North Bengal, 2001-10 that was under consideration of the *Parishad*. The State Government has proposed to allocate an amount of Rs. 112.53 crore for the Tenth Five Year Plan for this *Parishad* (*Lok Sabha Debates*, 2002).

But till date the progress of work of the *Parishad* is said to be unsatisfactory. Its style of functioning has been vehemently criticised. It has been alleged that allocation of funds for the *Parishad* has been gradually decreasing over the successive years since its inception in 1999. The allocations were Rs. 45 crore in 1999-2000, Rs. 42 crore in 2000-01, Rs. 13 crore in 2001-02 and about Rs. 5 crore only in 2002-03 (*Uttar Banga Sambad*, September 7, 2003, p. 9). It is also alleged that the projects that are undertaken are not completed within stipulated time. Another problem of the *Parishad* is that proper manning and other logistic supports have not been provided for the smooth functioning of the *Parishad*. People's representatives of the area complain that the Centre has failed to provide its share of the funds. It is reported that several projects conceived by the *Parishad* fell flat since the body did not have the requisite funds to support its ideas. However, it has also been reported that the State Government is planning to revive a "near defunct" *North Bengal Development Council* to boost development in the region (The *Telegraph*, September 1, 2003). Thus, it is clear that within its life span of 4 years the *Parishad* has not been able to deliver goods to the region and its people.

The Planning Commission's study report as mentioned earlier (*GoI*, 2002) has also brought into focus an inter-district disparity in West Bengal in different dimensions of development under the following heads: demographic attributes, economic indicators, infrastructure and human development and implementation of central schemes. This study has come out with the conclusion that 'the districts of North Bengal have lagged behind with regard to a number of development dimensions for over two decades'. It is not yet known as to what action the State and the Central Governments are going to take on the basis of this report. The report has suggested that for the reduction of regional disparities within the State, it is the State Government as well as *Panchayats* at district level who need to evolve a medium-term development strategy. However, from our above analysis about different dimensions of development and the regional disparities in West Bengal and comparative backwardness of North Bengal and some other districts of the State, we may suggest the following policies for the development of backward areas.

IV.1 Improving Economic Infrastructure

To remove backwardness of North Bengal, top priority should be given to build up social and economic infrastructure. Among economic infrastructure, status of road connectivity is poor in North Bengal region compared to other two regions (*Government of West Bengal*, 2002a, 2002b). The railway and road connectivity should be greatly improved and its remote areas need be linked to markets at the local, regional, national and global levels. Bagdogra airport should be upgraded to the international standard. Developments of such items of infrastructure are crucial in order to create economic opportunities. Such infrastructure will facilitate as well as reduce the cost of marketing of agricultural and industrial goods produced in the region and will make these more competitive in the national and world market. For example, certain kinds of flowers, fruits and vegetables of the region may get access to the national and even international markets if such links are strengthened. For improving agricultural productivity, measures should be taken to create more and more minor irrigation facilities. The current status of irrigation facilities is also low in North Bengal region (*Government of West Bengal*, 2002a). The Teesta canal irrigation project, which was started long ago, should be completed within a reasonable time frame. Schemes already undertaken by the NHPC to construct low dams over Teesta and Jaldhaka rivers for generation of electricity will satisfy power requirement of the region to some extent. But efforts should be made to utilize the full hydroelectric power potential of the region.

IV.2 Industrialisation

North Bengal has good potential for industrialisation. Agro-based industries, specially food processing industry based on mango, pineapples, oranges, potatoes and tomatoes can be profitably established in different parts of North Bengal. For example, fruit processing units may be set-up in Siliguri, Japaiguri, Darjeeling and Malda based on pineapples, jackfruits, oranges and mangoes. Vegetable-based food processing units may be set-up at

Dhupguri (based on potato) and Haldibari (based on tomato). Initiatives have already been started in this area. For example, a Food Park is coming up at Malda and a fruit-processing unit is coming up at Jalpaiguri with initiative from Pepsi. Employment opportunities will be created through the creation of forward and backward linkages with the coming up of more and more of such units in this region. Tourism industry has a bright potential in North Bengal due to its natural and situational advantages. Tourist resorts may be developed in many places of Terai and Duars region of North Bengal with its scenic beauty which includes the magnificent Kanchanjungha at the background, numerous streams and rivulets, beautiful tea gardens, forests with its wide variety of flora and fauna and pleasant weather for most parts of the year. Through a comprehensive planning tourism needs to be promoted to the optimum level.

IV.3 Improving Education and Health Infrastructure

The government, through the disinvestments of public sector enterprises, by closing down the sick public enterprises, by encouraging its employees to take voluntary retirement and in various other ways, is gradually withdrawing itself from economic activities and leaving most of the activities to the market. The government is, perhaps, not much willing to expand its social welfare services also. But it appears to us that the State shall have to play a more proactive role for the economic development of backward areas like North Bengal as well as for the provision of basic social services in the areas of primary health and primary education in the longer future too since such backward areas are predominantly inhabited by poor people. Data on health and education reveal that the government shall have to establish more schools, colleges and hospitals in the districts of North Bengal (*Bagchi and Sarkar*, 2003). The existing ones are to be run more effectively by employing more teachers, doctors, nurses and other staff. However, in the rapidly changing national and international scenario, improving education will no longer be only a matter of providing education for all, but also of enhancing the quality of education and making students to learn and think and become creative, and preparing them for lifelong learning. The knowledge-based economy will require changes in the curriculum and the teaching strategy, and changes in the attitude and the mind of every member of the community - the learners, the educated parents and society at large. The role of private sector in these areas is to be recognised and the government should provide proper facilities to them.

IV.4 Empowering the Poor and Strengthening Social Safety Nets

For the development of the people in the backward areas empowering the poor and strengthening safety nets for them are absolutely necessary. Organising the poor into rural and urban cooperatives and community-based savings and credit schemes can strengthen their position. The existing social safety nets like Targeted Public Distribution System, old age pension and other such schemes are to be run effectively and new, possibly community-based delivery mechanism for delivering social services need to be explored and researched. Voluntary organisations may be encouraged to provide social services to the poor and needy people.

IV.5 Revitalise the North Bengal Development Council

The *North Bengal Development Council* is to be revitalised so that it can perform its catalytic role in socio-economic development for which it has been constituted. More funds need to be allocated to the Council both by the State and the Centre to enable it to undertake and implement special plans and programmes of development for the region. The *Panchayati Raj* institutions and municipal bodies at the grassroots level are to be effectively involved in the implementation of various projects undertaken by the Council.

V. CONCLUSIONS

Our above analysis based on various indicators of development has made it clear that North Bengal and West Plain regions are the relatively backward regions in West Bengal. Between these two regions, North Bengal appears to be more underdeveloped and under-privileged region. It should, however, be noted that although North Bengal is more backward region, the position of West Plain region is also not much better. Therefore, any plan or programme for improving the level of development of these two backward regions should go together.

It may be noted that efforts have been made at the level of the State Government to develop growth centres in North Bengal region through the establishment of North Bengal Development Council and the most significant fact is that there has been a beginning to address the problem of the region. In the mean time Paschimanchal Unnayan Parishad has also been constituted for the development of the West Plain region. Such regional development agencies must be strengthened, since it can play a coordinating role for greater convergence of development efforts to prepare a blueprint for regional development involving local *Panchayats* and municipal bodies of the backward regions. These efforts are to be combined with the provision of adequate resources for the Development Councils to perform developmental activities properly and to attract outside investments.

References

Bagchi K.K. and S. Sarkar (2003): "Development of Social Sector in West Bengal: A Study in Inter-District Disparity", *Indian Journal of Regional Science*, Vol. 35, No. 2, pp. 115-30.

Banerjee, S. and Roy, S. (1998): "On Construction of District Development Index in West Bengal", *Economic and Political Weekly*, November 21, (3019-26).

Bengal Chamber of Commerce and Industry, Calcutta (1971): *West Bengal: An Analytical Study*, Oxford and IBH Publishing Co., New Delhi, pp. 44-51.

Bhat, P.N. Mari and Francis Zavier (1999): "Findings of National Family Health Survey: Regional Analysis," *Economic and Political Weekly*, October 16-23.

Bhattacharya, B. (1998): "Urbanisation and Human Development in West Bengal: A District Level Study and Comparison with Inter-State Variation", *Economic and Political Weekly*, November 21, pp. 3027-32.

Bose, A. (1994): *Demographic Zones in India*, B.R. Publishing, Delhi.

Census of India (2001): *Provisional Population Totals Paper-I of 2001 Census Supplement, India.*

ESCAP (2001): *Policy Issues for the ESCAP Region: Balanced Development of Urban and Rural Areas and Regions Within the Countries of Asia and the Pacific*, United Nations Economic and Social Council, Bangkok.

GoI (2002): *Report on the Comparative Backwardness of North Bengal Region*, Planning Commission, New Delhi.

Government of West Bengal (1997, 2000, 2001): *Bamfront Sarkar O Uttar*

Banga (in Bengali), Department of Information and Culture, Writers' Buildings, Kolkata.

Government of West Bengal (2002a): *Economic Review*, 2001-02, Bureau of Applied Economics and Statistics, pp. 89-90 and 173.

Government of West Bengal (2002b): *Statistical Abstract*, 2001-02, Bureau of Applied Economics and Statistics, p. 502.

Institute for Development of Backward Regions (IDBR), Bhubaneswar (2000): *Impact of Social Sector Development in West Bengal*, a report of the study sponsored by Planning Commission, New Delhi.

Khan, B. (1973): "The Regional Dimension", *Seminar*, No. 164, pp. 33-45.

Konar, D.N. (1999): "Patterns of Development of the Majority of States of India", *Economic Affairs*, Vol. 44, Qr. 4, pp. 225-26.

Lok Sabha Debates (2002): Synopsis of Debates, (Proceedings other than Questions and Answers), Calling Attention, Wednesday, May 15, http://1 64.100.24.208/ls/lsdeb/lsl 3/ses9/1 50502

Mitra, Asok (1965): *Levels of Regional Development in India, Census of India, 1961*, Series 1, Volume I, Part IA(i), Manager of Publications, Delhi.

Nath, V. (1970): "Regional Development in Indian Planning", *The Economic and Political Weekly*, Annual Number, January, pp. 242-60.

Pal, G.K. (1995): "Regional Disparities in Economic Development: An Inter-District Empirical Study of the State of West Bengal", *Artha Vijnana*, Vol. 3, September, pp. 276-96.

Pathak, C.R. (2003): *Spatial Structure and Process of Development in India*, Regional Science Association, India, Kolkata.

Pradhan, Tusar (2003): "Unnayaner Dekha Naire" (in Bengali), *Uttar Banga Sambad*, September 7, p. 9.

Rani, P. Geetha (1999): "Human Development Index in India: A District Profile", *Artha Vijnana*, Vol. 41, No. 1, p. 9.

Spate O.H.K. and A.T.A. Learmonth (1967): *India and Pakistan: A General and Regional Geography*, 3rd edition, Methuen, London.

Thorner, D. and A. Thorner (1962): *Land and Labour in India*, Asia, Bombay.

18

Regional Disparity and Secessionist Militancy in North Bengal

SUMIT MUKHERJEE

One of the most formidable challenges confronting the state in India is the growth and intensification of secessionist tendencies, which sap at the very roots of national unity. Centrifugal forces are threatening the country with the ominous prospect of Balkanization. Agitations for the cause of Bodoland, Nagaland, Kamtapuri and Greater Coochbihar are examples of separatist movements that have endangered the body politic of India. The present paper concentrates on the Kamtapuri movement of North Bengal, which assumed gigantic magnitude in the early part of the new millennium. It was accompanied by a high incidence of violence and thus assassination of political leaders and activists, gruesome massacre of civilians, extortion, kidnapping and other activities became the order of the day. The movement threatened to turn the region into a hotbed of violence and militancy when the Operation Flush Out was launched by the Bhutan government to evict the KLO (Karntapur Liberation Organization) militants who had been conducting their operations from the jungles of Bhutan. This brought the movement to a temporary halt but with the escalation of the Greater Coochbihar movement, signs of a revival of militancy are again discernible. The present paper addresses itself to the question whether militancy is a political or economic problem. It argues that though political in its external manifestation, militancy has a predominant economic dimension. On close scrutiny it is revealed that majority of the militants are youths from families afflicted with acute poverty and unemployment. Economic deprivation creates frustration and alienation, which lead a person to the path of militancy. Militants capitalize on the economic issues of poverty and unemployment and target those youths whose dreams of a prosperous and happy life are shattered by deprivation.

The seminal point of enquiry in the paper is whether regional disparities are responsible for the spurt of militancy in North Bengal. It examines the allegation that North Bengal has been long left in a state of neglect and that this has begun to boomerang. Taking into consideration the various ramifications of the problem, it seeks to offer a prescriptive analysis of the same providing recommendations of appropriate remedial measures. It concludes that though the ultimate solution of the problem should be undertaken at the political level, at the same time its economic and sociological dimensions should never be lost sight of.

Since the late nineties, North Bengal has gone through the trauma of secessionist militancy which has threatened the region with the ominous prospect of a blood bath.

The Kamtapuri movement unleashed at the dawn of the new millennium was characterised by widespread violence, murder, abduction, extortion, and intimidation, the civilian population being the main casualty. The 'Operation Flush Out' launched by the Government of Bhutan in 2004 to evict the K.L.O. (Kamtapur Liberation Organisation) militants who had established their bases of operation in that country, temporarily halted the rampage. However, the latent fire of discontent continued to simmer and sinister forebodings of a recrudescence of militancy in North Bengal, were conveyed by the Great Coochbihar movement of October 2005. One of the aberrations of contemporary Scholarship, is to exalt the effect over the cause. Thus instead of magnifying the effects of terroristic violence in North Bengal, it is worthwhile to explore the causes of the same. The present paper intends to answer the question whether regional disparity is the largest single factor contributing to militancy in North Bengal. For militancy is often the outcome of feeling of deprivation emanating from uneven economic development, favouring certain regions and neglecting others.

TWO CONTENDING VIEWPOINTS

Two alternative explanations of militancy in North Bengal have been provided by scholars. According to one group, militancy is the result of the faulty, discriminatory policies of the state government which subject certain regions to chronic poverty at the expense of others.

Poverty stricken unemployed youths are thus driven into the fold of the militants who brainwash them with the vision of a prosperous future. Thus many promising youths are transformed into militants by the unbearable pain of starvation and frustration of their long cherished dreams and aspirations.

At the other end of the spectrum, there is the contending view that the myth of deprivation is a deliberate fabrication of secessionist elements. The policies of the state government have in no way meted out step motherly treatment to North Bengal. It is rather the Central government which is responsible for creating regional disparities and North Bengal may have suffered from it. The exponents of this view say that militancy in North Bengal is a reactionary phenomenon as it unable to carry the common people which is the first condition for the establishment of a society free from exploitation. Thus there can be no compromise on the question of militancy.

Neither of the above viewpoints is sacrosanct though both contain elements of truth. The first treats militancy as an economic problem while the second considers it predominantly political. Actually militancy is often the result of the interplay of politics and economics. Both are important though not deterministic factors and hence their relative validity deserves in depth study.

REGIONAL DISPARITY—MYTH OR REALITY?

Those who seek to disprove the conclusion that regional disparities perpetuated by the state government, have fomented Militancy in North Bengal, argue that the allegation of regional disparity is not borne out by facts in this case. One scholar contends on the basis of the following statistical information that if education is regarded as the main indicator of development, then North Bengal is at par with West Bengal. In 1975-76, there were 40,723 primary schools in West Bengal of which 7,292 were in North Bengal. In 1998-99 the corresponding figures were 52,123 and 9472. In 1984-85, West Bengal had 291 Colleges and North Bengal 38 while in 1997-98, the figures were 327 and 68. In 1998-99, the state government spent Rs. 12,306.57 for district development of which 41.88% was allogaced for North Bengal.

These figures, he asserts, conclusively repudiate the charge of regional disparity and completely exonerate the State Government.[1]

Without contesting the authenticity of the above information, it may be observed that they reflect a part of reality, not the whole. The proponents of the disparity argument also provide ample statistical data in support of their stand. According to the Human Development Report West Bengal 2004, 'both material and human development in West Bengal have strong regional dimensions'.[2]

The report identifies North Bengal as a region characterised by imbalance. Darjeeling is the second richest district of West Bengal but North Dinajpur is the poorest. Jalpaiguri has the third highest per capita income in the state but also one of the highest head count poverty ratio at more than 45% of the population. The report states portentously that 'There is a common perception among residents of North Bengal region that distance from Kolkata is associated with some degree of neglect by the state government.'[3] According to a survey conducted by the Planning Commission in 2002, North Bengal is poorly placed in comparison to West Bengal in terms of electricity, sanitation and safe drinking water. The report observed that in North Bengal, "development gravitates towards those pockets where a semblance of infrastructure is already available. Regionally there are gainers and losers. The democratic federal structure cannot be sustained if such disparities continue to accentuate."[4] According to the survey, per capita income was low in all the districts of North Bengal in comparison with West Bengal with the exception of Darjeeling. It noted further that North Bengal lagged behind in employment generation despite the Swaranjayanti Gram Svarojgar Yojna (S.G.S.Y.) and the Jawahar Gram Samridhi Yojna (J.G.S.Y.). Under the J.G.S.Y. the number of mandays employment generated declined from 46.4 lakh in 2000-01 to 29.2 lakh in 2002. The report criticizes the state government for making substantial allocations for infrastructural programmes but lower in case of employment generation programmes. Moreover, Coochbihar has received priority while Malda and Dinajpur have received less allocations. The number of self-employed persons assisted by the S.G.S.Y. programme declined from 13,408 in 1999-2000 to 5841 in 2000-01 and 2317 in 2001-02. According to the report North Bengal's achievement in employment generation in terms of lakh man-days was 18.23% of the envisaged target as against 25.75% achieved by West Bengal.

In an informative paper, K.K. Bagchi and S. Sarkar have sought to relate the Kamtapuri movement in North Bengal with the socio-economic backwardness of the region. Some of the relevant data cited by them are as follows. The per capita income of North Bengal was lower both in 1960-82 and 2000-01 than the West Plain and South Delta regions. So far as the Human Development Index is concerned, North Bengal in 1981 happened to be the least developed region with average value of 0.1996 compared to 0.5739 for the West Plain and 0.3473 for the South Delta regions. This pattern was replicated in 1991. In terms of social development based on indicators like access to toilets, rural water supply, availability of doctors, availability of beds in state government health system, infant mortality and percentage of safe delivery total literacy rate, number of primary schools per ten thousand population, teacher-student ratio at primary level, Scheduled Caste and Scheduled Tribe literacy rate and percentage of schools having drinking water facilities, all the six districts of Darjeeling happened to belong to the less developed category while 3 out of the 4 West Plain districts belonged to the developed category.[5]

The above data provide very strong foundation for the disparity view point. From the Lok Sabha debates it is known that on February 4, 2004, Mr. Priya Ranjan Das Munshi draw the attention of the Minister of State in the Ministry of Planning to the situation arising out of the regional imbalance in the development of North Bengal due to the plan process of the seventh, eighth, ninth and tenth five years Plans. This does not appear a baseless apprehension in view of the comparative backwardness of North Bengal. Though one cannot hold the state government entirely responsible for this, yet it would be mere wishful thinking to consider regional disparity a myth. As far back as 1971, the Bengal Chamber of Commerce and Industry stated that "While the Calcutta Metropolitan District or the district of Burdwan in the coal iron ore belt represents a relatively high level of development, the outlying regions like Darjeeling-Coochbihar-Jalpaiguri in the North or Purulia-Bankura-Murshidabad in the West reflect the sorry plight of stagnation and decay." Interestingly the rate of agricultural productivity in Coochbihar and Jalpaiguri is lower than even the drought prone Purulia. Thus regional disparity appears to be an inescapable fact which cannot be disproved by statistical jugglery. It is also indubitably true that disparity has been a hallmark of development in North Bengal. Statistics alone proves nothing because the inference drawn from it depends on the mode and method of interpretation of the same. There may be considerable-logic behind the contention that the allegation of political disempowerment of the ethnic communities is misplaced but economic empowerment in North Bengal has proved elusive. At this stage we have to address ourselves to two important questions. Firstly, is regional disparity the cause of militancy in North Bengal? Secondly, is militancy a political or an economic problem?

MILITANCY AND REGIONAL DISPARITY—IN SEARCH OF A CORRELATION

Taking an overview of the North Bengal region, one is instantly inclined to identify poverty and unemployment as two of its pressing problems. The theory of Relative Deprivation developed by Ted Robert Gurr in his classical work 'Why Men Rebel' postulates that a gap between expectations and perceived capabilities of a person *vis-a-vis* his economic situation, political power and social status in relation to the other leads ethnic minority groups to the violent revolutionary path. Here the psychological element combines with the economic as it is the feeling of being exploited rather than exploitation itself which creates a revolutionary mentality. Social scientists like Watson have argued that uneven pace of modernization and industrialization in multiethnic societies tends to benefit some regions at the expense of the others and thus leads to a potentially explosive situation. The grievances articulated and ventilated by minority nationalism are often integrally linked to economic deprivation.

Unemployment which is a perennial problem in North Bengal, is not merely an economic problem but has deep socio-psychological ramifications. Some instructive individual case studies in North Bengal may be used, as explanatory, illustrative variables for establishing a positive correlation between disparity and militancy. One has to consider the compositional character of the militant movements. To take the case of North Bengal, the militants accused of affiliation with the K.L.O. happened to be originally extremely peace-loving. To quote the testimony of Ahindra Dhar Chowdhury, Ex-Head Master of Kumar Gram Madan Singh High School, those who took up arms were all very good students. According to Intelligence reports, they are now eager to return to the mainstream of national life.[6] The arrested militants have been found to belong to poverty stricken families. Disillusionment and frustration have driven unemployed youths into the fold of militant outfits like the K.L.O. who have offered them monetary benefits.[7] The K.L.O. has entrusted a band of recruiting militants with the task of targetting the youths of regions like Mathabhanga, Tufangunj, Dhupguri, Hazrahat, Maynaguri, Kumar gramduar, etc.[8] Subhas Roy a militant trained in Batch 10 of Bhutan who was instructed by the K.L.O. to organize militant movement in Jalpaiguri, confessed during interrogation that he was promised a good job once the dream of Kamtapur became a reality. He was found to be very cultured and well-behaved.[9] Khalimohan Singh, another K.L.O. militant also confessed that the belief was instilled in him that with the creation of a separate Kamtapur State, poverty would go once and for all and he would get a permanent job.[10]

Tamir Das who could not complete his graduation from North Bengal University because of poverty, testified in the same vein that he was forced to collude with the militants and so did Milton Burma and Gajen Singh Kongar.[11] Takura Das also revealed that the pains of poverty and starvation led him to become a K.L.O. linkman.[12] The above examples provide the rule rather than the exception. They clearly show that there is a positive relationship between unemployment and militancy. Almost all the militants are misguided youths who have no political ideology as such. The writer of this paper was told by a police officer Sisir Basu Roy that the militants were basically gullible, impressionable and emotional rather than politically motivated. The militant organizations could capitalize on this because of their economic distress.[13]

The above examples demonstrate that regional disparity leads to poverty which leads to unemployment which in turn creates frustration which intensifies into social alienation and finds its culmination in anti-state activities. This perpetuates a headlong collision between the militants and the government but the fundamental problem of disparity continues unabated and the 'vicious circle' is repeated and replicated with its cyclical constellation of forces. This may be termed the 'Militancy Cycle' because most militant youths are entangled in it. They are ideologically immature and inarticulate. The masterminds of the secessionist militant movements capitalize on the 'Militancy Cycle' and make it the basis of their recruitment policy. Under the circumstances, it would be in the fitness of things to concentrate on the vital aspect of policy formulation by the government.

A REALISTIC ANTIDOTE

If the Militancy Cycle is to be attacked, it must be attacked at its roots. While one root cause is economic deprivation, the concomitant cause of psychological disenchantment with the state apparatus must also be duly emphasized. The lesson to be drawn from the North Bengal experience, is that militancy is not merely a political or economic problem. It is an amalgam of diverse factors, political, social, economic, cultural and psychological. It is a dependent variable which is a function of numerous independent variables. Thus an adequate response to the challenge must be as multi-faceted, as the problem itself and must be launched on several fronts. Some experts are of the opinion that in other regions of Bengal and India, poverty end unemployment are rampant and yet no militant uprising has occurred there. This line of reasoning ignores the geostrategic significance of North Bengal which is flanked by Nepal and Bhutan on the one hand, and the Bangladesh border on the other. The huge corridor provides the militants with a convenient pathway for infilteration. No other region of Bengal can be called the epicenter of militancy with Darjeeling under the shadow of the Gorkhaland movement and Coochbihar and Jalpaiguri reeling under the Kamtapuri and Greater Coochbihar movement. The Maoist movement too has intensified which has made the region most vulnerable. North Bengal provides the corridor for the flow of trade and Commerce from North-East India to the rest of the country in the form of tea, timber and oil. This is bound to be jeopardised of militancy is not curbed. One way of doing this is to ensure that the K.L.O. militants who have secret linkages with the U.L.F.A. militants of eastern Assam, cannot establish their psychological foothold in North Bengal by ensure that these youths do not fall into the trap laid by them, the government must address the unemployment problem with special care. Kailash Chandra Mina, Ex-S.P. of Coochbihar testified. In 2000 that the K.L.O. recruited a number of unemployed Rajbansi Youths with the temptation of a good job.[14] Thus employment generation through industrial development appears a viable solution. Mr. Jyoti Basu, Ex-Chief Minister of West Bengal admitted in Coochbihar that no heavy industry had developed in this region. He recommended the establishment of agro-industries.[15] The moribund agricultural system needs to be revived particularly through the resuscitation of the jute industry. In some regions, the jute industry has been found to prosper but its market is not assured. The cold and damp weather of North Bengal prevents Rabi crops from flourishing and progress in the agricultural sphere is thus stultified which causes displacement of many peasant workers who migrate to urban areas and unemployment intensifies. It may be recalled in this connection that when Punjab became explosive, K.P.S. Gill, the Chief of Punjab Police provided an employment package for the militants and recruited some of them in the police force. This helped him win the confidence of Rural youths. Here the cue may be taken from the Punjab experience. The rejuvenation of the Tourist Industry can provide employment to a large chunck of unemployed youths of North Bengal. The current decision by the West Bengal government to increase the number of primary and Secondary Schools in the region, is also very correct in view of the close correlation of education and employment. While any violent movement cannot be curbed through economic packages alone, yet such packages do provide a viable antidote to the malady, and are worth-experimenting with. The Chief Minister of West Bengal declared in a public meeting at Dinhata Coochbihar on December 21, 2004 that he was willing to discuss issues like unemployment with the Kamtapuri leaders on condition that they would lay down arms. This is both realistic and reasonable because armed resistance against the state apparatus cannot be justified under the pretext of poverty and unemployment.

Unemployment does not legitimate the right to murder because the sacrosanctity of the right to life is guaranteed under the constitution. Conversely, it may be argued that poverty and unemployment render this right meaningless which may provide a temporary justification for militancy, but if the state government is responsive, continuation of militancy would be suicidal.

Since the hard core militants who are bent on carrying out a separate homeland by Balkanizing India, cannot be pacified through economic packages, it would be expedient to distinguish between politically sensitive and apolitical militants. The latter comprise the bulk of the Task Force of the militants and for them, it is a decent life that matters rather than a separate state. Two distinct types of response need to be devised. The former should be addressed in the political language while the latter is likely to be influenced more by the language of economics. Here lies the potential opportunity for conversion of the militants. If the Militancy cycle is drastically weakened and reduced if not eliminated, the entire cycle is likely to collapse. In this case, the antidote might hold the key to the final solution.

Militancy in North Bengal is basically a political problem with a pronounced economic dimension. Since economics cannot be a substitute for politics, the fundamental character of government's response to militancy must be political. But economics can provide a palliative which may greatly facilitate the greater political solution by restoring the dwindling confidence of the people. Not only can economic development provide an overall tranquillizing effect on the psyche of the people by extirpating entrenched beliefs and complexes from their minds but can also provide a bulwark against the recruitment policy of the militants by generating employment opportunities for the youth. Without stepping into the shoes of Marxian economic determinism, economics can be used as a catalytic agent for peaceful political change. Economic measures by themselves cannot contain the rising tide of militancy, but can put a temporary check on it and the resultant breathing space can be utilized for the purpose of enduring peace. In the case of North Bengal, economics can blunt the edge of the militant movement because its ideological foundations are not very strong. By assigning a catalytic rather than deterministic role to economics, Marx may be rediscovered in the new millennium where globalization is the order of the day. But even in the era of globalization, the time is not ripe for writing the epitaph of Marx because the benefits of market economy have not percolated to the lowest layers of the society and thus islands of prosperity have crystallized around a vast ocean of poverty. Poverty dehumanizes man and neither politics nor economics is sufficient by itself to restore his humanity. In the context of North Bengal, therefore, the rediscovery of Marx in a new from appears promising both intellectually and practically.

It is a lasting alliance between politics and economics which provides the surest guarantee for fertilizing the soil of North Bengal with the seeds of lasting peace.

Notes and References

1. Manik Sanyal Kamtapuri Andolan: Paschatpot O Abhimukh, *Sangrami Hatiyar*, 2001, pp. 89-92.
2. *Human Development Report, West Bengal, 2004*, Ch. 10, p. 195.
3. *Ibid*., p. 198.
4. Survey Sponsored by the Planning Commission, November 2002, *Report on the Comparative Backwardness of the North Bengal Region.*
5. K.K. Bagchi and S. Sarkar, Comparative Backwardness of North Bengal: Strategies for its improvement in *Artha Beekshan*, Vol. 14, Nos. 3 and 4, Dec. 2005-March 2006, pp. 205-10.
6. *Uttarbanga Sambad*, August 15, 2002
7. *Ananda Bazar Patrika*, August 21, 2002.
8. *Uttarbanga Sambad*, August 21, 2002
9. *Ibid*., August 27, 2002.
10. *Ibid*., August 30, 2002.
11. *Ibid*., December 21, 200 2.
12. *Ibid*., September 2, 2002.
13. Interview with Sisir Basu Roy, May 10, 2003.
14. *The Telegraphs*, December 10, 2000
15. *Uttarbanga Sambad*, December 13, 2000.

Index